STUDY GUIDE TO ACCOMPANY

MACRO ECONOMICS

SIXTH CANADIAN EDITION

STUDY GUIDE TO ACCOMPANY

MACRO ECONOMICS

SIXTH CANADIAN EDITION

William B. Walstad
UNIVERSITY OF NEBRASKA-LINCOLN

Robert C. Bingham

Cyril J. Grant
ST. FRANCIS XAVIER UNIVERSITY

McGraw-Hill Ryerson Limited

Toronto Montreal New York Auckland Bogota
Caracas Lisbon London Madrid Mexico Milan
New Delhi Paris San Juan Singapore Sydney Tokyo

STUDY GUIDE to accompany
MACROECONOMICS
Sixth Canadian Edition

ISBN: 0-07-551436-2

 2 3 4 5 6 7 8 9 10 MD 2 1 0 9 8 7 6 5 4

Printed and bound in Canada

Care has been taken to trace ownership of copyright
material contained in this text. The publisher will
gladly take any information that will enable them to
rectify any reference or credit in subsequent editions.

SPONSORING EDITOR: Jennifer Mix
SUPERVISING EDITOR: Margaret Henderson
COPY EDITOR: Gail Marsden
COVER DESIGN: Brant Cowie/ArtPlus Limited
TYPESETTING/PAGING: Jay Tee Graphics Ltd.
PRINTING & BINDING: Moore Data Management Services

Canadian Cataloguing in Publication Data

Walstad, William B.
   Study guide to accompany Macroeconomics, sixth
Canadian edition

Supplement to: McConnell, Campbell R. Macroeconomics. 6th Canadian ed.
ISBN 0-07-551436-2

1. Macroeconomics. 2. Macroeconomics – Problems,
exercises, etc. I. Bingham, Robert C.
II. Grant, Cyril J. III. McConnell, Campbell R.
Macroeconomics, 6th Canadian ed. IV. Title.

HB172.5.M312 1993   339   C93-093027-1

Contents

PART 1 An Introduction to Economics   1

   1. The Nature and Method of Economics   *3*
      Appendix to Chapter 1   11
   2. The Economizing Problem   *20*
   3. Overview of the Market System and the Circular Flow   *30*
   4. Understanding Individual Markets: Supply and Demand   *37*

PART 2 National Income, Employment, and Fiscal Policy   51

   5. Measuring Domestic Output, National Income, and the Price Level   *53*
   6. Macroeconomic Instability: Unemployment and Inflation   *65*
   7. The Determination of National Income in a Closed Economy: The Short Run   *76*
   8. Determination of the Price Level and National Income in an Open Economy: The Short Run   *93*
   9. Fiscal Policy   *106*

PART 3 Money, Banking, and Monetary Policy   121

   10. Money and Banking in Canada   *123*
   11. How Banks Create Money   *130*
   12. The Bank of Canada and Monetary Policy   *141*
   13. The Inflation–Unemployment Relationship: Short-Run Versus Long-Run Analysis   *155*

PART 4 Problems and Controversies in Macroeconomics   171

   14. The Evolution of Macroeconomics and Recent Controversies   *173*
   15. Budget Deficits and the Public Debt   *188*
   16. Economic Growth   *198*

PART 5 International Economics and the World Economy *209*

17. International Trade: Comparative Advantage and Protectionism *211*
18. Exchange Rates and the Balance of Payments *227*
19. Macroeconomic Policy in an Open Economy *242*
20. Growth and the Less-Developed Countries *249*

GLOSSARY *261*

- - - - - - - - - - - cut here - - - - - - - - - - -

STUDENT REPLY CARD

You can help us to develop better textbooks. Please answer the following questions about the *Study Guide to accompany Macroeconomics*, Sixth Canadian Edition by Walstad/Bingham/Grant. Then, return this form via Business Reply Mail. Your opinions matter: thank you in advance for sharing them with us!

Name of your college or university: _____

Major program of study: _____

Course title: _____

Were you required to buy this Study Guide? _____ yes _____ no

Did you buy this book new or used? _____ new _____ used ($_____)

Do you plan to keep or sell this book? _____ keep _____ sell

What did you like most about this Study Guide?

cut here

- - - - - - - - - - - - - fold here - - - - - - - - - - -

What did you like least?

Were there topics covered in your text that are not included in this Study Guide? If so, please specify:

Did this Study Guide assist you in learning concepts and techniques used in the text?

How could we make this Study Guide more useful in future editions?

- *cut here* -

- *fold here* - - - - - - - - - - - - - - - - - - -

cut here

Postage will be paid by

0183560299-L1N9B6-BR01

Attn.: Sponsoring Editor
College Division

MCGRAW-HILL RYERSON LIMITED
300 WATER ST
WHITBY ON   L1N 9Z9

tape shut

MACRO ECONOMICS

An Introduction to Economics

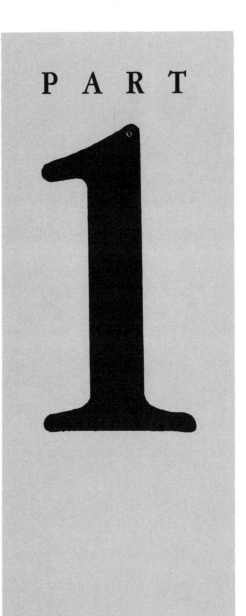

CHAPTER

1

The Nature and Method of Economics

Chapter 1 introduces you to economics—the study of how people decide to use scarce productive resources to satisfy wants. Knowledge of economics is important because it is essential for well-informed citizenship and it has many practical applications to personal decisions. The purpose of this chapter is to explain the nature of the subject and to describe the methods that economists use to study economic questions.

Economists use different approaches to examine economic topics. Knowledge of economic relationships is obtained through the accumulation of relevant facts sometimes referred to as *descriptive* or *empirical economics*. Using the knowledge gained from an examination of these facts to directly propose economic principles is termed *inductive economics*. Utilizing the knowledge as background information to suggest general relationships among variables results in the construction of economic models; from these models economic principles are deduced using rules of logic. *Policy economics* is the formulation of recommendations based on economic principles to overcome specific economic problems or to reach predetermined economic objectives.

The heart of the chapter is the discussion of economic principles in the economic theory section. Economic principles are not, in themselves, answers to economic problems but are tools the investigator uses in analysing economic problems and for suggesting policies and programs to solve these problems. Our society has five fairly well accepted goals: economic growth, full employment, price level stability, equitable income distribution, and a balance in foreign trade. The degree to which all five goals can be reached with our limited resources is dependent upon the economic policies put in place by the public authorities. Economists envision individuals and institutions making rational decisions on the basis of benefits and costs. Programs, based on principles that follow from this economic perspective, are designed to reach a specific goal with the minimum use of resources.

The selection of what economic policies to follow depends not only on economic principles, but also on the value judgments and the weight given to particular economic goals. Here we move from economic theory and positive economics, which investigates *what is*, to normative economics, which incorporates subjective or value-laden views of *what ought to be*. Many of the apparent disagreements among economists are over normative policy issues and involve deciding which economic goals for our economy are most important in making the case for a policy solution.

Economics is divided into two broad categories, micro- and macroeconomics. Microeconomics is concerned with the interaction of individual economic units such as business firms or households and concentrates on the determination of output and prices. Macroeconomics is the study of the determinants of economy-wide aggregates, such as total output, national or regional unemployment rates, or the flow of capital into Canada.

Clear thinking about economic questions requires that the beginning student avoid many pitfalls. Errors of commission and omission can occur from bias, loaded terminology, imprecise definitions, fallacies of composition, and confusing correlation with causation. If you can guard against these potential hazards, you can use the economic perspective to improve your understanding of people's actions and events in the economy at the microeconomic or the macroeconomic level.

CHECKLIST

When you have studied this chapter, you should be able to:
- Write the formal definition of economics.
- Give two reasons for studying economics.
- Define descriptive economics, economic theory, and policy economics.
- Distinguish between induction and deduction in economic reasoning.

- Explain what an economic principle is and how economic principles are obtained.
- Explain what the "other things equal" (*ceteris paribus*) assumption is and why this assumption is employed in economics.
- Discuss the distinction between macroeconomics and microeconomics.
- Distinguish between positive economics and normative economics and provide examples of both.
- Identify the five economic goals.
- Recognize the "pitfalls to straight thinking" when confronted with examples of them.
- Outline the basic steps in policy formulation.
- Describe the economic perspective.

CHAPTER OUTLINE

1. Economics is concerned with the efficient use of scarce productive resources to achieve maximum satisfaction from the fulfilment of human wants.

2. In order to comprehend some of the present-day problems of their society citizens must have an understanding of economic principles.

3. Economists gather relevant facts both as an aid in formulating hypotheses and as a test of the predictions that flow from economic models.
(a) Descriptive economics is the gathering of relevant facts about the production, exchange, and consumption of goods and services.
(b) Theoretical economics is the derivation of economic principles.
(1) Economic principles are also called laws, theories, and models.
(2) Each of these principles is a generalization.
(3) Economics employ the *ceteris paribus* (or "other things equal") assumption to obtain these generalizations.
(4) These principles are also abstractions from reality.
(5) To obtain and test their principles economists use both the inductive and the deductive method.
(6) Economists express their principles or models with words, tables, equations, and graphs.
(7) Economists can derive principles about economic behaviour at the macroeconomic or the microeconomic level.
(8) Economic models can be quite useful; but there are at least three dangers in building and using them.
(c) Policy economics is the application of economic principles to reach specific goals. The goal itself is often

determined by the value judgments of the investigator.
(1) Values are the judgments people make about what is desirable (good, just) and what is undesirable (bad, unjust).
(2) Positive economics concerns *what is*, or the scientific analysis of economic behaviour; normative economics suggest *what ought to be* in offering answers to policy questions.
(3) Canada appears to have at least five major economic goals; but several of these goals may be conflicting or mutually exclusive.
(4) There are four steps in creating a policy designed to achieve an economic goal.
(i) Define the goal.
(ii) Apply economic principles in designing alternative policies to achieve the goal.
(iii) Choose the policy that achieves the goal at least cost.
(iv) Evaluate the effect of the policy selected after it has been put in operation.

4. Pitfalls encountered by beginning students in studying and applying economic principles include:
(a) bias or preconceived beliefs not warranted by facts;
(b) loaded terminology or the use of terms in a way that appeals to emotions and leads to a nonobjective analysis of the issues;
(c) the definition of terms by economists different from the way these terms are ordinarily used;
(d) the fallacy of composition or the assumption that what is true of the part is necessarily true of the whole;
(e) the *post hoc* fallacy, or the mistaken belief that when one event precedes another, the first event is the cause of the second.

5. The economic perspective is a cost-benefit perspective. People, either as individuals or in groups, make economic choices by evaluating the costs and benefits of decisions.

IMPORTANT TERMS

ceteris paribus or "other things being equal"
  assumption
correlation and causation
descriptive economics
economics
economic perspective
economic theory
fallacy of composition
induction and deduction hypothesis

macroeconomics and microeconomics

policy economics

positive and normative economics

post hoc, ergo propter hoc or "after this, therefore because of this" fallacy

principles or generalizations

FILL-IN QUESTIONS

1. Economics is concerned with the _____ use of _____ _____ for the purpose of attaining the _____ _____ from the fulfilment of human material wants.

2. An understanding of economics is essential if we are to be well-informed _____ and it has many personal applications even though it is an academic and not a _____ subject.

3. Economics, like other sciences, begins with the facts found in the world around us.
(a) The gathering of relevant facts is the part of economics called _____ economics.
(b) Economic _____ involves deriving general principles about the economic behaviour of people and institutions. When economists develop economic principles from studying facts, they are using the _____ method; whereas the _____ method uses facts to test real-world applicability of economic principles derived from formal economic models.
(c) The formulation of recommended solutions or remedies for economic problems is referred to as _____ economics.

4. The economic principles (often called _____, or _____) derived from facts are all _____ about human economic behaviour and, as such, necessarily involve _____ from reality.

5. Economists hypothesize that the number of units of a particular good a consumer purchases depends upon the price of that good, and several other factors such as income and tastes. To isolate the relationship between the price of the good and the quantity purchased

economists often assume that these other factors are constant and do not change and this is termed the _____ assumption.

6. There are two different types of statements that can be made about economic topics. A (positive, normative) _____ statement explains *what is* by offering a scientific proposition about economic behaviour that is based on economic theory and facts. A _____ statement includes a value judgment about an economic policy or the economy that suggests *what ought to be*. Many of the reported disagreements among economists usually involve _____ statements.

7. Increases in economic growth that promote full employment would be an example of a set of (conflicting, complementary, mutually exclusive) _____ economic goals. Efforts to achieve an equitable distribution of income that reduce economic efficiency and growth would be an example of a set of _____ economic goals.

8. Macroeconomics deals with the economy _____ _____ _____. Microeconomics deals with _____ economic units such as the output level of a _____ or the price of a _____ good.

9. Five widely accepted economic goals in Canada are:
(a) _____
(b) _____
(c) _____
(d) _____
(e) _____

10. The four steps involved in the formulation of economic policy are:
(a) _____
(b) _____
(c) _____
(d) _____

11. There are many obstacles to logical consistency in economic reasoning. For example, the conclusion that what is true for an individual must necessarily be true

of the group is known as the _____

_____ _____. The con-
clusion that because one event precedes another the first
is necessarily the cause of the second is known as the

_____ fallacy.

12.   The economic perspective is a _____

_____ perspective.

PROBLEMS AND PROJECTS

1.   ''In 1987 the scientific claim that fish products were
low in cholesterol-producing substances caused the price
of fish throughout North America to rise.'' This is a
specific instance of a more general economic principle.
Of which economic generalization is this a particular
example?

_____

_____

2.   Below are five statements. Each of them is an example of one of the pitfalls frequently encountered in the
study of economics. Indicate, in the space following each
statement, the type of pitfall involved.
(a)   The Second World War resulted in forty five years

of economic expansion in Canada. _____

_____

(b)   ''An unemployed worker can find a job if he or she
looks diligently and conscientiously for employment;
therefore, all unemployed workers can find employment
if they are diligent and conscientious in looking for a

job.'' _____
(c)   ''Just tell me when rain will be needed and I will

schedule my vacation for that week.'' _____

_____

(d)   Individual renters are made better off by a law that
fixes rents below market clearing prices. Therefore to promote the well-being of that segment of society that rents
housing the government should institute rent control

legislation. _____
(e)   '' Employment in Canadian manufacturing fell
250,000 in the two years after the signing of the Free
Trade Agreement. Free trade is disastrous for the Cana-

dian worker.'' _____

3.   Below is a list of economic statements. Indicate in
the space to the right of each whether they are positive

(P) or normative (N). Then in lines (g), (h), (i), and (j)
below, write two of your own examples of positive statements and two examples of normative economic
statements.
(a)   The leading commercial banks in Canada are too

big to fail. _____
(b)   The supply management system in agriculture pro-
tects our small family farms from unfair competition by

large corporate agricultural enterprises. _____
(c)   Resources are used most efficiently in a competi-

tively based market economy. _____
(d)   The Unemployment Insurance program is used as

a welfare program. _____
(e)   Free trade can improve the standard of living of a

country. _____
(f)   The federal government should do more to

eliminate regional disparity in Canada. _____

(g)   P _____

(h)   P _____

(i)   N_____

(j)   N_____

4.   Below is an exercise in making graphs. On the graph,
plot the economic relationships contained in the exercise. Be sure to label each axis of the graph and to indicate the unit of measurement and scale used on each axis.

National income (billions of dollars)	Consumption expenditures (billions of dollars)
$600	$660
650	700
700	740
750	780
800	820
850	860
900	900

Graph national income on the horizontal axis and consumption expenditures on the vertical axis; connect the
seven points and label the curve ''Consumption
Schedule.''

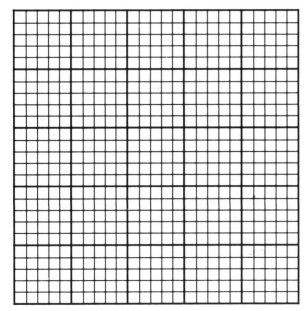

0

The relationship between national income and consumption expenditures is a(n) (direct, inverse) _____ one and the Consumption Schedule a(n) (up-, down-) _____ sloping curve.

SELF-TEST

Circle T if the statement is true, F if it is false.

1. Economics deals with the activities by which people earn their living and improve their standard of living.
T F

2. The study of economics provides the student with specific skills which are highly valued by incorporated businesses. **T F**

3. Gathering the relevant economic facts from which economic principles are derived is the part of economics called economic analysis. **T F**

4. In economics, the terms "law," "principle, " and "theory, " mean essentially the same thing. **T F**

5. The "other things equal" or *ceteris paribus* assumption is made in order to simplify the reasoning process.
T F

6. The application of economic principles enables economists to propose programs that achieve specific goals with the least cost use of resources. **T F**

7. The free trade agreement with the United States is an example of a policy based upon economic principles.
T F

8. The first step in the formulation of an economic policy, the statement of the goal or desired result, may be an occasion for disagreement because different people may have different and conflicting goals. **T F**

9. Making value judgments as to preferred goals of an economy is known as positive economic analysis. **T F**

10. Normative statements are expressions about desired states of the economy as seen by the speaker. **T F**

11. If you speak of "capital" to the average person, he or she understands you to be referring to money. The economist, therefore, is obligated to use the term "capital" to mean money. **T F**

12. The statement: "Increased patent protection for the Canadian pharmaceutical industry will result in increased investment by that industry in Canada" is a positive statement. **T F**

13. The economic perspective views individuals or institutions as making rational choices based on the analysis of the costs and benefits of the decision. **T F**

14. Complete equity in regional income per person and sustained national economic growth may be conflicting goals for any economy. **T F**

15. Microeconomic analysis is concerned with the behaviour of individual households and business firms.
T F

MULTIPLE-CHOICE

Circle the letter that corresponds to the best answer.

1. Which statement would be the best one to use to complete a short definition of economics? "Economics is a study of"
(a) the capitalistic system
(b) the triumph of the capitalistic system over communism
(c) monetary transactions
(d) the efficient use of scarce resources
(e) the roles of business and government in providing a rising standard of living for the nation

2. Economics is a practical field of study in several ways. Which one of the following is *not* an element of its practicality?
(a) every person affects and is affected by the operation of the economy

(b)   every person has to earn a living in some manner, and economics develops skills and trains the student in the art of making a living

(c)   every person in a democracy is confronted with its political problems and many of them are economic in nature

(d)   every person who understands the overall operation of the economy is in a better position to solve personal economic problems

3.   One economic principle states that, *ceteris paribus*, the lower the price of a commodity the greater will be the quantity of the commodity consumers will wish to purchase. On the basis of this principle alone, it can be concluded that

(a)   if the price of mink coats is seen to fall, one can conclude that more mink coats will be purchased by consumers

(b)   if the price of mink coats falls, there must have been a decrease in the demand for clothes made of fur

(c)   if the price of mink coats falls and there are no important changes in the other factors affecting their demand, the public will probably purchase a greater quantity of mink coats than it did at the higher price

(d)   if more mink coats are purchased this month than last month, it is because the price of mink coats has fallen

4.   An economic model is not

(a)   an ideal type of economy or an economic policy for which we ought to work

(b)   a tool economists employ to enable them to predict

(c)   one or a collection of economic principles

(d)   an explanation of how the economy or a part of the economy functions in its essential details

5.   Which of the following is not a danger to be encountered in the construction or application of economic models?

(a)   it may contain irrelevant facts and omit more relevant data

(b)   it may come to be accepted as "what ought to be" rather than as "what is"

(c)   it may be overly simplified and so be a very poor approximation of the reality it explains

(d)   it may result in a conclusion that is unacceptable to the citizens or the government of a nation

6.   A theory in economics is

(a)   useless if simplifying assumptions are used

(b)   of little use because it is too abstract

(c)   useful if the predictions of the theory correspond to actual economic occurrences

(d)   would never contradict another economic theory if both were derived using the rules of logic

7.   The method of reasoning in which economic principles are derived from an analysis of historical data is called

(a)   descriptive statistics

(b)   historical determinism

(c)   induction

(d)   fallacy of composition

(e)   deduction

8.   An economic theory may contain all but which of the following?

(a)   predictions that are deduced from that theory

(b)   definitions that clearly set out the variables included in the model

(c)   statements as to the relationships among the variables in the model

(d)   normative statements as to the most preferred outcomes

9.   During World War II, Canada employed price controls to prevent inflation; this was referred to as "a fascist and arbitrary restriction of economic freedom" by some and as "a necessary and democratic means of preventing ruinous inflation" by others. Both labels are examples of

(a)   economic bias

(b)   the fallacy of composition

(c)   the misuse of common-sense definitions

(d)   loaded terminology

10.   If one individual decides to decrease the consumption of beef, there will be little or no effect on beef prices. To argue, therefore, that if all individuals do likewise there should be little or no effect on beef prices is an example of

(a)   the *post hoc, ergo propter hoc* fallacy

(b)   the fallacy of composition

(c)   a generalization that is true during a depression but untrue during prosperity

(d)   using loaded terminology

11.   The Great Depression that began in 1929 was preceded by a stock market crash. To argue that the depression was then caused by the decline in the stock market is an example of

(a)   the *post hoc, ergo propter hoc* fallacy

(b)   the fallacy of composition

(c)   the *ceteris paribus* assumption

(d)   using loaded terminology

12.   Microeconomics deals with

(a)   the output of the entire economy

(b)   the output, employment, and income of the entire economy

(c)   the effect of changing the money supply on the Consumer Price Index

(d)   the economic decisions made by individuals

13.   If economic growth tends to produce a more equitable distribution of income among people in a nation, then this relationship between the two economic goals appears to be

(a)   deductive
(b)   conflicting
(c)   complementary
(d)   mutually exclusive

14.   Which of the following is associated with macroeconomics

(a)   the effect of the National Energy Program on the price of oil in Ontario

(b)   the effect of government set stumpage fees on the amount of lumber being exported to the United States

(c)   the effect of the Hibernia oil development on the economy of Newfoundland

(d)   the effect of the Free Trade Agreement on the price of computers in Canada

15.   When studying the relationship between two variables economists frequently assume that ''other things are equal.'' This is the use of

(a)   the *post hoc, ergo propter hoc* fallacy
(b)   the fallacy of composition
(c)   *ceteris paribus* assumption
(d)   using loaded terminology

DISCUSSION QUESTIONS

1.   Define economics in both a less and a more sophisticated way. In your second definition, explain the meaning of ''resources'' and ''wants.''

2.   Fresh water that cannot be exported from British Columbia flows into the Pacific and has no monetary value attached to it. If the government grants an export permit for shipment to the United States the same water suddenly becomes valuable. What changed to turn the water from a noneconomic good to an economic good?

3.   What is the relationship between facts and theory?

4.   Define and explain the relationships between descriptive economics, economic theory, and applied economics.

5.   Why do economic theories sometimes yield different predictions when dealing with identical economic circumstances?

6.   Why do economic models use very general assumptions?

7.   In what ways are the construction and application of economic models dangerous?

8.   What does it mean to say that economic principles can be used for prediction and control?

9.   A perusal of theoretical economic models discloses extensive use of quantitative methods. Why do economists have a bias for the use of mathematical techniques?

10.   Explain each of the following
(a)   fallacy of composition; (b)   loaded terminology; (c)   the *post hoc, ergo propter hoc* fallacy.

11.   Explain briefly the difference between
(a)   macroeconomics and microeconomics; (b)   deduction and induction; and (c)   correlation and causation.

12.   In the discussion in Box 1-1 exactly what economic perspective was used to understand the behaviour of fast-food customers?

ANSWERS

Fill-in questions

1.   efficient, scarce resources, maximum satisfaction

2.   citizens, vocational

3.   (a) descriptive; (b) theory, inductive, deductive; (c) policy

4.   theories, laws, generalizations, abstractions

5.   ''other things equal'' (*ceteris paribus*)

6.   positive, normative, normative

7.   complementary, conflicting or mutually exclusive

8.   as a whole; individual, firm, particular

9.   (a) full employment; (b) economic growth; (c) reasonable price stability; (d) viable balance of payments; (e) equitable distribution of rising incomes

10.   (a) define the goal; (b) suggest alternative policies, based on economic principles, to meet the goal; (c) choose the least cost alternative; (d) evaluate the effects of the policy

11.   fallacy of composition; *post hoc, ergo propter hoc*

12.   benefit, cost

Problems and projects

1.   An increase in the demand for an economic good will, *ceteris paribus*, cause the price of that good to rise.

2. (a) *post hoc ergo propter hoc* fallacy; (b) the fallacy of composition; (c) *post hoc ergo propter hoc* fallacy; (d) loaded terminology; (e) *post hoc ergo propter hoc* fallacy and loaded terminology

3. (a) N; (b) N; (c) P; (d) N; (e)P; (f) N

4. direct, up;

Self-test

1. T; 2. F; 3. F; 4. T; 5. T; 6. T; 7. T;

8. T; 9. F; 10. T; 11. F; 12. F; 13. T; 14. T; 15. T;

Multiple-choice

1. (d); 2. (b); 3. (c); 4. (a); 5. (d); 6. (c); 7. (c); 8. (d); 9. (d); 10. (b); 11. (a); 12. (d); 13. (c); 14. (c); 15. (c)

Appendix to Chapter 1: Graphs and Their Meaning

This appendix provides an introduction to graphing in economics. Graphs help illustrate and simplify the economic theories and models that will be presented throughout this book. The old saying that "a picture is worth a thousand words" applies to economics; graphs are the way that economists "picture" relationships between economic variables.

You will need to master the basics of graphing if these "pictures" are to be of any help to you. The appendix explains how to achieve that mastery. It begins by showing you how to construct a graph from a table of data on two variables, such as income and consumption. Economists usually, but not always, place the independent variable (income) on the horizontal axis and the dependent variable (consumption) on the vertical axis of the graph. Once the data points are plotted and a line drawn to connect the plotted points, you can determine whether there is a direct or inverse relationship between the variables. Identifying a direct and inverse relationship between variables is an essential skill that will be used repeatedly in this book.

Information from data in graphs and tables can be written in an equation. This work involves determining the slope and intercept from a straight line in a graph or data in a table. Using values for the slope and intercept, you can write a linear equation that will enable you to calculate what the dependent variable would be for a given level of the independent variable.

Some graphs used in the book are nonlinear. With nonlinear curves, the slope of the line is no longer constant throughout but varies as one moves along the curve. This slope can be estimated at a point by determining the slope of a straight line that is drawn tangent to the curve at that point. Similar calculations can be made for other points to see how the slope changes along the curve.

There is a particularly useful graph used in macroeconomics that is referred to as a 45° diagram. Construct an arithmetic graph with the same scale on the vertical and horizontal axes. Through the origin draw a straight line that has a slope of +1. This line makes an angle of 45° as measured from either axis. At any point on this line drop a perpendicular to the horizontal axis and a line parallel to the horizontal axis over to the vertical axis. The intersected values will be the same on both axes.

CHECKLIST

When you have studied this appendix, you should be able to:

- Understand why economists use graphs.
- Construct a graph of two variables using the numerical data from a table.
- Construct a table with two variables from an algebraic function or from data on a graph.
- Distinguish between a direct and an inverse relationship when given data on two variables.
- Identify dependent and independent variables in economic examples and graphs.
- Calculate the slope of a straight line between two points and determine the vertical intercept for the line.
- Write a linear equation using the slope of a line and the vertical intercept, and when given values for the independent variable, determine values for the independent variable.
- Estimate the slope of a nonlinear curve at a point using a line that is tangent to the curve at that point.

APPENDIX OUTLINE

1. A graph is a visual representation of the relationship between variables and serves as an aid in describing the economic theories and models.

2. The construction of a simple graph involves the plotting of numerical data about two variables from a table.

The tabular data can be obtained from the mathematical expression of the relationship between the variables.
(a)   Each graph has a horizontal and a vertical axis that can be labelled for each variable and then scaled for the range of the data points that will be measured on the axis. Arithmetic graphs are used extensively in the text and possess the characteristic that along a given axis equal distances represent equal numerical values.
(b)   Data points are plotted on the graph by drawing perpendiculars from the scaled points on the two axes to the place on the graph where the perpendiculars intersect.
(c)   A line or curve can then be drawn to connect the points plotted on the graph.

3.   A graph provides information about relationships between variables.
(a)   A line that is upward sloping to the right on a graph indicates that there is a positive or direct relationship between two variables: an increase in one is associated with an increase in the other; a decrease in one is associated with an increase in the other.
(b)   A line that is downward sloping to the right means that there is a negative or inverse relationship between the two variables because the variables are changing in opposite directions: an increase in one is associated with a decrease in the other; a decrease in one is associated with an increase in the other.

4.   Economists are often concerned with determining cause and effect in economic events.
(a)   A dependent variable changes (increases or decreases) because of a change in another variable.
(b)   An independent variable produces or "causes" the change in the dependent variable.
(c)   In a graph, mathematicians place an independent variable on the horizontal axis and a dependent variable on the vertical axis; economists are more arbitrary about which variable is placed on an axis.

5.   Economic graphs are simplifications of economic relationships. When graphs are plotted, there is usually an implicit assumption made that all other factors are being held constant. This "other things equal" or *ceteris paribus* assumption is used to simplify the analysis so the study can focus on the two variables of interest.

6.   A slope and intercept can be calculated for a straight line and written in the form of a linear equation.
(a)   The slope of a straight line is the ratio of the vertical change to the horizontal change between two points. Roughly, the slope measures the change in the dependent variable as a result of a one unit change in the independent variable. It is given the symbol: $\Delta y / \Delta x$.

A positive slope indicates that the relationship between two variables is direct; a negative slope means there is an inverse relationship between the variables.
(b)   Where the line intersects the vertical axis of the graph is the vertical intercept.
(c) A linear equation is written as $y = a + bx$. Once the values for the intercept a and the slope b are calculated, then given any value of the independent variable x, the value of the dependent variable y can be determined.

7.   The slope of a straight line is constant, but the slope of a nonlinear curve changes throughout. To estimate the slope of a nonlinear curve at a point, the slope of a line tangent to the curve at that point is calculated.

IMPORTANT TERMS

dependent and independent variables
direct and inverse relationships
slope of a straight line
tangent
vertical and horizontal axes
vertical intercept

FILL-IN QUESTIONS

1.   The relationship between two economic variables can be visualized with the aid of a two-dimensional graph.
(a)   Customarily, the (dependent, independent) _____ variable is placed on the horizontal axis and the _____ variable is placed on the vertical axis. The _____ variable is said to change because of a change in the _____ variable.
(b)   The vertical and horizontal (scales, ranges) _____ on the graph are calibrated to reflect the _____ of values in a table of data points on which the graph is based.
(c)   Other variables, beyond the two in the graph, that might affect the economic relationship are assumed to be (changing, held constant) _____.
Ceteris paribus also means that other variables are

_____.

2.   The graph of a straight line that slopes downward to the right indicates that there is (a direct, an inverse)

_____ relationship between the two variables. A graph of a straight line that slopes upward to the right tells us that the relationship is (direct, inverse) _____. When the value of one variable increases and the value of the other variable increases, then the relationship is _____; when the value of one increases, while the other decreases, the relationship is _____

3. The slope of a straight line between two points is defined as the ratio of the (vertical, horizontal) _____ change to the _____ change. When two variables move in the same direction, the slope will be (negative, positive) _____; when the variables move in opposite directions, the slope will be _____. The point at which the line meets the vertical axis is called the _____ _____.

4. We can express the graph of a straight line with a linear equation that can be written as $y = a + bx$.

(a) a is the (slope, intercept) _____ and b is the _____.

(b) y is the (dependent, independent) _____ variable and x is the _____ variable.

(c) If a was 2, b was 4, and x was 5, then y would be _____. If the value of x changed to 7, then y would be _____. If the value of x changed to 3, then y would be _____.

5. The slope of a (straight line, nonlinear) _____ curve is constant throughout; the slope of a _____ curve varies from point to point. An estimate of the slope of a nonlinear curve at a point can be made by calculating the slope of a straight line that is _____ to the point on the curve.

PROBLEMS AND PROJECTS

1. Below are two exercises in making graphs. On the graphs plot the economic relationships contained in each exercise. Be sure to label each axis of the graph and to indicate the unit of measurement. Use the same scale on both axes.

(a) Graph national income on the horizontal axis and consumption expenditures on the vertical axis; locate the various national-consumption combinations given in the table below; connect the seven points and label the curve "Consumption Schedule." You have constructed a graph of a consumption function that is used extensively in macroeconomics.

The relationship between national income and consumption expenditures is a(n) (direct, inverse) _____ one and the Consumption Schedule a(n) (up-, down-) _____ sloping curve.

National income (billions of dollars)	Consumption expenditures (billions of dollars)
$ 600	$ 600
700	640
800	780
900	870
1000	960
1100	1050
1200	1140

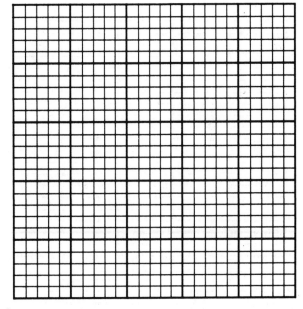

0

Suppose that national income goes from 600 to 700. The change in national income is + _____ . At the same time consumption increases from 600 to 670 so the accompanying change in consumption is _____. Given that income is the independent variable, the slope of the function at this point is equal to _____/_____ or

_____. The slope of this function (is, is

not) _____ constant.

(b)   Graph investment expenditures on the horizontal axis and the rate of interest on the vertical axis; connect the seven points and label the curve "Investment Schedule." The relationship between the rate of interest and

investment expenditures is a(n) _____

one and the Investment Schedule is a(n) _____ sloping curve.

Rate of Interest (%)	Investment Expenditures (Billions of Dollars)
9	$220
7	280
6	330
5	370
4	400
3	420
2	430

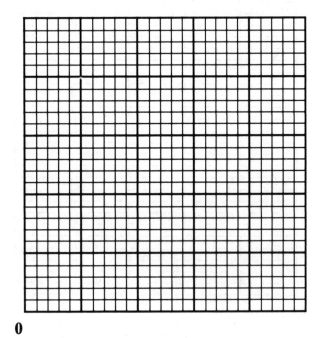

0

2.   This question is based on the graph in the next column.

(a)   Construct a table for points *A-I* from the data shown in the graph.

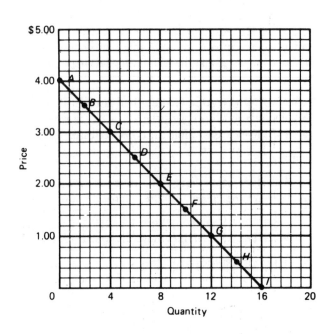

(b)   Economists generally treat price as the independent

variable and quantity as the _____ variable. The graph of the relationship between price and

quantity is a (downward, upward) _____ sloping straight line. The slope of the function is (posi-

tive, negative) _____ and since the graph

is a straight line the slope is some _____.

3.   To obtain a linear equation that summarizes the data the following steps can be followed.

The function is a _____ line so is of the form $p = a + bq$ where p is price and q is quantity.

a is   the   _____ and b is   the

_____.

To obtain the intercept term just note the value where the graph crosses the p axis. The intercept value is

_____. The slope is given by: (change in the p value/change in the q value). Consider the combinations (4, $3.00); (8, $2.00). The change in q is

_____ and the change in p is

_____. The slope is

_____/_____ =

_____.

The equation of the function is _____.

Notice that the function shows that price is a function of quantity. However, economists often place quantity as a function of price. To do this take the previous equation $p = a + bq$ and solve for q. Then $q = -a/b + (1/b).p$. The equation that shows q as a function of p is obtained by substituting the values of a and b found for the original equation:

$$q = \underline{\hspace{3cm}} - \underline{\hspace{3cm}} \, p$$

4. This problem is based on the graph below.

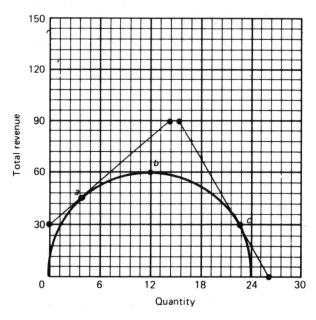

(a) The slope of the straight line through point a is?

_____

(b) The slope of the straight line through point b is?

_____

(c) The slope of the straight line through point c is?

_____

5. A dependent variable is sometimes related to more than one independent variable. For example quantity purchased may be a function of the price of the good, the price of other goods and incomes. Such a relationship cannot be placed on two-dimensional graphs. Economists fix the value of all but one of the independent variables at specific values. The function has now been reduced to one dependent and one independent variable. For example suppose the demand function is: $Q_x = (P_y.M)/P_x$ where Q_x is the quantity of good x, P_y is the price of a related good y, M is income and P_x is the price of good x. Set $P_y = 4$ and $M = 100$ and substitute into the function to yield: $Q_x = (4.100)/P_x$ or $Q_x =$

$400/P_x$. Complete the following table and place on a graph.

P_x	Q_x
8	_____
6	_____
4	_____
2	_____

This demand curve is (linear, nonlinear) _____.

SELF-TEST

Circle the T if the statement is true; the F if it is false.

1. Graphs provide a visual representation of the relationship between two variables.　**T F**

2. If the straight line on a two-variable graph is downward sloping to the right, then there is a positive relationship between the two variables.　**T F**

3. A variable that changes as a consequence of a change in another variable is considered to be a dependent variable.　**T F**

4. Economists always put the independent variable on the horizontal axis and the dependent variable on the variable axis of a two-variable graph.　**T F**

5. *Ceteris paribus* means that the value of all other variables is set equal to 0.　**T F**

6. In the ratio for the calculation of the slope of a straight line, the vertical change is divided by the horizontal change.　**T F**

7. If the slope of the linear relationship between consumption and income is 0.90, then it tells us that for every $1 increase in income there will be a $0.90 increase in consumption.　**T F**

8. The slope of a straight line is 0.　**T F**

9. If a linear equation is $y = 10 + 5x$, the vertical intercept is 10.　**T F**

10. A function with a constant slope becomes steeper as the independent variable increases.　**T F**

11. If the slope of a straight line on a two-variable (x, y) graph is 0.5 and the vertical intercept was 5, then a value of 10 for x means y is also 10.　**T F**

12. A slope of 4 for a straight line in a two-variable graph indicates that there is an inverse relationship between the two variables.　**T F**

13. If there is an inverse relation between price and quantity demanded, the graph of this function will be downward sloping.   **T F**

14. An upward slope for a straight line that is tangent to a nonlinear curve would indicate that the slope of the line is positive.   **T F**

15. If one pair of (x, y) points is (13, 10) and the other is (8, 20), then the slope of the straight line between the two sets of points in the two-variable graph, with x on the horizontal axis and y on the vertical axis, would be 2.   **T F**

16. When the value of x is 2, a value of 10 for y would be calculated from a linear equation of $y = -2 + 6x$.   **T F**

MULTIPLE-CHOICE

Circle the letter that corresponds to the best answer.

1. If an increase in one variable is associated with a decrease in another variable, then we can conclude that the variables are
(a) nonlinear
(b) directly related
(c) inversely related
(d) positively related

2. The ratio of the absolute vertical change to the absolute horizontal change between two points of a straight line is the
(a) slope
(b) vertical intercept
(c) horizontal intercept
(d) point of tangency

3. Economists
(a) always put the independent variable on the vertical axis
(b) always put the independent variable on the horizontal axis
(c) sometimes put the dependent variable on the horizontal axis
(d) use only linear function

4. In a two-variable graph of data on the price and quantity of a product, economists place
(a) price on the horizontal axis because it is the independent variable and quantity on the vertical axis because it is the dependent variable
(b) price on the vertical axis because it is the dependent variable and quantity on the horizontal because it is the independent variable

(c) price on the vertical axis even though it is the independent variable and quantity on the horizontal axis even though it is the dependent variable
(d) price on the horizontal axis even though it is the dependent variable and quantity on the vertical axis even though it is the independent variable

5. When the slope of a straight line to a point tangent to a nonlinear curve is zero, then the straight line is
(a) vertical
(b) horizontal
(c) upward sloping
(d) downward sloping

6. Assume a household has the following relationship between consumption (C) and income (Y): $C = 100 + .75Y$. At what level of income will consumption and income be equal?
(a) $Y = 0$
(b) $Y = 100$
(c) $Y = 200$
(d) $Y = 300$
(e) $Y = 400$

Answer the next four questions (7, 8, 9, and 10) on the basis of the following diagram.

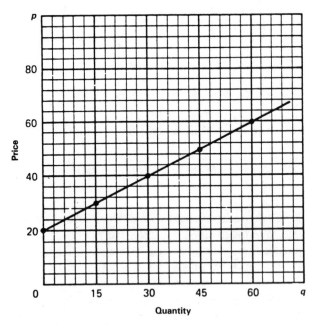

7. The graph indicates that price and quantity supplied are
(a) positively related
(b) negatively related
(c) indirectly related
(d) nonlinear

8. The slope of the line is
(a)   0.33
(b)   0.67
(c)   1.50
(d)   3.00

9. The vertical intercept is
(a)   80
(b)   60
(c)   40
(d)   20

10. The linear equation for the function is
(a) $p = 20 + 0.33q$
(b) $q = 20 + 0.33p$
(c) $p = 20 + 0.67q$
(d) $q = 20 + 0.67p$

11. There is a second relationship between p and q that can be displayed on the same graph. This new function has an intercept value on the p axis of 80 and an intercept value of 60 on the q axis. Join these two points with a straight line. The slope of this function is
(a)   1.00
(b)   -1.00
(c)   1.33
(d)   -1.33
(e)   -.67

12. The equation for the new function is
(a) $p = 80—q$
(b) $p = 80 + q$
(c) $p = 80—1.33q$
(d) $p = 80 + 1.33q$
(e) $p = 80 -.67q$

13. The two functions are equal to each other at a q value of
(a)   15
(b)   30
(c)   45
(d)   60

Answer the next three questions on the basis of the diagram in the next column.

14. The slope of the line tangent to the curve at point A is
(a)   -2
(b)   2
(c)   1.5
(d)   0.5

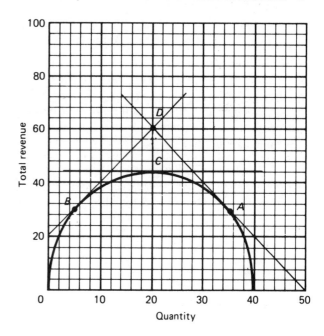

15. The slope of the line tangent to the curve at point B is
(a)   – 2
(b)   2
(c)   3
(d)   0.5

16. The slope of the line tangent to the curve at point C is:
(a)   – 1
(b)   1
(c)   0
(d)   undefined

DISCUSSION QUESTIONS

1. Why do economists use graphs in their work? Give two examples of a graph that illustrates the relationship between two economic variables.

2. Construct graphs for straight line functions with slopes of: -1, 0, infinity.

3. If the vertical intercept increases in value but the slope of a straight line stays the same, what happens to the graph of the line? If the vertical intercept decreases in value, what will happen to the line?

4. When you know that the price and quantity of a product are inversely related, what does this tell you about the slope of a line? What do you know about the slope when the two variables are positively related?

5.   Which variable is the dependent and which is the independent in the following economic statement: "A decrease in business taxes had a positive effect on investment spending." How do you tell the difference between a dependent and independent variable when examining economic relationships?

6.   Why is an assumption made that all other variables are held constant when we construct a two-variable graph of the price and quantity of a product?

7.   How do mathematicians and economists differ at times in the way that they construct two-dimensional graphs? Give an example.

8.   If you know that the equation relating price to quantity demanded is: $q = 60 - 2p$. What would quantity demanded be if price is 6? Construct a price-quantity demanded schedule for five different levels of price.

9.   How do the slopes of a straight line and a nonlinear curve differ? How do you estimate the slope of a nonlinear curve?

ANSWERS

Fill-in questions

1. (a) independent, dependent; dependent, independent (b) scales, ranges (c) held constant; held constant

2. an inverse; direct; direct, inverse

3. vertical, horizontal; positive, negative; vertical intercept

4. (a) intercept, slope (b) dependent, independent; (c) 22; 30; 14

5. straight line, nonlinear, tangent

Problems and projects

1. (a) direct, up; 100; 70; 70/100,. 70; is (b) inverse, down-

2. (a)

Point	Price	Quantity
A	$4.00	0
B	3.50	2
C	3.00	4
D	2.50	6
E	2.00	8
F	1.50	10
G	1.00	12
H	0.50	14
I	0.00	16

(b) dependent; downward; negative, constant

3. straight; intercept, slope; $4.00; 4, 1; (-1/4) = -.25; $p = 4 - .25q$; $q = 16 - 4p$

4. (a) 4; (b) 0; (c)- 8.75

5. 50, 66.6, 100, 200; nonlinear

Self-test

1. T; **2.** F; **3.** T; **4.** F; **5.** F; **6.** T; **7.** T; **8.** F; **9.** T; **10.** F; **11.** T; **12.** F; **13.** T; **14.** T; **15.** F; **16.** T

Multiple-choice

1. (c); **2.** (a); **3.** (c); **4.** (c); **5.** (b); **6.** (e); **7.** (a); **8.** (b); **9.** (d); **10.** (c); **11.** (d); **12.** (c); **13.** (b); **14.** (a); **15.** (b); **16.** (c)

CHAPTER

2

The Economizing Problem

The central problem of economics is that resources—the ultimate means of satisfying material wants—are scarce *relative* to the insatiable wants of society. Resources possess varying characteristics as to their durability. Some productive factors, such as labour, are reproducible while others, such as iron ore or the environmental carrying capacity, tend to be fixed in volume. The capital stock, which is a produced factor of production, lasts more than one period so the type of goods produced in one period affects the productive capacity for some future periods. Given these interrelationships the science of economics is the study of how society should determine the allocation of scarce resources over time and choose a specific array of goods and services to be produced in order to achieve maximum satisfaction from fulfilling some of its unlimited wants. In this chapter the four factors of production—land, labour, capital, and entrepreneurial ability—are set fixed and only one time period is considered. Since these inputs are scarce, they must be used in the most efficient manner (productive efficiency) to produce the goods most wanted by society (allocative efficiency).

The production possibilities table and curve are used in this chapter to illustrate the meaning of the scarcity of resources and of opportunity costs. It is both an illustrative device that will help you to understand several economic concepts and problems and a tool that has many applications in the real world.

Every economy is faced with the problem of scarcity and has to find ways to allocate resources for the production of different goods and services. But no two economies arrive at answers to their fundamental economic problems in the same way. Between the extremes of pure (or *laissez-faire*) capitalism and the command economy (or communism) are various economic systems; all of these systems are different methods of organization for finding solutions to the problem of scarcity in the face of unlimited wants.

CHECKLIST

When you have studied this chapter, you should be able to:

- Write a definition of economics that incorporates the relationship between scarce resources and unlimited wants.

- Be able to differentiate between wants and needs.

- Understand that choice is necessitated because scarce resources imply limited output and wants are unlimited.

- Identify the four economic resources and the type of income associated with each.

- State the four assumptions made when a production possibilities table or curve is constructed.

- Construct a production possibilities curve when you are given the appropriate data.

- Define opportunity cost and utilize a production possibilities curve to explain the concept.

- State the law of increasing opportunity costs and, in as few words as possible, present the economic rationale for this law.

- Be able to construct production possibilities tables that display increasing and constant opportunity costs.

- Use a production possibilities curve to illustrate technical change, underemployment of resources, constant and increasing opportunity costs.

- Define productive and allocative efficiency and indicate their relationship to the production possibilities curve.

- Describe some economic characteristics of pure capitalism, the command economy, and a mixed economic system.

CHAPTER OUTLINE

1. The bases upon which the study of economics rests are

(a) An assumption that society's material wants are unlimited.

(b) The economic resources that are the ultimate means of satisfying these wants are scarce in relation to the wants.

(1) Economic resources are classified as land, capital, labour, and entrepreneurial ability. The passage of time as a factor affecting resource supply is ignored.

(2) The payments received by those who provide the economy with these four resources are rental income, interest income, wage, and profits, respectively.

(3) Because these resources are scarce (or limited), the output the economy is able to produce is also limited.

2. Economics, then, is the study of how society's scarce resources are used (allocated) to obtain the greatest satisfaction from the fulfilment of some of its material wants.

3. The production possibilities table indicates the alternative combinations of goods and services an economy is capable of producing when it has achieved productive efficiency.

4. Four assumptions are made when a production possibilities table is constructed.

(a) efficiency
(b) fixed resources
(c) fixed technology
(d) two products

5. The data contained in the production possibilities table can be plotted on a graph to obtain a production possibilities curve.

6. The scarcity of resources together with unlimited wants implies that society is better off when maximum output is obtained from output usage or, in other words, resources are used efficiently. When productive efficiency is achieved maximum output is obtained and with full employment of resources society will be on and not inside it's production possibilities curve.

7. Every point on the production possibilities curve can be attained. Society must choose one combination of goods and when this combination provides the greatest satisfaction the economy is said to be allocatively efficient.

8. When both productive and allocative efficiency are achieved the economy has reached full production.

9. Which of the different combinations of goods is selected depends upon the choice mechanism utilized by society to reflect preferences.

10. The production possibilities curve illustrates the concepts of scarcity, choice, and opportunity cost.

11. Given full employment and full production the increase in production of one good necessitates a decrease in the production of the other good. This foregone output is termed the opportunity cost and arises because resources must be shifted from the production of one good to the production of the other.

12. Economists often assume that the opportunity cost of producing additional units of a product increases as more of that product is produced.

(a) Increasing opportunity costs are assumed to arise because resources are not perfectly substitutable in the production of different goods.

(b) Increasing opportunity cost is reflected in a production possibilities curve that is concave (bowed out from the origin).

13. The following modifications make the production possibilities concept more realistic.

(a) The failure to achieve full employment and full production reduces the output of the economy. Production is occurring to the left of the production possibilities curve.

(b) Improvements in technology and increased amounts of resources expand the output the economy is capable of producing. The production possibilities curve shifts to the right.

(c) The combination of goods and services an economy chooses to produce today helps to determine its production possibilities in the future. By using its resources for the production of capital today society increases tomorrow's productive capacity.

14. Different economic systems are used by different societies to coordinate and direct economic activity.

(a) At one extreme is pure capitalism, which relies upon the private ownership of its economic resources, the profit motive, and the market system to determine the goods to be produced.

(b) At the other extreme, the command economy uses public ownership of its resources and central planning.

(c) Economies in the real world lie between these two extremes and are hybrid systems.

(d) Some underdeveloped nations have traditional (or customary) economies, in which the answers to the central economic problem are provided by the customs and traditions of the society.

15. Canada has a "mixed" economy with varying degrees of private control and governmental regulation in different sectors.

IMPORTANT TERMS

allocative efficiency
authoritarian capitalism
capital goods
command economy or communism
consumer goods
economic growth
economizing problem
full employment
full production
investment
land, labour, capital, and entrepreneurial ability
law of increasing opportunity costs
market socialism
production possibilities table (curve)
productive efficiency
pure or laissez-faire capitalism
traditional or customary economies
utility

FILL-IN QUESTIONS

1. The two fundamental facts that provide the foundation of economics are:

(a) _____

(b) _____

2. Complete the following classification of resources.

(a) _____

(1) _____

(2) _____

(b) _____

(1) _____

(2) _____

3. Both consumer goods and capital goods satisfy human wants. The consumer goods satisfy these wants (directly, indirectly) _____ and the capital goods satisfy them _____.

4. The incomes of individuals are received from supplying resources. Four types of incomes are:

_____ _____, _____

_____, _____, and

_____.

5. Economics can be defined as _____

_____.

6. Economic efficiency requires that there be both full _____ of resources and full

_____.

7. When a production possibilities table or curve is constructed, four assumptions are made. These assumptions are

(a) _____

(b) _____

(c) _____

(d) _____

8. Below is a production possibilities curve for tractors and suits of clothing.

(a)   If the economy moves from point A to point B, it will produce (more, fewer) _____ tractors and (more, fewer) _____ suits of clothing.

(b)   If the economy is producing at point X, some of the resources of the economy are either _____ or _____.

(c)   If the economy moves from point X to point B (more, fewer) _____ tractors and (more, fewer) _____ suits will be produced.

(d)   If the economy is to produce at point Y, it must either _____ or _____.

9. All the combinations of products shown in the production possibilities table (or on the curve) can be achieved only if there are both full employment and productive efficiency in the economy; the best combination of products depends upon the (values, resources, technology) _____ of that society and is a (scientific, nonscientific) _____ matter.

10. The quantity of other goods and services an economy must go without in order to produce more low-cost housing is the _____ of producing the additional low-cost housing.

11. The cost of producing a commodity tends to increase as more of the commodity is produced because

_____.

12. The more an economy consumes of its current production, the (more, less) _____ it will be capable of producing in future years if other things are equal.

13. The changes that occur almost continuously in modern industrial economies, and that these economies must accommodate if they are to be efficient, are changes in

(a) _____

(b) _____

(c) _____

14. Productive efficiency is met when the economy, with full employment, is (to the right of, on) _____ its production possibilities curve.

15. Productive efficiency means that the _____ _____ production techniques are used in the production of wanted goods and services.

16. Production is allocatively efficient when, given the distribution of resources and assets, the economy produces that combination of goods _____ _____ by society.

17. All points on the production possibilities curve are _____ efficient but some points are not _____ efficient.

18. Full production implies that two kinds of efficiency, _____ and _____, are achieved.

19. In pure capitalism property resources are (publicly, privately) _____ owned; in a command economy resources are _____ owned.

20. The term "laissez-faire" can be roughly translated as _____ _____ _____ and means a _____ role for government in the economy.

21. The Canadian economy leans toward _____ _____ but the government plays an active role in some sectors.

PROBLEMS AND PROJECTS

1. Below is a list of resources. Indicate in the space to the right of each whether the resource is land (Ld), capital (K), labour (L), entrepreneurial ability (EA), or some combination of these.
(a) fishing grounds in the North Atlantic
(b) the wheat inventory held by the Canadian Wheat Board
(c) an irrigation ditch in Saskatchewan
(d) the Saddledome in Calgary
(e) the work performed by the late Henry Ford
(f) the oxygen breathed by human beings
(g) Cavendish beach in Prince Edward Island
(h) the Steel Company of Canada plant in Hamilton, Ontario
(i) the tasks accomplished in making Apple Computer a commercial success
(j) the goods on the shelf of a retail store
(k) the work done by a welder on an assembly line
(l) the Jacques Cartier bridge over the St. Lawrence river

2. Suppose an economy produces two products: timber (T) and fish (F) with the use of one input, which we will call labour (L). The production relation is give by:

$$T^2 + F^2 = L$$

Suppose in the economy there are 1600 units of L. Therefore $T^2 + F^2 = 1600$. Solve for T.

$$T = +\sqrt{1600 - F^2}$$

Now we have a relation between the amount of timber and fish an economy can produce so a production possibilities schedule can be constructed. Complete the following production possibilities schedule.

Place the production possibilities schedule on the graph below. Place T on the vertical axis and F on the horizontal axis.

T	F
0	40
19.36	35
40	0

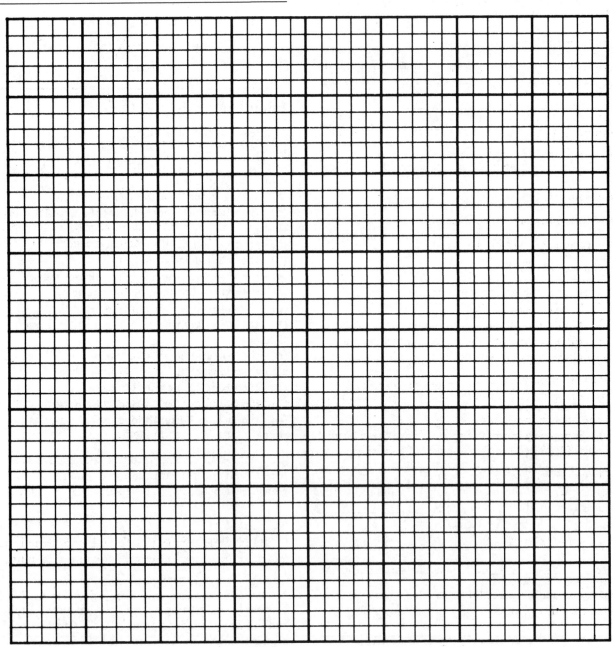

0

(a)   Can the economy produce 30 of F and 35 of T?

_____ If you answered "no" state the reason

for your answer. _____
(b)   Assume the economy is at full employment of input
L and is producing 0 of F and 40 of T and the decision
is made to produce 5 of F. How many units of T must

be given up? _____
(c)   Assume that the economy is at full employment of
L and is producing 5 of F. The decision is made to produce 5 more of F. How many of T must be given up?

_____

(d)   Assume the economy is at full employment of L
and is producing 35 of F and the decision is made to produce 40 of F. How many units of T must be given up?

_____

(e)   As the number of units of F produced increases what
can be said about the number of units of T that must

be given up to get the extra F? _____
(f)   What can you say about the opportunity cost of an

extra unit of F? _____

(g)   Since the opportunity cost of F _____

the production possibilities curve will be _____

or bowed out from the _____.

3.   Suppose the production relation changed to T +
F = L. Again assume that L = 1600.
(a)   Would the production possibilities curve shift to
the right or to the left if you placed the new production
possibilities schedule on the same graph as you con-

structed for question 2? _____
(b)   Along the new production possibilities curve what

is the opportunity cost of one unit of F? _____
(c)   Suppose with the new production relation output
is 600 of F and 600 of T. What would be the opportu-

nity cost of producing one more of F? _____
(d)   What does this economy lose by using only 1599

units of L? _____

4.   In the next column is a production possibilities curve.

Draw on this graph
(a)   a production possibilities curve that indicates greater
efficiency in the production of good A;

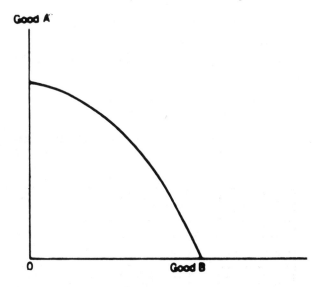

(b)   a production possibilities curve that indicates greater
efficiency in the production of good B;
(c)   a production possibilities curve that indicates an
increase in the resources available to the community.

5.   Below is a list of economic goods. Indicate in the
space to the right of each whether the good is a consumer
food (C), a capital good (K), or that it depends (D) upon
who is using it and for what purpose.
(a)   a dairy cow
(b)   a tractor
(c)   a parking lot
(d)   a telephone pole
(e)   a telephone
(f)   Highway 401 in Ontario
(g)   a refrigerator in a meat packing plant
(h)   hockey skates worn by Brett Hull
(i)   a book in the library at your educational institution
(j)   my VCR in my home
(k)   a rented VCR in my home
(l)   a screwdriver

SELF-TEST

Circle T if the statement is true, F if it is false.

1.   Since the government can print money there is no
opportunity cost connected with government spending.
                                          T F

2.   Money is a resource and is classified as "capital."**T F**

3.   A Canada Savings Bond is classified as a capital good.
                                          T F

4. A natural gas pipeline is an example of a capital good. **T F**

5. Profit is the reward paid to those who provide the economy with capital. **T F**

6. The World Series share paid to the members of the losing team is a rent payment. **T F**

7. The payment to Quebec Hydro for electricity service by a resident of Montreal is a rent payment. **T F**

8. The fundamental problem of Canadian economics is the lack of employment opportunities for Canadian youth. **T F**

9. The main opportunity cost of going to college is the foregone earnings. **T F**

10. Other things being equal university enrolment should increase during periods of recession. **T F**

11. Rising living standards in the capitalistic economies is proof that the scarcity problem has been overcome. **T F**

12. The opportunity cost of producing a good tends to increase as more of it is produced because resources less suitable to its production must be employed. **T F**

13. Drawing a production possibilities curve concave to the origin is the geometric way of stating the law of increasing opportunity costs. **T F**

14. A downward sloping production possibilities curve that is bowed out from the origin indicates constant opportunity costs. **T F**

15. An economy cannot produce outside its production possibilities curve because resources are limited. **T F**

16. Every person in a society would prefer any point on the production possibilities curve to every point off the curve. **T F**

17. Roundabout methods of production are used because they result in the production possibilities curve shifting to the right over time. **T F**

18. Economic growth means an increase in the ability of an economy to produce goods and services; this is shown by a movement of the production possibilities curve to the right. **T F**

19. Most economies are arrayed between the extremes of pure capitalism and the command economy. **T F**

20. An economy that is employing the least cost productive methods has achieved allocative efficiency. **T F**

MULTIPLE-CHOICE

Circle the letter that corresponds to the best answer.

1. An "innovator" is defined as an entrepreneur who
(a) makes basic policy decisions in a business firm
(b) combines factors of production to produce a good or service
(c) invents a new product or process for producing a product
(d) introduces new products on the market or employs a new method to produce a product

2. An economy is efficient when it has achieved
(a) full employment
(b) full production
(c) either full employment or full production
(d) both full employment and full production

3. When a production possibilities schedule is written (or a production possibilities curve is drawn), four assumptions are made. Which of the following is *not* one of those assumptions?
(a) only two goods are produced
(b) wants are unlimited
(c) the economy has both full employment and full production
(d) the quantities of all resources available to the economy are fixed

Answer the next four questions on the basis of the following diagram.

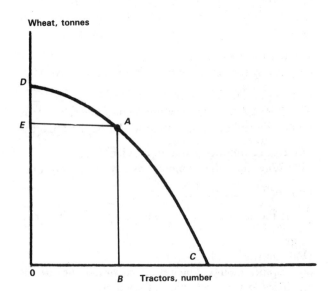

4. At point *A* on the production possibilities curve
(a) less wheat than tractors is being produced
(b) less tractors than wheat are being produced

(c) the economy is employing all its resources
(d) the economy is not employing all its resources

5. The opportunity cost of producing 0B of tractors is:
(a) 0D of wheat
(b) 0E of wheat
(c) ED of wheat
(d) 0C of tractors
(e) BC of tractors

6. If there occured a technological improvement in the production of tractors but not wheat,
(a) point D would remain fixed and point C shift to the left
(b) point C would remain fixed and point D shift upward
(c) point D would remain fixed and point C shift to the right
(d) point C would remain fixed and point D shift inward
(e) point D would shift upward and point C shift to the left

7. The production possibilities curve is
(a) concave
(b) convex
(c) linear
(d) positive

8. For a movement along a production possibilities curve
(a) resources remain fixed but are reallocated between the production of the two goods
(b) resources are increased and are reallocated between the two goods
(c) resources are increased and production of both goods increased
(d) idle resources are put to work to increase the production of one good

9. A production possibilities curve that displays constant opportunity costs will be
(a) concave to the origin
(b) convex to the origin
(c) a downward sloping straight line
(d) parallel to the horizontal axis

10. Which of the following would cause a nation's production possibilities curve to shift inward toward the origin?
(a) increase in the labour force
(b) a shift in employment from manufacturing to service industries
(c) increased international trade
(d) increased employment
(e) not replacing the capital stock as it wears out

11. Which of the following will cause the movement of the Canadian production possibilities curve to the right to slow down?
(a) increasing rate of technological change
(b) increased immigration
(c) decrease in the birth rate
(d) decreased impediments to the interprovincial flow of goods and services

12. The opportunity cost of providing a governmentally financed stadium for the city's baseball team is
(a) the interest on the money borrowed to finance the stadium
(b) the future tax increase the public will be forced to contribute to pay for the stadium
(c) there is no opportunity cost since Ottawa will finance the stadium under a regional development program
(d) the other goods and services that must be sacrificed so that resources can be used for stadium construction.

13. The private ownership of property resources, use of the market system to direct and coordinate economic activity and the presence of the profit motive is characteristic of
(a) pure capitalism
(b) the command economy
(c) market socialism
(d) the traditional economy

14. In Canada the presence of some public ownership and numerous governmental regulations together with an emphasis on private ownership, profit motive, and market determined prices can be described as a
(a) pure capitalistic system
(b) market socialism
(c) mixed capitalistic system
(d) command economy
(e) traditional economy

15. The public ownership of property resources and use of a market system to direct and coordinate economic activity is characteristic of
(a) pure capitalism
(b) the command economy
(c) market socialism
(d) authoritarian capitalism

16. To decide how to use its scarce resources to satisfy human wants, pure capitalism relies on
(a) central planning
(b) roundabout production
(c) a price system together with the profit motive
(d) the coincidence of wants

17. Factors that change the potential output of an economy include all but
(a) technological change
(b) increased resource supplies
(c) improved resource quality
(d) moving labour out of the service industries and back into manufacturing industries

18. Productive efficiency is attained when
(a) resources are all employed
(b) output is produced at least possible cost
(c) there is no government involvement in the economy
(d) the production possibilities curve is concave

19. The term "laissez faire" refers to
(a) the absence of monopoly
(b) the absence of government involvement in the economy
(c) the efficient use of employed resources
(d) the view that government is responsible for achieving full employment but should operate through the private sector to reach this goal.

DISCUSSION QUESTIONS

1. Explain what is meant by the "economizing problem." Why are resources scarce?

2. In what sense are wants satiable, and in what sense are they insatiable?

3. What are the four economic resources? How is each of these resources defined? What is the income earned by each of them called?

4. When is a society economically efficient? What is meant by "full production," and how does it differ from "full employment"?

5. What four assumptions are made in drawing a production possibilities curve or schedule? How do technological advance and an increased supply of resources in the economy affect the curve schedule?

6. Why cannot an economist determine which combination in the production possibilities table is "best"? What determines the optimum product-mix?

7. What is opportunity cost? What is the law of increasing cost? Why do costs increase?

8. Would the economic problem disappear if the affluent countries offered to pay more for the products of the Third World countries? Explain.

9. Would the economic problem disappear if every country abolished all trade restrictions? If your answer is "no" then explain why so much emphasis was placed on the Canada–U.S. Free Trade Agreement. In your answer make use of the economic concepts introduced in this chapter.

10. Suppose resources in an economy are fully employed. What would be the effect on living standards if the government decided to increase the output of capital? Explain using the production possibilities curve introduced in this chapter.

11. Explain why you agree or disagree with the statement: "The opportunity cost of increased production during a recession is different from the opportunity cost during a period of full employment."

12. What is the important relationship between the composition of the economy's current output and the location of future production possibilities curves?

13. Explain the difference between productive and allocative efficiency.

14. How is the "what to produce" question solved under the pure capitalistic system as compared to a mixed capitalistic system?

ANSWERS

Fill-in questions

1. (a) society's material wants are unlimited; (b) economic resources, which are the ultimate means of satisfying these wants, are scarce in relation to these wants

2. (a) property resources; (1) land or raw materials, (2) capital;. (b) human resources; (1) labour, (2) entrepreneurial ability

3. directly, indirectly

4. rental income, interest income, wages, profits

5. a social science concerned with the problem of allocating scarce resources to attain maximum satisfaction from fulfilling some of society's unlimited wants

6. employment, production

7. (a) full employment; (b) fixed factor supplies; (c) fixed technology; (d) two goods are produced

8. (a) fewer, more;. (b) unemployed, underemployed;. (c) more, more;. (d) increase resource supplies, improve technology

9. values, nonscientific

10. opportunity

11. resources are not perfectly substitutable in the production of various goods

12. less

13. (a) consumers' tastes; (b) resource supplies; (c) technology

14. on

15. least costly

16. most wanted

17. productively, allocatively

18. productive, allocative

19. (a) privately, publicly

20. let it be, limited

21. pure capitalism

Problems and projects

1. (a) Ld; (b) K; (c) K; (d) K; (e) EA; (f) Ld; (g) Ld; (h) K; (i) EA; (j) K; (k) L, (l) K

2.

T	F
0	40
19.36	35
26.46	30
31.22	25
34.64	20
37.08	15
38.73	10
39.69	5
40	0

(a) No; $30^2 + 35^2 > 1600$; (b) .31; (c) .96; (d) 19.36; (e) increases; (f) increasing; (g) increases, concave, origin

3. (a) right; (b) 1 T; (c) 0 (unemployed resources); (d) 1 F or 1 T

5. (a) K, (b) K, (c) K, (d) K, (e) D, (f) K, (g) K, (h) D, (i) K, (j) C, (k) K, (l) D

Self-test

1. F, 2. F, 3. F, 4. T, 5. F, 6. F, 7. F, 8. F, 9. T, 10. T, 11. F, 12. T, 13. T, 14. F, 15. T, 16. F, 17. T, 18. T, 19. T, 20. F

Multiple-choice

1. (d), 2. (d), 3. (b), 4. (c), 5. (c), 6. (c), 7. (a), 8. (a), 9. (c), 10. (e), 11. (c), 12. (d), 13. (a), 14. (c), 15. (c), 16. (c), 17. (d), 18. (b), 19. (b)

CHAPTER

3

Overview of the Market System and the Circular Flow

Chapter 2 outlined the central economic problem faced by every economy. Throughout history different forms of economic organization have been used to provide solutions. The system used in Canada is termed "mixed capitalistic" and it is the aim of this chapter to begin a description of our economy. To start, an idealized market system, which is called pure capitalism, is described and the determinants of its production and distribution activities outlined. The model is altered in a number of later chapters so the system that finally emerges at the close of the course does represent the present-day Canadian economy.

In the pure capitalist system resources are privately owned; prices, which are determined in competitive markets, reflect the desires of buyers and sellers; self-interest is the motivating factor, and the role of the government strictly limited. Competitive forces lead society to produce at some point on the production possibilities curve where productive and allocative efficiency are realized. Prices, set in a system of competitive markets and indicative of profit opportunities, determine resource allocation.

The central economic problem can now be expressed as five problems or questions that must be answered: the level at which resources will be utilized; what will be produced; how it will be produced; how the output will be distributed; and how the economic system can be made to accommodate changes. These five questions are answered by a form of economic organization that will automatically result in the least cost production of goods and services that are deemed to be most valuable by society's members.

In the capitalist system self-interest of the individual, through the discipline of competition, is led to work for the well-being of society. It is as though the participants are led by an "invisible hand" to promote society's interest even though each individual is concerned solely with his/her own profit. Forced by unending competition to produce at least cost, the producer uses a mini-

mum of society's scarce resources. Prices, which reflect society's marginal valuation of goods and services, determine profits and hence the goods produced. Productive and allocative efficiency are met so society is obtaining maximum satisfaction from its scarce resources. The five fundamental questions are answered by a self-regulating market system without the need for any outside interference. The system automatically responds to changes in consumers' tastes, technology, or resource supplies.

The three practices of all modern economies are: the employment of large amounts of capital, extensive specialization, and the use of money. Economies use capital and engage in specialization because it is a more efficient use of their resources in that a larger total output results. Greater satisfaction results from fulfilling a greater number of wants. But, when workers, business firms, and regions within an economy specialize, trade must occur to obtain goods and services produced by others. Exchange results in the creation of markets in which buyers and sellers communicate their offers and exchange ratios among the traded goods and services are determined. The use of money allows the exchange ratios to be expressed in terms of units of a currency and are referred to as prices. Trade is facilitated since a common denominator—units of currency—is used to express value. In the market milk is quoted at a price of $1.50 per litre and oranges $3.00 a dozen rather than the exchange ratio of one dozen oranges for two litres of milk.

The circular-flow-of-income model is a device that illustrates, for a capitalistic economy, the relation between households and businesses, the flow of money and economic goods and services between households and businesses, their dual role as buyers and sellers, and the two basic types of markets essential to the capitalistic system. Economists differentiate between real flows, which are exchanges of goods and services for other goods and services, and money flows, which are exchanges of units of currency for goods and services.

CHECKLIST

When you have studied this chapter, you should be able to:

■ Identify and explain the six important institutional characteristics of capitalism.

■ List the Five Fundamental Questions every economy must answer and explain how the answers are determined in a capitalistic system.

■ Name and explain the three characteristics of all modern economies.

■ Explain why specialization requires trade and trade, in turn, results in the formation of markets and the determination of trading ratios or prices.

■ Know the difference between real and monetary flows.

■ Explain how the use of money facilitates trade.

■ Draw the circular flow diagram and correctly label the *real* and *money* flows and the two major types of markets.

CHAPTER OUTLINE

1. Capitalism is defined as an economic system possessing the characteristics of: private property, freedom of enterprise and choice, self-interest, competition, reliance upon markets, and a limited role for government.

2. In the capitalist model prices are determined in the market by buyers and sellers seeking their own well-being. These prices are the signalling device for the allocation of society's scarce resources. Because of the pivotal role markets play the capitalistic model is often referred to as the market system or market economy.

3. Private property refers to the individual ownership of assets. Not all property is of a material nature but consists of rights attached to assets or granted by society.

4. The working of the market system results in output that meets the criteria of productive and allocative efficiency.

5. The market mechanism communicates the intensity of the wants of consumers to business people who, forced by competition and motivated by self-interest, use the minimum of resources to produce the indicated good or service.

6. Faced with unlimited wants and scarce resources, every economy must find answers for the Five Fundamental Questions: the level of resource use; what goods and services to produce; how to organize the production of these goods and services; how to divide this output among the citizens of society; and how to accommodate changes in tastes, resources, and technology.

7. The market system provides an answer to these five questions by basing business survival on the efficient use of resources for the production of goods most wanted by society.

8. In common with other advanced economies of the world, the Canadian economy has three main characteristics:
(a) It employs complicated and advanced methods of production and large amounts of capital equipment to produce goods and services efficiently.
(b) It is a specialized economy and this specialization increases the productive efficiency of the economy.
(c) It also uses money to facilitate trade.

9. The use of capital means that resources are not used to directly produce goods or services but to produce goods that, in turn, produce the goods and services that are consumed. Resources are used to build bulldozers that are then used in road construction. Roundabout productive methods are utilized because of their efficiency.

10. Specialization, which increases productive efficiency, requires trade and has led to the formation of markets in which trading ratios are determined. Trade is facilitated by the use of money through which the trading ratios between goods and services are indicated by their prices.

11. The circular flow model is a device used to clarify the relationships between households and business firms in a purely capitalistic economy. In resource markets, households supply and firms demand resources. In the product markets the firms supply and households demand products. The real flow is the exchange of services for goods. Households use the money they get for services to purchase the products of firms. There is a money flow of incomes to households and product expenditures to firms.

12. Although the market system leads to the efficient use of resources the operation of the pure capitalistic system is often modified in real world activity because:
(a) markets sometimes do not exist, i.e. pollution rights
(b) private ownership of resources does not exist, i.e. the fishery
(c) the presence of interrelationships in production or consumption may be ignored
(d) the resulting distribution of income may not meet society's minimum standards for some individuals
(e) specialization can lead to some disadvantages

IMPORTANT TERMS

bartering
circular flow model
coincidence of wants
competition
firms
Five Fundamental Questions
freedom of choice
freedom of enterprise
household
''invisible hand''
market economy
medium of exchange
money
private property
resource and product markets
roundabout production
self-interest
specialization and division of labour

FILL-IN QUESTIONS

1. The ownership of property resources by private individuals and organizations is the institution of _private property_.

2. Two basic freedoms encountered in the market system are the freedoms of _choice_ and _enterprise_.

3. According to the assumption of self-interest each economic unit attempts to do what _is best for_.

4. The market economy presumes _self-interest_ as the fundamental method of operation for the various economic units.

5. Competition is present if two conditions prevail; these two conditions are

(a) _free entrepreneurship_

(b) _large number of buyers and sellers_

6. Market determined prices are the _guideposts_ upon which economic units make and revise their choices in furthering their own _self interest_.

7. Market prices are determined by the _demand_

of the _consumer_ and the _supply_ of the producers.

8. The concept of the pure market system as a self-regulating economy precludes any significant role for _government_.

9. List the six characteristics of the capitalist system.

(a) _private property_

(b) _freedom of enterprise_

(c) _freedom of choice_

(d) _self-interest_

(e) _competition_

(f) _reliance upon market_
limited role for government

10. Economic units seeking to further their own self-interest and operating within the capitalistic system will simultaneously, as though directed by an _invisible hand_, promote the _social_ or _public_ interest.

11. The output mix of the competitive market system is determined by _price_.

12. Competition forces firms to use the _least cost_ production methods.

13. List the Five Fundamental Questions to which every society must respond.

(a) _what is the level of ressources use?_

(b) _what good and services to produce_

(c) _how to organise the production_

(d) _how to divide the output_

(e) _how to accomodate changes_

14. Changes in consumer _tastes_ cause competitive markets to _reallocate_ resources.

15. The three practices or institutions common to modern economies are:

(a) _Specialization_

(b) _use of money_

(c) _roundabout production_

16. Specialization tends to _increase_ productive efficiency.

17. If an economy engages in extensive specialization, the individuals living in the economy are extremely _independent_ and if these individuals are to enjoy the benefits of specialization there must be _trade_ among them.

18. Bartering refers to trading _good_ for _good_.

19. Exchange by barter requires a _coincidence_ _of_ _wants_.

20. Money is a social invention for _faciliting_ exchange.

21. For an item to serve as money it needs to pass only one test: _generally acceptable by buyer and seller_.

22. In the circular flow model there are two groups of decision makers: _households_ and _business firm_.

23. In the circular flow model,
(a) households are demanders and businesses are suppliers in the _product_ markets; and businesses are demanders and householders are suppliers in the _ressources_ markets of the economy.

(b) the two real flows are called the _ressource_ flow and the _product_ flow.

(c) the expenditures made by firms are _expenses_ to them and _income_ to resource owners.

PROBLEMS AND PROJECTS

1. Various cities have put in place programs to overcome smog and pollution conditions generated mainly by automobile emissions. This question considers two such programs. City A placed a tax on cars so that at present a medium-sized car costs $80, 000. City B allows cars with licence plates ending with an odd number to drive on city streets on Monday, Wednesday and Friday. Cars with plates ending with an even number can use city streets on Tuesday, Thursday and Saturday. Only one licence plate is issued per car.
(a) You are a university student. What program do you prefer? Why? Suppose you are a local T. V. personality making $2.5 million a year. What program would you prefer?

(b) If different programs are chosen by the student and T. V. personality how is a city to decide what program to implement?
(c) Why not simply scrap the present programs, put in place a capitalistic system, and allow the price to allocate the scarce fresh air?
(d) What does the capitalistic model predict happened to the rent charged for privately owned accommodations close to the universities when both cities implemented their plans?
(e) Is it "fair" that students who can't afford a car should have to pay higher rents because of pollution problems caused by car owners?

2. Suppose the price of oil rose to $40 a barrel in international trade. Trace some of the consequences and economic reactions that would occur for the following if Canada operated under a pure capitalistic system.
(a) Imperial Oil or Shell Oil
(b) Joe's Energy Mart—a local furnace oil dealer in Red Deer
(c) Ace Drilling Company Limited—an oil drilling company in Lloydminster
(d) Quebec Hydro
(e) an accountant in Moncton who heats her home with furnace oil
(f) a mechanic in Burnaby who heats his home with natural gas
(g) Anne's Auto—a car dealership in Blind River
(h) the coal miners of Cape Breton

3. In the circular flow diagram below, the upper pair of flows (*a* and *b*) represent the product market and the lower pair (*c* and *d*) the resource market.

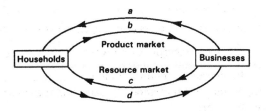

Supply labels for each of the four flows.
(a) _goods and services_
(b) _expenditures for goods ..._
(c) _money, income_
(d) _service of ressources_

4. Under Canada's supply management system the right to produce some agricultural products is limited and is allocated to existing industry producers on some

agreed-on basis. Generally the rights are saleable and tend to command a high price. To what extent are these rights a form of private property? Suppose you had a yearly quota or production right of 50,000 dozen eggs. What would happen to the value of your production right if supply management was abolished and anyone could produce and sell eggs?

SELF-TEST

Circle T if the statement is true, F if it is false.

1. The Canadian economy can be correctly called "pure capitalism."   T **F**

2. The United States economy can be correctly called "pure capitalism."   T **F**

3. Private property can refer to rights that are granted by society to individuals or institutions.   **T** F

4. In the real world there are usually legal limits placed on the rights of private property.   **T** F

5. A price system is used only in capitalistic economies.   T **F**

6. In the capitalistic system prices are set by a governmental agency.   **T** F

7. In the capitalistic system prices serve as guideposts for the allocation of resources.   **T** F

8. The capitalistic system promotes productive efficiency.   **T** F

9. Since the capitalistic system is efficient in resource use it must follow that every individual is better off under this form of economic organization than any alternative.   T **F**

10. The distribution of output in the market economy depends upon the distribution of resources.   **T** F

11. In a purely capitalistic economy, it is the firm that ultimately determines what will be produced.   T **F**

12. Competition serves to regulate self-interest for the benefit of society in the market model.   **T** F

13. The employment of capital to produce goods and services implies that there will be roundabout means of production.   **T** F

14. Roundabout means of production is used because it is more efficient than direct production.   **T** F

15. Specialization allows for a more efficient use of resources.   **T** F

16. Money is a device for facilitating the exchange of goods and services.   **T** F

17. The only real money is gold.   T **F**

18. "Coincidence of wants" means that two persons desire to acquire the same good or service.   T **F**

19. In the circular flow model households demand product and supply resources.   **T** F

20. In the circular flow model households purchase goods for money from firms. This is an example of an exchange of real goods and services.   **T** F

MULTIPLE-CHOICE

Choose the letter that corresponds to the best answer.

1. Which of the following is not one of the six characteristics of capitalism?
(a) competition
(b) freedom of enterprise and choice
(c) self-interest
(d) private property
(e) central economic planning

2. In the capitalist system the price of a good in the output market does all of the following except
(a) provides information on prospective profits and therefore affects resource allocation
(b) reflects the intensity of the desire for the good by consumers and the supply offered by sellers
(c) indicates the least cost combination of resources used in the production of the good
(d) is a determinant of the price that will be paid to the resources used in the production of that good

3. To decide how to use its scarce resources to satisfy human wants, pure capitalism relies on
(a) central planning
(b) roundabout production
(c) a price system together with the profit motive
(d) the coincidence of wants

4. The "invisible hand" is used to explain how in the capitalistic system
(a) prices are determined
(b) resources are allocated
(c) the self-interest of individuals is harnessed for the benefit of society
(d) allocative efficiency is achieved

5. In the capitalistic system a decrease in the demand for a good should result in all but
(a) an increase in the price of the resources producing the good

(b)   a decrease in the profitability of producing the good

(c)   a movement of resources out of the production of the good

(d)   a decrease in the price of the good

6.   Roundabout production refers to

(a)   the use of resources by government

(b)   the use of resources to produce consumer goods directly

(c)   the use of resources to produce services

(d)   the use of resources to produce capital goods that in turn are used to produce other goods

7.   The basis for competition, or economic rivalry, entails all but

(a)   the presence of a large number of buyers

(b)   the freedom to enter or leave a particular market

(c)   the presence of a large number of sellers

(d)   a fair price determined by a public agency

8.   Specialization in production is more efficient because

(a)   increasing opportunity costs reduce the resources used in the production of an extra unit of output

(b)   constant opportunity costs reduce the resources used in the production of an extra unit of output

(c)   regions and individuals possess unique resources and talents

(d)   experience or ''learning-by-doing'' results in increased output

(e)   (c) and (d)

9.   Which of the following is not a necessary consequence of specialization?

(a)   people will use money

(b)   people will engage in trade

(c)   people will be dependent upon each other

(d)   people will produce more of one thing than they would produce in the absence of specialization

10.   Barter

(a)   is the major method of trading in capitalistic economies

(b)   is the main method of trading in socialist economies

(c)   is the exchange of a good for money

(d)   is the exchange of a good for a good

11.   One of the following is not a disadvantage of specialization

(a)   increased interdependence among economic units

(b)   the performance of repetitive and boring tasks

(c)   increased production

(d)   need for exchange

12.   In the circular flow of income

(a)   households demand products and resources

(b)   businesses demand products and resources

(c)   households supply resources and demand products

(d)   businesses supply resources and demand products

13.   The two kinds of markets found in the circular flow model are

(a)   the real and money market

(b)   the real and product market

(c)   the money and resource market

(d)   the product and resource market

14.   In the circular flow model a real flow occurs when

(a)   goods are exchanged for money

(b)   resource inputs are exchanged for money

(c)   goods are exchanged for resource inputs

(d)   specialization occurs

15.   All modern economies have the following characteristics with the exception of

(a)   specialization

(b)   limited government interference

(c)   use of money

(d)   roundabout means of production

(e)   trade

DISCUSSION QUESTIONS

1.   List the Five Fundamental Questions that all economies must answer. Explain how the market system determines the answers to these questions.

2.   How does the pursuit of self-interest by all economic units in the capitalist model end up benefitting society?

3.   If the basic decisions are not made in a capitalist economy by a central authority, how are they made?

4.   At one time it was expected that the price of oil would hit $100 a barrel by 1992. Explain how, in a capitalist system, this expectation led to exploration in the Beaufort Sea in the far north of Canada?

5.   What explanation would the capitalist system offer for the decreased oil exploration in Alberta and the Canadian Arctic since 1982?

6.   Some students from Nova Scotia spent the summer of 1980 working on the oil rigs in the Beaufort Sea. Explain how the price system operated to allocate their labour effort to the oil industry so far away from home.

7.   What are the advantages of ''indirect'' or ''roundabout'' production?

8.   If capital intensive productive methods are more efficient does this imply that there must be high rates of unemployment for labour resources? Explain.

9. How does an economy benefit from specialization and division of labour?

10. What is money? What important function does it perform? Explain how money performs this function and how it overcomes the disadvantages associated with barter. Why are people willing to accept paper money in exchange for goods and services they have to sell?

11. In the circular-flow-of-income model:
(a) What two markets are involved? (b) What roles do households play in each of these markets? (c) What roles do businesses play in each of these markets? (d) What two income flows are pictured in money terms? In real terms? (e) What two expenditure flows are pictured in money terms? In real terms?

12. In the pure capitalistic model what determines the living standards of a particular individual?

ANSWERS

Fill-in questions

1. private property

2. enterprise, choice

3. is best for itself

4. self-interest

5. (a) large number of buyers and sellers; (b) freedom of exit from and entry to any market

6. guideposts, self-interest

7. demand, consumer, supply

8. government

9. (a) private property; (b) freedom of enterprise and choice; (c) self-interest; (d) markets and prices; (e) competition; (f) limited government

10. "invisible hand," social, public

11. price

12. least cost

13. (a) How much is to be produced?; (b) What is to be produced?; (c) How is the output to be produced?; (d) Who is to receive the output?; (e) How can the system adapt to change to remain efficient?

14. tastes, reallocate

15. (a) specialization; (b) use of money; (c) roundabout production

16. increase

17. interdependent, trade

18. good, good

19. coincidence of wants

20. facilitating

21. generally acceptable by buyer and seller

22. households, business firms

23. (a) product, resource; (b) product, resource; (c) expenses, income

Problems and projects

3. (a) goods and services; (b) expenditures for goods and services; (c) money income payments (rent, wages, interest, profits); (d) services of resources (land, labour, capital, entrepreneurial ability)

Self-test

1. F,   2. F,   3. T,   4. T,   5. F,   6. F,   7. T,   8. T,
9. F,   10. T,   11. F,   12. T,   13. T,   14. T,   15. T,
16. T,   17. F,   18. F,   19. T,   20. F

Multiple-choice

1. (e);   2. (c);   3. (c);   4. (c);   5. (a);   6. (d);
7. (d);   8. (e);   9. (a);   10. (d);   11. (c);   12. (c);
13. (d);   14. (c);   15. (b)

CHAPTER

4 Understanding Individual Markets: Supply and Demand

Chapter 4 is an introduction to the most fundamental model of economic analysis: the demand and supply model. It is the model most often used by economists to forecast levels and changes in prices and quantities. Although not all prices in the modern economy are determined by the demand and supply forces as defined in this model, the predictions derived from applying the model have conformed to actual price changes in many industries and over a long period of time. An understanding of the material in later chapters requires that you have knowledge of the content and operation of this model.

Demand and supply are simply "boxes" or categories into which all the forces and factors that affect the price and the quantity of a good bought and sold in a competitive market can conveniently be placed. Demand and supply determine price and quantity exchanged, and it is necessary to see why and how they do this.

In order to keep track of the various determinants of supply and demand this model applies the *ceteris paribus* assumption. All factors (independent variables), except its own price, that affect the quantity taken off the market by demanders or placed on the market by profit-maximizing firms are given fixed values. Emphasis is then placed on the relationship between price and quantity for both buyers and sellers. This also allows the model to be explained with the aid of two-dimensional diagrams. The demand and supply relationships can be expressed in the form of an algebraic equation, schedules placed in tabular form, or in the geometrical figures extensively used in this chapter. It is necessary to understand the construction of and the information conveyed by the demand and supply curves.

Many students never understand how to apply the model because they never learn to define demand and supply exactly and because they never learn: (1) what is meant by an increase or decrease in demand or supply; (2) the important distinctions between "demand" and "quantity demanded" and between "supply" and "quantity supplied"; and (3) the equally important distinction between an increase (or decrease) in demand and an increase (or decrease) in quantity demanded and between an increase (or decrease) in supply and an increase (or decrease) in quantity supplied. These distinctions arise from the use of the *ceteris paribus* assumption.

Once all the nonprice factors affecting demand and supply are set at specified levels it is possible to obtain the price at which the quantity consumers take off the market exactly equals the quantity profit-maximizing sellers offer for sale on the market. This price is called the equilibrium price and is the price at which the market clears. At this price the quantity demanded and the quantity supplied are equal. The equilibrium quantity is the quantity demanded and supplied at the equilibrium price. If you can determine the equilibrium price and quantity under one set of demand and supply conditions, you can determine them under any other set, and so will be able to analyse for yourself the effects of changes in the nonprice factors on the equilibrium price and quantity. It is then possible, for example, to predict the direction of change in car prices in Canada when import quotas are enforced on Japanese cars or in wheat prices when the European Economic Community decreases subsidies for wheat production.

If you wonder why an entire chapter has been devoted to demand and supply, you will find the answer in the last major section of the chapter. Demand and supply have so many applications that they are the most important single tool in economics. You will use supply and demand over and over again. It will turn out to be as important as jet propulsion is to the pilot of a Boeing 747: you can't get off the ground without it.

CHECKLIST

When you have studied this chapter, you should be able to

- Define a market.
- Define demand schedule, supply schedule.
- Define quantity demanded, quantity supplied.
- Derive a demand schedule from a given algebraic demand function.
- Graph demand and supply curves when you are given demand and supply schedules.
- State the law of demand and the law of supply.
- List the major determinants of demand and of supply.
- Determine, when you are given the demand for and the supply of a good, what the equilibrium price and the equilibrium quantity will be.
- Explain the underlying actions of consumers and business firms that bring about an equilibrium price in this model.
- Recognize the nonprice factors that cause shifts in the demand and supply curves and the direction of change.
- Predict the effects of changes in demand and supply on equilibrium price and equilibrium quantity; and on the prices of substitute and complementary goods.
- Explain the meaning of the rationing function of prices.

CHAPTER OUTLINE

1. A market is any institution or mechanism that brings together the buyers and the sellers of a particular good or service; and in this chapter it is assumed that markets are perfectly competitive.

2. The market demand for a good indicates the number of units of a good consumers will purchase as determined by: 1) the price of the good, 2) the price of related goods, 3)consumer's income, 4) consumer's tastes, 5) and number of consumers. The market demand is obtained by "adding up" the demand of individual consumers.

3. By fixing all other factors except its own price a relation between the quantity purchased and the price of the good is obtained.

4. A demand schedule is a list of prices and the quantity that buyers will purchase at each of these prices during some period of time.
(a) As price rises, buyers will purchase smaller quantities, and as price falls, they will purchase larger quantities; this is the law of demand.
(b) The demand curve is a graphic representation of the demand schedule and the law of demand is reflected in the demand curve being downward sloping.
(c) The law of demand holds because of:
1) the substitution effect — when the price of a good falls that good becomes cheaper relative to or compared with the price of other goods. Consumers compare relative prices when shopping and so will purchase more of the good;
2) the income effect — when the price of a good falls the purchasing power of a consumer's fixed money income rises and the consumer tends to purchase more.
(d) Market (or total) demand for a good is a summation of the demands of all individuals in the market for that good.
(e) A change in quantity demanded is a movement along a demand schedule or demand curve as a result of a change in the price of the good, all other nonprice determinants remaining fixed.
(f) A change in demand is brought about by a change in the nonprice determinants — the price of related goods or consumer's tastes or income or the number of purchasers.
(g) A change (either an increase or a decrease) in demand means that the quantities in the demand schedule have increased or decreased for a given price and the demand curve has shifted to the right or left.
(h) A change in demand and a change in the quantity demanded are not the same thing. A change in quantity demanded is a movement along a demand curve and is caused by a change in the price of the good. A change in demand results in the whole demand curve moving to the right or the left on a graph and is caused by changes in the price of other goods, consumer's income or tastes, or the number of purchasers.

5. If the demand for good x increases as a result of an increase in the price of good y, then goods x and y are termed substitutes. If the demand for good x decreases as a result of an increase in the price of good y, then good x and good y are termed complements.

6. If the demand for good x increases as a result of an increase in income, good x is termed a normal good. If the demand for good x decreases as a result of an increase in income, then good x is termed an inferior good.

7. Market supply indicates the number of units of a good a profit- maximizing firm will place on the market for sale as related to the price of the good, the price of inputs, technology, taxes and subsidies, prices of other goods, and expectations.

8. By fixing all factors except the price of the product a relation between the price of a good and the number

of units placed on the market for sale is obtained.

9. A supply schedule is a list of prices and the quantities producers will offer for sale at each of these prices during some period of time, other factors being fixed. (a) The law of supply states that, as the price of the good rises, larger quantities will be offered for sale, and that, as the price of the good falls, smaller quantities will be offered for sale. (b) The supply curve is a graphic representation of the supply schedule and the law of supply; the market supply of a good is the sum of the supplies of all sellers of the good. (c) A change in quantity supplied is a movement along a given supply curve and is caused by a change in the price of the good. (d) A change in supply is a change in the entire supply schedule or curve and is caused by a change in any of the factors listed in 7 except the price of the good. A change in supply causes the supply curve to move to the right or left. (e) A change in supply must be distinguished from a change in quantity supplied.

10. The market or equilibrium price of a commodity is that price at which quantity demanded and quantity supplied are equal; and the quantity exchanged in the market (the equilibrium quantity) is equal to the quantity demanded and supplied at the equilibrium price. At a price above the equilibrium, price of quantity demanded is less than quantity supplied and the surplus will cause the price to fall. At a price below the equilibrium, quantity demanded is greater than quantity supplied and the shortage will cause the price to rise.

11. A change in the nonprice determinants results in the demand or supply curves shifting and a new equilibrium price and quantity realized.

12. Given the supply curve, there is a direct relationship between a change in demand and the resulting change in equilibrium price and quantity.

13. Given the demand curve, there is an inverse relationship between a change in supply and the resulting change in equilibrium price, and a direct relationship between a change in supply and the resulting change in equilibrium quantity.

14. The rationing function of price is the elimination of shortages and surpluses of the commodity.

15. In resource markets, suppliers are households and demanders are business firms, and in product markets, suppliers are business firms and demanders are households. Supply and demand are useful in the analysis of prices and quantities exchanged in both types of markets.

IMPORTANT TERMS

change in demand (supply) versus change in the
   quantity demanded (supplied)
complementary goods
demand
demand schedule
diminishing marginal utility
equilibrium price and quantity
income and substitution effects
inferior goods
law of demand
law of supply
market
normal (superior) good
rationing function of prices
shortage
substitute goods
supply
supply schedule
surplus

FILL-IN QUESTIONS

1. (a) A market is the institution or mechanism that brings together the ___buyers___ and the ___seller___ of a particular good or service.
(b) In resource markets, prices are determined by the demand decisions of (business firms, households) ___buisness firm___ and the supply decisions of ___households___.
(c) In the product markets, prices are determined by the demand decisions of ___households___ and the supply decisions of ___firms___.

2. The quantity of a good that consumers will purchase per unit of time depends upon six factors: 1) ___price___, 2) ___taste___, 3) ___income___, 4) ___price___, 5) ___expectation___, and 6) ___number of buyer___

3. "Demand is a schedule that shows the units of a product consumers are willing and able to purchase at

each specific price in a series of possible prices during a specific period of time, all other things being equal.''

The "all other things" are _____, _____, _____, _____, and _____. They are sometimes referred to as the _____ determinants.

4.   When demand or supply is graphed, price is placed on the _____ axis and quantity on the _____ axis.

5.   The graph of the demand schedule is called the demand _____ and according to the law of demand is _____ _____.

6.   When there is a change in quantity demanded the _____ of the good is changed and results in a movement _____ the demand curve.

7.   A change in demand occurs as a result of a change in one of the _____ _____ and the whole demand curve shifts to the _____ or to the _____. An _____ _____ _____ shifts the demand curve to the right; a _____ _____ _____ shifts the demand curve to the left.

8.   The relationship between price and quantity in the demand schedule is a(n) (direct, inverse) _____ relationship; in the supply schedule it is a(n) _____ one.

9.   A consumer tends to buy more of a product as its price falls because
(a)   the purchasing power of the consumer is increased and the consumer tends to buy more of this and other products; this is called the _____ effect.
(b)   the product becomes less expensive relative to similar products and the consumer tends to buy more of this and less of the other products; and this is called the _____ effect.

10.   Along a given demand curve for good x the price of other goods stays _____. Suppose the price of the good called y is fixed at $1 and the price of x changes from $6 to $4. At a price of $6, a unit of x is _____ times as expensive as a unit of y; while at a price of $4.00, a unit of x is _____ times as expensive as a unit of y. The price of x as compared to or relative to the price of y has _____. Moving down the demand curve for x the relative price of x _____.

11.   The fundamental factors that determine the supply of any commodity in the produce market are:

(a)   _____

(b)   _____

(c)   _____

(d)   _____

(e)   _____

(f)   _____

(g)   _____

12.   Fixing the nonprice factors a supply schedule is obtained showing the relationship between quantity placed on the market and the _____ of the good.

13.   A _____ _____ _____ _____ is the result of a change in the price of the good and is a movement _____ a supply curve.

14.   A change in supply is the result of a change in the _____ factors. An increase in supply is shown by a movement of the entire supply curve to the _____. A decrease in supply is shown by a movement of the entire supply curve to the _____.

15.   The equilibrium price of a commodity is the price at which _____.

16.   If quantity demanded exceeds quantity supplied, price is (above, below) _____ the equilibrium price; and the (shortage, surplus) _____ will cause the price to (rise, fall) _____.

17.   In the spaces after each of the following, indicate

the effect [increase (+), decrease(-), or indeterminate (?)] upon the equilibrium price and equilibrium quantity of each of these changes in demand and/or supply.

(a)   Increase in demand, supply constant _____

(b)   Increase in supply, demand constant _____

(c)   Decrease in demand, supply constant _____

(d)   Decrease in supply, demand constant _____

(e)   Increase in demand, increase in supply _____

(f)   Increase in demand, decrease in supply _____

(g)   Decrease in demand, decrease in supply _____

(h)   Decrease in demand, increase in supply _____

18.   If supply and demand establish a price for a good such that there is no shortage of the good, then price is successfully performing its _____ function.

19.   Graphically the market demand curve is found by summing _____ the individual demand curves in the market.

20.   Given the supply curve, an increase in demand will have a price _____effect and a quantity _____ effect. A decrease in demand will have price _____ and quantity _____ effects.

21.   Given the demand curve, an increase in supply will have price _____ and quantity _____ effects. A decrease in supply will have price _____ and quantity _____ effects.

PROBLEMS AND PROJECTS

1.   (a)   Plot the demand and supply schedule below on the graph on page 42. Indicate on the graph the equilibrium price and quantity by drawing lines from the intersection of the demand and supply curves to the price and quantity axes.

Quantity Demanded	Price per Unit	Quantity Supplied
61	$13	91
64	$12	84
67	$11	77
70	$10	70
73	$ 9	63
76	$ 8	56
79	$ 7	49
82	$ 6	42

(b)   Obtain: Equilibrium Price   _____

         Equilibrium Quantity _____

(c)   A price of $13 is not the equilibrium price because

_____.

(d)   The government puts in place a fixed price of $6. At this price the quantity demanded will be _____; the quantity supplied will be _____. At this price there will be a (surplus, shortage) _____ of _____ units. Indicate the fixed price, the quantity demanded and quantity supplied, and shortage on the graph.

2.   The demand schedules of three individuals (Robert, Charles, Lynn) for loaves of bread are shown below. Assuming there are only three buyers of bread, draw up the total or market demand schedule for bread.

Price	Quantity Demanded (Loaves of Bread)			Total
	Robert	Charles	Lynn	
$1.15	1	4	0	_____
$1.10	3	5	1	_____
$1.05	6	6	5	_____
$1.00	10	7	10	_____
$ .95	15	8	16	_____

3.   Assume that O'Rourke has, when his income is $300 per week, the demand schedule for good A shown in columns 1 and 2 of the table on page 43 and the demand schedule for good B shown in columns 4 and 5. Assume that the prices of A and B are $0.80 and $5 respectively.

(a)   How much A will O'Rourke buy? _____;

How much B? _____.

(b)   Suppose that as a consequence of a $30 increase in O'Rourke's weekly income, the quantities demanded of A become those shown in column 3 and quantities demanded of B those shown in column 6.

1) How much A will O'Rourke now buy? _____;

how much B? _____.

2) Good A is (normal, inferior) _____.

3) Good B is (normal, inferior) _____.

Price

0

Quantity

Table for question 3 (page 41)

Demand for A per week			Demand for B per week		
(1) Price	**(2)** Quantity Demanded	**(3)** Quantity Demanded	**(4)** Price	**(5)** Quantity Demanded	**(6)** Quantity Demanded
$.90	10	0	$5.00	4	7
.85	20	10	4.50	5	8
.80	30	20	4.00	6	9
.75	40	30	3.50	7	10
.70	50	40	3.00	8	11
.65	60	50	2.50	9	12
.60	70	60	2.00	10	13

4. Suppose that the demand-supply model is applicable to the Canadian beef market. What will be the effect of the following occurrences on the equilibrium price and quantity of beef in Canada.

(a) A popular singer remarks that red meat in the diet may be a contributory factor in heart and circulatory diseases. _____

(b) The East coast fishery is closed due to failure of the fish stock. _____

(c) The United States government places an embargo on the importation of beef from Canada claiming the Canadian beef industry is unfairly subsidized by provincial governments._____

(d) The price of livestock feed grains falls sharply due to a record harvest._____

(e) A new growth hormone that will increase the weight of beef cattle by 20% with the same feed intake is discovered by Agriculture Canada._____

(f) Most people that work in outlets that serve beef receive the minimum wage. The governments of all Canadian provinces declare a 50% increase in the minimum wage._____

5. This question uses an algebraic expression for demand to illustrate some of the concepts introduced in the chapter. Suppose the market demand for good x is given by: $Q_x = 100 - 2P_x - .5P_y$ where Q_x is quantity of good x, P_x is the price of good x, and P_y is the price of good y.

(a) Set the price of y equal to 4. The market demand becomes: $Q_x = 98 - 2P_x$. Complete the following demand schedule:

Table 1

P_x	Q_x	Q_x^*
20	_____	_____
18	_____	_____
16	_____	_____
14	_____	_____
12	_____	_____
10	_____	_____

Place the demand schedule in the graph on page 44.

(b) Suppose that the price of y increases to 12. The new market demand is: $Q_x^* =$ _____.

(c) Complete the new demand schedule in table 1.

(d) Place the new demand schedule on the graph.

(e) The increase in P_y shifted the demand curve for x to the (left, right) _____. The increase in the price of y resulted in a(n) (increase, decrease) _____ in the demand for x. The goods x and y would be called (substitutes, complements) _____ because when the price of y rises the demand for x _____.

6. Use demand and supply models to explain the changes that occurred in hog and beef prices as detailed in the following report. '' Hog prices for fall and winter delivery plunged yesterday on the Chicago Mercantile Exchange after a U. S. Agriculture Department report projected rising supplies through the second quarter of next year... and cattle futures fell as selling pressures spilled over from the neighbouring pork pits'' [*The Globe and Mail*, June 16, 1992]

7. One of the factors that shift the supply curve is a change in tax. Suppose the supply schedule is given

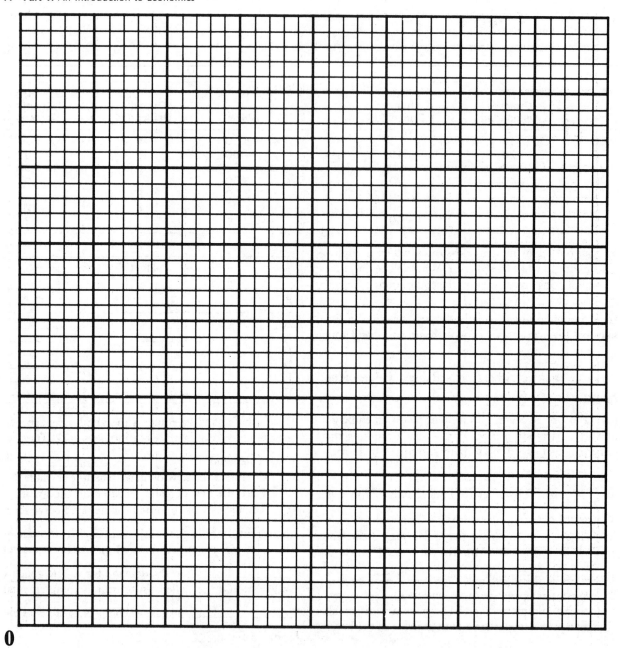

0

below where Q_s is quantity supplied and P is price.

P	Q_s
$1.5	.5
2	4
3	11
4	18
5	25
6	32
7	39
8	46

Place on the graph on page 45.

Suppose that the government imposes a tax of $1 per unit sold. The tax is collected by the producer and remitted to the government. If the consumer pays $8 per unit, the producer gets to keep $8-$1 = $7. If the consumer pays $5 per unit the producer gets to keep _____. Check the supply schedule.

To produce 32 units the producer must now receive $7 per unit because $1 must be sent to the government. Locate the point ($7, 32) on the graph.

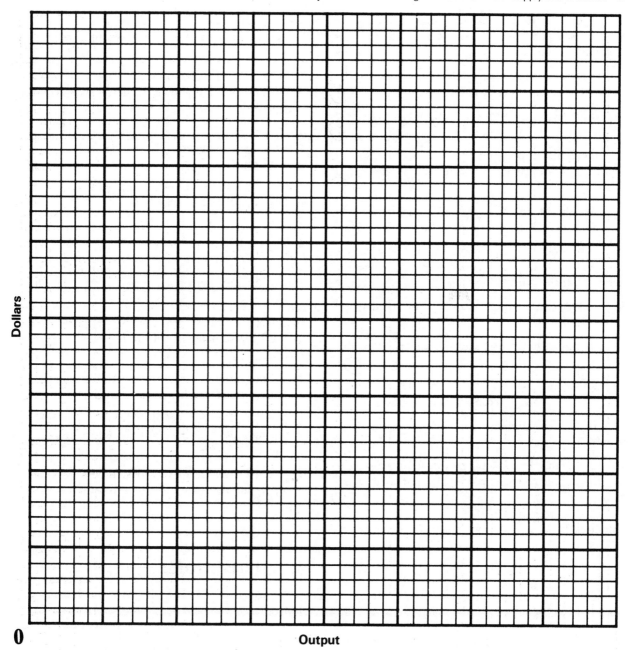

0   **Output**

To produce 25 units the producer must receive _____ per unit since $_____ per unit must be sent to the government. Locate this combination on the graph.

For every output in your supply schedule obtain the amount the producer must receive and plot the combination on the graph. Join the various points. A new supply curve is obtained that is above the original supply curve. The supply curve will move upward by the amount of the tax.

On the same graph place a downward sloping demand curve. The effect of the unit tax is to _____ equilibrium price and to _____ equilibrium quantity.

SELF-TEST

Circle T if the statement is true, F if it is false.

1. A market is any arrangement that brings the buyers and sellers of a particular good or service together. **T** F

2.   Demand is the amount of a commodity or service a buyer will purchase at various prices, other things remaining constant.   **T F**

3.   The law of demand states that as price increases, the quantity of the product demanded increases.   **T F**

4.   The effect of a decrease in the price of oranges is an increase in the demand for oranges.   **T F**

5.   In graphing supply and demand schedules, supply is put on the horizontal axis and demand on the vertical axis.   **T F**

6.   A fall in the price of a good will cause the demand for goods that are substitutes for it to decrease.   **T F**

7.   If two goods are complements, such as beer and pickled eggs, an increase in the price of one will cause the demand for the other to decrease.   **T F**

8.   A change in buyers' tastes will cause the demand curve to shift.   **T F**

9.   An increase in income increases the demand for normal goods.   **T F**

10.   An inferior good is a lower quality good that is consumed by the bottom income group in society.   **T F**

11.   In all markets prices are determined by demand and supply.   **T F**

12.   Since the amount purchased must equal the amount sold then demand and supply must always equal each other.   **T F**

Questions 13–15 are based on the accompanying graph.

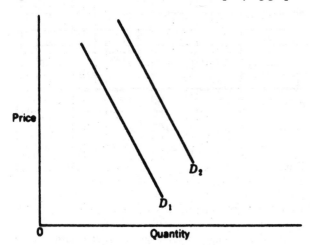

13.   If the demand curve moves from D_1 to D_2 demand has increased.   **T F**

14.   The movement of the demand curve from D_1 to D_2 could be caused by an improvement in technology.   **T F**

15.   The law of demand says that the demand curves would move from D_1 to D_2 if the price of substitutes increased.   **T F**

16.   A supply curve indicates the maximum amount that a profit- maximizing firm would offer for sale at various prices.   **T F**

17.   A decrease in quantity supplied is caused by an increase in production costs.   **T F**

18.   A shift to the right of the supply curve is called a decrease in supply.   **T F**

19.   The equilibrium price of a good is the price that equates quantity demanded and quantity supplied.   **T F**

20.   If the market price of a commodity is for a time below its equilibrium price, the market price will tend to rise because demand will decrease and supply will increase.   **T F**

21.   The rationing function of prices is the elimination of shortages and surpluses.   **T F**

22.   A change in demand alters both equilibrium price and equilibrium quantity in the opposite direction to the change in demand.   **T F**

23.   There is an inverse relationship between a change in supply and the resulting change in equilibrium price.   **T F**

MULTIPLE-CHOICE

Circle the letter that corresponds to the best answer.

1.   A market demand curve shows
(a)   the equilibrium price that will prevail in the market
(b)   various prices and quantities where demand equals supply
(c)   various prices and quantities where quantity demanded equals quantity supplied
(d)   the minimum price consumers will pay to get a specified quantity
(e)   the various amounts of a product consumers are willing and able to purchase at each specific price in a series of possible prices

2.   An increase in the quantity demanded of oranges can be caused by

(a)   a shift to the left of the supply curve of oranges
(b)   a shift to the right of the supply curve of oranges
(c)   a decline in the demand for orange juice
(d)   a rise in the demand for orange juice
(e)   a decrease in the price of salt

3.   A decrease in the quantity demanded
(a)   moves the demand curve to the left
(b)   moves the demand curve to the right
(c)   is a movement down along the demand curve
(d)   is a movement up along the demand curve

4.   If two goods are substitutes for each other, an increase in the price of one will necessarily
(a)   decrease the demand for the other
(b)   increase the demand for the other
(c)   decrease the quantity demanded of the other
(d)   increase the quantity demanded of the other

5.   The income of a consumer decreases and as a result the demand for a particular good decreases. It can be concluded that the good is
(a)   normal
(b)   inferior
(c)   substitute
(d)   complement

6.   According to the law of supply
(a)   equilibrium quantity will always increase when equilibrium price increases
(b)   equilibrium quantity will always decrease when equilibrium price increases
(c)   the supply curve has a negative slope
(d)   other things remaining the same the quantity supplied increases whenever price increases

7.   A supply curve indicates
(a)   the profit-maximizing quantities sellers place on the market at alternative prices
(b)   the minimum quantities sellers place on the market at alternative prices
(c)   the maximum quantities sellers will place on the market at different prices for inputs
(d)   the quantities sellers place on the market in order to meet consumer demand at that price

8.   The supply curve of the firm slopes upward in the short run because
(a)   the increased production requires the use of inferior inputs
(b)   hiring more inputs for the extra production requires the payment of higher input prices
(c)   of increasing opportunity costs
(d)   productive efficiency declines because certain productive resources cannot be expanded in a short period of time

9.   A movement along a supply curve for a good would be caused by
(a)   an improvement in the technology of production
(b)   an increase in the price of the good
(c)   an increase in the number of suppliers of the good
(d)   a change in expectations

10.   A market is in equilibrium when
(a)   inventories of the good are not rising
(b)   suppliers can sell all of the good they decide to produce at the prevailing price
(c)   quantity demanded equals quantity supplied
(d)   demanders can purchase all of the good they want at the prevailing price

11.   An increase in the demand for potatoes is expected this year. The demand-supply model predicts, other things being equal,
(a)   an increase in the supply of potatoes
(b)   a decrease in the quantity exchanged of potatoes
(c)   an increase in equilibrium price and a decrease in equilibrium quantity
(d)   an increase in the equilibrium price of potatoes

Questions 12 to 15 are based on the following diagram.

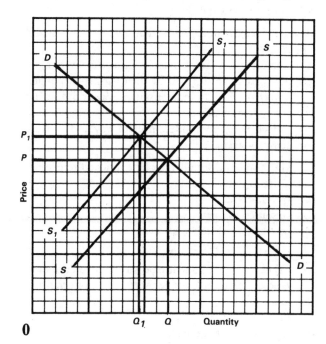

12.   Given the original demand and supply curves are *DD* and *SS*
(a)   the equilibrium price and quantity were P and Q_1
(b)   the equilibrium price and quantity were P and P_1
(c)   the equilibrium price and quantity were P_1 and Q
(d)   the equilibrium price and quantity were Q and Q_1

(e)   the equilibrium price and quantity were P and Q

13.   The shift of the supply curve from SS to S_1S_1 is termed
(a)   an increase in supply
(b)   an increase in quantity supplied
(c)   a decrease in supply
(d)   a decrease in quantity supplied

14.   The shift in the supply curve from SS to S_1S_1 could be caused by
(a)   an increase in the price of the good
(b)   a decrease in the price of the good
(c)   a technological improvement in the production of the good
(d)   a decrease in demand
(e)   an increase in the cost of the resources used in the production of the good

15.   The shift in the supply curve from SS to S_1S_1 resulted in
(a)   an increase in both equilibrium price and quantity
(b)   a decrease in both equilibrium price and quantity
(c)   an increase in equilibrium price and a decrease in equilibrium quantity
(d)   a decrease in equilibrium price and an increase in equilibrium quantity

16.   An increase in supply and an increase in demand will
(a)   increase price and increase the quantity exchanged
(b)   decrease price and increase the quantity exchanged
(c)   affect price in an indeterminate way and decrease the quantity exchanged
(d)   affect price in an indeterminate way and increase the quantity exchanged

17.   Demand and supply may be employed to explain how price is determined in
(a)   product markets
(b)   resource markets
(c)   markets for foreign currency
(d)   all of the above markets

18.   When the government places a ceiling on the price of a good and that ceiling is below the equilibrium price, the result will be
(a)   a surplus of the good
(b)   a shortage of the good
(c)   an increase in the demand for the good
(d)   a decrease in the supply of the good

DISCUSSION QUESTIONS

1.   What are the determinants of market demand? How is a demand schedule obtained from market demand? How is a demand curve constructed from a demand schedule?

2.   Carefully state the law of demand and explain the two reasons put forth in this chapter to justify downward sloping demand curves.

3.   Explain the difference between an increase in demand and an increase in quantity demanded.

4.   Define supply and explain why supply curves are upward sloping.

5.   Neither demand nor supply remains constant for long. Economic circumstances are always changing so the actual prices we see are not equilibrium prices. Why then do economists spend so much time trying to determine the equilibrium price and quantity if these magnitudes are going to change so frequently?

6.   How are normal, inferior, substitute, complementary, and independent goods defined? How can these concepts be used to predict the way in which a change in income or in the price of another good will affect the demand for a given good?

7.   Given the demand for and the supply of a commodity, what price will be the equilibrium price of this commodity? Explain why this price will tend to prevail in the market and why higher (lower) prices, if they do exist temporarily, will tend to fall (rise).

8.   Analyse the following quotation and explain the fallacies contained in it. "An increase in demand will cause price to rise; with a rise in price, supply will increase and the increase in supply will push price down. Therefore, an increase in demand results in little change in price because supply will increase also."

9.   Given the law of demand does a higher price always yield a greater expenditure on a good? Construct a demand schedule and determine the price that results in the highest consumer expenditure on that good. Given there were no production costs and you were the only producer, would you charge the highest price possible in order to maximize profits?

10.   The interest rate is a price. It is the price paid by borrowers for the use of money and the price received by the lenders of the money. Unless government interferes, the demand for borrowed money and the supply of loanable money determine the interest rate. What would be the effect of (a) a government imposed interest-rate ceiling on this money market; (b) the deduction of interest expenses from the taxable incomes of borrowers on the demand for borrowed money and the rate of interest; and (c) the exclusion of interest incomes from the taxable incomes of lenders on the supply of loanable money and the rate of interest?

ANSWERS

Fill-in questions

1. (a) buyers (demanders), sellers (suppliers) (either order) (b) business firms, households (c) households, business firms

2. 1) price of the good, 2) tastes, 3) income, 4) price of related goods, 5) expectations, 6) number of buyers

3. tastes, income, price of related goods, expectations, number of buyers; nonprice

4. vertical, horizontal

5. curve, downward sloping

6. price, along

7. nonprice factors, left, right; increase in demand, decrease in demand

8. inverse, direct

9. (a) income (b) substitution

10. fixed; 6, 4; decreased; decreases

11. (a) price of the product (b) resource prices (c) technology (d) taxes and subsidies (e) prices of other goods (f) expectations (g) number of sellers

12. price

13. change in quantity supplied, along

14. nonprice; right; left

15. quantity demanded equals quantity supplied

16. below, shortage, rise

17. (a) +, +; (b) -, +; (c) -, -; (d) +, -; (e) ?, +; (f) +, ?; (g) ?, -; (h) -, ?

18. rationing

19. horizontally

20. increasing, increasing; decreasing, decreasing

21. decreasing, increasing; increasing, decreasing

Problems and projects

1. (b) equilibrium price: 10; equilibrium quantity: 70 (c) quantity demanded is less than quantity supplied (surplus of 30) (d) 82, 42; shortage, 40

2. Total: 5, 9, 17, 27, 39

3. (a) 30, 4 (b) (1) 20, 7, (2) inferior, (3) normal

4. (a) P-, Q- (b) P +, Q + (c) P-, Q + (d) P-, Q + (e) P-, Q + (f) P +, Q-

5. (a) Q_x = 58, 62, 66, 70, 74, 78 (b) 94-2P_x (c) Q_x* = 54, 58, 62, 66, 70, 74 (e) left; decrease; complements, decreases

7. $4; $6, $1; increase, decrease

Self-test

1. T; 2. F; 3. F; 4. F; 5. F; 6. T; 7. T; 8. T; 9. T; 10. F; 11. F; 12. F; 13. T; 14. F; 15. F; 16. T; 17. F; 18. F; 19. T; 20. F; 21. T; 22. F; 23. T

Multiple choice

1. (e); 2. (b); 3. (c); 4. (b); 5. (a); 6. (d); 7. (a); 8. (d); 9. (b); 10. (c); 11. (d); 12. (e); 13. (c); 14. (e); 15. (c); 16. (d); 17. (d); 18. (b)

National Income, Employment, and Fiscal Policy

CHAPTER

5

Measuring Domestic Output, National Income, and The Price Level

The subject matter of Chapter 5 is national income (or social) accounting. This type of accounting measures or estimates the size of (1) the gross domestic product, (2) the gross national product, (3) the national income, (4) the personal income, and (5) the disposable income of the economy. These terms represent different measurements of the value of the output produced and/or income generated in an economy over a year.

National income (or social) accounting involves estimating output or income for the nation or society as a whole, rather than for an individual business firm or family. Note that the terms "output" and "income" are interchangeable because the nation's output and its income are identical (except for "net investment income from nonresidents"). The value of the nation's output equals the total expenditure for this output, and these expenditures become the income of those in the nation who have produced this output. Consequently, there are two equally acceptable methods, both discussed in the chapter, for obtaining each of the five income-output measures listed above. These two methods are the expenditures method and the income method.

Accounting is essentially an adding-up process. This chapter explains in detail how to obtain by both methods each of the five income-output measures. It even lists the items to be added. It is up to you to learn precisely what to add; that is, how to compute GDP, GNP, NI, PI, and DI by both methods. This is a fairly difficult chapter and the only way to learn the material is simply to sit down and learn it—memorize it if necessary! A careful reading of the chapter, however, will enable you to avoid the necessity of memorizing. You should first try to understand each of the five income-output measures and the two alternative approaches to these measurements. Remembering the items to be added will then be much simpler.

In addition to explaining the two methods of computing the five income-output measures and each of the items used in the computation process, the chapter dis-

cusses the measurement of the price level in the economy. By measuring the price level, economists are able to determine how much inflation (an increase in the price level) or deflation (a decrease in the price level) has occurred in the economy. This information is important because income-output measures are expressed in monetary units, so if accurate comparisons are to be made between years, these monetary measures must be adjusted to take account of changes in the price level. A simple example is presented to show how a GDP price index or deflator is constructed and then the index is used to adjust nominal GDP to determine real GDP for comparison purposes. But, as the last section of the chapter points out, it is especially dangerous to assume that GDP is a good measure of the welfare of the society.

Chapter 5 is the essential background for Parts 2 and 3, which explain the history of and the factors that determine the level of total output and income in the economy. This chapter is important because it explains the several methods used to measure the performance of the economy in a given year and make the adjustments necessary to ensure accurate measurements of performance over time.

CHECKLIST

When you have studied this chapter, you should be able to:

- State the purposes of national income accounting.
- Define GDP and explain why it is a monetary measure.
- Explain what is meant by "final goods and services" and describe how double counting is avoided in constructing the accounts.
- Provide some examples of the transactions that are excluded from GDP.
- Describe the four basic expenditure components that are summed in the expenditure approach to GDP.

■ Be able to compute the GDP for a particular year when provided with the expenditure data.

■ Explain: (1) the difference between gross and net investment; (2) why changes in inventories are investment; and (3) the relation between net investment and economic growth.

■ Identify the major income and nonincome components of GDP utilized in the income approach to GDP.

■ Be able to compute the GDP using the income approach, when provided with the necessary data.

■ Define each of the following and, when you are given the needed data, be able to compute: GNP, NI, PI, and DI.

■ Explain how the GDP price index or deflator is calculated and, given relevant data, how to calculate an index number.

■ Know why nominal GDP figures are adjusted for price changes.

■ Adjust the nominal GDP, when you are given the relevant price index, to find the real GDP.

■ Present seven reasons why GDP may not be a good measure of social welfare.

CHAPTER OUTLINE

1. National income accounting consists of concepts that enable those who use them to measure the economy's output, to compare it with past outputs, to explain its size and the reasons for changes in its size, and to formulate policies designed to increase it.

2. The gross domestic product (GDP) is the total market value of all final goods and services produced in the economy during a year.
(a) GDP is measured in dollar terms rather than in terms of physical units of output.
(b) To avoid double counting, GDP includes only final goods and services (goods and services that will not be processed further during the current year).
(c) Nonproductive transactions are not included in GDP; purely financial transactions and second-hand sales are, therefore, excluded.
(d) Measurement of GDP can be accomplished by either the expenditures or the income approach, but the same result is obtained by the two methods.

3. Computation of the GDP by the expenditures method requires the addition of the total amounts of the four types of spending for final goods and services:
(a) Personal consumption expenditures (C) are the expenditures of households for durable, semi-durable, and nondurable goods and for services.
(b) Gross capital formation or gross investment (I_g) is the sum of the spending by governments and business firms for machinery, equipment, and tools; spending by firms and households for new buildings; and the changes in the inventories of business firms.
(1) A change in inventories is included in investment because it is the part of output of the economy that was not sold during the year.
(2) Investment does not include expenditures for stocks or bonds or for second-hand capital goods.
(3) Gross investment exceeds net investment by the value of the capital goods worn out during the year.
(4) An economy in which net investment is positive (zero, negative) is an expanding (a static, a declining) economy.
(c) Government purchases of goods and services (G) are the current expenditures (that is, excluding investment) made by all governments in the economy for products produced by business firms and for resource services from households.
(d) Net exports (X_n) in an economy equal the expenditures made by foreigners for goods and services produced in the economy less the expenditures made by the consumers, government, and investors of the economy for goods and services produced in foreign nations.
(e) In symbols, $C + I_g + G + X_n = $ GDP.

4. Computation of GDP by the income method requires the addition of the eight uses to which the income derived from the production and sale of final goods and services are put. These eight items are:
(a) wages, salaries, and supplementary labour income;
(b) corporation profits before taxes;
(c) interest and miscellaneous investment income;
(d) accrued net income of farm operators from farm production;
(e) net income of nonfarm unincorporated business, including rent;
(f) inventory valuation adjustment;
(g) indirect taxes less subsidies;
(h) capital consumption allowances (depreciation).

5. In addition to GDP, four other national income measures are important in evaluating the performance of the economy. Each has a distinct definition and can be computed by making additions to or deductions from another measure.
(a) GNP is GDP less net investment income from nonresidents (''less'' because it is always negative in Canada).
(b) NI is the total income earned by owners of land and capital and by the suppliers of labour and entrepreneu-

rial ability during the year; and equals GNP less indirect taxes and depreciation (capital consumption allowances).

(c)   PI is the total income received—whether it is earned or unearned—by the households of the economy before the payment of personal taxes. It is found by adding transfer payments to and subtracting other earnings not paid out to persons, corporation income taxes, and undistributed corporation profits from the NI.

(d)   DI is the total income available to households after the payment of personal taxes; and is equal to PI less personal taxes and also equal to personal consumption expenditures plus personal saving and the interest paid by consumers.

(e)   The relations among the five income-output measures are summarized for you in Table 5-5 in the text.

(f)   Figure 5-2 is a more realistic and complex circular flow diagram that shows the flows of expenditures and incomes among the households, business firms, and governments in the economy.

6.   Because price levels change from year to year, it is necessary to adjust the money or nominal GDP computed for any year to obtain the real GDP before year-to-year comparisons between the outputs of final goods and services can be made.

(a)   The price level is stated as an index number that measures the combined price of a market basket of goods in a given year relative to a combined price of a market basket of goods in a base year, and that ratio is multiplied by 100.

(b)   Although there are many price indices, the GNP price index or deflator is used to adjust GDP measures for changes in the price level.

(c)   To adjust the GDP figures, divide the nominal GDP in any year by the price index for that year. The result is the adjusted or real GDP.

(d)   When the price index in a year is below (above) the 100 it was in the base year the nominal GDP figure for that year is inflated (deflated) by this adjustment.

7.   GDP is not, for the following reasons, a measure of social welfare in the economy.

(a)   It excludes the value of final goods and services not bought and sold in the markets of the economy.

(b)   It excludes the amount of leisure the citizens of the economy are able to have.

(c)   It does not record the improvements in the quality of products that occur over the years.

(d)   It does not measure changes in the composition and the distribution of the domestic output.

(e)   It is not a measure of per capita output because it does not take into account changes in the size of the economy's population.

(f)   It does not record the pollution costs to the environment of producing final goods and services.

(g)   It does not measure the market value of the final goods and services produced in the hidden or underground sector of the economy.

IMPORTANT TERMS

base year
capital consumption allowances
corporation income taxes
disposable income
dividends
double counting
expenditure and income approaches
GDP deflator
government current purchases of goods and services
gross and net investment
gross domestic product
gross national product
income or factor payment
indirect taxes
inflating and deflating
national income
national income accounting
net domestic income
net exports
nominal GDP
personal consumption expenditure
personal income
price index
real GDP
undistributed corporation profits
value added

FILL-IN QUESTIONS

1.   National income accounting is valuable because it provides a means of keeping track of the level of

_____ in the economy and the course it has followed over the long run; it also provides the information required to devise and put into effect the public

_____ that will improve the performance of the economy.

2.   Gross domestic product is defined as the total

market _____ of all final goods and services (produced, sold) _____ in an economy in a year. The goods and services are valued at their

_____ _____.

3. In measuring GDP, only final goods and services are included; if intermediate goods and services were included, the accountant would be _____

_____ .

4. Value added is the difference between the market value of a firm's _____ and its _____ from other firms. A firm buys materials for $200 from other firms in the economy and produces from them a product that sells for $315. Value added by the firm is _____.

5. The total value added to a product at all stages of production equals the _____ of the final product; and the total value added to all products produced in the economy during a year is the _____ _____ product.

6. Excluded from the computation of GDP are two types of nonproduction transactions:
(a) financial transactions that can be further subdivided into:

(1) _____;

(2) _____;

(3) _____;

(b) _____-_____ sales

7. GDP can be computed by adding up all that is spent on this year's final goods and services production and this method is called the _____ or _____ approach. GDP can also be computed by adding all the incomes derived from the production of this year's output and this method is called the _____ or _____ approach.

8. In using the expenditure approach, national income accountants divide expenditures on final goods and services into four categories or expenditure streams:

(a) _____ _____ _____

(b) _____ _____

(c) _____

(d) _____ _____

9. In symbols, the GDP by the expenditures approach = _____ + _____ + _____ + _____

10. Personal consumption expenditures are the expenditures of households for _____, _____, and _____ goods and for _____.

11. Gross investment includes _____, _____, and _____.

Goods that have been produced but not sold in a given year are counted as investment and included in the category _____.

12. Net investment is less than gross investment by an amount equal to _____ or _____ _____.

13. If gross investment is less than depreciation, net investment is (positive, zero, negative) _____ and the economy's stock of capital is (constant, declining, increasing) _____.

14. Government transfer payments are not counted as part of government purchase of goods and services because transfer payments do not represent a payment for _____ _____.

15. An economy's net exports equal its _____ less its _____.

16. In the income approach, GDP is computed by adding the incomes earned by inputs to the productive process to two nonincome charges: _____ and _____.

17. The actual income flow categories used by national income accountants are:

(a) wages, _____ and _____ _____ _____

(b) corporation _____

_____

(c) _____ and miscellaneous investment income

(d) accrued net income of _____

_____ from farm production

(e) net income of nonfarm _____

_____

18. Supplementary labour income consists of the payments employers make to social _____ programs and to _____ pension funds.

19. Corporation profits are disposed of in three ways:

(a) _____

(b) _____

(c) _____

20. Net investment income from nonresidents is the difference between gross domestic product and

_____ _____

_____. This latter aggregate measures income received from production by (resident/nonresident) _____ factors of production. GNP in Canada has always been (greater than/less than/equal to) _____ GDP because net investment income from nonresidents has been (positive/negative/zero) _____.

21. National income equals gross national product minus _____ _____ and

_____ _____ _____ .

22. Personal income

(a) equals national income plus _____ and minus the sum of _____ ,

_____ ,

and _____

(b) also equals _____ ,

plus _____ ,

plus _____ .

23. Disposable income
(a) equals personal income minus _____

_____ ;

(b) also equals _____

_____ .

24. A price index is the ratio of the combined price of a market basket of goods and services in a given year to the combined _____ of an _____ basket of goods and services in the _____ year, with the ratio being multiplied by 100.

25. The price index used to adjust the nominal GDP for changes in the price level is called the _____ _____. To obtain real or _____ dollar GDP, _____ the year's nominal GDP by that year's GDP deflator expressed in hundredths.

26. For several reasons the real GDP is not a measure of social welfare in an economy.

(a) It does not include the _____ transactions that result in the production of goods and services or the amount of _____ enjoyed by the citizens of the economy.

(b) It fails to record improvements in the _____ of the products produced, changes in the composition and distribution of the economy's total _____ , the undesirable effects of producing the GDP upon the _____ of the economy, and the goods and services produced in the _____ economy.

(c) And because it is a measure of the total output of the economy it does not measure the _____

_____ output of the economy.

27. When the population of an economy grows at a more rapid rate than its real GDP grows, the standard of living in the economy (rises, falls, remains constant)

_____.

PROBLEMS AND PROJECTS

1. Below are actual national accounts figures for Canada in 1990.
(a) Compute each of the following using the method outlined in the simplified accounts presented in Table 5-6 of the text.

	Billions of Dollars
Exports	$169
Corporation profits before taxes	46
Capital consumption allowances	76
Government current purchases of goods and services	133
Net investment income from nonresidents	-24
Accrued net income of farm operators from farm production	4
Indirect taxes (less subsidies)	75
Wages, salaries, supplementary labour income	373
Gross investment	139
Personal saving	49
Corporation income taxes	17
Government transfer payments	149
Interest and miscellaneous investment income	59
Net income from nonfarm unincorporated business, including rent	36
Personal consumption expenditures	398
Imports	170
Other earnings not paid out to persons	-37
Undistributed corporation profits	7
Personal taxes	136

(a)   (1) Dividends $_____

(2) Net Exports $_____

(3) Net Investment $_____

(b)   Use any of these figures and any of your computations in (a) above to prepare in the table below an Income Statement for the Economy similar to the one found in Table 5-6 (on page 85 of the text).

Receipts: Expenditure Approach		Allocations: Income Approach	
$_____		$_____	
_____		_____	
_____		_____	
_____		_____	
		_____	
		_____	
		_____	
		_____	
GDP $_____		$_____	

(c)   In this economy:

(1) Net domestic income is $ _____.

(2) National income is $ _____.

(3) Personal income is $ _____.

(4) Disposable income is $ _____.

(5) Personal saving is $ _____.

2.   The following table contains data on the nominal GDP, constant dollar GDP, and the GDP price deflator in Canada for a number of years. Complete the missing entries based on the information provided by the table.

Year	Nominal $ GDP (Billions)	Constant $ GDP (Billions)	GDP Deflator
1984	$444.7	$_____	95.2
1985	477.9	489.6	_____
1986	_____	505.7	100.
1987	551.6	526.8	
1988	605.9	_____	109.5
1989	_____	565.6	114.9

3.   The following tables show financial data for three firms in the toy producing industry. The firms are a wood producer, a toy manufacturer, and a toy retailer.

Wood Producer			
Purchase of material inputs	$0	Sales to toy manufacturer	$84
Wages	65		
Profits	19		

Toy Manufacturer			
Purchases from wood producer	$84	Sales to toy retailer	$110
Wages	16		
Profits	10		

Toy Retailer			
Purchases from toy manufacturers	$110	Sales to consumers	$150
Wages	30		
Profits	10		

(a)   Complete the table:

Firm	Gross Value of Production	Purchases from other Firms	Value Added
Wood producer	$_____	$_____	$_____
Toy manufacturer	_____	_____	_____
Toy retailer	_____	_____	_____
Totals	_____	_____	_____

(b)   The total incomes earned: Wages $_____

Profits $_____

Total Incomes $ _____

4. In the table below are nominal GDP figures for three years and the price indices for each of the three years. (The GDP figures are in billions.)

Year	Nominal GDP	Price Index	Real GDP
1929	$104	121	$_____
1933	56	91	$_____
1939	91	100	$_____

(a) Which of the three years appears to be the base year? _____

(b) Between

(1) 1929 and 1933 the economy experienced (inflation, deflation) _____;

(2) 1933 and 1939 it experienced (inflation, deflation) _____;

(c) Use the price indices to compute the real GDP in each year. (You may round your answer to the nearest billion dollars.)

(d) The nominal GDP figure:

(1) for 1929 was (deflated, inflated, neither) _____.

(2) for 1933 was _____

(3) for 1939 was _____

(e) The price level

(1) fell by _____% from 1929 to 1933;

(2) rose by _____% from 1933 to 1939.

5. Using the information below calculate the nominal GDP for 1993 and 1994; the real GDP for 1993 and 1994, using 1986 as the base year; and the GDP deflator for 1993 and 1994.

Product	Production in 1993	Production in 1994	Price in 1993	Price in 1994	Price in 1986
Wheat	2	2	$6	$ 5	$4
Skates	1	2	$9	$10	$5
Tables	1	1	$3	$ 4	$3
Books	2	1	$2	$ 1	$1

(a) 1993 nominal GDP $_____

(b) 1994 nominal GDP $_____

(c) 1993 real GDP $_____

(d) 1994 real GDP $_____

(e) 1993 GDP deflator _____

(f) 1994 GDP deflator _____

6. Following is a list of four production and income measures and a number of items that may or may not be included in those measures. Indicate, in the space to the right of each item, which of the income-output measures includes this item by placing the appropriate letter in the blanks. It is possible for the item to be included in none, one, two, or three of the measures.

Production and Income Measures

(a) Gross Domestic Product
(b) Personal Income
(c) Disposable Income
(d) Not included in any of the measures

Items:

(1) Interest on the public debt. _____

_____ _____

(2) The sale of a used computer. _____

_____ _____

(3) The production of shoes that are not sold by the manufacturer._____ _____

_____

(4) The purchase of a share of common stock on the Vancouver Stock Exchange. _____ _____

_____

(5) The interest paid on the bonds of Quebec Hydro.

_____ _____ _____

(6) The labour performed by a homemaker. _____

_____ _____

(7) A student loan from a commercial bank. _____

_____ _____

(8) The purchase of a new tractor by a farmer.

_____ _____ _____

(9) The labour performed by an assembly line worker in repapering his or her own kitchen. _____

_____ _____

(10) The services of a provincial civil servant.

_____ _____ _____

SELF-TEST

Circle T if the statement is true, F if it is false.

1. The gross domestic product is a measure of the total market value of all final goods and services produced in the economy in one year. **T F**

2. Both the nominal GDP and the real GDP of the Canadian economy are measured in constant dollars. **T F**

3. The total market value of the wine produced in Canada during a year is equal to the number of bottles of wine produced in that year multiplied by the average price at which a bottle is sold during that year. **T F**

4. Value added is the market value of a firm's output less the value of the inputs it has purchased from others. **T F**

5. If the value added by all firms in an economy were summed, the resulting figure would be equal to gross domestic product. **T F**

6. The gross domestic product would be understated if intermediate goods were erroneously included in its calculation. **T F**

7. Goods purchased with public transfer payments are not included in the gross domestic product. **T F**

8. If a car was produced in 1991 and sold in 1992, it would be included in 1992's gross domestic product. **T F**

9. The two approaches to the measurement of the gross domestic product yield identical results because one approach measures the total amount spent on the products produced by business firms during a year, while the second approach measures the total income of business firms during the year. **T F**

10. In computing gross domestic product, net domestic income and national income by the expenditure approach, transfer payments are excluded because they do not represent payments for currently produced goods and services. **T F**

11. The expenditure made by a household to have a new home built is a personal consumption expenditure. **T F**

12. In national income accounting any increase in the inventories of business firms is included in gross investment. **T F**

13. The revenue from the sale of new issues of stocks is included in gross investment but not in net investment. **T F**

14. If gross investment is greater than capital consump-tion during a given year, the economy's stock of capital has increased. **T F**

15. Gross investment cannot have a negative value. **T F**

16. The net exports of an economy equal its exports of goods and services less its imports of goods and services. **T F**

17. Dividends are the only part of corporate profits that are included in calculating gross domestic product by the income approach. **T F**

18. In the income approach, all income received by people in the economy over a year is summed and increased by depreciation expenditures and indirect taxes less subsidies to obtain GDP. **T F**

The data in the following table should be used to answer true-false questions 19 to 22 and multiple-choice questions 10 to 16.

	Billions
Net investment	$32
Personal taxes	39
Government transfer payments	19
Indirect taxes	8
Corporation income taxes	11
Personal consumption expenditures	217
Capital consumption allowances	7
Exports	15
Dividends	15
Government current purchases of goods and services	51
Undistributed corporation profits	10
Other earnings not paid out to persons	4
Imports	12
Net investment income from nonresidents	-5

19. The stock of capital goods in the economy has expanded. **T F**

20. Gross investment is equal to $25 billion. **T F**

21. National income equals the net domestic income minus $5 billion. **T F**

22. Disposable income is equal to $245 billion. **T F**

23. A price index measures the combined price of a par-ticular collection of goods and services in a given period relative to the combined price of identical or similar goods and services in a reference period. **T F**

24. The base year of a price index must always be the first year of the period covered. **T F**

25. Comparison of a gross domestic product with the gross domestic product of an earlier year when the price level has risen between the two years necessitates the "inflation" of the GDP figure in the later year. **T F**

26. To adjust nominal gross domestic product for a given year so that a comparison between GDP in that year and in the base year can be made, it is necessary to divide nominal GDP in the given year by the price index—expressed as a decimal—for that year. **T F**

27. The price index used to adjust nominal GDP to measure the real GDP is the consumer price index (CPI). **T F**

28. If the price index for 1990 is 126 and the price index for 1991 is 130, the price level rose by 4% between 1990 and 1991. **T F**

29. The Consumer Price tends to overstate the increases in the cost of living. **T F**

30. A GDP value that reflects current prices is called current dollar or nominal GDP. **T F**

31. A constant dollar GDP value arises when the nominal GDP has not changed over two consecutive years. **T F**

32. Nominal GDP figures are adjusted for price changes over time by expressing each year's price index in hundredths and dividing it into the nominal GDP of that year. **T F**

33. GDP is a measure of the social welfare of society. **T F**

34. The presence of an underground economy results in an overstatement of the GDP value. **T F**

MULTIPLE-CHOICE

Circle the letter that corresponds to the best answer.

1. Which of the following is not an important use to which national accounting is put?
(a) provides a basis for the formulation and application of policies designed to improve the economy's performance
(b) permits measurement of the economic efficiency of the economy
(c) makes possible an estimate of the output of final goods and services in the economy
(d) enables the economist to chart the growth of the economy over a period of time

2. To include the value of the parts used in producing the automobiles turned out during a year in gross domestic product for that year would be an example of
(a) including a nonmarket transaction
(b) including a nonproductive transaction
(c) including a noninvestment transaction
(d) double counting

3. In the definition of GDP the term "final goods and services" refers to
(a) goods and services that are in the final stage of production
(b) goods and services that have been produced and purchased this year
(c) goods and services purchased this year for final use and not for resale or further processing
(d) goods and services produced in prior years and finally sold this year

4. Excluded from the measurement of GDP are all of the following with the exception of
(a) government transfer payments
(b) purchases of stocks and bonds
(c) second-hand sales
(d) investment expenditures by business firms

5. Net investment equals gross investment less
(a) gross national product
(b) net inventory change
(c) capital consumption allowances
(d) government investment expenditure

6. If net investment is a positive value, a nation's stock of capital is
(a) increasing
(b) declining
(c) staying constant
(d) not enough information provided to reach a conclusion

7. Which of the following does not represent investment?
(a) an increase in the quantity of shoes on the shelves of a shoe store
(b) the construction of a house that will be occupied by its owner
(c) the purchase of newly issued shares of stock in Canadian Pacific Limited
(d) the construction of a factory building using money borrowed from a bank

8. A refrigerator is produced by its manufacturer in 1991, sold during 1991 to a retailer, and sold by the retailer to a final consumer in 1992. The refrigerator is
(a) counted as consumption in 1991

(b)   counted as investment in 1992
(c)   counted as investment in 1991
(d)   not included in the gross domestic product of 1991

9.   The income approach to GDP sums the total income earned by resource suppliers and adds two nonincome charges
(a)   saving and investment
(b)   depreciation and indirect taxes less subsidies
(c)   indirect business taxes and undistributed corporate profits
(d)   depreciation and net investment

Questions 10 to 16 use the national income accounting data given in the table in the true-false section.

10.   The nonincome charges are equal to
(a) $11 billion
(b) $15 billion
(c) $17 billion
(d) $19 billion

11.   Corporate profits are equal to
(a) $15 billion
(b) $25 billion
(c) $36 billion
(d) $19 billion

12.   Net exports are equal to
(a) $3 billion
(b) $2 billion
(c)   -$32 billion
(d) $32 billion

13.   The gross domestic product is equal to
(a) $245 billion
(b) $284 billion
(c) $298 billion
(d) $310 billion

14.   The net domestic income is equal to
(a) $295 billion
(b) $302 billion
(c) $317 billion
(d) $321 billion

15.   National income exceeds personal income by
(a) $6 billion
(b) $15 billion
(c) $21 billion
(d) $44 billion

16.   Personal saving is equal to
(a)   -$28 billion
(b)   -$8 billion
(c) $8 billion
(d) $28 billion

17.   In national income accounting personal income is defined as
(a)   income earned by the factors of production for their current contribution to production
(b)   income received by households before personal taxes
(c)   income received by households less savings
(d)   income received by households less personal consumption expenditure

18.   If both nominal gross domestic product and the level of prices are rising, it is evident that
(a)   real GDP is constant
(b)   real GDP is rising but not as rapidly as prices
(c)   real GDP is declining
(d)   no conclusion can be drawn concerning the real GDP of the economy on the basis of this information.

19.   In 1971 the Canadian nominal GDP was $97 billion and in 1991 the nominal GDP was $674 billion. The GDP deflator (1986 = 100) was 33.8 in 1971 and 122 in 1991. The percentage change in real GDP was approximately
(a)   22%
(b)   67.2%
(c)   93%
(d)   594%

20.   The real GDP in Canada(1986 = 100) in 1989 was $566 billion and in 1991 it was $553 billion. It can be concluded that
(a)   the price level in Canada declined between 1989 and 1991
(b)   the price level in Canada rose between 1989 and 1991
(c)   the quantity of goods and services produced in Canada fell between 1989 and 1991
(d)   the quantity of goods and services produced in Canada increased between 1989 and 1991
(e)   none of the above

21.   In an economy, the total expenditure for a market basket of goods in year 1 (the base year) was $4,000 million. In year 2, the total expenditure for the same basket of goods was $4,500 million. What was the GDP price index for the economy in year 2?
(a)   88
(b)   112.5
(c)   188
(d)   103

22.   Changes in the real GDP from one year to the next do not reflect
(a)   changes in the quality of the goods and services produced

(b) changes in the size of the population of the economy
(c) changes in the average length of the work week
(d) any of the above changes

23. A price index one year was 145 and the next year it was 167. What is the approximate percentage change in the price level from one year to the next as measured by that index?
(a) 12%
(b) 13%
(c) 14%
(d) 15%

24. GDP is deficient as a measure of social welfare because GDP does not reflect
(a) increased leisure enjoyed by members of society
(b) the composition and distribution of output
(c) per capita output
(d) transactions in the underground economy
(e) all of the above

DISCUSSION QUESTIONS

1. Of what use are national income accounts to the economist and to the policy makers in the economy?

2. Why are GDP, GNP, and so on, monetary measures, and why is it necessary that they be monetary measures?

3. Why does GDP exclude nonproductive transactions? What are the two principal types of nonproductive transactions? List some examples of each.

4. Why are there two ways, both of which yield the same answers, of computing GDP, net domestic income, and so on?

5. Why are transfer payments excluded from GDP, GNP, and NI but included in PI?

6. Is residential construction counted as investment or consumption? Why? Why is a change in inventories counted as an investment?

7. How do you define a static, an expanding, and a declining economy? What is the relationship between gross investment and the capital consumption allowances in these three economies?

8. What is meant by a nonincome charge or allocation? What are the two principal nonincome charges included in GDP? Why are they excluded from NI?

9. Why do economists find it necessary to inflate and deflate GDP when comparing GDP in different years? How do they do this?

10. Why is GDP not a measure of the social welfare of society?

ANSWERS

Fill-in questions

1. production, policies

2. value, produced; market prices

3. double counting

4. output, purchases; $115

5. price; gross domestic

6. (a) (1) public transfer payments, (2) private transfer payments, (3) security transactions (b) second-hand

7. output, expenditure; earnings, income

8. (a) personal consumption expenditure (b) gross investment (c) government current purchase of goods and services (d) net exports

9. C; I_g; G; X_n

10. durable, semi-durable, nondurable, services

11. final purchases of machinery, equipment, and tools; all construction; changes in inventory; changes in inventory

12. depreciation, capital consumption allowances

13. negative, declining

14. current production

15. exports, imports

16. depreciation, indirect taxes less subsidies

17. (a) salaries, supplementary labour income (b) profits before tax (c) interest (d) farm operators (e) unincorporated businesses

18. insurance, private

19. (a) corporation income tax (b) dividends (c) undistributed corporate profits

20. gross national product; resident; less than, negative

21. indirect taxes, capital consumption allowances

22. (a) transfer payments; corporation income taxes, undistributed corporation profits, other earnings not paid out to persons (b) personal taxes, personal consumption expenditures (including interest paid by consumers), personal saving

23. (a) personal taxes; (b) personal consumption expenditures (including interest paid by consumers) plus personal saving

24. price, identical, base

25. GDP deflator, constant, divide

26. (a) nonmarket, leisure (b) quality, output, environment, hidden (c) per capita

27. falls

Problems and projects

1. (a) (1) $22, (2) $-1, (3) $63

(b)

Receipts:	Allocations:	
Expenditure Approach	Income Approach	
C $398	Wages, salaries & supp.	
G $133	labour income	$373
I_g $139	Corp. profits	
X_n $-1	before taxes	$46
	Interest & misc.	
	investment income	$59
	Accrued net income	
	of farm operators	$4
	Net income of nonfarm	
	unincorp. business	$36
	Net domestic income	$518
	Indirect taxes (less	
	subsidies)	$75
	Capital consumption	
	allowances	$76
GDP $669	GDP	$669

(c) (1) $518, (2) $494 (3) $582, (4)$446, (5) $48

2. 1984: $467; 1985: 97.61; 1986: $505.7; 1987: 104.7; 1988: $553.3; 1989: $649.8

3. (a) Wood producer: $84; 0; $84
Toy manufacturer: $110; $84; $26
Toy retailer: $150; $110; $40
Totals: $344; $194; $150
(b) 111; 39; 150

4. (a) 1939; (b) (1) deflation,(2) inflation; (c) 86, 62, 91; (d) (1) deflated, (2) inflated, (3) neither; (e) (1) 24.8, (2) 9.9

5. (a) $28; (b) $35; (c) $18; (d) $22; (e) 155; (f) 159

6. (1) b,c; (2) d; (3) a,b,c; (4) d; (5) a,b,c; (6) d; (7) d; (8) a,b,c; (9) d; (10) a, b, c

Self-test

1. T; 2. F; 3. T; 4. T; 5. T; 6. F; 7. F; 8. F;
9. F; 10. T; 11. F; 12. T; 13. F; 14. T; 15. T;
16. T; 17. F; 18. F; 19. T; 20. F: 21. T; 22. T;
23. T; 24. F; 25. F; 26. T; 27. F; 28. F; 29. T;
30. T; 31. F; 32. T; 33. F; 34. F

Multiple-choice

1. (b); 2. (d); 3. (c); 4. (d); 5. (c); 6. (a);
7. (c); 8. (c); 9. (b); 10. (b); 11. (c); 12. (a);
13. (d); 14. (a); 15. (a); 16. (d); 17. (b);
18. (d); 19. (c); 20. (c); 21. (b); 22. (d); 23. (d);
24. (e)

CHAPTER

6

Macroeconomic Instability: Unemployment and Inflation

In the last chapter you learned how to define and how to compute various measures of the nominal and real value of national output and income in any year. This chapter begins the explanation of what determines how large each of these income-output measures will tend to be. In the chapters that follow you will learn what causes the income and output of the economy to be what they are, what causes them to change, and how they might be controlled for the welfare of society.

Chapter 6 is concerned with the instability of the Canadian economy, or with what is commonly called the business cycle: the ups and downs in employment of labour and the real output of the economy and changes in the general level of prices that occur over the years. That there have been expansions and contractions in economic (or business) activity since before Confederation is evident from even a casual look at Canadian economic history. What is not immediately evident, however, is that these alternating and relatively short periods of prosperity and "hard times" have taken place over a very long period in which the trends in per capita output, employment, and the standard of living have been upward. During this long history, booms and busts have occurred quite irregularly; and their duration and intensity have been so varied that it is better to think of economic instability than of business cycles.

The first section of the chapter describes the four phases of a typical business cycle and its impact on the production of different kinds of goods. Attention is then turned to an examination of the unemployment that accompanies a downturn in the level of economic activity in the economy. You will discover that there are different kinds of unemployment, that full employment means about 7-8% of the labour force is unemployed, and that there are at least three problems encountered in measuring what percentage of the labour force is actually unemployed at any time. Unemployment has an economic cost—the lost production that the unemployed resources could have produced—and this cost is unequally distributed among different sectors of our society. Moreover, widespread unemployment can be the cause of other social problems.

A second problem that can result from economic instability is inflation, and it is examined in the remainder of the chapter. Inflation is an increase in the general (or average) level of prices in an economy. Unanticipated inflation can redistribute income and wealth and so can work a real hardship on some individuals while benefiting others. History teaches us that if inflation occurs at too rapid a rate, a severe breakdown in the economy can occur.

One last word. The thing to keep your eye on when you consider economic fluctuations and unemployment and inflation in the Canadian economy is the change in total or aggregate spending that can occur because consumers, business firms, the public sector, or nonresidents decide to spend more or less for goods and services.

CHECKLIST

When you have studied this chapter, you should be able to:

■ Explain what the term "macroeconomic stability" implies with regard to prices, employment, and growth.

■ Explain what is meant by the business cycle; describe the four phases of an idealized cycle; and identify the two types of noncyclical fluctuations.

■ Identify the phase of the business cycle the Canadian economy is presently passing through.

■ Identify the "immediate determinant" or cause of changes in the levels of output and employment.

■ Distinguish between the impact of cyclical fluctuations on output and prices in industries producing capital and consumer durable goods and on those producing consumer semi- and nondurable goods;

and on high- and low-concentration industries.

■ Provide some explanation for the differences among industries in their reactions to downturns in economic activity.

■ Distinguish between frictional, structural, and cyclical unemployment; and explain the causes of these three kinds of unemployment.

■ Define full employment and the full-employment unemployment rate (the natural rate of unemployment).

■ Describe the process employed (by Statistics Canada) to measure the rate of unemployment; and list the three criticisms of Statscan data.

■ Given the necessary data be able to obtain measures for employment, unemployment, and the unemployment rate.

■ Define the GDP gap, and state Okun's law.

■ Identify the economic cost of unemployment and the groups that bear the unequal burdens of unemployment.

■ Define inflation and the rate of inflation, and describe the index used to measure changes in the general price level.

■ Describe the trends in the inflation rate in Canada since 1980; make international comparisons of inflation rate and unemployment rate data.

■ Describe how inflation can redistribute income among groups and how lenders can protect the purchasing power of their savings if inflation is correctly anticipated.

■ List the groups and institutions that are hurt by and those that benefit from inflation.

■ Distinguish between nominal and real income and,given the data on nominal income and the price level, calculate real income.

■ Explain the relationship between the nominal and real interest rate.

CHAPTER OUTLINE

1. The history of the Canadian economy is a record of long-term economic growth.
(a) But this growth has been characterized by periods of inflation and of depression or of both entwined around the upward growth trend.
(b) The business cycle means alternating periods of prosperity and depression. These recurrent periods of ups and downs in employment, output, and prices are irregular in their duration and intensity. But the typical pattern is: peak, recession, trough, and recovery to another peak.
(c) Changes in the levels of output and employment in a market economy are largely the result of changes in the level of total spending or demand.
(d) Not all changes in employment and output that occur in the economy are cyclical; some are due to seasonal and secular influences.
(e) The business cycle affects the entire economy, but it does not affect all parts in the same way and to the same degree. In particular, the production of capital and durable consumer goods fluctuates more than the production of consumer nondurable and semi-durable goods during a cycle because (1) the purchase of capital and durable consumer goods can be postponed, and (2) the industries producing these goods are largely dominated by a few large firms that hold prices constant and let output decline when demand falls.

2. Full employment does not mean that all workers in the labour force are employed and that there is zero unemployment; some unemployment is normal.
(a) There are at least three kinds of unemployment.
(1) Frictional unemployment arises from the search for a first time or alternative job opportunity. Such unemployment is characteristic of a growing and dynamic economy and is generally desirable.
(2) Structural unemployment is the result of changes in technology and in the type of goods and services consumers wish to buy. A difference between worker skills and job required skills make structural employment a serious and longer term problem.
(3) Cyclical unemployment is the result of insufficient aggregate spending in the economy.
(b) Because some frictional and structural unemployment is unavoidable, the full-employment unemployment rate (the natural rate of unemployment) is the sum of frictional and structural unemployment. It is achieved when cyclical unemployment is zero (real output of the economy is equal to its potential output) and, in Canada,has been estimated at about 7%-8% of the labour force.
(c) Surveying 55,000 households each month, Statistics Canada finds the unemployment rate by dividing the number of persons in the civilian labour force who are unemployed by the number of people in the civilian labour force; but the figures collected in the survey have been criticized because of biases in the counting of both the employed and the unemployed.
(d) Unemployment has an economic cost.
(1) The economic cost is the forgone output (or the GDP gap). Okun's law is that for every 1% the actual unem-

ployment rate exceeds the natural rate of unemployment there is a 2.5% GDP gap.

(2) This cost is unequally distributed among different groups of workers in the labour force.

(e) Unemployment also leads to serious social problems.

3. Over its history the Canadian economy has experienced not only periods of unemployment but periods of inflation.

(a) Inflation is an increase in the general level of prices in the economy; and a decline in the level of prices is deflation.

(b) The rate of inflation in any year is equal to the percentage change in the price index between that year and the preceding year. The rule of 70 can be used to calculate the number of years it will take for the price level to double at any given rate of inflation.

(c) The inflation rate in Canada tended to slowly accelerate in the 1960s and 1970s, reach a peak yearly rate of increase of 12.4% in 1981, and decline irregularly to its present yearly rate of under 2%.

4. Even if the total output of the economy did not change, unanticipated inflation would arbitrarily redistribute real income and wealth. This would benefit some groups and hurt other groups in the economy.

(a) Whether someone benefits or is hurt by inflation is measured by what happens to real income. Inflation injures those whose real income falls, and it benefits those whose real income rises as the result of the inflation.

(1) Real income is determined by dividing nominal income by the price level expressed in hundredths.

(2) The percentage change in real income can be approximated by subtracting the percentage change in the price level from the percentage change in nominal income.

(b) It also injures savers because it decreases the real value of any savings, the nominal value of which is fixed.

(c) It benefits debtors and hurts creditors because it lowers the purchasing power or the real value of the debt when it is repaid.

(d) But when the inflation is anticipated and people can adjust their nominal incomes to reflect the expected rise in the price level, the redistribution of income and wealth is lessened.

(e) Since World War II, inflation in Canada has redistributed wealth from the household to the public sector of the economy.

(f) In short, inflation acts to tax some groups and to subsidize other groups.

IMPORTANT TERMS

anticipated versus unanticipated inflation
business cycle
civilian labour force
cost-of-living adjustment (COLA)
discouraged workers
frictional, structural, and cyclical unemployment
GDP gap
hyperinflation
labour force population
natural rate of unemployment
nominal and real income
Okun's law
participation rate
peak
potential output
recession
recovery
rule of 70
seasonal variations
secular trend
trough

FILL-IN QUESTIONS

1. Macroeconomic stability refers to (a) steady _____ _____; (b) _____ _____ and (c) _____ _____.

2. The history of the Canadian economy is one of (steady, unsteady) _____ long-term economic growth; at times, this growth has been accompanied by _____ and at other times its expansion has been interrupted by low levels of _____ and _____.

3. The business cycle is a term that means the recurrent _____ and _____ in the level of business activity in the economy. The four phases of a typical business cycle are peak, _____, _____, and _____.

Although having common phases, business cycles vary greatly in _____ and _____.

4. In addition to the changes brought about by the operation of the business cycle, changes in output and employment may be due to _____ variations and to a _____ trend.

5. Business cycles are _____ around the long-run growth trend in the economy.

6. Production and employment in the (durable, non-durable) _____ and (capital, consumer) _____ goods industries are affected to a greater extent by the expansion and contraction of the economy than they are in the _____ goods industries. On the demand side the purchase of consumer durables and capital goods can be _____, while on the supply side the exercise of _____ _____results in the lowering of _____ rather than _____.

7. The three types of unemployment are:

(a) _____

(b) _____

(c) _____

8. Frictional unemployment refers to that group of workers who are _____ for jobs or waiting to take jobs in the near future. Structural unemployment means the lack of job opportunities due to changes in product _____ or _____. Cyclical unemployment arises in the _____ phase of the business cycle which is caused by _____ _____ _____.

9. Full employment (does, does not) _____ mean zero unemployment. The full-employment unemployment rate is: (a) sometimes called the _____ rate of unemployment; (b) equals the total of the _____ and the _____ unemployment in the economy; (c) realized when the _____ unemployment in the economy is equal to zero and when the _____ output of the economy is equal to its _____ output; and (d) assumed in this chapter to be about _____%.

10. When the economy achieves its natural rate of unemployment, the number of jobseekers is (greater than, less than, equal to) _____ the number of job vacancies; and the price level is (rising, falling, constant) _____.

11. The unemployment rate is found by dividing _____ by the _____.

12. The cost to society of unemployment is the lost _____ that the unemployed resources could have produced.

13. The GDP gap is equal to _____ GDP minus _____ GDP; and for every percentage point the unemployment rate rises above the natural rate of unemployment the GDP gap will, according to Okun's law, (increase, decrease) _____ by _____%.

14. The unemployment rate as measured by Statistics Canada may be understated due to:

(a) _____

(b) _____;

while (c) _____ _____ may lead to an overstatement of the rate.

15. An unemployed worker who has no job prospects and who has not actively sought work would be classified as ''_____ _____ _____ _____ _____,'' and (would, would not) _____ count as one of the unemployed by Statistics Canada.

16. The burdens of unemployment are borne more heavily by (adult, teenage) _____ and (educated, uneducated) _____ workers.

17. Inflation means a _____ in the general level of _____ in the economy. The rate of inflation in year 1991 is equal to the price index for year _____ less the price index for year _____ all divided by the price

index for year _____.

18. The amount of goods and services one's nominal income can buy is called _____ _____.

(a)   If one's nominal income rises by 10% and the price level rose by 7%, the percentage increase in _____ _____ would be _____.

(b)   If nominal income was $30,000 and the price index, expressed in hundredths, was 1.06, then _____ _____would be _____.

19.   Inflation

(a)   hurts those whose money incomes are relatively (fixed, flexible) _____;

(b)   penalizes savers when the inflation is (expected, unexpected) _____;

(c)   hurts (creditors, debtors) _____ and benefits _____;

(d)   has since World War II shifted wealth from (the public sector, households) _____ to _____.

20.   The redistributive effects of inflation are less severe when it is (anticipated, unanticipated) _____.

(a)   Clauses in labour contracts that call for automatic adjustments of workers' income from the effects of inflation are called _____.

(b)   The percentage increase in purchasing power that the lender receives from the borrower is the (real rate of interest, nominal rate of interest) _____; the percentage increase in money that the lender receives is the _____.

21.   Real income measures the _____ _____ of nominal income. To obtain real income for a year divide the _____ income by a _____ _____ expressed in hundreds for that year. If nominal income increases at a faster rate than the price index, real income will _____; while, if the price index is increasing at a faster rate, real income will _____.

PROBLEMS AND PROJECTS

1.   In the following table are Canadian labour force statistics for a number of recent years. (Numbers of persons are in thousands.)

| | Year | | |
---	1983	1989	1990
Civilian noninstitutional pop. (15+)	18,805	20,141	20,430
Labour force participation rate (%)	64.4	67.04	67.0
Civilian labour force	___	___	___
Employed	10,675	___	12,486
Unemployed	___	1018	___
Unemployment rate	___	___	___

(a)   Fill in the missing entries in the table.

(b)   How is it possible that both employment and unemployment increased in 1990?

(c)   Would you say that any of the years 1983, 1989, and 1990 was a year of full employment?

(d)   Why is the task of maintaining full employment over the years more than just a problem of finding jobs for those who happen to be unemployed at any given time?

2.   Janice consumes only one good, "Pepsi," and measures purchasing power in terms of litres of "Pepsi."

(a)   At the beginning of the year when "Pepsi" was $1 a litre Janice loaned $100 interest free for one year to a friend. During the course of the year the price of "Pepsi" increased to $1.25.

(1) How many litres of "Pepsi" did Janice lend to her friend?

(2) How many litres of "Pepsi" were returned to Janice when the loan was paid back?

(3) By how much did the unanticipated inflation reduce Janice's wealth?

(b)   Suppose that Janice knew that the price of "Pepsi" would increase to $1.25. What nominal interest rate would she charge in order to keep the purchasing power of the loan constant?

(c)   Suppose that Janice wants to receive a 3% increase in purchasing power from the loan. Given that she knows that the price of "Pepsi" will increase to $1.25, how much money must she receive when the loan is repaid? What nominal interest rate will she charge?

3.   Peter is in the 45% marginal tax bracket so that 45 cents of every extra dollar of nominal income is paid in taxes. He is considering the purchase of a $1000 Canada Savings Bond, which carries a 6% nominal interest rate.

Peter anticipates a rate of inflation of 4% for the year. If Peter is correct, what is the approximate real rate of return he would receive on the Savings Bond?

4. Indicate in the space to the right of each of the following, the effect [beneficial (B), detrimental (D), or indeterminate (I)] of inflation on these persons:
(a) A retired, self-employed business executive who now lives by spending, each month, a part of the amount saved and deposited in a trust company. _____
(b) A retired private-school teacher who lives on the dividends she receives from the shares of stocks she owns.

_____

(c) A farmer who (by mortgaging his farm) borrowed at the local bank $500,000 that must be repaid during the next ten years. _____
(d) A retired couple whose sole source of income is the fixed nominal pension they receive from her former employer. _____
(e) A widow whose income consists entirely of interest received from the corporate bonds she owns.

_____

(f) A member of a union that negotiated a contract containing a COLA clause. _____
(g) A retired person with a guaranteed fully indexed pension plan. _____

(h) The Canadian government. _____

5. Suppose that in 1990 the Canadian economy is at full employment, has a potential and actual real GDP of $566 billion, and has an unemployment rate of 7.5%.
(a) Compute the GDP gap in 1989 and enter it in the table below. Data is in billions of dollars. The natural rate of unemployment is estimated as 7.5%.

Year	Potential Real GDP	Actual Real GDP	GDP Real Gap (in Billions)
1990	$566	$566	$_____
1991	571	563	_____
1992	591	553	_____

(b) The potential and actual real GDPs in 1990 and 1991 are also shown in the table. Compute and enter into the table the GDP gaps in these two years.

(c) In 1991 the actual real GDP is _____% of the potential real GDP. (Hint: Divide the actual real GDP by the potential real GDP.)

(1) The actual real GDP is _____ % less than the potential real GDP.
(2) Using Okun's law, the unemployment rate will rise from 7.5% in 1990 and be _____% in 1991.

(d) In 1992 the actual real GDP is _____% of the potential real GDP.

(1) The actual real GDP is _____% less than the potential real GDP.
(2) The unemployment rate, according to Okun's law, will be _____%.

6. The following table shows the price index in the economy at the end of four different years.

Year	Price Index	Rate of Inflation
1	100.00	
2	112.00	_____
3	123.20	_____
4	129.36	_____

(a) Compute and enter in the table the rates of inflation in years 2, 3, and 4.
(b) Employing the "rule of 70," how many years would it take for the price level to double at each of these three inflation rates?
(c) If nominal income increased by 15% from year 1 to year 2, what was the approximate percentage change in real income?
(d) If nominal income increased by 7% from year 2 to year 3, what was the approximate percentage change in real income?
(e) If nominal income was $25,000 in year 2, what was real income that year?
(f) If nominal income was $25,000 in year 3, what was real income that year?
(g) If the nominal interest rate was 14% to borrow money from year 1 to year 2, what was the approximate real rate of interest over that period?
(h) If the nominal interest rate was 8% to borrow money from year 3 to year 4, what was the approximate real rate of interest over that period?

7. The table on page 71 shows the Canadian GDP in 1986 dollars since 1971. (Shown in millions of dollars.)

Year	GDP	% Change	Year	GDP	% Change
1971	$286,998		1981	$440,127	
1972	303,447		1982	425,970	
1973	326,848		1983	439,448	
1974	341,235		1984	467,167	
1975	350,113		1985	489,437	
1976	371,688		1986	505,666	
1977	385,122		1987	526,730	
1978	402,737		1988	552,958	
1979	418,328		1989	565,779	
1980	424,537		1990	563,060	

(a) Complete the columns indicating the % change in real GDP.

(b) The average rate of change per year over the time period was approximately 3.34%. Construct a graph with years (1971-1990) placed on the X axis and percent change (-4 to + 7) on the Y axis. Draw a horizontal line on the graph at the 3.34 percent change level. Place on the graph the various years and associated percent change in real GDP values. The graph indicates the variability in the growth rates in real GDP over this time period and is partly the result of cyclical activity.

SELF-TEST

Circle T if the statement is true, F if it is false.

1. The long-term trend of economic growth in Canada has not been smooth but has been interrupted by periods of unemployment or inflation or both. **T F**

2. The business cycle is best defined as alternating periods of increases and decreases in the rate of inflation in the economy. **T F**

3. The typical business cycle has four phases: peak, recession, trough, and secular trend. **T F**

4. Individual business cycles tend to be of roughly equal duration and intensity. **T F**

5. Not all changes that occur in output and employment in the economy are due to the business cycle. **T F**

6. Industries that are highly concentrated show small relative decreases in output and large relative decreases in prices during a downswing of the business cycle. **T F**

7. Structural unemployment can be described as a mismatch between worker skills and the skills required by job vacancies. **T F**

8. The essential difference between frictionally and structurally unemployed workers is that the former do not have and the latter do have saleable skills. **T F**

9. Cyclical unemployment is sometimes termed deficient demand unemployment. **T F**

10. Full employment means zero unemployment. **T F**

11. The full-employment unemployment rate is equal to the total of the frictional and structural unemployment rates. **T F**

12. If unemployment in the economy is at its natural rate, the actual and potential outputs of the economy are equal. **T F**

13. The natural rate of unemployment in the Canadian economy has remained a constant 6% of the labour force since the 1950s. **T F**

14. The unemployment rate is equal to the number of persons who are unemployed divided by the civilian labour force. **T F**

15. The participation rate plus the unemployment rate must add up to 100%. **T F**

16. By not counting discouraged workers as unemployed, the official unemployment data tends to understate the unemployment rate. **T F**

17. The economy's GDP gap is measured by deducting its actual GDP from its potential GDP. **T F**

18. An economy cannot produce an actual real GDP that exceeds its potential real GDP. **T F**

19. Because of gender discrimination, the unemployment rate for females is higher than the unemployment rate for males. **T F**

20. Teenagers, because they will work for lower wages, have a lower unemployment rate than persons 25 years of age and older. **T F**

21. The economic costs of cyclical unemployment are the goods and services that are not produced. **T F**

22. Inflation is defined as an increase in the total output of an economy. **T F**

23. Between 1989 and 1990 the consumer price index rose from 114.0 to 119.5. The rate of inflation was, therefore, 5.5%. **T F**

24. If the price level increases by 10% each year, the price level will double every ten years. **T F**

25. A person's real income is the amount of goods and

services that the person's money (or nominal) income will enable him or her to purchase. **T F**

26. If the rate of inflation is greater than the percent increase in nominal income, real income will decline. **T F**

27. Since a Canada Savings Bond can always be cashed in for its purchase price, the purchasing power of the bond remains constant. **T F**

28. Inflation lowers the living standard of those individuals living on a fixed nominal income. **T F**

29. Unanticipated deflation would benefit creditors (lenders) and hurt debtors (borrowers). **T F**

30. The real interest rate equals the nominal interest rate plus the expected rate of inflation. **T F**

31. Whether the inflation is anticipated or unanticipated, the effects of inflation on the distribution of income are much the same. **T F**

32. Inflation reduces the real burden of existing government debt. **T F**

MULTIPLE-CHOICE

Circle the letter that corresponds to the best answer.

1. Which one of the following is not one of the four phases of an idealized business cycle?
(a) inflation
(b) recession
(c) recovery
(d) trough

2. Most economists believe that the immediate determinant of the levels of domestic output and employment is
(a) the price level
(b) the size of the civilian labour force
(c) the nation's stock of capital good
(d) the level of aggregate spending

3. Changes in business activity are the result of
(a) seasonal variation
(b) the business cycle
(c) secular trend
(d) all of the above

4. Total employment in December of this year was greater than total employment in December 1928. This is no doubt due to the effect of
(a) seasonal variations
(b) secular trend

(c) the business cycle
(d) business fluctuations

5. If employment in the forest products sector of the Canadian economy during last August and September was 112% of what it normally is in those months, this is probably a consequence of
(a) seasonal variations
(b) secular trend
(c) the business cycle
(d) both seasonal variations and the business cycle

6. Production and employment in which of the following industries would be least affected by a depression?
(a) nondurable consumer goods
(b) durable consumer goods
(c) capital goods
(d) iron and steel

7. A worker who loses his job at a petroleum refinery because electricity is being generated by using a nuclear reactor rather than the burning of oil is an example of
(a) frictional unemployment
(b) structural unemployment
(c) cyclical unemployment
(d) disguised unemployment

8. A worker who has quit one job and is taking two weeks off before reporting to a new job is an example of
(a) frictional unemployment
(b) structural unemployment
(c) cyclical unemployment
(d) disguised unemployment

9. Insufficient aggregate demand results in
(a) frictional unemployment
(b) structural unemployment
(c) cyclical unemployment
(d) disguised unemployment

10. The unemployment rate is computed by dividing the number unemployed by
(a) the labour force population
(b) the civilian labour force
(c) the number employed
(d) total population

11. The civilian labour force in an economy is 150. If the unemployment rate is 10%, the number of employed workers in the economy is
(a) 120
(b) 135
(c) 125
(d) 130

12.   The labour force data collected by Statistics Canada have been criticized because
(a)   part-time workers are not counted in the number of workers employed
(b)   discouraged workers are treated as a part of the civilian labour force
(c)   some workers who are not looking for work are included in the civilian labour force
(d)   all of the above

13.   The full-employment unemployment rate in the economy has been achieved when
(a)   frictional unemployment is zero
(b)   structural unemployment is zero
(c)   cyclical unemployment is zero
(d)   the natural rate of unemployment is zero

14.   Which of the following has increased the natural rate of unemployment in Canada?
(a)   the increased participation of women and teenagers in the Canadian labour force
(b)   the expansion of unemployment insurance benefits in Canada
(c)   the increases in the legal minimum wage
(d)   all of the above

15.   The GDP gap is calculated as the value of
(a)   potential output minus actual output
(b)   actual output minus potential output
(c)   output achieved if the natural rate of employment was zero minus actual output
(d)   nominal GDP minus nominal GNP in any one year

16.   Okun's law predicts that when the actual unemployment rate exceeds the natural rate of unemployment by two percentage points the GDP gap will equal
(a)   2% of the potential GDP
(b)   3% of the potential GDP
(c)   4% of the potential GDP
(d)   5% of the potential GDP

17.   If the GDP gap were equal to 7.5% of the potential GDP, the actual unemployment rate would exceed the natural rate of unemployment by
(a)   two percentage points
(b)   three percentage points
(c)   four percentage points
(d)   five percentage points

18.   The rate of unemployment is lowest among the following groups:
(a)   the uneducated
(b)   teenagers
(c)   workers 15–24 years of age
(d)   workers 25 years of age and older

19.   During periods of inflation the purchasing power of $1
(a)   rises
(b)   falls
(c)   stays constant
(d)   not enough information given to arrive at a conclusion

20.   If a person's nominal income increases by 8% while the price level increases by 10%, the person's real income will have
(a)   increased by 2%
(b)   increased by 18%
(c)   decreased by 18%
(d)   decreased by 2%

21.   If no inflation were anticipated, a bank would be willing to lend a business firm $10 million at an annual interest of 8%. If the rate of inflation were expected to be 6%, the bank would charge the firm an annual interest rate of
(a)   2%
(b)   6%
(c)   8%
(d)   14%

22.   Of the following, who would not be hurt by inflation?
(a)   those living on fixed money incomes
(b)   those who find prices rising more rapidly than their money incomes
(c)   those who have money savings
(d)   those who became debtors when prices were lower

23.   A cost-of-living adjustment clause (COLA) in a union contract
(a)   states that the last worker hired will be the first one fired in a cyclical downturn
(b)   guarantees a worker a stated percentage of regular income during layoffs
(c)   adjusts worker incomes automatically to inflation
(d)   provides early retirement benefits for long-term employees in case of permanent layoffs

24.   The consumer price index was 104.4 in 1987 and 108.6 in 1988. The rate of inflation over this time period was
(a)   4%
(b)   4.02%
(c)   2.04%
(d)   4.20%

25.   Which of the following is not associated with hyperinflation?

(a) war or its aftermath

(b) rising output in the economy

(c) the hoarding of goods and speculation

(d) a halt to the use of money as both a medium of exchange and a standard of value

26. In general, since 1983 in Canada,

(a) both the rate of inflation and the unemployment rate have increased

(b) the rate of inflation has increased and the unemployment rate has increased

(c) the rate of inflation has increased and the unemployment rate has decreased

(d) the rate of inflation has decreased and the unemployment rate first decreased and later increased

DISCUSSION QUESTIONS

1. What is the historical record of the Canadian economy with respect to economic growth, full employment, and price-level stability?

2. Define the business cycle. Why do some economists prefer the term "business fluctuation" to "business cycle"? Describe the four phases of an idealized cycle.

3. What, in the opinion of most economists, is the immediate determinant or cause of the levels of output and employment in the economy?

4. The business cycle is only one of three general causes of changes in output and employment in the economy. What are the other influences that affect these variables?

5. Compare the manner in which the business cycle affects output and employment in the industries producing capital and durable goods and services. What causes these differences?

6. Distinguish between frictional, structural, and cyclical unemployment.

7. When is there full employment in the Canadian economy? (Answer in terms of the unemployment rate, the actual and potential output of the economy, and the markets for labour.)

8. How is the unemployment rate measured in Canada? What criticisms have been made of Statistics Canada's method of determining the unemployment rate?

9. What is the economic cost of unemployment, and how is the cost measured? What is the quantitative relationship (called Okun's law) between the unemployment rate and the cost of unemployment?

10. What groups in the economy tend to bear the burdens of unemployment? How are blue-collar workers affected by unemployment, and how is the percentage of the labour force unemployed fourteen or more weeks related to the unemployment rate in the economy?

11. What is inflation and how is the rate of inflation measured?

12. What is real income and how can the real income be obtained from nominal income figures?

13. What groups benefit from and what groups are hurt by inflation, and how has the public sector of the economy been affected by it?

14. What is the difference between the effects of unanticipated and the effects of anticipated inflation on the redistribution of real incomes in the economy?

15. Write three scenarios that describe the effects of inflation on the real domestic output.

16. How does the unemployment rate and the inflation rate in Canada compare with those for other industrialized nations in recent years?

ANSWERS

Fill-in questions

1. (a) economic growth (b) full employment (c) price stability

2. unsteady, inflation, output, employment

3. ups (increases), downs (decreases); recession, trough, recovery; duration, intensity

4. seasonal, secular

5. fluctuations

6. durable, capital, consumer; postponed, monopoly power, production, prices

7. (a) frictional unemployment (b) structural unemployment; (c) cyclical unemployment

8. looking; demand, technology; recession, deficient aggregate expenditure

9. does not (a) natural; (b) frictional, structural (either order); (c) cyclical, actual, potential (either order); (d) 7-8

10. equal to, constant

11. the number of persons unemployed, civilian labour force

12. output

13. the potential, the actual, increase, 2.5

14. (a) part-time employees counted as full-time (b) discouraged workers (c) false information

15. not in the labour force, would not

16. teenage, uneducated

17. rise, prices; 1991, 1990, 1990

18. real income; (a) real income, 3; (b) real income, $28,301.88

19. (a) fixed; (b) unexpected; (c) creditors, debtors; (d) households, the public sector

20. anticipated; (a) cost-of-living adjustments (COLA); (b) real rate of interest, nominal rate of interest

21. purchasing power; nominal, price index; increase, decrease

Problems and projects

1. (a) The following figures complete the table:
1983: 12,109, 1434, 11.8%
1989: 13,503, 12,486, 7.5%
1990: 13,681, 1109, 8.1%
(b) The civilian labour force increased more than employment increased.
(c) Given a natural rate of unemployment of 7%-8%, 1989 and probably 1990 were years of full employment.
(d) The number of people looking for work expands.

2. (a) (1) 100; (2) 80: (3) 20 litres

(b) 25%
(c) $128.75;28.75%

3. a negative 7/10 of 1% or -.007

4. (a) D; (b) I; (c) B; (d) D; (e) D; (f) I; (g) B;(h) B

5. (a) $ 0; (b) $8; $38 (c) 98.6, (1) 1.4 (2) 8.06 (d) 93.5 (1) 6.4 (2) 10.07

6. (a) 12, 10, 5; (b) 5.83, 7, 14; (c) 3; (d) 3; (e) $22,321; (f) $20,292; (g) 2; (h) 3

7. (a) (% change rounded): 5.7, 7.7, 4.6, 2.6, 6.1, 3.7, 4.6, 4.0, 1.5, 3.7, (-3.2), 3.1, 6.3, 4.8, 3.2, 4.1, 4.9, 2.39, —.

Self-test

1. T; 2. F; 3. F; 4. F; 5. T; 6. F; 7. T;
8. F; 9. T; 10. F; 11. T; 12. T; 13. F; 14. T;
15. F; 16. T; 17. T; 18. F; 19. F; 20. F; 21. T;
22. F; 23. F; 24. F; 25. T; 26. T; 27. F; 28. T;
29. T; 30. F; 31. F; 32. T

Multiple-choice

1. (a); 2. (d); 3. (d); 4. (b); 5. (c); 6. (a);
7. (b); 8. (a); 9. (c); 10. (b); 11. (b); 12. (d);
13. (c); 14. (d); 15. (a); 16. (d); 17. (b); 18. (d);
19. (b); 20. (d); 21. (d); 22. (d); 23. (c); 24. (b);
25. (b); 26. (d)

CHAPTER

7

The Determination of National Income in a Closed Economy: The Short Run

The level of output and employment in the market economy depends upon the level of total or aggregate spending. In Chapter 5 you calculated the GDP for the Canadian economy by summing the final expenditures on goods and services. This chapter at first proceeds in a similar manner with the spending streams limited to consumption and investment. In Chapter 6 economic instability was discussed and it was pointed out that business cycles result in lost output. If the factors determining the spending flows could be identified, business cycles could be controlled and lost output avoided. An equilibrium level of output for given levels of spending is first obtained. The equilibrium level, once attained, remains constant from one period to another as long as the spending flows remain the same. This level provides a starting point from which to measure the effect on the equilibrium level of GDP of changing one of the spending streams. By noting and changing the factors that affect the spending stream, a new equilibrium level of GDP is reached. Given the assumption of unemployed resources and stable prices, an increase in spending will always increase real GDP. By comparing equilibrium levels of income before and after the change in the spending streams, it becomes possible to predict not only the direction but also the amount of change. By changing a factor such as the interest rate, which determines a spending stream, it is possible to overcome some economic instability.

The chapter analyses the economic factors that determine two principal components of aggregate expenditures—consumption expenditures and planned investment expenditures. The main determinant of consumption spending is the level of disposable income that, with the assumptions of this chapter, is equal to GDP. You should pay particular attention to the relationships called the consumption schedule, the saving schedule, and their characteristics; to the four propensity concepts; and to the "nonincome" determinants of consumption. Since disposable income can be either consumed or saved

there also exists a relationship between saving and disposable income.

Investment expenditures—that is, the purchase of capital goods—depend upon the rate of net profits that business firms expect to earn from an investment and upon the real rate of interest they have to pay for the use of money. Because firms are anxious to make profitable investments and to avoid unprofitable ones, they undertake all investments that have an expected rate of net profit greater than (or equal to) the real rate of interest. They do not undertake an investment when the expected rate of net profit is less than the real interest rate.

You should see that because business firms behave this way the lower the real rate of interest the larger will be the dollar amount invested. This relationship between the real interest rate and the level of investment spending, called the investment-demand schedule, is an inverse one. Five noninterest determinants of investment spending influence the profit expectations of business firms. You should learn how changes in these determinants affect investment, and why investment spending is unstable.

At the equilibrium level of output, planned aggregate spending is just sufficient to purchase that output. The determination of the equilibrium level of real GDP is explained with both tables and graphs, first by using the expenditures–output approach and then by employing the leakages–injections approach. These two approaches are complementary and are two different ways of analysing the same process and of reaching the same conclusions. For each approach it is important for you to know, given the consumption (or saving) schedule and the level of net investment expenditures, what real GDP will tend to be produced and why this will be the real GDP that will be produced.

It is also important that you understand the significant distinction between planned investment and actual investment. Saving and actual investment are always equal because they are defined in exactly the same way:

the output of the economy minus its consumption. But saving and planned investment are not, however, equal by definition. They are equal only when real GDP is at its equilibrium level. When real GDP is not at its equilibrium level, saving and planned investment are not equal; even though saving and actual investment are, as always, equal because the actual investment includes unplanned investment or disinvestment. Remember: Equilibrium real GDP is achieved when saving and planned investment—not saving and actual investment—are equal.

The consumption (and the saving) schedule and the investment schedule—especially the latter—are subject to change, and when they change equilibrium real GDP will also change. The relationship between an initial change in the investment or consumption schedules and a change in equilibrium real GDP is called the multiplier. Three things to note here are: how the multiplier is defined, why there is a multiplier effect, and upon what the size of the multiplier depends. Because of the multiplier, the paradoxical consequence of an attempt by the economy to save more is either no increase or a decrease in the level of saving in the economy. The explanation of this paradox will be evident to you when you understand the equilibrium real GDP and the multiplier effect.

CHECKLIST

When you have studied this chapter, you should be able to:

■ State the assumptions on which the aggregate expenditure model is built in this chapter.

■ State what determines the amount of goods and services produced and the level of employment in the aggregate expenditure model.

■ Explain how consumption and saving are related to disposable income.

■ Compute, when you are given the necessary data, the four propensities.

■ Explain what happens to the size of the two average propensities as income increases, given the consumption schedule.

■ Explain the relationship that holds between the marginal propensity to consume and marginal propensity to save in the model in this chapter.

■ List five nonincome determinants of consumption and saving. Explain how a change in each of these determinants will affect (shift) the consumption and saving schedules.

■ Explain the difference between a change in the

amount consumed (or saved) and a change or shift in the consumption (or saving) schedule.

■ List the two basic determinants of investment; explain when a firm will and will not invest.

■ Compute, when given the appropriate data, the investment-demand schedule; explain why the relationship between investment spending and the real rate of interest is inverse.

■ List the five noninterest determinants of investment; and explain how a change in each of these determinants will shift the investment-demand curve.

■ List the four factors that explain why investment spending tends to be unstable.

■ Explain for a market economy the determinants of the level of aggregate output and employment.

■ Explain why economists take such an interest in the equilibrium level of output since that level is not necessarily the full employment level of output.

■ Find the equilibrium GDP when you are given the necessary tabular or graphical data, by employing either the aggregate expenditures–domestic output or the leakages–injections approach.

■ List the conditions that are met at the equilibrium level of output using the aggregate expenditure and the leakages–injections approach.

■ State the difference between planned investment and actual investment.

■ Explain how it is possible for saving and actual investment to be equal when saving and planned investment are not equal.

■ Explain why the economy will tend to produce its equilibrium GDP rather than some smaller or larger GDP.

■ Determine the economy's new equilibrium GDP when there is a change in any of the schedules.

■ Find the value of the multiplier when you are given the needed information; and cite the two facts upon which the multiplier effect (a multiplier greater than one) is based.

■ Use a graph as an aid in explaining the paradox of thrift.

CHAPTER OUTLINE

1. Output and employment are directly related to the level of total or aggregate expenditures in the economy. To understand what determines the level of total expenditures at any time it is necessary to explain the factors that determine the levels of the various expenditure

flows, which, in Chapter 7, are confined to consumption and investment expenditures.

2. Consumption is the largest component of aggregate expenditures; saving is disposable income not spent for consumer goods.

(a) Disposable income, which equals GDP under the assumptions of this chapter, is the most important determinant of both consumption and saving; the relationships between income and consumption and between income and saving are both direct (positive) ones.

(b) The consumption schedule shows the amounts that households plan to spend for consumer goods at various levels of income, given a price level.

(c) The saving schedule indicates the amounts households plan to save at different income levels, given a price level.

(d) The average propensities to consume and to save and the marginal propensities to consume and to save can be computed from the consumption and saving schedules.

(1) The APC and the APS are, respectively, the percentages of income spent for consumption and saved; and their sum is equal to 1.

(2) The MPC and the MPS are, respectively, the percentages of additional income spent for consumption and saved; and their sum is equal to 1.

(e) In addition to income, there are several other important determinants of consumption and saving; and changes in these nonincome determinants will cause the consumption and saving schedules to change.

(f) A change in the amount consumed (or saved) is not the same thing as a change in the consumption (or saving) schedule. If these two schedules change, they change in opposite directions; but the schedules are usually very stable.

3. The two important determinants of the level of net investment spending in the economy are the expected rate of net profits from the purchase of additional capital goods and the real rate of interest.

(a) The expected rate of net profits is directly related to the net profits (revenues less operating costs) that are expected to result from an investment and inversely related to the cost of making the investment (purchasing capital goods).

(b) The rate of interest is the price paid for the use of money. When the expected real rate of net profits is greater (less) than the real rate of interest, a business will (will not) invest because the investment will be profitable (unprofitable).

(c) For this reason, the lower (higher) the real rate of interest, the greater (smaller) will be the level of invest-

ment spending in the economy; and the investment-demand curve (schedule) indicates this inverse relationship between the real rate of interest and the level of spending for capital goods.

(d) There are at least five noninterest determinants of investment demand; and a change in any of these determinants will shift the investment-demand curve (schedule).

(e) Investment spending in the economy may also be either independent or directly related to the real GDP; and the investment schedule may show that investment either remains constant or increases as real GDP increases. In the model developed in this chapter investment is independent of the level of real GDP.

(f) Because the five noninterest determinants of investment are subject to sudden changes, investment spending tends to be unstable.

4. In this chapter it is assumed that the price level is constant and that all saving is personal saving. Two approaches are then used to explain what real GDP the economy will produce; but both approaches yield the same conclusion.

(a) Employing the aggregate expenditures–national output approach, the equilibrium real GDP is the real GDP at which:

(1) aggregate expenditures (consumption plus planned investment) equal the real GDP; or

(2) in graphical terms, the aggregate expenditures curve crosses the 45° line.

(b) Using the leakages–injections approach, the equilibrium real GDP is the real GDP at which:

(1) saving and planned investment are equal; or

(2) in graphical terms, the saving curve crosses the planned investment curve.

5. The investment schedule indicates what investors plan to do, and when saving is greater (less) than planned investment.

(a) Unplanned investment (disinvestment) in inventories will occur; and

(b) producers will reduce (expand) their production and the real GDP will fall (rise) until there is no unplanned investment (disinvestment); but the actual net investment and saving are always equal because the former includes unplanned investment or disinvestment.

6. Changes in planned net investment (or in the consumption and saving schedules) will cause the equilibrium real GDP to change in the same direction by an amount greater than the initial change in investment (or consumption).

(a) This is called the multiplier effect; and the multiplier is equal to the ratio of the change in the real GDP to the initial change in spending.

(1) The multiplier effect occurs because a change in the dollars spent by one person alters the income of another person in the same direction, and because any change in the income of one person will change the person's consumption and saving in the same direction by a fraction of the change in income.

(2) The value of the simple multiplier is equal to the reciprocal of the marginal propensity to save.

(3) The significance of the multiplier is that relatively small changes in the spending plans of business firms or households bring about large changes in the equilibrium real GDP.

(4) The simple multiplier has this value only in an economy in which the only leakage is saving.

7. The paradox of thrift is that an increase in the saving schedule results in no increase, and may result in a decrease, in saving. The increase in the saving schedule causes a multiple contraction in real GDP, and at the lower real GDP the same amount or even less saving takes place.

IMPORTANT TERMS

aggregate expenditures–domestic output approach
average propensities to consume and save
consumption and saving schedules
equilibrium GDP
45° line
investment-demand curve
investment schedule
leakages–injections approach
marginal propensities to consume and save
multiplier effect
paradox of thrift
planned and actual investment

FILL-IN QUESTIONS

1. With the assumptions of no government sector, no business saving, and constant prices, GDP equals _____ _____ and real GDP equals _____ GDP.

2. The level of output and employment in the market economy depends directly on the level of _____

or _____ _____.

3. In the model presented in this chapter aggregate expenditure is composed of _____ and _____ spending.

4. The most important determinant of consumption and of saving in the economy is the economy's _____ _____; and both consumption and saving are (directly, inversely) _____ related to this determinant.

5. As disposable income falls, the average propensity to consume will (rise, fall) _____ and the average propensity to save will _____.

6. The most important determinants of consumption spending, other than the level of income, are:

(a) the wealth or the sum of the _____ and the _____ assets households have accumulated

(b) _____

(c) _____

(d) _____

(e) _____

7. In the simple model of aggregate expenditure, the sum of the marginal propensity to consume and the marginal propensity to save equals _____.

8. A change in the consumption (or saving) schedule means that _____, but a change in the amount consumed (or saved) means that _____.

9. Investment is defined as spending for additional _____ _____; and the total amount of investment spending in the economy depends upon:

(a) the _____ rate of net _____;

(b) the real rate of _____.

10. A business firm will invest in more capital if the expected rate of net profits on this investment is (greater, less) _____ than the real rate of interest

it must pay for the use of money.

11. The relation between the rate of interest and the total amount of investment in the economy is (direct, inverse) _____ .
This means that if the real rate of interest:

(a)   rises, investment will _____ ;

(b)   falls, investment will _____ .

12. Five noninterest determinants of investment demand are:

(a)_____

(b)_____

(c)_____

(d)_____

(e)_____

13. The consumption schedule and the saving schedule tend to be (stable or unstable) _____ , while investment demand tends to be _____ .

14. The demand for new capital goods tends to be unstable because of the _____ of capital goods, the _____ of innovation, and the _____ of actual and expected profits.

15. Two complementary approaches that are employed to explain the equilibrium level of real national output are the _____ _____ approach and the _____ _____ approach.

16. Assuming a private and closed economy, the equilibrium level of real GDP is the real GDP at which:

(a)   aggregate _____ equal real national _____ ;

(b)   real GDP equals _____ plus _____ _____ ;

(c)   the aggregate expenditures schedule or curve intersects the _____ line.

17. When the leakages–injections approach is used in this chapter, the only leakage considered is _____ and the only injection considered is _____

_____ . In the graphical portrayal of this approach equilibrium real GDP is that level of GDP at which _____ _____ equals _____ .

18. If

(a)   aggregate expenditures are greater than the real national output, saving is (greater, less) _____ than planned investment, there is unplanned (investment, disinvestment) _____ in inventories, and the real GDP will (rise, fall) _____ .

(b)   aggregate expenditures are less than the real national output, savings is _____ than planned investment, there is unplanned _____ in inventories, and the real GDP will _____ .

(c)   aggregate expenditures are equal to the real national output, saving is _____ _____ planned investment, unplanned investment in inventories is _____ , and the real GDP will _____ .

19. At every level of real GDP, saving is equal to (planned, actual) _____ investment.
(a)   But if planned investment is greater than saving by $10,
(1) there is $10 of unplanned (investment, disinvestment) _____ ;

(2) the real GDP will (rise, fall) _____ .
(b)   And if planned investment is less than saving by $5,

(1) there is $5 of unplanned _____ ;

(2) the real GDP will _____ .

20. The multiplier

(a)   is the ratio of the change in _____ _____ to an initial change in spending in the economy;
(b)   has a value equal to the one divided by the _____ which is the same thing as one divided by the value of one minus _____ .

21. The multiplier effect is based on two facts:
(a)   an initial increase in spending by business firms or consumers will increase the _____ of the

households in the economy; and

(b) the latter increase will expand the (consumption, investment) _____ spending of the households by an amount equal to the increase in income times the _____.

22. When planned investment spending increases, the equilibrium real GDP (increases, decreases) _____, and when planned investment spending decreases, the equilibrium real GDP _____.

(a) The changes in the equilibrium real GDP are (greater, less) _____ than the changes in planned investment spending.

(b) The size of the multiplier varies (directly, inversely) _____ with the size of the marginal propensity to consume.

23. If the economy decides to save more (consume less) at every level of GDP, the equilibrium real GDP will (increase, decrease) _____ and the equilibrium level of saving in the economy will either remain the same or (increase, decrease) _____. This consequence of an increased desire to save is called the _____.

PROBLEMS AND PROJECTS

1. Following is a consumption schedule. Assume taxes and transfer payments are zero and that all saving is personal saving.

GDP	C	S	APC, %	APS, %
$1500	$1540	$_____	1.027	0.027
1600	1620	_____	1.025	0.025
1700	1700	_____		
1800	1780	_____	0.989	0.011
1900	1860	_____	0.979	0.021
2000	1940	_____		
2100	2020	_____	0.962	0.038
2200	2100	_____		

(a) Compute saving at each of the eight levels of GDP and the missing average propensities to consume and to save.

(b) The break-even level of income (GDP) is $_____.

(c) As GDP rises the marginal propensity to consume remains constant. Between each two GDPs the MPC can be found by dividing $_____ by $_____; and is equal to _____%.

(d) The marginal propensity to save also remains constant when the GDP rises. Between each two GDPs the MPS is equal to $_____ divided by $_____; or to _____%.

(e) Plot the consumption schedule, the saving schedule, and the 45° line on the graph on page 82.

2. Indicate in the space to the right of each of the following events whether the event will tend to increase (+) or decrease (–) the saving schedule.

(a) Development of consumer expectations that prices will be higher in the future. _____

(b) Gradual shrinkage in the quantity of real assets owned by consumers. _____

(c) Increase in the volume of consumer indebtedness. _____

(d) Growing belief that disposable income will be lower in the future. _____

(e) Rumours that a current shortage of consumer goods will soon disappear. _____

(f) Rise in the actual level of disposable income. _____

(g) A build-up in the dollar size of the financial assets owned by consumers. _____

(h) Development of a belief by consumers that the federal government can and will prevent depressions in the future. _____

3. The following schedule shows eight different rates of net profit and the dollar amounts of the investment projects expected to have each of these net profit rates.

Expected Rate of Net Profit	Investment Projects (Billions)
18%	$ 0
16	10
14	20
12	30
10	40
8	50
6	60
4	70

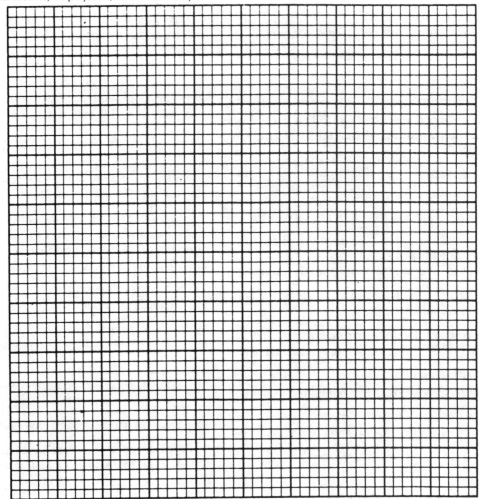

0

(a)   If the real rate of interest in the economy were 18%, business firms would plan to spend $_____ billion for investment; but if the real interest rate were 16% they would plan to spend $_____ for investment.

(b)   Should the real interest rate be 14%, they would still wish to make the investments they were willing to make at real interest rates of 18% and 16%; they would also plan to spend an additional $_____ billion for investment; and their total investment would be $_____ billion.

(c)   Were the real rate of interest 12%, they would make all the investments they had planned to make at higher real interest rates plus an additional $_____ billion; and their total investment spending would be $_____ billion.

(d)   Complete the table below by computing the amount of planned investment at the four remaining real

interest rates.

Real Rate of Interest	Amount of Investment (Billions)
18%	$ 0
16	10
14	30
12	60
10	_____
8	_____
6	_____
4	_____

(e)   Graph the schedule you completed on the graph on page 83. Plot the real rate of interest on the vertical axis and the amount of investment planned at each real rate of interest on the horizontal axis.

(f)   Both the graph and the table show that the relation between the real rate of interest and the amount of investment spending in the economy is _____.

0

This means that when the real rate of interest
(1) increases, investment will (increase, decrease)

_____;

(2) decreases, investment will _____.

(g) It also means that should we wish to

(1) increase investment, we would need to _____
the real rate of interest;

(2) decrease investment, we would have to _____
the real rate of interest.

(h) This graph (or table) is the _____-

_____ curve (or schedule).

4. Indicate in the space to the right of the following
events whether the event would tend to increase (+) or
decrease (–) investment expenditures.

(a) Rising stock-market prices. _____
(b) Development of expectations by businesspeople
that business taxes will be higher in the future.

_____

(c) Step-up in the rates at which new products and new

production processes are being introduced. _____
(d) Business belief that wage rates may be lower in the

future._____

(e) A mild recession._____
(f) A belief that business is "too good" and the economy is due for a period of "slow" consumer demand.

_____

(g) Rising costs in the construction industry.

_____

(h) A rapid increase in the size of the economy's popu-

lation. _____
(i) A period of a high level of investment spending
that has resulted in productive capacity in excess of the

current demand for goods and services. _____

5. (a) The table below shows consumption and saving
at some levels of real GDP. The equation for the consumption schedule is:
$C = 250 + .80\,GDP$. Assume the price level is constant,
the economy is closed, there is no government sector,
and business saving is 0.

The table on page 84 is an investment-demand schedule that shows the net amounts investors plan to invest
at different rates of interest (i). Assume the rate of interest

Real GDP	C	S	I	C + I	UI	Tendency of GDP
$1300	$1290	$10	$22	$1312	-$12	+
1310	1298	12	22	1320	-10	+
1320	_____	_____	_____	_____	_____	_____
1330	_____	_____	_____	_____	_____	_____
1340	_____	_____	_____	_____	_____	_____
1350	_____	_____	_____	_____	_____	_____
1360	_____	_____	_____	_____	_____	_____
1370	_____	_____	_____	_____	_____	_____
1380	_____	_____	_____	_____	_____	_____
1390	1362	28	22	1384	+6	-
1400	1370	30	22	1392	+8	-

is 6% and complete the table at the bottom of page 83 indicating consumption (*C*), saving (*S*), investment (*I*), aggregate expenditure (*C* + *I*), unplanned investment (*UI*) with unplanned accumulation shown by + and unplanned disinvestment by −, and the tendency of GDP to rise (+) or fall (−).

i	*I*
10%	$ 0
9	7
8	13
7	18
6	22
5	25
4	27
3	28

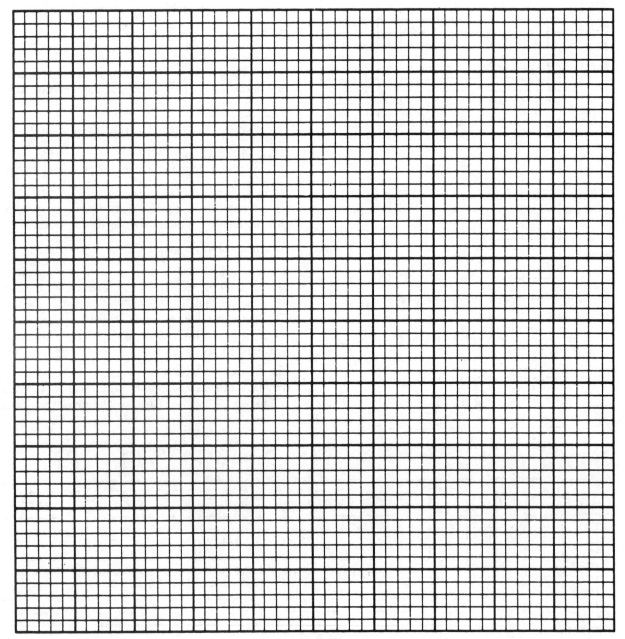

0   **Real GDP**

(b)   The equilibrium real GDP will be $_____.

(c)   The value of the marginal propensity to consume in this problem is_____ and the value of the marginal propensity to save is _____.

(d)   The value of the simple multiplier is _____.

(e)   If the rate of interest should fall from 6% to 5%, planned investment would (increase, decrease) _____ by $_____; and the equilibrium real GDP would, as a result, (increase, decrease) _____ by $_____.

(f)   Suppose the rate of interest were to rise from 6% to 7%. Planned investment would _____ by $_____; and the equilibrium real GDP would _____ by $_____.

(g)   Assume the rate of interest is 6%.

(1) On the graph on page 84, plot C, C + I, and the 45° line, and indicate the equilibrium real GDP.

(2) On the graph below plot S and I and indicate the equilibrium real GDP.

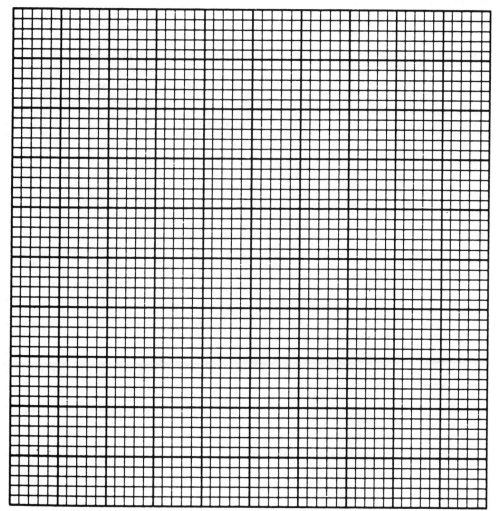

0

Real GDP

6. In part (e) of question 5 above an increase of $3 in planned investment resulted in an increase of $15 in real GDP. Given that the marginal propensity to consume is .8, complete the table below, modelled after Table 7-5 (page 135 in the text).

	Change in Income	Change in Consumption	Change in Saving
Increase in investment of $3	+ $3	$_____	$_____
Second round	_____	_____	_____
Third round	_____	_____	_____
Fourth round	_____	_____	_____
Fifth round	_____	_____	_____
All other rounds	_____	_____	_____
Total	_____	_____	_____

7. In the next table are a saving schedule (S) and an investment schedule (I) indicating that planned investment is constant.

Real GDP	S	I_a
$300	$ 5	$15
310	7	15
320	9	15
330	11	15
340	13	15
350	15	15
360	17	15
370	19	15
380	21	15
390	23	15
400	25	15

(a) The equilibrium real GDP is $_____,

and saving and planned investment are both $_____.

(b) The marginal propensity to save is _____

and the simple multiplier is _____.

(c) Use the investment schedule given in the table and assume a $2 increase in the saving schedule in the table—that is, saving at every real GDP increases by $2.

(1) Equilibrium real GDP will _____

to $_____, and at this real GDP saving

will be $_____.

(2) The effect of the increase in the saving schedule is

to _____ equilibrium real GDP. Society

tried to save more but ended up saving the same amount.

This is called the _____ _____

_____.

SELF-TEST

1. In the aggregate expenditure model presented in this chapter the two types of spending are consumption and investment. **T F**

2. In the model in this chapter the price level remains constant so any change in GDP is a change in real output. **T F**

3. The consumption schedule indicates the relationship between consumption and disposable income. **T F**

The next four questions (4, 5, 6, and 7) are based on the data in the following table. Assume that there is no government and no business saving, so GDP and disposable income (DI) are equal.

GDP = DI	C
160	172
200	200
240	228
280	256
320	284
360	312
400	340
440	368
480	396

4. At a GDP level of 240 the average propensity to consume is .95. **T F**

5. At a GDP level of 320 there is dissaving. **T F**

6. The "break-even" level of GDP is 240. **T F**

7. The marginal propensity to consume in the table is .95 at all income levels. **T F**

8. If the graph of a consumption schedule is a straight line, the marginal propensity to consume is a constant value. **T F**

9. The marginal propensity to consume is the numerical value of the slope of the consumption schedule. **T F**

10. If when disposable income increases by 100 consumption increases by 75, the marginal propensity to consume is .75. **T F**

11. The level of saving depends primarily upon the level of disposable income. **T F**

12. The marginal propensity to save is the fraction of any change in disposable income that is saved. **T F**

13. If the marginal propensity to consume is positive, the marginal propensity to save must be negative. **T F**

14. Other things being equal, an increase in wealth will shift the consumption schedule upward and result in an increase in saving out of any given level of income. **T F**

15. An increase in the price level will increase the consumption schedule (shift the consumption curve upward). **T F**

16. An increase in the taxes paid by consumers will decrease both the amount they spend for consumption and the amount they save. **T F**

17. Both the consumption schedule and the saving schedule tend to be relatively stable over time. **T F**

18. The basic determinants of investment are the expected rate of net profits and the wage rate. **T F**

19. A business firm will purchase additional capital goods if the real rate of interest it must pay exceeds the expected rate of net profits from the investment. **T F**

20. If a firm can finance investment spending out of internally generated funds, the interest will have no role to play in the investment decision. **T F**

21. The investment-demand curve for the economy shows the relationship between the real interest rate and the aggregate quantity of capital goods demanded. **T F**

22. A rapid rate of technological change will shift the investment demand schedule to the left. **T F**

23. A decrease in the corporate profits tax will shift the investment-demand schedule to the left. **T F**

24. The investment-demand schedule is assumed to be independent of the level of real income in the aggregate expenditure model of this chapter. **T F**

25. In explaining the determination of the equilibrium level of income two distinct but interrelated approaches are used: the *aggregate expenditure-domestic output* approach and the *demand-supply* approach. **T F**

26. The equilibrium level of output is that output level that generates planned spending exactly equal to the value of production. **T F**

27. At the equilibrium level of income, potential and actual GDP are equal. **T F**

28. Using the 45° diagram the equilibrium level of income is that GDP that corresponds to the intersection of the aggregate expenditure schedule and the 45° line. **T F**

29. The actual amounts saved and invested are always equal by definition, but it is only at the equilibrium level of GDP that planned investment and saving are equal. **T F**

30. The investment schedule is a schedule of actual investment rather than a schedule of planned investment. **T F**

31. The multiplier is the ratio of the change in equilibrium GDP to the change in spending that caused the GDP change. **T F**

32. In the model in this chapter the multiplier is equal to the reciprocal of the marginal propensity to consume. **T F**

33. The larger the size of the marginal propensity to consume, the smaller the multiplier. **T F**

34. The paradox of thrift is the idea that, if a nation tries to save more, it may wind up saving less. **T F**

MULTIPLE-CHOICE

Circle the letter that corresponds to the best answer.

1. In developing the aggregate expenditure model in this chapter the following assumptions are made, with the exception of
(a) the price level is constant
(b) business saving is zero
(c) there is no government sector
(d) investment spending is related to the level of income

2. In the aggregate expenditure model, output and employment in the economy depend
(a) directly on the level of total expenditures
(b) inversely on the quantity of resources available to it
(c) directly on the level of saving
(d) directly on the rate of interest

3. As disposable income decreases, *ceteris paribus*,
(a) both consumption and saving increase
(b) consumption increases and saving decreases
(c) consumption decreases and saving increases
(d) both consumption and saving decrease

4. If consumption spending increases from $358 to $367 billion when disposable income increases from $412 to $427 billion, it can be concluded that the marginal propensity to consume is
(a) 0.4
(b) 0.6
(c) 0.8
(d) 0.9

5. If when disposable income is $375 billion the average propensity to consume is 0.8, it can be concluded that
(a) the marginal propensity to consume is also 0.8
(b) consumption is $325 billion
(c) saving is $75 billion
(d) the marginal propensity to save is 0.2

6. Suppose that the equation for the consumption schedule is given by: $C = 20 + .75 DI$ where DI is disposable income. If the level of disposable income is 100, consumption will be
(a) 75
(b) 20
(c) 95
(d) 100

7. Which of the following would not cause the consumption schedule to increase (that is, cause the consumption curve to rise)?
(a) a decrease in the expected price level
(b) an increase in consumers' ownership of financial assets
(c) a decrease in the amount of consumers' indebtedness
(d) an increase in the income received by consumers

8. A decrease in the price level tends to
(a) increase the amount consumed
(b) decrease the amount consumed
(c) shift the consumption schedule upward
(d) shift the consumption schedule downward

9. A shift to the left in the investment demand curve would be a consequence of
(a) a decline in the rate of interest
(b) a decline in the level of wages paid
(c) a decline in business taxes
(d) a pessimistic outlook on the part of businesspeople

10. Which of the following relationships is an inverse one in the aggregate expenditure model?
(a) the relationship between consumption spending and disposable income
(b) the relationship between investment spending and the rate of interest
(c) the relationship between saving and the level of income

(d) the relationship between investment spending and GDP

11. The slope of the consumption schedule or line for a given economy is the
(a) marginal propensity to consume
(b) average propensity to consume
(c) marginal propensity to save
(d) average propensity to save

12. The proportion of the extra income that is consumed is called the
(a) marginal propensity to save
(b) marginal propensity to consume
(c) average propensity to save
(d) average propensity to consume

Answer the next five questions (13, 14, 15, 16 and 17) on the basis of the following diagram.

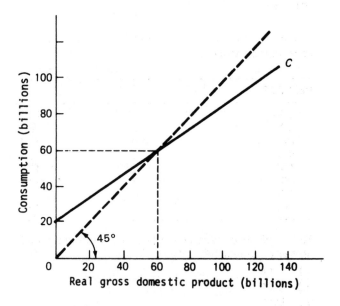

13. This diagram indicates that
(a) consumption decreases after the $60 billion level of GDP
(b) the marginal propensity to consume decreases after the $60 billion level of GDP
(c) the marginal propensity to consume is a constant
(d) consumption increases as GDP decreases

14. Saving equals zero at a GDP level (in billions) of
(a) 0
(b) 20
(c) 60
(d) 100

15. If the relevant saving schedule were constructed, one would find that
(a) the marginal propensity to save is negative up to the $60 billion level of GDP
(b) the marginal propensity to save increases after the $60 billion level of GDP
(c) saving is $20 billion at the $0 level of GDP
(d) saving is negative or there is dissaving at income levels less than 60 billion

16. If real GDP increases from 0 to 60 billion, consumption will increase (in billions) by
(a) 20
(b) 40
(c) 60
(d) 80

17. The marginal propensity to consume is
(a) .67
(b) .70
(c) .75
(d) .80

The next 3 questions (18, 19 and 20) are based on the consumption schedule below.

Real GDP	C
$250	240
300	280
350	320
400	360
450	400
500	440
550	480
600	520

18. If planned investment is $60, the equilibrium level of real GDP will be
(a) $300
(b) $400
(c) $500
(d) $600

19. If planned investment were to increase by $10, the equilibrium real GDP would rise to
(a) $450
(b) $500
(c) $550
(d) $600

20. The multiplier in this economy is
(a) 3
(b) 4
(c) 5
(d) 6

21. If the real GDP in an economy is $275 billion, consumption $250 billion, and planned gross investment $30 billion, real GDP
(a) will tend to remain constant
(b) will tend to increase
(c) will tend to decrease
(d) none of the above

The next 5 questions (22, 23, 24, 25, and 26) are based on the following diagram. The equation for the consumption is given by $C = 50 + .50$ GDP.

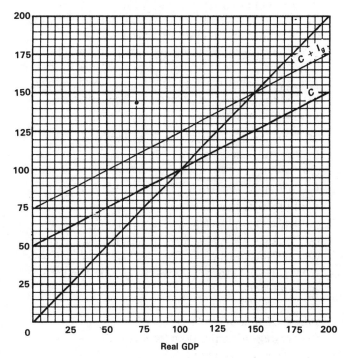

22. The level of planned investment is
(a) $15
(b) $20
(c) $25
(d) $30

23. The equilibrium level of real GDP is
(a) $100
(b) $150
(c) $175
(d) $200

24. At an income level of $200, unintended investment is
(a) $25
(b) $50
(c) $75
(d) cannot be calculated with the information supplied

25. The multiplier is
(a) 1
(b) 2
(c) 3
(d) 4

26. In this economy an increase in planned investment spending of $5 will increase equilibrium income by
(a) $5
(b) $20
(c) $15
(d) $10

27. In the leakages–injections approach, the equilibrium GDP is characterized by
(a) the equality of saving and actual investment
(b) the equality of saving and planned investment
(c) the equality of planned and unplanned investment
(d) the equality of actual investment with planned plus unplanned investment

28. Which of the following is an injection?
(a) investment
(b) saving
(c) consumption
(d) imports

29. If saving is greater than planned investment,
(a) businesspeople will be motivated to increase planned investment
(b) aggregate expenditure will be greater than the real domestic output
(c) real GDP will be greater than planned investment plus consumption
(d) saving will tend to increase

30. If the marginal propensity to consume is 0.67 and if both planned investment and the saving schedule increase by $25, real GDP will
(a) increase by $75
(b) not change
(c) decrease by $75
(d) increase by $25

31. The multiplier equals
(a) the change in real GDP divided by the marginal propensity to save
(b) the change in real GDP divided by the marginal propensity to consume
(c) the change in equilibrium GDP divided by the change in spending that caused that change in real GDP
(d) the marginal propensity to consume divided by the marginal propensity to save

32. The multiplier will be larger,

(a) the greater the marginal propensity to consume
(b) the greater the marginal propensity to save
(c) the greater the level of real GDP
(d) the lower the rate of interest

33. The paradox of thrift means that
(a) an increase in saving lowers the real GDP
(b) an increase in the average propensity to save lowers or leaves unchanged the level of savings
(c) an increase in the marginal propensity to save lowers the value of the multiplier
(d) an increase in real GDP increases investment demand

DISCUSSION QUESTIONS

1. Define aggregate expenditure and explain why, in a market economy, aggregate expenditure determines the level of output and income.

2. Describe the relation between consumption and disposable income called the consumption schedule and the one between saving and disposable income known as the saving schedule; and then define the two average propensities and the two marginal propensities.

3. Explain briefly how the average propensity to consume and the average propensity to save vary as disposable income varies if (a) the graph of the consumption schedule is a straight line through the origin as in Figure 7-1 and if (b) the graph intersects the consumption axis as in Figure 7-2 in the text. What happens to consumption and saving as disposable income varies?

4. Why do the sum of the APC and the APS and the sum of the MPC and the MPS always equal exactly one?

5. Explain briefly and explicitly how changes in the five nonincome determinants will affect the consumption schedule and the saving schedule and why such changes will affect consumption and saving in the way you have indicated.

6. Explain (a) when a business firm will or will not purchase additional capital goods; (b) how changes in the five noninterest determinants of investment spending will affect the investment-demand curve; (c) why investment spending tends to rise when the rate of interest falls; and (d) how changes in GDP might affect investment spending.

7. Why does the level of investment spending tend to be highly unstable?

8. Why is the equilibrium level of real GDP that level

of real GDP at which national output equals aggregate expenditure and at which savings equals planned investment? What will cause real GDP to rise if it is below this level and what will cause it to fall if it is above this level.

9. Explain what is meant by a leakage and by an injection. Which leakages and which injections are considered in this chapter? Why is the output at which leakages equals investment the equilibrium level of real GDP.

10. What is meant by "the distinction between savings and investment plans and the actual amounts that households manage to save and business to invest"? Is the investment schedule planned or actual investment? What adjustment causes planned and actual investment to become equal?

11. What is the multiplier effect? Why does there tend to be a multiplier effect? What determines how large the multiplier effect will be?

12. What is meant by the paradox of thrift? How does the paradox of thrift suggest that "thrift, which has always been held in high esteem in our economy, can be a social vice"?

ANSWERS

Fill-in questions

1. disposable income, nominal

2. total, aggregate expenditure

3. consumption, investment

4. disposable income; directly

5. rise, fall

6. (a) real, financial (b) price level (c) expectations (d) consumer indebtedness (e) taxation

7. one

8. the amount consumers plan to consume (save) will be different at every level of income, the level of income has changed and that consumers will change their planned consumption (saving) as a result

9. capital goods; (a) expected, profits; (b) interest

10. greater

11. inverse; (a) decrease; (b) increase

12. (a) the cost of acquiring, maintaining, and operating the capital goods; (b) business taxes; (c) technological change; (d) the stock of capital goods on hand; (e) expectations

13. stable, unstable

14. durability, irregularity, variability

15. aggregate expenditure, leakages–injections

16. (a) expenditures, output (b) consumption, planned investment (c) 45°

17. saving, planned investment; planned investment, savings

18. (a) less, disinvestment, rise (b) greater, investment, fall (c) equal to, zero, neither rise nor fall

19. actual, (a) (1) disinvestment, (2) rise (b) (1) investment, (2) fall

20. (a) equilibrium GDP; (b) marginal propensity to save, marginal propensity to consume

21. (a) income, (b) consumption, marginal propensity to consume

22. increases, decreases, (a) greater; (b) directly

23. decrease, decrease; paradox of thrift

Problems and projects

1. (a) S: – 40, – 20, 0, 20, 40, 60, 80, 100; APC: 1.000, 0.970, 0.955; APS: 0.000, 0.030, 0.045; (b) 1700; (c) 80, 100, 80; (d) 20, 100, 20

2. (a) -; (b) + ; (c) + ; (d) + ; (e) + ; (f) none; (g) -; (h) -

3. (a) 0, 10; (b) 20, 30; (c) 30, 60; (d) 100, 150, 210, 280; (f) inverse, (1) decrease, (2) increase; (g) (1) lower, (2) raise; (h) investment-demand

4. (a) + ; (b) -; (c) + ; (d) + ; (e) -; (f) -; (g) -; (h) + ; (i) -

5. (a) C: 1306, 1314, 1322, 1330, 1338, 1346, 1354; S: 14, 16, 18, 20, 22, 24, 26
I: 22, 22, 22, 22, 22, 22, 22
(C + I): 1328, 1336, 1344, 1352, 1360, 1368, 1376
UI: -8, -6, -4, -2, 0, + 2, + 4
Tendency of GDP: +, +, +, +, equilibrium, −, −
(b) 1360; (c) 0.8, 0.2; (d) 5; (e) increase, 3, increase, 15 (f) decrease, 4, decrease, 20

6.

	Change in Income	Change in Consumption	Change in Saving
Increase in investment	$3	$2.40	$0.60
Round 2	2.40	1.92	.48
Round 3	1.92	1.54	.38
Round 4	1.54	1.23	.31
Round 5	1.23	.98	.25
All other rounds	4.91	3.93	.98
Total	15.00	12.00	3.00

7. (a) 350, 15; (b) 0.20, 5; (c) (1) fall, 340, 15; (2) decrease, paradox of thrift

Self-test

1. T; 2. T; 3. T; 4. T; 5. F; 6. F; 7. F;
8. T; 9. T; 10. T; 11. T; 12. T; 13. F; 14. F;
15. F; 16. T; 17. T; 18. F; 19. F; 20. F;
21. T; 22. F; 23. F; 24. T; 25. F; 26. T;
27. F; 28. T; 29. T; 30. F; 31. T; 32. F;
33. F; 34. T

Multiple-choice

1. (d); 2. (a); 3. (d); 4. (b); 5. (c); 6. (c);
7. (d); 8. (c); 9. (d); 10. (b); 11. (a); 12. (b);
13. (c); 14. (c); 15. (d); 16. (b); 17. (a);
18. (c); 19. (c); 20. (c); 21. (b); 22. (c); 23. (b);
24. (a); 25. (b); 26. (d); 27. (b); 28. (a); 29. (c);
30. (b); 31. (c); 32. (a); 33. (b)

CHAPTER

8

Determination of the Price Level and National Income in an Open Economy: The Short Run

In the aggregate expenditure model of the economy the equilibrium level of real GDP is determined only by the level of aggregate expenditures. The two components of aggregate expenditures in an economy that is closed (neither exports nor imports goods and services) and in which governments do not spend or tax are: consumption expenditures and planned investment expenditures. These were analysed in the last chapter. The aggregate expenditure model of the economy can be extended by adding the net exports of an economy to the aggregate expenditures schedule. Net exports are nothing more than the economy's exports less its imports of goods and services. Like investment, the exports of a nation are an injection into its circular flow of income, and they increase the flow. But imports are, like saving, a leakage from the circular flow, and they decrease the flow.

The generalization used to find the equilibrium real GDP in an open economy (one that exports and imports) is the same one as for a closed economy: the economy will tend to produce a real GDP that is equal to aggregate expenditures. The only difference is that the aggregate expenditures include not only consumption and planned investment expenditures but the expenditures for net exports. So the equilibrium real GDP will equal $C + I + X_n$ (when X_n is the symbol used for net exports).

An increase in X_n, like an increase in I, will increase the equilibrium real GDP; and a decrease in X_n will decrease the equilibrium real GDP. Like a change in I, a change in X_n has a multiplier effect on real GDP. Imports, like savings, are a leakage from the spending flow; and the higher the marginal propensity to import, the lower the value of the multiplier.

The assumption of a constant price level is now relaxed in Chapter 8 and the model is expanded so that changes in both the price level and the level of output result from changes in the spending flows. This is accomplished by expanding the aggregate expenditure model to an aggregate demand–aggregate supply model. The Chapter 7 model and this model, which allows for price changes, do not, however, contradict each other. The important thing to understand is that prices can be constant at different levels. The price index in the economy, for example, might be constant at 100, at 75, or at 120. An aggregate demand (AD) curve is derived from the expenditure model by letting prices be constant at different levels. It is no great problem to see that the lower (the higher) the level at which prices are constant in the aggregate expenditure model, the larger (the smaller) will be the equilibrium real GDP, and therefore the AD curve slopes downward.

The tools employed to explain what determines the economy's real output and price level are demand and supply. You first encountered these tools in Chapter 3, where they were used to explain what determines the output and the price of a particular product. These same tools are now employed in a slightly different way. To use these tools of aggregate demand and aggregate supply, you will have to think not of the price of a particular good or service but of the price level in the economy. And, instead of thinking about the quantity of a particular good or service demanded or supplied, it is necessary to think about the total (the aggregate) quantity of all final goods and services demanded (purchased) and supplied (produced) in the economy. You will have no difficulty with the way demand and supply are used in this chapter once you adjust the way you think about them from a particular good or service and its price to all final goods and services and their average price.

Having made this adjustment in your way of thinking about demand and supply, the rest is not too difficult. The aggregate demand curve is downsloping because of the interest-rate, real-balances, and foreign-trade effects of changes in the price level. With the downsloping aggregate demand, changes in the price level cause changes in the level of spending by domestic consumers, businesses, government, and foreign buyers that affect the amount of real national output, assuming other things equal. This change would be equivalent to a movement along an existing aggregate demand curve; a lower price level increases the quantity of real domestic output and a higher price level decreases the quantity of real output. The entire aggregate demand curve can also shift because of a change in one of the nonprice-level determinants of aggregate demand. You should pay attention to these "aggregate demand shifters" that are outlined in Table 8-3 in the textbook.

The aggregate supply curve shows the level of real domestic production at different price levels during the time period that input prices remain constant. A rising price level implies greater profits in the market economy, and producers respond by increasing output or aggregate supply. The larger the pool of unemployed resources, the flatter the aggregate supply curve, which then becomes progressively steeper as capacity utilization approaches 100%. In the long run, analysed in Chapter 13, the aggregate supply curve becomes vertical.

You should remember that an assumption has also been made that other things are equal, when one moves along an aggregate supply curve. When other things change, then the aggregate supply curve can shift. The nonprice-level determinants of aggregate supply include changes in input prices, changes in productivity, and changes in the legal and institutional environment for production.

Like the ordinary demand and supply curves of Chapter 3, the intersection of the aggregate demand and the aggregate supply curves determine equilibrium quantity and price: the equilibrium quantity is the equilibrium real domestic output and the equilibrium price is the equilibrium price level. With the knowledge of how aggregate demand and supply determine the real domestic output and the price level, you have acquired the ability to explain the basic causes of inflation (an increase in demand or a decrease in supply), or of a decrease in domestic output and employment (a decrease in demand or in supply).

Aggregate demand and aggregate supply are the skeleton upon which macroeconomic theory and policies are based. The next six chapters "flesh-out" this skeleton. As you study these chapters you may forget the aggregate demand–aggregate supply framework. Don't!

It is important to be aware that the equilibrium real GDP is not necessarily the real GDP at which full employment without inflationary pressures is achieved. Aggregate expenditures may be greater or less than the full-employment noninflationary real GDP. If they are greater, there is an inflationary gap; and if they are less, there exists a recessionary gap. Be sure that you know how to measure the size of each of these gaps: the amount by which the equilibrium GDP must change to bring the economy to its full-employment real GDP without there being inflation in the economy.

The AD curve derived in this way from the aggregate expenditure model and the AS curve together determine the price level and the equilibrium real GDP in the aggregate demand–aggregate supply model. But aggregate demand can increase (or decrease), and when it does both the price level and the equilibrium real GDP may change. How the price level and real GDP are affected depends upon the slope of the aggregate supply curve. Here the important thing to see is that because the change in AD may also affect the price level in the economy, the change in AD may not have its full multiplier effect on the real GDP.

CHECKLIST

When you have studied this chapter, you should be able to:

■ Identify the major determinant of a nation's exports and the major determinant of its imports.

■ Compute, when you are given the necessary data, the marginal propensity to import and the net export schedule.

■ Use the concept of net exports to define aggregate expenditures in an open economy.

■ Explain what the equilibrium real GDP in an open economy will be when net exports are positive and when net exports are negative.

■ Find the equilibrium real GDP in an open economy when you are given the appropriate data.

■ Outline the linkage between the real GDP and the level of employment in one nation with the real GDP and employment in other nations.

■ Find the equilibrium GDP when you are given the necessary tabular or graphical data for an open economy by employing either the aggregate expenditures–domestic output or the leakages–injections approach.

■ Define aggregate demand and aggregate supply.

■ Explain why the aggregate demand curve slopes downward and the short-run aggregate supply curve upward.

■ Derive the aggregate demand curve (or schedule) from the aggregate expenditure model when you are supplied with the necessary price level data, and explain the effect of a change in aggregate expenditures on the aggregate demand curve (or schedule).

■ Identify the major nonprice-level determinants of aggregate demand and explain how they shift the aggregate demand curve.

- List the major nonprice-level determinants of aggregate supply and describe how they shift the aggregate supply curve.

- Explain, using the aggregate demand–aggregate supply model, what the equilibrium real domestic output and the equilibrium price level will be; and why the economy will tend to produce this output (rather than a larger or smaller one).

- Predict the effects of a change in aggregate demand on the price level and the equilibrium real GDP, and explain what determines how large the multiplier effect on the equilibrium real GDP will be in the aggregate demand–aggregate supply model.

- Explain why a decrease in aggregate demand will not reduce the price level so much as an equal increase in aggregate demand would have raised it.

- Distinguish between the equilibrium GDP and the full-employment, noninflationary level of GDP.

- Find the recessionary and the inflationary gaps when you are provided with the relevant data.

CHAPTER OUTLINE

1. In an open economy the exports (X) of a nation increase and its imports (M) decrease aggregate expenditures in that economy; and the aggregate expenditures are equal to the sum of consumption spending, planned investment spending, and net exports (X_n) when X_n is defined as X minus M.

(a) The equilibrium real GDP in an open economy occurs where the real GDP is equal to consumption plus planned investment plus net export spending and:

(1) a nation's exports depend directly upon the GDPs of foreign nations, while its imports depend directly upon its own GDP;

(2) the marginal propensity to import (MPM) is the percentage of additional income spent for imports.

(b) Any increase (decrease) in its X_n will increase (decrease) its equilibrium real GDP with a multiplier effect.

(c) If imports are related to the level of domestic GDP, the open economy multiplier will be smaller than the closed economy multiplier and its value given by: $1/(MPS + MPM)$.

(d) In an open economy model, circumstances and policies abroad (such as a change in the level of domestic incomes of trading partners), changes in tariffs or quotas, or changes in exchange rates will affect domestic GDP.

2. Aggregate demand and aggregate supply determine the real domestic output and the price level of the econ-

omy. They are used in this chapter to explain both why output and the price level fluctuate.

3. The aggregate expenditure model and the aggregate demand model are reconciled by recalling that the price level is assumed to be constant in the former and is a variable (can rise or fall) in the latter model.

(a) The AD curve is derived from the intersections of the aggregate expenditures curve and the 45° curve: as the price level falls (rises) the aggregate expenditures curve shifts upward (downward) and the equilibrium real GDP increases (decreases). This inverse relationship between the price level and the equilibrium real GDP is the AD schedule (or curve).

(1) As the price level falls (rises), the consumption curve shifts upward (downward) because of the real-balance or wealth effect;

(2) the investment curve shifts upward (downward) because of the interest-rate effect; and

(3) the net export curve shifts upward (downward) because of the foreign-trade effect.

The aggregate demand then is a curve that shows the total quantity of goods and services that will be purchased (demanded) at different price levels.

(b) Spending by domestic consumers, businesses, government, and foreign buyers (that is independent of changes in the price level) shifts aggregate demand, as outlined in Table 8-3 in the textbook.

(1) For domestic consumers, increases in wealth, improved expectations, reductions indebtedness, or lower taxes can increase consumer spending and aggregate demand; decreases in consumer wealth, less positive expectations, increases in indebtedness, and higher taxes decrease consumer spending and aggregate demand.

(2) For businesses, lower interest rates, improved profit expectations, lower taxes, improved technology, and less excess capacity may increase investment spending and aggregate demand; whereas higher interest rates, worse profit expectations, higher taxes, and more excess capacity may retard investment spending and aggregate demand.

(3) More government spending tends to increase aggregate demand and less government spending will decrease it, assuming that tax collections and interest rates do not change as a result.

(4) Net export spending and aggregate demand is increased by increases in the national incomes of other nations and by a dollar depreciation; declines in the incomes of foreign buyers and a dollar appreciation tend to reduce net exports and aggregate demand.

(c) Aggregate supply is a curve that shows the total quantity of goods and services that will be produced (supplied) at different price levels. In Chapter 8 aggregate supply slopes upward since, in the short run, unit costs rise with output. The steepness of the aggregate supply curve then depends on the rate of capacity utilization.

Factors that shift the aggregate supply curve include changes in the prices of inputs for production, changes in productivity, and changes in the legal and institutional environment in the economy, as outlined in Table 8-4.
(1) Lower prices for productive domestic resources (land, labour, capital, and entrepreneurial ability) and imported resources tend to reduce unit costs of production and increase aggregate supply; whereas higher input prices, which may be brought about by more market power on the part of resource suppliers, will tend to increase aggregate supply.
(2) As productivity improves, per unit production costs fall and aggregate supply increases; the converse occurs when productivity falls.
(3) A decrease in the level of business taxation or reduced regulation of business may improve the business environment and increase aggregate supply; the opposite actions may reduce aggregate supply.
(d) The equilibrium real domestic output and the equilibrium price level occur at the intersection of the aggregate demand and the aggregate supply curves. Were the actual output greater (less) than the equilibrium output, producers would find that their inventories were increasing (decreasing) and they would contract (expand) their output to the equilibrium output.
(1) An increase in aggregate demand will result in an increase in both real domestic output and the price level.
(2) An increase (a decrease) in the costs of producing goods and services will decrease (increase) aggregate supply—move the aggregate supply curve to the left (right)—and reduce (expand) the real domestic output and push the price level upward (downward).
Both aggregate demand and aggregate supply affect real domestic output and the price level.
(e) If the price level is constant, any change in the nonprice-level determinants of consumption and planned investment that shifts the aggregate expenditures curve upward (downward) will increase (decrease) the equilibrium real GDP and shift the AD curve to the right (left) by an amount equal to the increase (decrease) in aggregate expenditures times the multiplier.

4. The equilibrium level of real GDP may turn out to be an equilibrium at less than full employment, at full employment, or at full employment with inflation.
(a) If the equilibrium real GDP is less than the real GDP consistent with full employment, there exists a recessionary gap. The size of the recessionary gap equals the amount by which the actual real GDP is short of the noninflationary full-employment real GDP.
(b) If equilibrium real GDP is greater than the real GDP consistent with stable prices, there is an inflationary gap. The size of the inflationary gap equals the amount by which actual GDP exceeds the noninflationary full-employment GDP.
(c) The multiplier effect on real GDP of any increase in the spending flows will be smaller the larger the increase in the price level.

IMPORTANT TERMS

aggregate demand
aggregate supply
appreciation
capacity utilization
depreciation
determinants of aggregate demand
determinants of aggregate supply
equilibrium price level
equilibrium real domestic product
foreign-trade effect
interest-rate effect
marginal propensity to import
net exports
net export schedule
open-economy multiplier
productivity
recessionary and inflationary gaps
wealth or real-balances-effect

FILL-IN QUESTIONS

1. When a nation is able to export and import goods and services,

(a) its net exports equal its _____ minus its _____.
(b) In an open economy:
(1) aggregate expenditures are equal to consumption plus planned investment plus _____ _____;
(2) the equilibrium real GDP is the real GDP that is equal to _____ _____.

2. What would be the effect—increase (+) or decrease (−)—of each of the following upon an open economy's equilibrium real GDP?

(a) An increase in its imports _____

(b) An increase in its exports _____

(c) A decrease in its imports _____

(d) A decrease in its exports _____

(e) An increasing level of national income among trading partners _____

(f) An increase in trade barriers imposed by trading partners _____

(g) A depreciation in the value of the economy's currency _____

3. The demand for Canadian exports depends upon the _____ in other countries, the _____ _____ between Canadian and foreign currencies, and the _____ price levels in Canada and foreign countries.

4. Canadian imports depend upon the exchange rate, relative price levels, and on _____ GDP.

5. Generally an appreciation of the Canadian dollar results in a(n) _____ in imports and a(n) _____ in exports.

6. The marginal propensity to import is defined as: (_____ _____ _____)/ (change in GDP). If exports are constant at all levels of income the marginal propensity to import is the _____ of the graph of the net export schedule.

7. The aggregate expenditure schedule is given by

_____ + _____ +

_____.

8. If exports are constant and imports increase with an increasing domestic GDP, the open economy multiplier will be (greater, less than) _____ the closed economy multiplier and is given by 1/(_____ + _____).

9. The aggregate demand curve shows the quantity of goods and services that will be _____ at various price _____.

(a) It slopes (upward, downward) _____ because of the _____, the _____, and the _____ effects.

10. The aggregate supply curve shows the quantity of goods and services that will be _____ at various price _____.

11. Aggregate demand and aggregate supply together determine the equilibrium real domestic _____ and the equilibrium _____ _____.

12. In the aggregate demand–aggregate supply model the price level is a (constant, variable) _____; in the aggregate expenditures model it is a _____.

(a) But if the price level were lower in the aggregate expenditures model, the _____ effect would (raise, lower) _____ the consumption, investment, net exports, and aggregate expenditures curves; and the equilibrium real GDP would (rise, fall) _____.

(b) And if the price level were higher in the aggregate expenditure model this effect would _____ the consumption, investment, net exports, and aggregate expenditure curves; and the equilibrium real GDP would

_____.

(c) This (direct, inverse) _____ relationship between the price level and the equilibrium real GDP in the aggregate expenditure model is the aggregate (demand, supply) _____ curve (or schedule).

13. For the aggregate demand curve:
(a) an increase in the price level leads to a(n) (increase, decrease) _____ in the quantity of real national output;
(b) whereas a decrease in the price level leads to a(n) _____ in the quantity of real national output, assuming _____.

14. When the price level changes
(a) there is a (movement along, change in) _____ the aggregate demand curve.
(b) When the entire aggregate demand curve shifts,

there is a (change in the quantity of real output demanded, change in aggregate demand) _____

_____,

(c) and that change is caused by one or more of the

_____ _____ of aggregate demand.

15. List the nonprice-level determinants of aggregate demand by type:
(a) From changes in consumer spending due to changes in:

(1) _____

(2) _____

(3) _____

(4) _____
(b) From changes in investment spending due to changes in:

(1) _____

(2) _____

(3) _____

(4) _____

(5) _____

(c) From changes in government _____
(d) From net export spending due to changes in:

(1) _____

(2) _____

16. The basic cause of the aggregate supply curve being upward sloping is a(n) (increase, decrease) _____ in the per unit costs of producing goods and services as output expands in the short run.

17. List the nonprice-level determinants of aggregate supply:
(a) From a change in input prices due to a change in:

(1) _____

(2) _____

(3) _____

(b) From a change in _____
(c) From a change in the legal and institutional environment due to a change in:

(1) _____

(2) _____

18. If the price level were a constant, a(n)
(a) increase in the aggregate expenditures curve would shift the aggregate demand curve to the (right, left)

_____ by an amount equal to the upward shift in aggregate expenditures times the

_____;
(b) decrease in the aggregate expenditures curve would shift the aggregate demand curve to the _____ by an amount equal to the _____.

19. Were aggregate demand to increase,
(a) the flatter the aggregate supply curve, the (greater, smaller) _____ is the multiplier effect on the real equilibrium GDP and the _____ is the effect on the equilibrium price level; and
(b) the steeper the aggregate supply curve, the

_____ is the multiplier effect on the equilibrium real GDP and the _____ is the effect on the equilibrium price level.

20. A recessionary gap exists when equilibrium real GDP is (greater, less) _____ than the full-employment real GDP. To bring real GDP to the full-employment level, the aggregate expenditures schedule must (increase, decrease) _____.

21. When the equilibrium money GDP is greater than the full-employment real GDP at which prices are stable, there is a(n) _____ gap; to eliminate this gap _____ _____ must decrease.

PROBLEMS AND PROJECTS

1. The table at the top of page 99 is a schedule showing what aggregate expenditures (consumption plus planned investment) would be at various levels of real GDP product in a closed economy. The equation for the consumption schedule is given by:

$$C = \$76 + .80GDP, \text{ and } I = \$100.$$

(a) Were this economy to become an open economy the volume of exports would be a constant $90; and the volume of imports would be a constant $86. At each of the seven levels of real GDP, net exports would be

$_____.

Possible Levels of Real GDP	Aggregate Expenditures, Closed Economy	Exports	Imports	Net Exports	Aggregate Expenditures, Open Economy
$810	$824	$90	$86	$_____	$_____
840	848	90	86	_____	_____
870	872	90	86	_____	_____
900	896	90	86	_____	_____
930	920	90	86	_____	_____
960	944	90	86	_____	_____
990	968	90	86	_____	_____

(b) Compute aggregate expenditures in this open economy at the seven real GDP levels and enter them in the table above.

(c) The equilibrium real GDP in this open economy would be $_____.

(d) The value of the multiplier in this open economy is equal to _____.

(e) Suppose the import schedule changes from a constant $86 to: $M = 5 + .10$ GDP.

(1) Complete the Import (M), Net Exports, and Aggregate Expenditures columns on the basis of this new information.

(2) The new equilibrium level of GDP is $_____.

(3) The new multiplier is _____.

2. In the list below, what will most likely happen as a result of each event to: (1) aggregate demand (AD);(2) aggregate supply (AS); (3) the equilibrium price level (P): and (4) equilibrium real domestic output (Q)? Assume that all other things remain constant when the event occurs and that the aggregate supply curve is upward sloping. Use the following symbols to indicate the expected effects: I = increase; D = decrease; S = remains the same; and U = uncertain.

(a) A decrease in labour productivity:

AD_____ AS_____ P_____ Q_____

(b) A fall in interest rates:

AD_____ AS_____ P_____ Q_____

(c) Consumers' incomes decline as the economy moves into a recession:

AD_____ AS_____ P_____ Q_____

(d) The price of oil on the world market falls to a low level:

AD_____ AS_____ P_____ Q_____

(e) There is a depreciation of the Canadian dollar:

AD_____ AS_____ P_____ Q_____

(f) An increase in personal income tax rates:

AD_____ AS_____ P_____ Q_____

(g) An economic recovery from a recession in the United States:

AD_____ AS_____ P_____ Q_____

3. This question asks for the derivation of a downward sloping aggregate demand curve from the aggregate expenditure model.

Suppose in a closed economy the equation for the consumption schedule is: $C = \$50 + .75$ GDP. At a particular price level investment spending is determined by the interest rate according to the following table:

Interest Rate	Investment Spending
12%	$100
11	150
10	200
9	250
8	300
7	350
6	400

At a price level of 1 the interest rate is 7% and rises one percentage point for each increase of 1 in the price level. Suppose that the price level is 2 and interest rates will be 8%.

(a) Complete the following table:

Real GDP	Consumption Expenditure	Investment Expenditure	Aggregate Expenditure
$800	$650	$300	$950
900	725	300	1025
1000	_____	_____	_____
1100	_____	_____	_____
1200	_____	_____	_____
1300	_____	_____	_____
1400	_____	_____	_____
1500	_____	_____	_____

(b) The equilibrium level of real GDP is $_____.
(c) Suppose the price level was 3. The equilibrium level of income is $_____.
(d) Complete the following table:

Price Level	Real GDP
5	_____
4	_____
3	_____
2	1400

You have derived the _____ _____ curve showing the relationship between the price level and the amount of real domestic output collectively demanded.

4. In the table below is a consumption and saving schedule for a closed economy. Assume that the level of real GDP at which full employment without inflation is achieved is $590.

Real GDP	C	S
$550	$520	$30
560	526	34
570	532	38
580	538	42
590	544	46
600	550	50
610	556	54
620	562	58
630	568	62

(a) The value of the multiplier is _____.
(b) If planned net investment is $58, the equilibrium money GDP is $_____ and exceeds the full-employment noninflationary real GDP by $_____. There is a(n) _____ gap of $_____.
(c) If planned investment is $38, the equilibrium real GDP is $_____ and is less than full-employment real GDP by $_____. There is a(n) _____ gap of $_____.

5. In the table below is an aggregate supply schedule.

Price Level	Real Domestic Output Produced
$7.00	2,000
6.00	2,000
5.00	1,900
4.00	1,700
3.00	1,400
2.00	1,000
2.00	500
2.00	0

(a) Plot this aggregate supply schedule on the graph below.

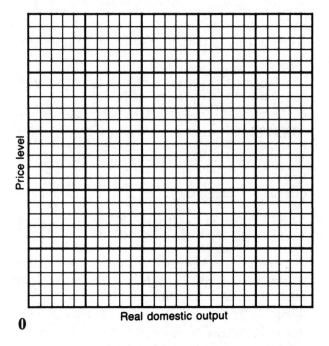

(b) In the following table on page 101 are three aggregate demand schedules.
(1) Plot the aggregate demand curve, shown in columns (1) and (2), on the graph; and label this curve D_1. At this level of aggregate demand the equilibrium real domestic output is _____ and the equilibrium price level is $_____.
(2) On the same graph plot the aggregate demand curve

REAL DOMESTIC OUTPUT PURCHASED

Price Level (1)	(2)	(3)	(4)
$7.00	1,400	1,900	400
6.00	1,500	2,000	500
5.00	1,600	2,100	600
4.00	1,700	2,200	700
3.00	1,800	2,300	800
2.00	1,900	2,400	900
1.00	2,000	2,500	1,000

shown in columns (1) and (3); and label this curve D_2.

The equilibrium real domestic output is _____

and the equilibrium price level is $_____.
(3) Now plot the aggregate demand curve in columns
(1) and (4) and label it D_3. The equilibrium real domes-

tic output is _____ and the equilibrium

price level is $_____.

SELF-TEST

Circle T if the statement is true, F if it is false.

1. The net exports of an economy equal the sum of its exports and imports of goods and services.   **T F**

2. The volume of Canadian imports depends upon the level of real GDP in other countries.   **T F**

3. Spending on Canadian exports is an addition to aggregate expenditure in Canada and increases Canadian GDP.   **T F**

4. If the GDP in the United States is growing, we can expect an increase in Canadian GDP.   **T F**

5. An increase in the imports of one nation will increase the exports of another nation.   **T F**

6. Canadian imports are dependent on the level of Canadian GDP.   **T F**

7. The price of a U.S dollar has risen from $1.15 Canadian to $1.28 Canadian. An increase in Canadian exports to the United States can be expected.   **T F**

8. The marginal propensity to import measures the extra spending in Canada from an extra dollar earned in foreign trade.   **T F**

9. Import spending, like investment spending, is an injection into the spending flow.   **T F**

10. The larger the marginal propensity to import, the smaller the multiplier.   **T F**

11. A rise in the price level of an economy (relative to foreign-price levels) tends to increase that economy's exports and to reduce its imports of goods and services.   **T F**

12. An aggregate demand schedule shows the net amounts of goods and services that consumers, businesses, governments, and foreigners collectively wish to purchase at different price levels.   **T F**

13. The aggregate demand curve slopes downward.   **T F**

14. A change in aggregate demand is caused by a change in the price level, other things equal.   **T F**

15. A fall in excess capacity, or unused existing capital goods, will retard the demand for new capital goods and therefore reduce aggregate demand.   **T F**

16. The wealth or real-balances effect is one of the nonprice-level determinants of aggregate demand.   **T F**

17. A high level of consumer indebtedness will tend to increase consumption spending and aggregate demand.   **T F**

18. A fall in the price level increases the real value of financial assets with fixed money values and, as a result, increases spending by the holders of these assets. **T F**

19. A fall in the price level reduces the demand for money in the economy and drives interest rates upward.   **T F**

20. A decrease in aggregate demand will lower the price level by the same amount as an equal increase in aggregate demand would have raised it.   **T F**

21. An increase in aggregate supply increases both the equilibrium real domestic output and the full-employment output of the economy.   **T F**

22. A decrease in aggregate supply is "doubly good" because it increases the real domestic output and prevents inflation.   **T F**

23. When the nonprice-level determinants of aggregate supply change, they alter the per unit production cost and thereby aggregate supply.   **T F**

24. Productivity is a measure of real output per unit of input.   **T F**

25.   An increase in productivity will shift the aggregate supply curve rightward.   **T F**

26.   A recessionary gap is the amount by which full-employment GDP falls short of actual GDP.   **T F**

27.   With an aggregate supply curve that is positively sloped, the multiplier effect of a change in a spending flow on real output is less than in the aggregate expenditure model of Chapter 7.   **T F**

28.   The greater the increase in the price level that results from an increase in aggregate demand, the greater will be the increase in real GDP.   **T F**

MULTIPLE-CHOICE

Circle the letter that corresponds to the best answer.

1.   The volume of Canadian exports depends upon
(a)   the price in foreign currency of a Canadian dollar
(b)   the level of Canadian prices relative to the price level abroad
(c)   the level of GDP in foreign countries
(d)   all of the above

2.   Generally a depreciation of the Canadian dollar will lead to
(a)   an increase in exports and an increase in imports
(b)   an increase in exports and no change in imports
(c)   a decrease in exports and an increase in imports
(d)   an increase in exports and a decrease in imports

3.   An increase in imports, other things remaining the same, will
(a)   shift the aggregate expenditure curve upward and the aggregate demand curve to the right
(b)   shift the aggregate expenditure curve downward and the aggregate demand curve to the left
(c)   shift the aggregate expenditure curve upward and the aggregate demand curve to the left
(d)   shift the aggregate expenditure curve downward and the aggregate demand curve to the right.

Use the data in the table below to answer questions 4 to 7.

Real GDP	C + I	Net Exports
$ 900	$ 913	$3
920	929	3
940	945	3
960	961	3
980	977	3
1000	993	3
1020	1009	3

4.   The equilibrium real GDP is
(a) $960
(b) $980
(c) $1000
(d) $1020

5.   If net exports are increased by $4 at each level of GDP, the equilibrium real GDP would be
(a) $960
(b) $980
(c) $1000
(d) $1020

6.   The multiplier in this economy is
(a)   5
(b)   4
(c)   3
(d)   2

7.   If the marginal propensity to save in this economy is .10, the marginal propensity to import must be
(a)   .10
(b)   .20
(c)   .30
(d)   .40

8.   Other things remaining constant, which of the following would decrease an economy's real GDP and employment.
(a)   the imposition of tariffs on goods imported from abroad
(b)   an increase in the level of national income among the trading partners for this economy
(c)   a decrease in the exchange rates for foreign currencies
(d)   an increase in the exchange rates for foreign currencies

9.   An increase in the real GDP of an economy will, other things remaining constant,
(a)   increase its imports and decrease the real GDPs in other economies
(b)   increase its imports and increase the real GDPs in other economies
(c)   decrease its imports and increase the real GDPs in other economies
(d)   decrease its imports and the real GDPs in other economies

10.   The effect of an increase in exports on GDP is similar to the effect of an increase in
(a)   interest rates
(b)   saving
(c)   investment
(d)   business taxes

11.   The aggregate demand curve is the relationship between the
(a)   price level and the real domestic output purchased
(b)   price level and the equilibrium real gross domestic product
(c)   price level producers are willing to accept and the price level purchasers are willing to pay
(d)   real domestic output purchased and the real domestic output produced

12.   The downward slope of the aggregate demand curve is the result of
(a)   the real-balances effect
(b)   the interest-rate effect
(c)   the foreign-trade effect
(d)   all of the above effects

13.   The aggregate supply curve is the relationship between the
(a)   price level and the real domestic output purchased
(b)   price level and the real domestic output produced
(c)   price level producers are willing to accept and the price level purchasers are willing to pay
(d)   real domestic output purchased and the real domestic output produced

14.   The aggregate supply curve is upward sloping in the short run due to
(a)   increased input prices as output rises
(b)   decreased input prices as output rises
(c)   rising per unit production costs as output rises
(d)   a shortage of domestic resources

15.   The aggregate demand curve will tend to be increased (shifted to the right) by
(a)   a decrease in the price level
(b)   an increase in the price level
(c)   an increase in the excess capacity of factories
(d)   a depreciation in the value of the Canadian dollar

16.   An increase in business taxes will tend to
(a)   decrease aggregate demand but not change aggregate supply
(b)   decrease aggregate supply but not change aggregate demand
(c)   decrease aggregate demand and decrease aggregate supply
(d)   decrease aggregate supply and increase aggregate demand

17.   When the price level rises,
(a)   holders of financial assets with fixed money values increase their spending
(b)   the demand for money and interest rates rise
(c)   spending that is sensitive to interest-rate changes increases

(d)   holders of financial assets with fixed money values have more purchasing power

18.   An increase in aggregate supply will
(a)   reduce the price level and real domestic output
(b)   reduce the price level and increase the real domestic output
(c)   increase the price level and real domestic output
(d)   reduce the price level and decrease the real domestic output

19.   If the Canadian prices of imported resources increase, then this event would most likely
(a)   decrease aggregate supply
(b)   increase aggregate supply
(c)   increase aggregate demand
(d)   decrease aggregate demand

20.   If Parliament passed much stricter laws to control the air pollution from business, then this action would tend to
(a)   increase per unit production costs and shift the aggregate supply curve to the right
(b)   increase per unit production costs and shift the aggregate supply curve to the left
(c)   increase per unit production costs and shift the aggregate demand curve to the left
(d)   decrease per unit production costs and shift the aggregate supply curve to the left

21.   If the price level in the aggregate expenditure model were lower, the consumption and aggregate expenditure curves would be
(a)   lower and the equilibrium real GDP would be smaller
(b)   lower and the equilibrium real GDP would be larger
(c)   higher and the equilibrium real GDP would be larger
(d)   higher and the equilibrium real GDP would be smaller

22.   An increase in aggregate expenditures in the aggregate expenditure model shifts the aggregate demand curve to the
(a)   right by the amount of the increase in aggregate expenditure
(b)   right by the amount of the increase in aggregate expenditure times the multiplier
(c)   left by the amount of the increase in aggregate expenditure
(d)   left by the amount of the increase in aggregate expenditure times the multiplier

23. A decrease in the price level will shift the
(a) consumption, investment, and net exports curves downward
(b) consumption, investment, and net exports curves upward
(c) consumption and investment curves downward and the net exports curve upward
(d) consumption and net exports curves upward, but the investment curve downward

Suppose that real domestic output in an economy is 50, the quantity of inputs is 10, and the price of each input is $2. Answer the next four questions (24, 25, 26, and 27) on the basis of this information.

24. The level of productivity in this economy is
(a) 5
(b) 4
(c) 3
(d) 2

25. The per unit cost of production is
(a) $0.40
(b) $0.50
(c) $0.75
(d) $1.00

26. If real domestic output in the economy rose to 60 units, then per unit production costs would
(a) remain unchanged and aggregate supply would remain unchanged
(b) increase and aggregate supply would decrease
(c) decrease and aggregate supply would increase
(d) decrease and aggregate supply would decrease

27. All else equal, if the price of each input increases from $2 to $4, productivity would
(a) decrease from $4 to $2 and aggregate supply would decrease
(b) decrease from $5 to $3 and aggregate supply would decrease
(c) increase from $4 to $2 and aggregate supply would increase
(d) remain unchanged and aggregate supply would decrease

28. The recessionary gap is
(a) the amount by which actual GDP falls short of full-employment GDP
(b) the amount by which actual GDP exceeds full employment GDP
(c) the number that would be employed at full employment minus the numbers actually employed
(d) the increase in investment spending needed to reach full-employment GDP from present GDP

29. In the aggregate demand–aggregate supply model, an increase in the price level will
(a) increase the marginal propensity to consume
(b) increase the strength of the multiplier
(c) decrease the strength of the multiplier
(d) have no effect on the strength of the multiplier

DISCUSSION QUESTIONS

1. How do exports and imports affect aggregate expenditure within a nation? In terms of injections and leakages, what condition is met at the equilibrium level of output for the open economy?

2. If imports rise whenever income increases, the open economy multiplier will be smaller than the closed economy multiplier. Why?

3. How does a change in the volume of exports and the volume of imports affect real GDP and the level of employment in an economy.

4. What are some examples of international economic linkages affecting the domestic level of GDP.

5. How would the economy of Canada be affected by increased spending undertaken by the United States government to combat a recession?

6. What is an aggregate demand and an aggregate supply curve?

7. How is the aggregate demand curve used in the aggregate demand–aggregate supply model of the economy derived from the aggregate expenditure model?

8. Explain why (a) the interest-rate effect, (b) the wealth effect, and (c) the foreign-trade effect cause the aggregate demand curve to be downward sloping.

9. What are the factors affecting investment spending that would .cause the aggregate demand curve to shift to the right?

10. What are the factors affecting consumption spending that would move the aggregate demand curve to the left?

11. Why does the aggregate supply curve slope upward in the short run?

12. Explain the effect of a change in input prices on the aggregate supply curve.

13. Define productivity and explain the effect on aggregate supply of an improvement in productivity.

14. What real domestic output is the equilibrium real domestic output? Why will business firms that produce the domestic output reduce or expand their production when they find themselves producing more or less than the equilibrium output?

15. What are the effects on the real domestic output and the price level when aggregate demand increases, and how are these effects related to the steepness of the aggregate supply curve?

16. What are the effects on the real domestic output and the price level of a decrease in aggregate supply? What are the effects of an increase in aggregate supply on the real domestic output, the price level, and the maximum real output the economy is able to produce?

17. Why is a decrease in aggregate supply "doubly bad" and an increase in aggregate supply "doubly good"?

18. Describe how changes in the international economy influence aggregate demand or supply.

19. Explain what is meant by a recessionary and an inflationary gap. What economic conditions are present in the economy when each of these gaps exist? How is the size of each of these gaps measured?

ANSWERS

Fill-in questions

1. (a) exports, imports; (b) (1) net exports (2) aggregate expenditures

2. (a) -; (b) +; (c) +; (d) -; (e) +; (f) -; (g) +

3. GDP, exchange rate, relative

4. Canadian

5. increase, decrease

6. change in imports; slope

7. C, I_g, X_n

8. less than, MPS + MPM

9. demanded (purchased), levels (a) downward, wealth (real-balances), interest-rate, foreign-trade (any order)

10. supplied (produced), levels

11. output, price level

12. variable, constant; (a) real-balance, raise, rise; (b) lower, fall; (c) inverse, demand

13. (a) decrease; (b) increase, other things equal

14. (a) movement along; (b) change in aggregate demand; (c) nonprice-level determinants

15. (a) (1) consumer wealth, (2) consumer expectations, (3) consumer indebtedness, (4) personal taxes (any order); (b) (1) interest rates, (2) profit expectations, (3) business taxes, (4) technology, (5) degree of excess capacity (any order); (c) purchases (d) (1) domestic income of other nations; (2) exchange rates (any order)

16. increase

17. (a) (1) domestic resource availability, (2) prices of imported resources, (3) market power (any order); (b) productivity; (c)(1) business taxes and subsidies, (2) government regulation (either order)

18. (a) right, multiplier; (b) left, downward shift in aggregate expenditure times the multiplier

19. (a) greater, smaller; (b) smaller, greater

20. less; increase

21. inflationary, aggregate expenditure

Problems and projects

1. (a) $4 (b) $828, 852, 876, 900, 924, 948, 972 (c) $900 (d) 5 (e) (1) Imports: $85, 89, 92, 95, 98, 101, 104; Net Exports: $5, 1, − 2, − 5, − 8, − 11, − 14; Aggregate Expenditures: $829, 849, 870, 891, 912, 933, 954 (2) $870 (3) 3.333

2. (a) S, D, I, D; (b) I, S, I, I; (c) D, S, D, D; (d) I, I, U, I (e) I, S, I, I; (f) D, S, D, D; (g) I, S, I, I

3. (a) C: $800, 875, 950, 1025, 1100, 1175; I: $300, 300, 300, 300, 300, 300
Aggregate Expenditure: $1100, 1175, 1250, 1325, 1400, 1475 (b) $1400 (c) $1200 (d) Real GDP: $800, 1000, 1200; aggregate demand

4. (a) 2.5; (b) 620, 30, inflationary, 30; (c) 570, 20; recessionary, 20

5. (b) (1) 1700, $4; (2) 2000, $6; (3) 900, $2

Self-test

1. F; 2. F; 3. T; 4. T; 5. T; 6. T; 7. T;
8. F; 9. F; 10. T; 11. F; 12. T; 13. T; 14. F;
15. F; 16. F; 17. F; 18. T; 19. F; 20. F; 21. T;
22. F; 23. T; 24. T; 25. T; 26. F; 27. T; 28. F

Multiple-choice

1. (d); 2. (d); 3. (b); 4. (b); 5. (c); 6. (a);
7. (a); 8. (d); 9. (b); 10. (c); 11. (a); 12. (d);
13. (b); 14. (c); 15. (d); 16. (c); 17. (b); 18. (b);
19. (c); 20. (b); 21. (c); 22. (b); 23. (b); 24. (a);
25. (a); 26. (c); 27. (d); 28. (a); 29. (c)

CHAPTER

9

Fiscal Policy

Chapter 9 is really an expansion of the aggregate expenditure and aggregate demand–aggregate supply model by adding one more spending stream—government spending—and one more leakage—taxes. It is a continuation of the preceding chapter and is concerned with the chief practical application of the principles discussed in it. The study of the model will suggest policies on the timing and volume of government spending and taxation that will help achieve full employment, maximum output, and stable prices. The student should carefully note the assumptions made in the aggregate expenditure model as some of the model's predictions will be modified as these assumptions are relaxed.

Government spending and taxing have a strong influence on the economy's output and employment and its price level. Federal expenditure and taxation policies designed to affect total production and employment and the level of prices are called fiscal policies. (The Bank of Canada is also able to affect these variables by applying monetary policy; but the study of monetary policy must wait until the effect of banks on the operation of the economy is examined in Chapters 10 and 11.)

The brief first section of the chapter makes it clear that since World War II the federal government has been committed to a full-employment objective to be achieved both through direct action and the elimination of barriers to the smooth functioning of the market system.

The section entitled ''Discretionary Fiscal Policy'' is, however, the crucial part of Chapter 9. It introduces government taxing and spending into the analysis of equilibrium real GDP. It is important to note that government purchases of goods and services add to aggregate demand; and that taxation reduces the disposable income of consumers, and thereby reduces both the amount of consumption and the amount of saving that will take place at any level of real GDP. Both ''approaches'' used in the explanation of equilibrium output in the aggregate expenditure model are again employed, and you are warned that you must know what

real GDP will tend to be produced and why. Special attention should be directed to the exact effect taxes have upon the consumption and saving schedules and to the multiplier effects of changes in government purchases and taxes.

Once you learn how government purchases and taxing affect the equilibrium real GDP, it is fairly easy to understand what fiscal policies can be used to offset the different phases of the business cycle. You should be aware that not only the difference between government spending and taxes affects the level of GDP, but also the absolute size of a balanced budget affects it.

Discretionary fiscal policy requires that the federal government take action to change tax rates, transfer payment programs, or purchases of goods and services. Nondiscretionary fiscal policy does not require the federal government to take any specific action, but built-in stabilizers automatically increase government deficits during recessions and increase government surplus during inflation. You should be sure that you understand why net taxes increase when the GDP rises and decrease when the GDP falls, and how this tends to stabilize the economy.

Unfortunately, nondiscretionary fiscal policy by itself may not be able to eliminate any recessionary or inflationary gap that might develop; discretionary fiscal policy will be necessary if the economy is to produce its full-employment GDP and avoid inflation. The built-in stabilizers make it more difficult to use discretionary fiscal policy to achieve this goal because they can create the illusion that the federal government's fiscal policy at different phases of the business cycle is expansionary or contractionary when, in fact, it is just the opposite. Because of the illusions created by the built-in stabilizers, economists developed the cyclically adjusted budget to enable them to discover whether federal fiscal policy was actually expansionary or contractionary and to determine what policy would have moved the economy toward full employment or slowed the rate of inflation.

In addition to the problems of timing and the political problems encountered in using fiscal policy in the real world, you will discover in the last major section of the chapter that many economists and other people are concerned by three additional important complications. They fear, first of all, that all expansionary fiscal policy that requires the federal government to borrow in the money market will raise the level of interest rates in the economy and reduce (or crowd out) investment spending. This is called the crowding-out effect, and if it is large it will reduce the effect of the expansionary fiscal policy on real GDP and unemployment. The second complication arises from the connection of the domestic economy to a world economy; aggregate demand shocks from abroad or a net export effect may increase or decrease the effectiveness of a given fiscal policy. The third fear is that an expansionary fiscal policy, with an upward sloping aggregate supply curve, will drive up the price level and may have only a limited effect on real output and employment. The supply-side economists argue that a reduction in tax rates will not only increase aggregate demand but will also expand aggregate supply. In this way, they contend, the real equilibrium GDP of the economy can be increased with little or no rise in the price level.

CHECKLIST

When you have studied this chapter, you should be able to:

■ Find the equilibrium GDP in an economy in which government purchases goods and services and levies net taxes when you are given the necessary data.

■ Determine the effect on equilibrium GDP of (1) a change in government expenditure, (2) a change in taxes, and (3) a change in transfer payments.

■ Be able to construct graphs to aid in the explanation of the effects of changes in government expenditures and taxes on equilibrium real GDP, using the aggregate–expenditures and leakages–injections approach.

■ Explain the balanced budget multiplier and indicate why in a closed economy it is equal to 1.

■ Explain when the government should pursue an expansionary and contractionary fiscal policy; what each of these policies might entail; and the effect of each on the budget.

■ Distinguish between discretionary and nondiscretionary fiscal policy.

■ Indicate how the built-in stabilizers help to elimi-

nate recession and inflationary pressures.

■ Describe the relationship between progressive, proportional, and regressive tax systems and the built-in stability of the economy.

■ Outline the timing and political problems encountered in applying fiscal policy in the real world.

■ Distinguish between the actual budget and the cyclically adjusted budget and explain why the latter indicates the government's fiscal stance.

■ Describe the crowding-out effect of an expansionary fiscal policy and how it may lessen the impact of an expansionary fiscal policy on real output and employment.

■ Explain the implications for fiscal policy of the Ricardian equivalence theorem.

■ Describe the effects of an expansionary fiscal policy using the aggregate demand–aggregate supply model and how an upward sloping aggregate supply curve lessens the impact of fiscal policy on output and employment.

■ State the effects supply-side economists argue a reduction in tax rates would have on aggregate supply, real GDP, and the price level, and explain why they believe it would have these effects.

CHAPTER OUTLINE

1. Fiscal policy is the manipulation by the federal government of its expenditures and tax receipts in order to expand or contract aggregate expenditures in the economy. By doing so either real output (and employment) is increased or the rate of inflation is decreased.

2. Since World War II, the federal government has used fiscal policy to counter the different phases of the business cycle.

3. Discretionary fiscal policy involves deliberate changes in tax rates and government spending to offset cyclical fluctuations and to increase economic growth.
(a) Six assumptions are made in order to simplify the explanation of the effects of government spending and taxes on the equilibrium real GDP.
(b) Government purchases of goods and services add to the aggregate-expenditures schedule and increase equilibrium real GDP; and an increase in these purchases has a multiplier effect upon equilibrium real GDP.
(c) Taxes decrease consumption and the aggregate-expenditures schedule by the amount of the tax times the MPC (and decrease saving by the amount of the tax times the MPS); and an increase in taxes has a negative

multiplier effect on the equilibrium real GDP. When government both taxes and purchases goods and services, the equilibrium GDP is the GDP at which (1) aggregate expenditures (consumption + planned investment + net exports + government purchases of goods and services) = the real national output (consumption + saving + taxes); or (2) using the leakages–injections approach, at which planned investment + exports + government purchases of goods and services = saving + imports + taxes.

(d)   Equal increases (decreases) in taxes and in government purchases, in a closed economy and under the assumptions of our model, increase (decrease) equilibrium real GDP by the amount of the change in taxes (or in expenditures).

(e)   The elimination of inflation (recession) is accomplished by contractionary (expansionary) fiscal policy, which is composed of an increase (decrease) in taxes, a decrease (increase) in government purchases, and incurring budget surpluses (deficits).

(f)   Whether government purchases or taxes should be altered to reduce recession and inflation depends to a large extent upon whether an expansion or a contraction of the public sector is desired.

(g)   In the aggregate demand–aggregate supply model, an expansionary fiscal policy (other things being equal) will shift the aggregate demand curve to the right, while a contractionary fiscal policy will shift the aggregate demand curve to the left.

4.   In the Canadian economy net tax revenues (tax receipts minus government transfer payments) are not a fixed amount or lump sum; they increase as the GDP rises and decrease as the GDP falls.

(a)   This net tax system serves as a built-in stabilizer of the economy because it reduces purchasing power during periods of inflation and expands purchasing power during periods of recession; but some economists contend that built-in stabilizers can only reduce and cannot eliminate economic fluctuations.

(1) AS GDP increases, the average tax rates will increase in progressive systems, remain constant in proportional systems, and decrease in regressive tax systems. There is more built-in stability for the economy in progressive tax systems.

(b)   The cyclically adjusted budget is a better index than the actual budget of the direction of government fiscal policy because it indicates what the federal budget deficit or surplus would be if the economy were to operate at full employment.

5.   Certain problems and complications arise in enacting and applying fiscal policy.

(a)   There will be problems of timing because it requires time to recognize the need for fiscal policy; for the federal government to take the appropriate steps; and for the action taken there to affect output and employment and the rate of inflation in the economy.

(b)   There will also be political problems because:

(1) the economy has goals other than full employment and stable prices;

(2) there is an expansionary bias (for budget deficits and against surpluses);

(3) there may be a political business cycle (if politicians lower taxes and increase expenditures before elections and then do the opposite after elections).

(c)   An expansionary fiscal policy may, by raising the level of interest rates in the economy, reduce (or crowd out) investment spending and weaken the effect of the policy on real GDP. But this crowding-out effect may be small and can be offset by an expansion in the nation's money supply.

(d)   The Ricardian equivalence theorem suggests that borrowing to finance a budget is offset by an increase in private saving as people save in anticipation of higher taxes in the future. Thus, the effects of deficit spending are offset by an equal increase in private saving.

(e)   The effect of an expansionary fiscal policy on the real GDP will also be weakened to the extent that it results in a rise in the price level (inflation).

(f)   Aggregate demand and aggregate supply curves can be used to show how crowding out and inflation weaken the effects of an expansionary fiscal policy on real GDP.

(g)   The connection of the domestic economy to a world economy means that fiscal policy will be inappropriate or less effective because of aggregate-demand shocks from the world economy or a net export effect that counteracts or reinforces domestic fiscal policy.

(h)   But an expansionary fiscal policy that includes a reduction in taxes (tax rates) may, by increasing aggregate supply in the economy, expand real GDP (and employment) and reduce inflation.

IMPORTANT TERMS

actual and cyclically adjusted budgets
actual and cyclically adjusted deficits
balanced-budget multiplier
built-in stabilizers
crowding-out effect
discretionary fiscal policy
expansionary and contractionary fiscal policy
lump-sum tax

political business cycle
progressive, proportional, and regressive tax systems
Ricardian equivalence theorem
supply-side economics

FILL-IN QUESTIONS

1.   The use of monetary and fiscal policy to reduce inflationary and recessionary gaps became national economic

policy at the end of _____.

2.   In order to increase real GDP during a recession,

taxes should be (increased, decreased) _____

and government purchases should be _____;
to decrease the rise in the price level during a period of inflation (according to the aggregate demand–aggregate

supply model), taxes should be _____

and government purchases should be _____.

3.   If fiscal policy is to have a counter-cyclical effect, it will probably be necessary for the federal government to

incur a budget (surplus, deficit) _____

during a recession and a budget _____
during inflation.

4.   Taxes tend to reduce consumption at each level of real GDP by an amount equal to the taxes multiplied

by the _____;
saving will decrease by an amount equal to the taxes

multiplied by the _____.

5.   In an economy in which government both taxes and purchases goods and services, the equilibrium level of real GDP is the real GDP at which:

(a)   aggregate _____ equal the domestic

_____;

(b)   GDP is equal to _____ plus

_____ _____ plus

_____ _____ plus

_____.

(c)   In the leakages–injection approach _____

_____ plus _____ plus

_____

equals _____ plus _____

6.   Equal reductions in taxes and government purchases

will (increase, decrease) _____ real GDP

by an amount equal to _____.

7.   A contractionary fiscal policy is composed of (1)

_____ _____ _____,

or (2) increased _____, or (3) a combination of both.

8.   Those who wish to expand the public sector of the economy would, during a period of inflation, advocate

a(n) (increase, decrease) _____ in govern-

ment (purchases, taxes) _____; and those who wish to contract the public sector during a recession

would advocate a(n) _____ in _____.

9.   Net taxes

(a)   equal _____ minus _____

_____;

(b)   in Canada will (increase, decrease) _____

_____ as the GDP rises and will

_____ as the GDP falls.

10.   When net tax receipts are directly related to the

GDP the economy has some _____
stability because
(a)   when the GDP rises, leakages (increase, decrease)

_____ and the budget surplus will

(increase, decrease) _____ (or the budget

deficit will _____);

(b)   when the GDP falls, leakages _____
and the budget deficit will _____ (or the

budget surplus will _____).

11.   As GDP increases, the average tax rate will increase

in (progressive, proportional, regressive) _____

systems, remain constant in _____ systems,

and decrease in _____ systems. There is

(more, less) _____ built-in stability for the
economy in progressive tax systems.

12.   The cyclically adjusted budget balance

(a)   indicates what the federal _____

would have been if the economy had operated at _____ during the year; (b) tells us whether the federal budget was in fact _____ or _____.

13. There is a problem of timing in the use of discretionary fiscal policy because of the _____, _____, and _____ lags.

14. Political problems arise in the application of discretionary fiscal policy to stabilize the economy because government has _____ goals; because voters have a bias in favour of budget (surpluses, deficits) _____; and because politicians use fiscal policies in a way that creates a _____ business cycle.

15. When the federal government employs an expansionary fiscal policy to increase real GDP and employment in the economy, it usually has a budget (surplus, deficit) _____ and (lends, borrows) _____ in the money market.
(a) This will (raise, lower) _____ interest rates in the economy and (contract, expand) _____ investment spending.
(b) This change in investment spending is the _____ effect of the expansionary fiscal policy, and it tends to (weaken, strengthen) _____ the impact of the expansionary fiscal policy on real GDP and employment.

16. The idea that public dissaving by borrowing to finance a budget deficit is offset by an increase in private saving to pay for the expected taxes in the future is associated with the _____ _____ _____. This idea suggests that fiscal policy may be (more, less) _____ effective than originally thought.

17. An expansionary fiscal policy in an economy with an upsloping aggregate supply curve will increase the real GDP and employment in the economy and (raise, lower) _____ the price level.
(a) This change in the price level will (weaken, strengthen) _____ the impact of the expansionary fiscal policy on output and employment in the economy.
(b) But if the expansionary fiscal policy is the result of reduction in taxes, the supply-side effects of the policy may be to (increase, decrease) _____ aggregate supply, to _____ the productive capacity of the economy, to _____ real GDP and employment, to _____ the rate of inflation, and to (weaken, strengthen) _____ the impact of the fiscal policy on output and employment.

18. An annually balanced budget is (pro-, counter-) _____ cyclical because governments would (raise, lower) _____ taxes and would _____ their purchases of goods and services during a recession (and to do just the opposite during an inflation).

19. A cyclically balanced budget suggests that to ensure full employment without inflation, the government incur deficits during periods of _____ and surpluses during periods of _____, with the deficits and surpluses equalling each other over the business cycle.

20. Fiscal policy is subject to further complications from _____ _____ with the world economy.
(a) The economy can be influenced by _____ _____ shocks that might reinforce or retard fiscal policy; or
(b) from a _____ effect that results from an expansionary or contractionary fiscal policy.
(1) When fiscal policy is expansionary, it tends to (increase, decrease) _____ interest rates, which in turn tends to _____ the value of the dollar, and _____ net exports.
(2) When fiscal policy is contractionary, it tends to (increase, decrease) _____ interest rates, which in turn tends to _____ the value of the dollar, and _____ net exports.

21. If an expansionary fiscal policy is the result of a reduction in taxes, the supply-side effects of the policy may be to (increase, decrease) _____ aggregate supply, to _____ productive capacity of the economy, to _____ real GDP and employment, to _____ the rate of inflation, and to (weaken, strengthen) _____ the impact of the fiscal policy on output and employment.

PROBLEMS AND PROJECTS

1. A consumption and saving schedule is shown in the table below.

(a) Assume government levies a lump-sum tax of $100. Also assume that imports are $5.

(1) Because the marginal propensity to consume in this problem is _____, the imposition of this tax will reduce consumption at all levels of real GDP by $_____. Complete the C_a column to show consumption at each real GDP after the levying of this tax.

(2) Because the marginal propensity to save in this problem is _____, this tax will reduce saving at all levels of real GDP by _____. Complete the S_a column to show saving at each real GDP after this tax has been levied.

(b) Compute the (after-tax) saving plus imports plus taxes at each real GDP and put them in the $S_a + M + T$ column.

(c) Suppose that planned investment is $150, exports are $5, and government purchases of goods and services equal $200. Complete the investment-plus-exports-plus-government-purchases column ($I + X + G$) and the (after-tax) consumption-plus-investment-plus-net-exports-plus-government-purchases column ($C_a + I + X_n + G$).

(d) The equilibrium real GDP is $_____.

(e) On the graphs on pages 112 and 113 plot:
(1) C_a, $I + X_n + G$, $C_a + I + X_n + G$, and the 45° line. Show the equilibrium real GDP.
(2) $S_a + M + T$ and $I + X + G$. Show the real equilibrium GDP. (To answer the questions below it is not necessary to recompute C, S, $S + M + T$, $I + X + G$, or $C + I + X_n + G$. They can be answered by using the multipliers.)

(f) If taxes remained at $100 and government purchases rose by $10, the equilibrium real GDP would (rise, fall) _____ by $_____.

(g) If government purchases remained at $200 and the lump-sum tax increased by $10, the equilibrium real GDP would _____ by $_____.

(h) The combined effect of a $10 increase in government purchases and a $10 increase in taxes is to _____ real GDP by $_____.

2. In the following table are seven real GDPs and the net tax revenues of government at each real GDP.

Real GDP	Net Tax Revenues	Government Purchases	Government Deficit/Surplus
$850	$170	$_____	$_____
900	180	_____	_____
950	190	_____	_____
1000	200	_____	_____
1050	210	_____	_____
1100	220	_____	_____
1150	230	_____	_____

(a) Looking at the two columns on the left of the table, it can be seen that:
(1) when real GDP increases by $50, net tax revenues (increase, decrease) _____ by $_____;

Real GDP	C	S	C_a	S_a	$(S_a + M + T)$	$(I + X + G)$	$(C_a + I + X_n + G)$
$1500	$1250	$250	$_____	$_____	$_____	$_____	$_____
1600	1340	260	_____	_____	_____	_____	_____
1700	1430	270	_____	_____	_____	_____	_____
1800	1520	280	_____	_____	_____	_____	_____
1900	1610	290	_____	_____	_____	_____	_____
2000	1700	300	_____	_____	_____	_____	_____
2100	1790	310	_____	_____	_____	_____	_____

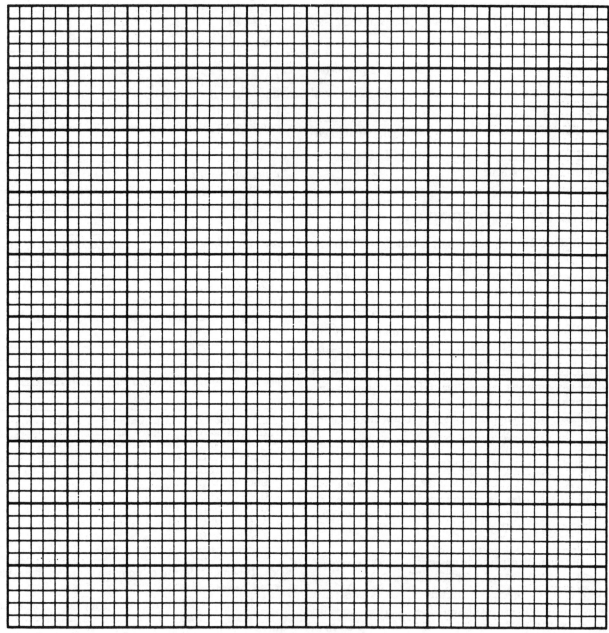

0   **Real GDP**

(2) when real GDP decreases by $100, net tax revenues

_____ by $_____;

(3) the relation between real GDP and net tax revenues

is (direct, inverse) _____.

(b)   Assume the investment multiplier has a value of 10 and that investment spending in the economy decreases by $10.

(1) If net tax revenues remained constant, the equilibrium real GDP would decrease by $_____.

(2) But when real GDP decreases, net tax revenues also decrease; and this decrease in net tax revenues will tend

to (increase, decrease) _____ the equilibrium real GDP.

(3) And, therefore, the decrease in real GDP brought about by the $10 decrease in investment spending will

be (more, less) _____ than $100.

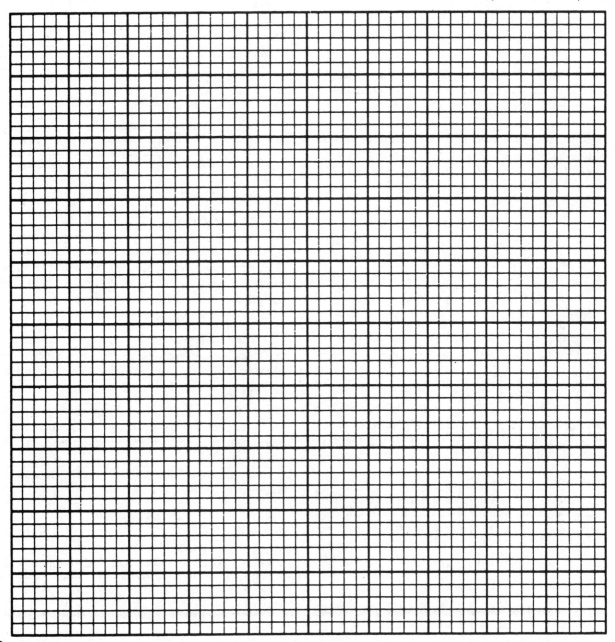

0   **Real GDP**

(4) The direct relationship between net tax revenues and

real GDP has (lessened, expanded) _____
the impact of the $10 decrease in investment spending
on real GDP.

(c) Suppose the government-purchases multiplier is also
10 and government wishes to increase the equilibrium
real GDP by $50.

(1) If net tax revenues remained constant, the government would have to increase its purchases of goods and

services by $_____.

(2) But when real GDP rises, net tax revenues also rise;
and this rise in net tax revenues will tend to (increase,

decrease) _____ the equilibrium real GDP.

(3) The effect, therefore, of the $5 increase in govern-
ment purchases will also be to increase the equilibrium

real GDP by (more, less) _____ than $50.

(4) The direct relation between net tax revenues and real

GDP has (lessened, expanded) _____
the effect of the $5 increase in government purchases;

and to raise the equilibrium real GDP by $50 government will have to increase its purchases by (more, less)

_____ than $5.

(d) Imagine that the full-employment real GDP of the economy is $1150 and that government purchases of goods and services are $200.

(1) Complete the table at the beginning of this question by entering the government purchases and by computing the budget surplus at each of the real GDPs. (Show a government deficit by placing a minus sign in front of the amount by which expenditures net tax receipts.)

(2) The full-employment surplus equals $_____.

(3) Were the economy in a recession and producing a real GDP of $900, the budget would show a (surplus,

deficit) _____ of $_____.

(4) This budget deficit or surplus makes it appear that government is pursuing a(n) (expansionary, contraction-

ary) _____ fiscal policy; but this deficit or surplus is not the result of counter-cyclical fiscal policy

but the result of the _____.

(5) If government did not change its net tax rates, it could increase the equilibrium real GDP from $900 to the full-employment real GDP of $1150 by increasing its purchases by (approximately) $70. At the full-employment real GDP the budget would show a (sur-

plus, deficit) _____ of $_____.

(6) If government did not change its purchases, it would increase the equilibrium real GDP from $900 to the full-employment real GDP of $1150 by decreasing net tax receipts at all real GDPs by a lump sum of (approximately) $80. The full-employment budget would have

a (surplus, deficit) _____ of $_____.

3. This question is designed to show that an economy with a proportional tax system is more stable than an economy with a lump-sum tax system. The analysis is presented in Table 9-2 in the text and is used in the text questions 10, 11, and 12 at the end of Chapter 9.

(a) Closed Economy
The consumption and investment schedules for a closed economy are given in the table below. The equation for the consumption schedule is: $C = 50 + .80GDP$ and investment is fixed at 30.

Real GDP	C	I	C_a	$(C_a + I + G)$
$200	$210	$30	$170	$250
250	250	30		
275	270	30		
300	290	30		
350	330	30		
400	370	30		
450	410	30		
500	450	30		
550	490	30		

(1) The equilibrium level of income is _____.

(2) The multiplier is _____.

(b) Add a public sector to the model; both government purchases and taxes equal $50 at all levels of income.
(1) Consumption (C_a) becomes related to after-tax income by replacing GDP with (GDP -$50) in the consumption schedule. Fill in the column for C_a and $(C_a + I + G)$ at various levels of GDP.

(2) The equilibrium level of income is $_____.
(c) Suppose the level of G (government expenditure) goes from $50 to 0. Taxes remain at $50. The new level

of GDP will be $_____.
(d) In this part of the question the consumption schedule is that given in part (a), investment spending is $30, government spending is $50 and taxes ($T$) equal 11.11% (.1111) of GDP.
(1) Complete the following table on the basis of the information in (d).

Real GDP	T	C_a	I	G	$(C_a + I + G)$
$200	$22.22	$192.22	$30	$50	$272.22
250	27.78	227.78	30	50	357.78
275					
300					
350					
400					
450					
500					
550					

(2) The equilibrium level of income is $_____.
(3) Reduce G to 0. The new equilibrium level of income

is (go through the same procedure as in (1)) $_____ (approximately).
(c) In part (c) when we started a lump-sum tax and an equilibrium GDP of $450 and reduced G by $50,

equilibrium GDP fell by $_____.
In part (d) (2) when we started with a proportional

tax and an equilibrium GDP of $450 and reduced *G* by $50, equilibrium GDP fell by $_____ (approximately). The GDP tended to be more stable under the _____ tax.

4. Columns (1) and (2) in the table below are the aggregate supply schedule and columns (1) and (3) are the aggregate demand schedule.

(1) Price Level	(2) Real GDP$_1$	(3) AQD$_1$	(4) AQD$_2$	(5) Real GDP$_2$
$2.20	$2390	$2100	$2200	$2490
2.00	2390	2200	2340	2490
1.90	2350	2255	2350	2450
1.80	2300	2300	2400	2400
1.60	2200	2400	2500	2300

(a) The equilibrium real GDP is $_____ and the price level is $_____.

(b) Suppose that an expansionary fiscal policy increases aggregate demand from that shown in columns (1) and (3) to that shown in columns (1) and (4).

(1) If the price level remained constant, the equilibrium real GDP would increase to $_____.

(2) But the increase in aggregate demand does raise the price level to $_____; and this rise in the price level results in real GDP increasing to only $_____.

(c) If the expansionary fiscal policy that increased aggregate demand also has supply-side effects and increased aggregate supply from that shown in columns (1) and (2) to that shown in columns (1) and (5),

(1) the equilibrium real GDP would increase to $_____; and

(2) the price level would _____.

SELF-TEST

Circle T if the statement is true, F if it is false.

1. The goal of fiscal policy is to stabilize economic activity at some desired level of employment.   **T F**

2. Fiscal policy is carried out by manipulating government spending, taxation, and the money supply.   **T F**

3. Fiscal policy can be one of two varieties; (1) expansionary and (2) contractionary.   **T F**

4. Increases in public spending, in the aggregate expenditure model utilized in this chapter, increase equilibrium GDP and have no effect on the price level.   **T F**

5. A decrease in taxes will result in an upward shift in the consumption schedule and an increase in equilibrium GDP.   **T F**

6. Equal increases in government spending and taxes will increase the level of equilibrium GDP.   **T F**

7. A governmental deficit is contractionary.   **T F**

8. Fiscal policy should move toward a surplus in the government's budget during the recession phase of the business cycle.   **T F**

9. Built-in stabilizers are not sufficiently strong to prevent recession or inflation, but they can reduce the severity of a recession or of inflation.   **T F**

10. Built-in stabilizers operate automatically to increase the government's deficit during inflation and increase its surplus during recessions.   **T F**

11. A progressive tax system provides an economy with greater built-in stability than would a proportional tax system.   **T F**

12. A look at the historical record of budgetary deficits and surpluses provides an accurate picture of the government's fiscal stance.   **T F**

13. The cyclically adjusted budget balance compares government spending to the tax revenue that would be forthcoming at full employment.   **T F**

14. Recognition, administrative, and operational lags in the timing of federal fiscal policy make fiscal policies more effective in reducing the rate of inflation and decreasing unemployment in the economy.   **T F**

15. The spending and taxing policies of the federal government are designed solely to reduce unemployment and limit inflation in the economy.   **T F**

16. Economists who see evidence of a political business cycle argue that the government tends to increase taxes and reduce expenditures before elections and to reduce taxes and increase expenditures after elections.   **T F**

17. If financing a deficit results in increased interest rates, investment spending will be reduced and the stimulative effect of the deficit on aggregate expenditure reduced.   **T F**

18. The Ricardian equivalence theorem states that increases in private and public spending have the same or equivalent effect on equilibrium real GDP.   **T F**

19. Supply-side economists maintain that reductions in tax rates decrease aggregate supply and are, therefore, inflationary.   **T F**

20. For the domestic economy there are gains from specialization and trade but also complications from interdependency with the world economy.   **T F**

MULTIPLE-CHOICE

Circle the letter that corresponds to the best answer.

1. Fiscal policy influences the level of economic activity by manipulating
(a)   the interest rate
(b)   the money supply
(c)   the foreign exchange rate
(d)   the level of government spending and taxes

2. Contractionary fiscal policy is composed of
(a)   a reduction in government expenditure and the money supply or some combination of both
(b)   an increase in government expenditure and taxes or some combination of both
(c)   a reduction in government expenditure and increase in taxes or some combination of both
(d)   a reduction in taxes and the money supply or some combination of both

3. In the aggregate expenditure model, taxes
(a)   are paid out of savings and have no effect on equilibrium output
(b)   reduce consumption at each level of GDP by an amount equal to the amount of the tax
(c)   reduce both consumption and saving at each level of GDP
(d)   are an injection into the spending flow

4. In the aggregate expenditure model (which has a business, foreign trade, and a government sector), at the equilibrium level of GDP
(a) $S_a + I_g = G + X$
(b) $S_a + M = I_g + X$
(c) $S_a + M + G = I_g + X + T$
(d) $S_a + M + T = I_g + X + G$

5. An equal increase in government expenditure and taxes in the closed aggregate expenditure model will lead to
(a)   no change in the equilibrium output
(b)   an increase in equilibrium GDP equal to the increase in government expenditure and taxes

(c)   a decrease in equilibrium GDP equal to the increase in government expenditure and taxes
(d)   an increase in equilibrium equal to the multiplier times the increase in government expenditure

6. The aggregate expenditure predicts that
(a)   an increase in G will have a greater impact on equilibrium GDP than an equal decrease in T
(b)   an increase in G or an equal decrease in T will have the same impact on equilibrium GDP
(c)   an increase in G will have a lesser impact on equilibrium GDP than an equal decrease in T
(d)   there is a multiplier effect connected only with an increase in G and not with a decrease in T

7. Which of the following policies would do the most to reduce inflation?
(a)   increase taxes by $5 billion
(b)   reduce government purchases of goods and services by $5 billion
(c)   increase taxes and government expenditures by $5 billion
(d)   reduce both taxes and government purchases by $5 billion

8. If the government wishes to increase the level of real GDP, it might
(a)   reduce taxes
(b)   reduce its purchases of goods and services
(c)   reduce transfer payments
(d)   reduce the size of the budget deficit

9. If the economy is to have built-in stability, when real GDP falls,
(a)   tax receipts and government transfer payments should fall
(b)   tax receipts and government transfer payments should rise
(c)   tax receipts should fall and government transfer payments should rise
(d)   tax receipts should rise and government transfer payments should fall

10. A direct relation between net tax receipts and real GDP
(a)   automatically produces budget surpluses during a recession
(b)   makes it easier for discretionary fiscal policy to move the economy out of a recession and toward full employment
(c)   makes it easier to maintain full employment in a growing economy
(d)   reduces the effect of a change in planned investment spending upon the national output and employment

11. The economy will have greater built-in stability with a
(a) progressive tax system
(b) proportional tax system
(c) regressive tax system
(d) property tax system

12. The crowding-out effect of an expansionary (deficit) fiscal policy is the result of government borrowing in the money market, which
(a) increases interest rates and net investment spending in the economy
(b) increases interest rates and decreases net investment spending
(c) decreases interest rates and increases net investment spending
(d) decreases interest rates and net investment spending

13. The Ricardian equivalence theorem states that
(a) an equal increase in government expenditure and taxes will leave the level of GDP unchanged
(b) financing a deficit by borrowing results in a downward shift of the investment schedule
(c) the increase in aggregate expenditure expected from an increase in the government deficit is offset by an upward shift in the saving schedule
(d) an increase in the government deficit increases prices, reduces export sales, and leaves the level of GDP unchanged

14. Aggregate expenditures in the open economy consist of
(a) $C_a + I_g + S_a + T$
(b) $C_a + I_g + X + M$
(c) $C_a + I_g + G + X_n$
(d) $C_a + S_a + T + M$

The next six questions (15, 16, 17, 18, 19, and 20) are based on the consumption schedule below. Investment figures are for planned investment.

Real GDP	C
$300	$290
310	298
320	306
330	314
340	322
350	330
360	338

15. If taxes were zero, government purchases of goods and services $10, investment $6, and net exports are zero, equilibrium real GDP would be

(a) $310
(b) $320
(c) $330
(d) $340

16. If taxes were $5, the consumption schedule becomes

GDP	(1)	(2)	(3)	(4)
$300	$290	$286	$294	$285
310	298	294	298	290
320	306	302	302	295
330	314	310	306	300
340	322	318	310	304
350	330	326	314	308
360	338	334	318	312

(a) 1
(b) 2
(c) 3
(d) 4

17. If taxes were $5, government purchases of goods and services $10, investment $6, and net exports are zero, equilibrium real GDP would be
(a) $300
(b) $310
(c) $320
(d) $330

18. To increase GDP to its equilibrium level of $330 in question 15, government spending would have to increase to
(a) $12
(b) $14
(c) $16
(d) $18

19. Given the consumption schedule in the table above question 15, assume investment is $42, taxes $40, net exports are zero, and government purchases of goods and services zero. If the full-employment level of real GDP is $340, the gap can be eliminated by reducing taxes by
(a) $8
(b) $10
(c) $13
(d) $40

20. Assume that investment is zero, that taxes are zero, net exports are zero, and the government purchases of goods and services are $20. If the full-employment-without-inflation level of real GDP is $330, the gap can be eliminated by decreasing government expenditures by
(a) $4
(b) $5

(c) $10

(d) $20

21. If APS is 0.2 and MPS is 0.10, a simultaneous increase in both taxes and government spending of $30 billion will

(a) reduce consumption by $27 billion, increase government spending by $30 billion, and increase GDP by $30 billion

(b) reduce consumption by $27 billion, increase government spending by $27 billion, and increase GDP by $27 billion

(c) reduce consumption by $24 billion, increase government spending by $30 billion, and increase GDP by $30 billion

(d) reduce consumption by $24 billion, increase government spending by $24 billion, and increase GDP by $24 billion

Answer the next two questions (22 and 23) on the basis of the following diagram:

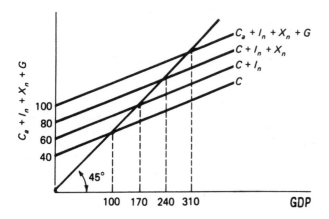

22. The size of the multiplier associated with changes in government spending in this economy is approximately

(a) 0.29

(b) 1.50

(c) 2.50

(d) 3.50

23. If this was an open economy without a government sector, the level of GDP would be

(a) $100

(b) $170

(c) $240

(d) $310

24. In which of the following situations for an open, mixed economy will the level of GDP contract?

(a) when $C_a + S + M$ is less than $I_n + X + T$

(b) when $I + M + T$ is less than $C + X + S$

(c) when $S_a + M + T$ is less than $I + X + G$

(d) when $I_n + X + G$ is less than $S_a + M + T$

Answer the next three questions (25, 26, and 27) on the basis of the following diagram:

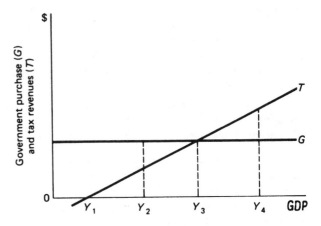

25. If the slope of the line T was steeper, there would be

(a) more built-in stability for the economy

(b) less built-in stability for the economy

(c) no change in the built-in stability in the economy

(d) the need for more emphasis on discretionary fiscal policy

26. If the slope of the line T was flatter, there would be

(a) larger cyclical deficits produced as GDP moved from Y_3 to Y_2

(b) smaller cyclical deficits produced as GDP moved from Y_3 to Y_2

(c) a recessionary gap at the equilibrium level of income

(d) larger cyclical surplus produced as GDP moved from Y_3 to Y_4.

27. Actions by the federal government to "index" personal income taxes and lower marginal tax rates would tend to

(a) flatten the slope of the T line and increase built-in stability

(b) flatten the slope of the T line and decrease built-in stability

(c) steepen the slope of line T and increase built-in stability

(d) steepen the slope of line T and decrease built-in stability

28. The length of time it takes for the fiscal action taken by the federal government to affect output, employment,

or the price level is referred to as the
(a)   administrative lag
(b)   operational lag
(c)   recognition lag
(d)   fiscal lag

29.   Suppose that the economies of Canada's trading partners improved substantially and at the same time Canada had adopted an expansionary fiscal policy. What would most likely happen in Canada?
(a)   there would be a rise in net exports, a rise in aggregate demand, and the potential for inflation
(b)   there would be a fall in interest rates, a rise in aggregate demand, and the potential for a recession
(c)   there would be a rise in the incomes of trading partners, less demand for Canadian goods, and the potential for a recession
(d)   there would be a rise in the employment in other nations, a· fall in net exports, and the potential for inflation

30.   The effect of an expansionary (deficit) fiscal policy on the real GDP of an economy with an upward sloping aggregate supply curve is lessened by
(a)   increases in aggregate supply
(b)   the crowding-out effect
(c)   increases in the price level
(d)   both (b) and (c)

DISCUSSION QUESTIONS

1.   What is meant by fiscal policy?

2.   What is the exact effect that taxes will have on the consumption schedule? On the saving schedule?

3.   Explain why, with government taxing and spending, the equilibrium real GDP is the real GDP at which real GDP equals consumption plus planned investment plus net exports plus government purchases of goods and services; and saving plus imports plus taxes equals planned investment plus exports plus government purchases. What will cause GDP to move to its equilibrium level?

4.   In the closed model used in this chapter, if both taxes and government purchases increase by equal amounts, real GDP will increase by that amount. Why?

5.   What three things might the federal government do if its fiscal policy were to be (a) expansionary and (b) contractionary? When would it invoke each of these two kinds of policy and what would be their effects on the federal budget?

6.   Explain the fiscal policy that would be advocated during a recession and during a period of inflation (a) by those who wish to expand the public sector and (b) by those who wish to contract the public sector.

7.   What is the difference between discretionary and nondiscretionary fiscal policy? How do the built-in stabilizers work to reduce rises and falls in the level of nominal GDP?

8.   Explain why a tax system in which net tax receipts vary directly with the level of nominal GDP makes it difficult to achieve and to sustain full employment.

9.   What is the cyclically adjusted budget balance? What was the problem that its use was designed to solve?

10.   Explain the three kinds of time lags that make it difficult to use fiscal policy to stabilize the economy.

11.   What are the three political problems that complicate the use of fiscal policy to stabilize the economy?

12.   How do (a) crowding out and (b) inflation reduce the effect of an expansionary (deficit) fiscal policy on real GDP and employment?

13.   What conclusions would be drawn about the effectiveness of fiscal policy from the Ricardian equivalence theorem?

14.   What might be the supply-side effects of a reduction in tax rates on the capacity output of the economy, the equilibrium levels of real GDP and employment, and the price level?

15.   What complications for fiscal policy arise from interdependency with the world economy? Explain how aggregate-demand shocks from abroad and the net export effect influence fiscal policy.

ANSWERS

Fill-in questions

1.   World War II

2.   decreased, increased, increased, decreased

3.   deficit, surplus

4.   marginal propensity to consume; marginal propensity to save

5.   (a) expenditures, output; (b) consumption, planned investment, net exports, government purchases of goods and services; (c) planned investment, exports, government purchases of goods and services, saving, imports, net taxes

6.   decrease; the decreases in taxes and government purchases

7.   decreased government spending, taxes

8.   increase, taxes, decrease, taxes

9.   (a) taxes, transfer payments; (b) increase, decrease

10.   built-in; (a) increase, increase, decrease; (b) decrease, increase, decrease

11.   progressive, proportional, regressive; more

12.   (a) budget surplus or deficit, at full employment (b) expansionary, contractionary

13.   recognition, administrative, operational

14.   other, deficits, political

15.   deficit, borrows; (a) raise, contract (b) crowding-out, weaken

16.   Ricardian equivalence theorem; less

17.   raise; (a) weaken; (b) increase, increase, increase, decrease, strengthen

18.   pro-, raise, lower

19.   recession, inflation

20.   mutual interdependency; (a) aggregate demand; (b) net-export, (1) increase, increase, decrease (2) decrease, decrease, increase

21.   increase, increase, increase, decrease, strengthen

Problems and projects

1.   (a) (1) 0.9, 90, C_a: 1160, 1250, 1340, 1430, 1520, 1610, 1700, (2) 0.1, 10, S_a: 240, 250, 260, 270, 280, 290, 300 (b) $S_a + M + T$: 345, 355, 365, 375, 385, 395, 405; (c) $I + X + G$: 355, 355, 355, 355, 355, 355, 355; $C_a + I + X_n + G$: 1510, 1600, 1690, 1780, 1870, 1960, 2050; (d) 1600; (f) rise, 100; (g) fall, 90; (h) raise, 10

2.   (a) (1) increase, $10, (2) decrease, $20, (3) direct (b) (1) $100, (2) increase, (3) less, (4) lessened (c) (1) $5, (2) decrease, (3) less, (4) lessened, more (d) (1) government expenditures are $200 at all NNPs, government surplus: − 30, − 20, − 10, 0, 10, 20, 30, (2) $30, (3) deficit, $20, (4) expansionary, recession, (5) deficit, $40, (6) deficit, $50

3.   (a) (1) $400; (2) 5
(b) (1) C_a: $ 210, 230, 250, 290, 330, 370, 410, 450
$(C_a + I + G)$: $290, 310, 330, 370, 410, 450, 490, 530
(2) 450 (c) $200 (d) (1) T: $30.55, 33.33, 38.89, 44.44, 50.00, 55.54, 61.09; C_a: $245.56, 263.33, 298.89, 334.44, 370.00, 405.55, 441.11; I: $30, 30, 30, 30, 30, 30, 30; G: $50, 50, 50, 50, 50, 50, 50
$(C_a + I = G)$: $325.56, 343.33, 369.89, 414.44, 450.00, 485.55, 521.11 (2) $450 (3) $275 (e) $250; $175; proportional

4.   (a) 2300, 1.80; (b) (1) 2400, (2) 1.90, 2350 (c) (1) 2400, (2) remain constant

Self-test

1. T;   2. F;   3. F;   4. T;   5. T;   6. T;   7. F;
8. F;   9. T;   10. F;   11. T;   12. F;   13. T;   14. F;
15. F;   16. F;   17. T;   18. F;   19. F;   20. T

Multiple-choice

1. (d);   2. (c);   3. (c);   4. (d);   5. (b);   6. (a);
7. (b);   8. (a);   9. (c);   10. (d);   11. (a);   12. (b);
13. (c);   14. (c);   15. (c);   16. (b);   17. (b);
18. (b);   19. (b);   20. (a);   21. (a);   22. (d);   23. (c);
24. (d);   25. (a);   26. (b);   27. (b);   28. (b);   29. (a);   30. (d)

Money, Banking, and Monetary Policy

CHAPTER

10 Money and Banking in Canada

By and large, Chapter 10 is descriptive and factual. It contains an explanation of the nature and functions of money and identifies some of the major institutions in the Canadian financial system. The purpose of this chapter is, however, to prepare you for a more detailed explanation (in Chapters 11 and 12) on the role that the changing money supply can play in promoting economic stability in the short run. Of special importance in this chapter are the many terms and definitions that will be new to you. These must be learned so that the following two chapters and their analysis of how the financial system affects the performance of the economy can be understood.

You will do well to pay particular attention to the following: (1) what money is and the functions it performs, what types of money exist in the Canadian economy and their relative importance, and how four measures of the money supply (M1, M2, M3, M2 +) are defined; (2) what gives value to, or "backs," Canadian money; (3) what determines the value of money; and (4) the two basic institutions of the Canadian banking system: the profit-maximizing chartered banks and the Bank of Canada — a regulatory bank owned and ultimately controlled by the government.

Several points are worth repeating here because so much depends upon their being fully understood. First, money is whatever performs the three functions of money, and in Canada money consists of Bank of Canada notes and the debts (promises to pay) of chartered banks. In Canada, this money is "backed" by the goods and services for which its owners can exchange it and not by gold or any other precious metal.

Second, chartered banks, like many other financial institutions, accept deposits and make loans, but they also — and this distinguishes them from financial intermediaries — are literally able to create money by lending deposits. However, trust companies, credit unions, and other such nonbank financial intermediaries, in effect, also create money when they lend chequable deposits — except that the Bank of Canada does not count these nonbank deposits in its official definition of M1, M2 or M3 money supply. Because banks are able to create money, they have a strong influence on the size of the money supply and the value of money. It is through the reactions of chartered banks to Bank of Canada initiatives that control of the money supply is achieved.

Third, financial institutions are market institutions that exist to maximize profits, and their success is measured by the numbers appearing on the bottom line of the income statement. Competition is a spur to efficiency and the whole Canadian financial system is being restructured to promote more competition. In the process, more financial institutions are being allowed to provide services previously reserved for designated types of banking, insurance, trust, and brokerage institutions.

Fourth, government controls actions of the financial intermediaries through legislation and it controls the money supply through the Bank of Canada, which operates as an agency of the federal government.

CHECKLIST

When you have studied this chapter, you should be able to:

- List the three functions of money, and explain the meaning of each function.
- Define the money supply, M1.
- Explain the meaning of near-money and identify the principal near-monies; and then define M2, M3, and M2 + .
- Present three reasons why near-monies are important.
- Explain why money in the Canadian economy is debt, and reveal whose debts paper money and deposits are.

- Present three reasons why currency and demand deposits are money and have value.

- Explain what gives money its value.

- Indicate the precise relationship between the value of money and the price level.

- Explain what is meant by stabilizing the value of money and enumerate the devices government could utilize to try to stabilize its value.

- Describe the structure of the Canadian banking system.

- List several kinds of financial intermediaries; explain the role played by these intermediaries; and state the distinction between a financial intermediary and a chartered bank.

- Identify the role played by the Canadian Payments Association in the banking sector.

CHAPTER OUTLINE

1. Money is whatever performs the three basic functions of money: a medium of exchange, a standard of value, and a store of value.

2. In the Canadian economy, money is whatever is generally used as a medium of exchange. It consists of the privately held currency issued by the Bank of Canada, debts of chartered banks, and, in effect, of other financial intermediaries that have set up chequing accounts.
(a)   The narrowly defined money supply is called M1 and consists of
(1) coins, which are token money and the smallest part of the total money supply;
(2) paper money, which is Bank of Canada notes; and
(3) demand deposits, which are bank-created money and the largest component of the money supply.
    Currency and deposits owned by the federal government and the chartered banks are not included in M1 or in any of the more broadly defined money supplies.
(b)   Other measures of the money, termed near money, are added to the M1 money supply to form the M2, M3 and M2 + money aggregates.
(c)   The amount of these near-monies held by the public is important for at least three reasons.
(d)   Credit cards are not money but are a device by which the cardholders obtain a loan (credit) from the issuer of the card.

3.   (a)   In Canada, money is largely the promise of either a chartered bank or the Bank of Canada to pay; but the central bank's "debts" cannot be redeemed for anything tangible. (All the Bank of Canada will give you

in exchange for a dollar bill is another one.)
(b)   Money has value only because people can exchange it for desirable goods and services.
(c)   The value of money is inversely related to the price level.
(d)   Money is "backed" by the confidence the public has that the value of money will remain stable. (The federal government can use monetary and fiscal policy to keep the value of money relatively stable.)

4.   The centralized Canadian banking system consists of privately owned and operated chartered banks (8 Canadian-owned) and the Bank of Canada, which is owned by the federal government. The foreign-owned banks will always remain a small part of the whole, because of legal restrictions on their growth.
(a)   The banking system is concentrated with each of the Canadian-owned banks having many branches. The five largest banks have more than a thousand branches each. The banks perform the two essential functions of holding deposits and making loans.
(b)   Both the chartered banks and the nonbank financial intermediaries act as intermediaries between savers and investors. Both create and destroy chequable deposit money, but the Bank of Canada counts only deposits in the chartered banks in its official definitions of the M1, M2, and M3 money supply.

5.   Banks are profit-maximizing market institutions, which gain revenue by providing various financial services and by using customers' deposits for extending interest-producing loans or purchasing revenue-producing assets. Our banking system is a fractional reserve system with banks keeping only a small percentage of deposit liabilities to meet everyday cash requirements.

IMPORTANT TERMS

Bank of Canada notes
Canadian Payments Association
chartered banks
demand deposits
fiat money
financial intermediaries
intrinsic value
legal tender
M1, M2, M3, M2 +
measure of value
medium of exchange
near-banks

near-monies
nonchequable savings accounts
prime rate
store of value
term deposits
token money

FILL-IN QUESTIONS

1. A properly functioning monetary system helps achieve full _____ and full _____.

2. Three functions of money are

(a) _____;

(b) _____;

(c) _____.

3. The supply of money, M1, in Canada consists of _____, _____ _____, and _____ _____ not owned by _____ or _____.

4. The other financial intermediaries

(a) include such institutions as _____ companies, _____ _____ companies, _____ unions, and _____ companies;

(b) channel funds from _____ to _____;

(c) like banks, can set up chequable deposits and thus can, like banks, _____ and _____ money. However, their deposits (are, are not) _____ counted in the money supply by the _____ unless it is majority-owned by a _____ _____.

5. The most important near-monies in the Canadian economy are _____, _____, and _____ deposits in chartered banks and _____ institutions. Another important near-money is Government of Canada _____

6. The M1 money supply is composed of _____, _____ and _____ _____ with the exclusion of _____ cash and _____ deposits.

7. List three reasons why the discussion of near-monies is important.

(a) _____

(b) _____

(c) _____

8. Money in Canada consists largely of _____ banknotes and the debts of _____ _____.

9. In Canada currency and chequable deposits

(a) (are, are not) _____ ''backed'' by gold and silver;

(b) are money because they are used as a medium of _____, they are (in the case of currency) _____ tender, and they are relatively (abundant, scarce)_____.

10. Money has value because it can be exchanged for _____ and its value varies (directly, inversely) _____ with changes in the _____ level.

11. The value of money is reflected in the quantity of _____ and _____ that $1 will _____ in the marketplace.

12. There are _____ Canadian chartered banks, each with _____ in different geographic locations.

13. Chartered banks are _____-_____ market institutions that lend out customers' deposits, retaining only a _____ _____ for daily cash requirements. This system of banking is termed a _____ _____ system.

14. The interest rate charged by chartered banks to their

best corporate borrowers is called the _____

_____.

15.   Chartered banks are banks that accept

_____, make loans, and in doing so

_____   _____.

PROBLEMS AND PROJECTS

1.   With the information given below obtain M1, M2, M3 and M2 + . (The figures are in millions of dollars.)

Currency outside banks:	$21,844
Demand deposits:	$24,151
Nonpersonal notice deposits:	$25,635
Personal savings deposits:	$224,062
Nonpersonal fixed-term deposits plus foreign currency deposits of residents booked in Canada:	$61,572
Deposits at trust and mortgage companies, credit unions, and *caisses populaires:*	$261,656

Calculate:

M1   _____

M2   _____

M3   _____

M2 +   _____

2.   Complete the following table showing the relationship between the percentage change in the price level and the percentage change in the value of money. Calculate the percentage change in the value of money to one decimal place.

Change in the price level	Change in the value of money
(a) rise by	
5%	– _____ . _____ %
10%	– _____ . _____
15%	– _____ . _____
20%	– _____ . _____
(b) fall by	
5%	+ _____ . _____ %
10%	+ _____ . _____
15%	+ _____ . _____

3.   The table at the bottom of this page shows the financial performance of some of Canada's chartered banks for their last two fiscal years. Profits are in millions of dollars.

Given that banks are profit-maximizing institutions, what factors account for the divergence in performance for some of the banks for 1991 and 1992?

4.   Indicate whether the following items belong to the M1, M2, M3, M2 + money supply or are not considered as part of any official measure of a money supply (N). Place the item in the smallest possible money supply measure.

(a)   Gold held by the Department of Finance

_____

(b)   Currency held by a chartered bank _____

(c)   Currency held in a credit union _____

	Profit		Return on assets		Return on equity	
	'92	'91	'92	'91	'92	'91
Royal Bank	107	983	0.08%	0.76%	-0.3%	15.5%
CIBC	12	811	0.01%	0.68%	-2.0%	13.9%
Bank of Montreal	640	595	0.61%	0.63%	14.1%	15.0%
Bank of Nova Scotia	676	633	0.72%	0.71%	15.7%	16.7%
Toronto-Dominion	408	497	0.58%	0.72%	8.4%	10.6%
National Bank	1	186	0.00%	0.51%	-2.6%	11.0%

(d) Notice deposits held in a trust company

_____

(e) Personal saving deposits held in a chartered bank _____

(f) Cash held in my wallet _____

(g) Government deposits held in chartered banks

_____

(h) A loan repayable to a chartered bank

_____

(i) A Canada Savings Bond _____

(j) A demand deposit held at a chartered bank

_____

SELF-TEST

Circle T if the statement is true, F if it is false.

1. Anything that is convertible into gold is money.
   T F

2. Money, by providing a convenient way to exchange goods and services, promotes specialization. **T F**

3. What we employ as money in Canada are actually debts of the chartered banks and other financial institutions and the federal government. **T F**

4. Money serves as a store of value when it is used for measuring the worth of goods. **T F**

5. When a person writes a cheque on a deposit in a chartered bank to pay for groceries at a checkout counter, money is being used as a medium of exchange.
   T F

6. The money supply designated M1 is the sum of currency and nonchequable deposits. **T F**

7. The currency component of M1 includes both coins and paper money. **T F**

8. If a coin is "token money," its face value is less than its intrinsic value. **T F**

9. Paper money is made up of Bank of Canada notes issued by the chartered banks. **T F**

10. Private demand deposits held in chartered banks are counted as part of the M1 money supply. **T F**

11. The demand deposits of the federal government in the chartered banks are a component of M1.
    T F

12. Both chartered banks and savings institutions accept chequable deposits. **T F**

13. The most inclusive measure of money is M2 + .
    T F

14. Economists and public officials are in general agreement on how to define the money supply in Canada.
    T F

15. A near-money is a medium of exchange. **T F**

16. The larger the volume of near-monies owned by consumers, the larger will be their average propensity to save. **T F**

17. The fastest growing part of the Canadian money supply is credit card money. **T F**

18. Currency and chequable deposits are money because they are acceptable to sellers in exchange for goods and services. **T F**

19. If money is to have a fairly stable value, its supply must be limited relative to the demand for it. **T F**

20. Gold has been designated as legal tender by the government. **T F**

21. In Canada our paper money will be redeemed for gold on demand by the monetary authorities. **T F**

22. A direct relationship exists between the general price level and the purchasing power of $1. **T F**

23. Canadian chartered banks are profit-maximizing financial institutions. **T F**

24. Banks in Canada operate under the Bank Act, which is usually updated whenever the constitution is amended. **T F**

25. For the chartered banking system, cash reserves equal demand deposits. **T F**

MULTIPLE-CHOICE

Circle the letter that corresponds to the best answer.

1. Which of the following is not one of the functions of money?
   (a) a factor of production
   (b) a medium of exchange
   (c) a store of value
   (d) a standard of value

2. Chequable deposits are
   (a) all deposits in chartered banks
   (b) demand deposits in chartered banks

(c)   deposits in thrift institutions on which cheques may be written
(d)   the sum of (b) and (c) above

3.   Which of the following constitutes the largest element in the nation's M1 money supply?
(a)   currency
(b)   Bank of Canada notes
(c)   term and notice deposits
(d)   demand deposits

4.   Demand deposits are money because they are
(a)   legal tender
(b)   fiat money
(c)   a medium of exchange
(d)   fully guaranteed by the chartered banks

5.   The supply of money, M1, consists almost entirely of the debts of
(a)   the federal government
(b)   the Bank of Canada
(c)   chartered banks
(d)   the Bank of Canada and chartered banks

6.   Which of the following best describes the "backing" of money in Canada?
(a)   the gold bullion stored in the Bank of Canada's vaults
(b)   the belief of holders of money that it can be exchanged for desirable goods and services
(c)   the willingness of banks and the government to surrender something of value in exchange for money
(d)   the faith and confidence of the public in the ability of government to pay its debts

7.   Bank of Canada notes are
(a)   "backed" by gold
(b)   count as part of the money supply when held by the chartered banks
(c)   legal tender in Canada
(d)   circulating assets of the Bank of Canada

8.   Whenever a person withdraws cash from a demand deposit at a chartered bank, the M1 money supply has
(a)   increased
(b)   decreased
(c)   stayed the same
(d)   not enough information provided to tell

9.   The supply of money in Canada is regulated by
(a)   the chartered banks
(b)   the chartered banks and the near-banks
(c)   the Department of Finance
(d)   the Bank of Canada

10.   The value of money flows from

(a)   being backed by gold
(b)   being a debt of the chartered banks and the Bank of Canada
(c)   what money can purchase
(d)   being declared legal tender

11.   The purchasing power of money would decrease whenever
(a)   the unemployment rate rises
(b)   the GDP deflator falls
(c)   the Consumer Price Index rises
(d)   the interest rate falls

12.   If the price level increases 20%, the value of money decreases
(a)   14.5%
(b)   16.67%
(c)   20%
(d)   25%

13.   To keep the value of money fairly constant, the federal government
(a)   utilizes price and wage controls
(b)   levies taxes that are progressive or proportional
(c)   controls the money supply
(d)   does both (b) and (c) above

14.   Which of the following functions distinguishes a commercial bank from other financial intermediaries?
(a)   accepts deposits
(b)   creates and destroys M1, M2, and M3 money as defined by the Bank of Canada
(c)   makes loans
(d)   deals in debts

15.   If all depositors wished to withdraw their money all at once from a chartered bank,
(a)   the chartered bank would meet the demand for funds out of cash reserves
(b)   the chartered bank would not be able to meet the demand for funds out of reserves
(c)   the chartered bank would print more currency to meet the demand for funds
(d)   the chartered bank would borrow currency from the Department of Finance

16.   The Canadian Payments Association
(a)   represents the eight Canadian chartered banks in discussions with the government
(b)   helps restructure loans for individuals and institutions who are unable to repay borrowings from the banks
(c)   operates the inter-bank cheque clearing system
(d)   determines the prices to be charged for different banking services

17. The prime rate of interest is
(a) the interest rate paid on Canada Savings Bonds
(b) the interest rate on long-term Government of Canada Bonds
(c) the interest rate charged by the chartered banks to their best corporate customers
(d) the interest rate charged by the chartered banks for home mortgages

DISCUSSION QUESTIONS

1. How would you define money? Where does money come from in Canada?

2. What are the components of the M1 money supply? Which of these components is the larger?

3. What is a near-money? What are the most important near-monies in the Canadian economy? Define M2 and explain why the existence of near-monies is important.

4. For what reasons are chequable deposits included in the money supply?

5. What "backs" the money used in Canada? What determines the value of money? Explain the relationship between the value of money and the price level.

6. Is there any relationship between the M1 money supply and the stock of gold held in the country?

7. What must government do if it is to stabilize the value of money?

8. What roles do financial intermediaries play in a modern economy? What is the difference between chartered banks and other financial intermediaries?

9. What is meant when our banking system is termed a "fractional banking system" ?

ANSWERS

Fill-in questions

1. production, employment

2. (a) medium of exchange; (b) standard of value; (c) store of value

3. coins, paper money, demand deposits, banks, the federal government

4. (a) trust, mortgage loan, credit, insurance (b) savers, investors (c) create, destroy; are not, Bank of Canada, chartered bank

5. savings, term, notice, savings, Savings Bonds

6. coin, currency, demand deposits, bank-held, government

7. (a) their existence influences consuming saving habits; (b) conversion from near money to money or from money to near-money may affect the stability of the economy; (c) important when monetary policy is to be employed

8. Bank of Canada, chartered banks

9. (a) are not; (b) exchange, legal, scarce

10. desirable goods and services, inversely, price

11. goods, services, purchase

12. eight, branches

13. profit-maximizing, small percentage; fractional reserve

14. prime rate

15. deposits, create money

Problems and projects

1. (millions) M1: $45,995; M2: $295,692; M3:$357,264;M2 + ; $618,920

2. (a) 4.8, 9.1, 13, 16.7; (b) 5.3, 11.1, 17.6

4. (a) N, (b) N, (c) M1, (d) M2 + , (e) M2, (f) M1, (g) N, (h) N, (i) N, (j) M1

Self-test

1. F; 2. T; 3. T; 4. F; 5. T; 6. F; 7. T; 8. F; 9. F; 10. T; 11. F; 12. T; 13. T; 14. F; 15. F; 16. F; 17. F; 18. T; 19. T; 20. F; 21. F; 22. F; 23. T; 24. F; 25. F

Multiple-choice

1. (a); 2. (d); 3. (d); 4. (c); 5. (d); 6. (b); 7. (c); 8. (c); 9. (d); 10. (c); 11. (c); 12. (b); 13. (c); 14. (b); 15. (b); 16. (c); 17. (c)

CHAPTER

11 How Banks Create Money

Chapter 10 explained the institutional structure of banking in Canada today, the functions that banks and money perform, and the composition of the money supply in Canada. Chapter 11 explains how banks literally create money — deposit account money — and the factors that determine and limit the money-creating ability of chartered banks. Even though the other depository institutions also create chequable deposits, this chapter focuses its attention on the chartered banks because they have and will continue to create a very large part of the total amount of money created by all the depository institutions in Canada. But where the term chartered bank (or bank) appears, it is legitimate to substitute depository institution; and it is permissible to substitute chequable deposit for demand deposit (or chequing account).

The device (and a most convenient and simple device it is) employed to explain chartered banking operations and money creation is the balance sheet. The balance sheet lists the assets, liabilities, and owners' equity for a firm. Based on accounting principles, the assets must equal liabilities plus owners' equity. The balance sheet for the Canadian chartered banks was presented in Table 10-2, and it should be noted from that table that a loan is a bank asset while a deposit is a bank liability. All banking transactions affect this balance sheet, and the first step to understanding how money is created is to understand the effect on the balance sheet of simple but typical transactions.

In reading this chapter, you must analyse for yourself the effect upon the balance sheet of each and every banking transaction discussed. The important terms in the balance sheet are deposits and reserves, because deposits are money, and the ability of a bank to create new deposits means that banks are able to create money. However, the volume of deposits that banks can create is determined by the amount of reserves the bank has. Expansion of the money supply depends upon the possession by the chartered banks of excess cash reserves. Excess reserves do not appear explicitly in the balance sheet, but

do appear there implicitly because excess reserves are the difference between the actual reserves and the required reserves of chartered banks. By the end of 1994 Canadian banks will no longer be required to hold a stated percentage of deposit liabilities in the form of reserves. However, reserves will still be kept, dictated by the need for clearing balances and for everyday transactions. Based on business considerations, banks will have a target reserve ratio.

Two cases — the single chartered bank and the banking system — are presented in order to help you build an understanding of banking and money creation. It is important here to understand that the money-creating potential of a single chartered bank differs in an important way from the money-creating potential of the entire banking system. It is equally important to understand how the money-creating ability of many single chartered banks is multiplied and results in the money-creating ability of the banking system as a whole.

Certain assumptions are used throughout most of the chapter to analyse money-creating ability; in certain instances, these assumptions may not be completely realistic and may need to be modified. The chapter concludes with a discussion of how the earlier analysis must be modified — but not changed in its essentials — to take account of these slightly unrealistic assumptions.

CHECKLIST

When you have studied this chapter, you should be able to:

■ Define the basic items in a bank's balance sheet.

■ Recount the story of how goldsmiths came to issue paper money and became bankers who created money and held fractional reserves.

■ Compute a bank's required and excess reserves when you are given the needed balance-sheet figures.

■ Explain why a chartered bank maintains a reserve;

and why this reserve is not sufficient to protect the depositors from losses.

■ Indicate how the deposit of a cheque drawn on one chartered bank in a second chartered bank will affect the reserves and excess reserves of the two banks.

■ Show what happens to the money supply when a chartered bank makes a loan (or buys securities); and what happens to the money supply when a loan is repaid (or a bank sells securities).

■ Explain what happens to a chartered bank's reserves and deposits after it has made a loan, a cheque has been written on the newly created deposit, deposited in another chartered bank, and cleared; and what happens to the reserves and deposits of the chartered bank in which the cheque was deposited.

■ Describe what would happen to a chartered bank's reserves if it made loans (or bought securities) in an amount that exceeded its excess reserves.

■ State the money-creating potential of a chartered bank (the amount of money a chartered bank can safely create by lending or buying securities).

■ State the money-creating potential of the banking system; and explain how it is possible for the banking system to create an amount of money that is a multiple of its excess reserves, when no individual chartered bank ever creates money in an amount greater than its excess reserves.

■ Compute the size of the monetary multiplier and the money-creating potential of the banking system when you are provided with the necessary data.

■ List the two leakages that reduce the money-creating potential of the banking system.

■ Explain why the size of the money supply needs to be controlled.

CHAPTER OUTLINE

1. The balance sheet of the chartered bank is a statement of the assets, liabilities, and net worth of the bank at a specific time. In the balance sheet the bank's assets equal its liabilities plus its net worth. Chartered banks can create demand deposit money, and the process of money creation is easily followed with the aid of a bank's balance sheet.

2. The history of the goldsmiths illustrates how paper money came into being; how they became bankers when they began to make loans and issue money in excess of their gold holdings; and how the currently used fractional reserve system, with its two significant characteristics, was developed.

3. By examining the ways in which the balance sheet of the chartered bank is affected by various transactions, it is possible to understand how a single chartered bank in a multibank system can create money.

(a) Once a chartered bank has been founded

(1) by selling shares of stock and obtaining cash in return;

(2) and acquired the property and equipment needed to carry on the banking business;

(3) the deposit of cash in the bank does not affect the total money supply; it only changes its composition by substituting deposits for currency in circulation.

(4) Three reserve concepts are essential to an understanding of the money-creating potential of a chartered bank:

(i) The primary or cash reserve deposit (required reserve), which a chartered bank must maintain at the Bank of Canada or as vault cash, is being phased out. This reserve will be replaced by a desired reserve based on a bank's business experience.

(ii) The actual reserves of a chartered bank are its deposits at the Bank of Canada plus the vault cash.

(iii) The excess reserves equal the actual reserves less the required reserves. Money creation depends upon the presence of excess reserves.

(5) The writing of a cheque upon the bank and its deposit in a second bank results in a loss of reserves and deposits for the first bank and a gain in reserves and deposits for the second bank.

(b) When a single chartered bank lends or buys securities, it increases its own deposit liabilities (and, therefore, the supply of money) by the amount of the loan or security purchase. But the bank only lends or buys in securities an amount equal to its excess reserves because it fears the loss of reserves to other chartered banks in the economy.

(c) An individual chartered bank balances its desire for profits (which result from the making of loans and the purchase of securities) with its desire for safety (which it achieves by having excess reserves).

4. The ability of a banking system composed of many individual chartered banks to lend and to create money is a multiple (greater than one) of its excess reserves; and is equal to the excess reserves of the banking system multiplied by the monetary (or deposit) multiplier.

(a) The banking system as a whole can do this even though no single chartered bank ever lends an amount greater than its excess reserve because the banking system, unlike a single chartered bank, does not lose reserves.

(b) The monetary multiplier is equal to the reciprocal of the required reserve ratio; the maximum expansion of demand deposits is equal to the excess reserves in the banking system times the monetary multiplier.

(c) The potential lending ability of the banking system may not be fully achieved if there are leakages because borrowers choose to have additional currency or if bankers choose to have excess reserves.

(d) If bankers lend as much as they are able during periods of prosperity and less than they are able during recessions, they add to the instability of the economy. To reduce the instability, the Bank of Canada must control the size of the money supply.

IMPORTANT TERMS

actual, desired, and excess cash reserves
balance sheet
cash reserve ratio
cash reserves
fractional reserve system of banking
leakages
money multiplier
vault cash

FILL-IN QUESTIONS

1. The balance sheet of a chartered bank is a statement of the bank's _____, _____, and _____ _____ at some specific point in time.

2. The fundamental balance sheet equation is: assets = _____ + _____ _____.

3. The coins and paper money that a bank has in its possession are called _____ cash or _____ money.

4. In a fractional reserve system of banking only a _____ of the bank's deposit liabilities are kept as a reserve.

5. In a fractional reserve system banks can _____ money.

6. Deposit liabilities of a bank are of two main types: _____ deposits and _____, _____ and _____ deposits.

7. When a person deposits cash in a chartered bank and receives a deposit account in return, the size of the money supply has (increased, decreased, not changed) _____.

8. When a person gets a loan at a bank and takes it in the form of a demand deposit, the money supply has (increased, decreased, not changed) _____.

9. The primary or cash reserves of a chartered bank (ignoring vault cash) must be kept in the _____ _____ and must equal (at least) its _____ _____ multiplied by the _____ _____.

10. In Canada the required bank reserves will be phased out by the end of _____.

11. The excess reserves of a chartered bank equal its _____ _____ less its _____ _____.

12. When a cheque is drawn upon bank X, deposited in bank Y, and cleared, the reserves of bank X are (increased, decreased, not changed) _____ and the reserves of bank Y are _____; deposits in bank X are _____, and deposits in bank Y are _____.

13. A single chartered bank in a multibank system can safely make loans or buy securities equal in amount to the _____ _____ of that chartered bank.

14. When a chartered bank makes a new loan of $10,000 by creating a deposit it (increases, decreases) _____ the supply of money by $_____.

15. When a chartered bank sells a $2,000 government bond to a securities dealer, the supply of money (increases, decreases) _____ by $_____.

16. When a chartered bank sells a security to the central bank, the central bank pays by increasing the _____ of the chartered bank kept at the _____ _____. These deposits are counted as part of the chartered bank's _____.

17. A bank ordinarily pursues two conflicting goals; they are _____ and _____.

18. The banking system can make loans (or buy securities) and create money in an amount equal to its excess reserves multiplied by the _____. Its lending potential per dollar of excess reserves is greater than the lending potential of a single chartered bank because it does not lose _____ to other banks.

19. The greater the reserve ratio is, the (larger, smaller) _____ is the monetary multiplier.

20. If the required cash reserve ratio is 5%, the banking system is $6 million short of reserves and the banking system is unable to increase its reserves, the banking system must _____ the money supply by $_____.

21. The money-creating potential of the chartered banking system is lessened by the withdrawal of _____ from banks and by the decision of bankers to keep _____ reserves.

22. Chartered banks, in the past,
(a) have kept considerable excess reserves during periods of (prosperity, recession) _____ and have kept few or no excess reserves during periods of _____;
(b) and by behaving in this way have made the economy (more, less) _____ unstable.

PROBLEMS AND PROJECTS

1. Indicate whether the following items would be an asset (A) or on the liabilities + owners' equity section (L) of a bank's balance sheet.
(a) Government of Canada securities held by the bank _____

(b) A loan to the general public _____
(c) The computer used in a bank branch in Portage La Prairie _____
(d) Demand deposits_____
(e) Cash held in a bank vault _____
(f) A government deposit held in the bank _____
(g) Bank reserves held in the central bank _____
(h) Common stock issued by the bank _____

2. Following is the simplified balance sheet of a chartered bank. Assume that the figures given show the bank's assets and the demand deposit liabilities prior to each of the following four transactions. Draw up the balance sheet as it would appear after each of these transactions is completed, and place the balance-sheet figures in the appropriate column. Do not use the figures you place in columns (a), (b), or (c) when you work the next part of the problem: start all parts of the problem with the printed figures. Cash is included in the Reserves total.

		(a)	(b)	(c)	(d)
Assets:					
Reserves	$100	$_____	$_____	$_____	$_____
Loans	700	_____	_____	_____	_____
Securities	200	_____	_____	_____	_____
Liabilities and net worth:					
Deposits	900	_____	_____	_____	_____
Capital stock	100	100	100	100	100

(a) A cheque for $50 is drawn by one of the depositors of the bank, given to a person who deposits it in another bank, and cleared [column (a)].
(b) A depositor withdraws $50 in cash from the bank, and the bank restores its vault cash by obtaining $50 in additional cash from the Bank of Canada [column (b)].
(c) A cheque for $60 drawn on another bank is deposited in this bank and cleared [column (c)].
(d) The bank sells $100 of government bonds to the Bank of Canada [column (d)].

3. In the table below are four balance sheets for a single chartered bank [columns (1a)-(4a)]. The required reserve ratio is 20%.
(a) Compute the required reserves (A), the excess reserves* (B) (cash counts as part of the reserve), and the amount of new loans it can extend (C).

_____

* If the bank is short of reserves and must reduce its loans or obtain additional reserves, show this by placing a minus sign in front of the amounts by which it is short of reserves.

(b)   For the individual bank, draw up the four balance sheets below as they appear after the bank has made the new loans that it is capable of making [columns (1b-4b)].

	(1a)	(2a)	(3a)	(4a)
Assets:				
Cash	$10	$10	$15	$10
Other Reserves	40	25	15	25
Loans	100	130	100	125
Securities	50	55	45	70
Liabilities and net worth:				
Deposits	175	200	150	180
Capital stock	25	20	25	50
A. Required reserves	$ ___	$ ___	$ ___	$ ___
B. Excess reserves	___	___	___	___
C. New loans	___	___	___	___

	(1b)	(2b)	(3b)	(4b)
Assets:				
Cash	$ ___	$ ___	$ ___	$ ___
Reserves	___	___	___	___
Loans	___	___	___	___
Securities	___	___	___	___
Liabilities and net worth:				
Deposits	___	___	___	___
Capital stock	___	___	___	___

4.   At the top of the next column are several reserve ratios. Compute the monetary multiplier for each of the reserve ratios and enter the figures in column 2.

In column 3, show the maximum amount by which a single chartered bank can increase its loans for each dollar's worth of excess reserves it possesses. In column 4, indicate the maximum amount by which the banking system can increase its loans for each dollar's worth of excess reserves in the system.

	(1)	(2)	(3)	(4)
5%		___	$ ___	$ ___
6%		___	___	___
6.25%		___	___	___
8%		___	___	___
10%		___	___	___
12%		___	___	___

5.   Below is the simplified consolidated balance sheet for all chartered banks in the economy. Assume that the figures given show the bank's assets and liabilities prior to each of the following three transactions, and that the reserve ratio is 5%. Do not use the figures you placed in columns 2 and 4 when you begin parts (b) and (c) of the problem. Start parts (a), (b), and (c) of the problem with the printed figures.

(a)   The public deposits $5 in cash in the banks, and the banks send the $5 to the Bank of Canada, where it is added to their reserves. Fill in column 1. If the banking system extends the new loans it is capable of extending, show in column 2 the balance sheet as it would then appear.

(b)   The banking system sells $8 worth of securities to the Bank of Canada. Complete column 3. Assuming the system extends the maximum amount of credit of which it is capable, fill in column 4.

(c)   The Bank of Canada sells $1 worth of securities to the chartered banks. Complete column 5. Complete column 6 showing the condition of the banks after they have contracted their loans by the amount necessary to meet the reserve requirement.

6.   There are no excess reserves in a banking system made up of many banks. The reserve ratio is 25%. A customer deposits $1000 in cash in Bank A. Cash is counted as part of bank reserves. Trace out the sequence of loan and deposit creation by succeeding banks

	(1)	(2)	(3)	(4)	(5)	(6)
Assets:						
Reserves	$ 25	$ ___	$ ___	$ ___	$ ___	$ ___	$ ___
Loans	425	___	___	___	___	___
Securities	100	___	___	___	___	___
Liabilities and net worth:						
Deposits	500	___	___	___	___	___
Capital Stock	50	50	50	50	50	50	50
Advances (loans) from Bank of Canada	0	___	___	___	___	___	___
Excess Reserves		___	___	___	___	___
Maximum possible expansion of the money supply		___	___	___	___	___	___

Bank	(1) Acquired Cash Reserves and Deposits	(2) Required Cash Reserves	(3) Excess Cash Reserves	(4) Amount the Bank Can Lend
Bank A	$1000	$250	$750	$750
Bank B	_____	_____	_____	_____
Bank C	_____	_____	_____	_____
Bank D	_____	_____	_____	_____
Bank E	_____	_____	_____	_____
Total for first 5 banks	_____	_____	_____	_____
Remaining banks	_____	_____	_____	_____
Total for the system	_____	_____	_____	_____

in the table above, until the maximum amount of new deposits is reached.

SELF-TEST

Circle T if the statement is true, F if it is false.

1. The balance sheet of a chartered bank shows the transactions in which the bank has engaged during a given period of time.   **T F**

2. A chartered bank's assets plus its net worth equal the bank's liabilities.   **T F**

3. Banks, operating under a fractional reserve system, can create money.   **T F**

4. If a borrower is unable to pay a loan that was not backed by some asset, a bank's before-tax profit will be reduced by the amount of the loan.   **T F**

5. Some of a bank's income is obtained from the interest earned on loans extended out of deposits created by the bank.   **T F**

6. Goldsmiths increased the money supply when they accepted deposits of gold and issued paper receipts to the depositors.   **T F**

7. Roberta Lynn, the dancing star, deposits a $30,000 cheque from the Royal Alex in a chartered bank and receives a deposit account in return. An hour later, the Manfred Iron and Coal Company borrows $30,000 from the same bank. The money supply has increased $30,000 as a result of the two transactions.   **T F**

8. A chartered bank may maintain its required cash reserves either as a deposit in the Bank of Canada or as government bonds in its own vault.   **T F**

9. Required reserves for banks are being phased out in Canada.   **T F**

10. Once required reserves are completely phased out, the banks will not hold any reserves whatsoever since reserves do not yield any interest income.   **T F**

11. When a borrower takes a loan in the form of a currency withdrawal rather than in the form of a demand deposit the money supply does not change.   **T F**

12. Until reserve requirements are eliminated the required cash reserves that a chartered bank maintains must equal its own deposit liabilities multiplied by the required reserve ratio.   **T F**

13. The actual reserves of a chartered bank equal excess reserves plus required reserves.   **T F**

14. The main purpose of reserves is to have cash on hand to meet depositors' cash demands if there ever should be a bank panic.   **T F**

15. The reserves of a chartered bank in the Bank of Canada are an asset of the Bank of Canada.   **T F**

16. A cheque for $1,000 drawn on bank X by a depositor and deposited in bank Y will increase the excess reserves of bank Y by $1,000.   **T F**

17. Excess reserves measure the amount by which actual reserves exceed required (desired) reserves.   **T F**

18. A single chartered bank can safely loan an amount equal to its excess reserves multiplied by the required reserve ratio.   **T F**

19. While a single chartered bank can only increase its loans by an amount equal to its excess reserves, the entire banking system can increase its loans by an amount equal to its excess reserves multiplied by the reciprocal of the reserve ratio.   **T F**

20. If the banking system has $10 million in excess reserves and if the reserve ratio is 5%, it can increase its loans by $200 million.   **T F**

21. When a borrower repays a loan of $500, either in cash or by cheque, the supply of money is reduced by $500.   **T F**

22. The granting of a $5,000 loan and the purchase of a $5,000 government bond from a securities dealer by a chartered bank have the same effect on the money supply.   **T F**

23. When borrowers from a chartered bank wish to have cash rather than demand deposits, the money-creating potential of the banking system is increased.
                                                              T F

24. The simple money multiplier is the reciprocal of the required reserve ratio.   **T F**

25. The money multiplier indicates the increase in nominal GDP as the result of increasing the money supply by $1.   **T F**

26. Profit-seeking banks will tend to make changes in the money supply that are pro-cyclical.   **T F**

27. A chartered bank seeks both profits and liquidity, but these are conflicting goals.   **T F**

MULTIPLE-CHOICE

Circle the letter that corresponds to the best answer.

1. The fundamental balance identity is
(a)   assets = liabilities – net worth
(b)   assets = liabilities + net worth
(c)   assets = liabilities
(d)   assets + liabilities = net worth

2. On the balance sheet of a bank, loans are recorded as
(a)   part of net worth
(b)   an asset
(c)   a liability
(d)   none of the above since loans are recorded on the income statement and not the balance sheet

3. The entry on the balance sheet of a bank that counts as part of the money supply is
(a)   cash held by the bank
(b)   bank loans
(c)   reserves held at the central bank
(d)   demand deposits

4. The goldsmiths became bankers when
(a)   they accepted deposits of gold for safe storage

(b)   they issued receipts for the gold stored with them
(c)   their receipts for deposited gold were used as paper money
(d)   they issued paper money in excess of the amount of gold stored with them

5. When cash is deposited in a deposit account in a chartered bank, there is
(a)   a decrease in the money supply
(b)   an increase in the money supply
(c)   no change in the composition of the money supply
(d)   a change in the composition of the money supply

6. A chartered bank has actual reserves of $2,000 and deposit liabilities of $30,000; the required reserve ratio is 5%. The excess reserves of the bank are
(a) $500
(b) $0
(c)   minus $1,000
(d) $1,500

7. A chartered bank was required to maintain a cash reserve, either on deposit in the Bank of Canada or as vault cash, in order
(a)   to protect the deposits in the chartered bank against losses
(b)   to provide the means by which cheques drawn on the chartered bank and deposited in other chartered banks can be collected
(c)   to add to the liquidity of the chartered bank and protect it against a "run" on the bank
(d)   to provide the Bank of Canada with a means of controlling the lending ability of the chartered bank

8. A depositor places $1,000 in cash in a chartered bank, and the reserve ratio is 5%; the bank sends the $1,000 to the Bank of Canada. As a result, the reserves and the excess reserves of the bank have been increased, respectively, by
(a) $1,000 and $50
(b) $1,000 and $950
(c) $1,000 and $1,000
(d) $500 and $500

9. A chartered bank has no excess reserves, but then a depositor places $600 in cash in the bank, and the bank adds the $600 to its reserves by sending it to the Bank of Canada. The bank then loans $300 to a borrower. As a consequence of these transactions, the size of the money supply has
(a)   not been affected
(b)   increased by $300
(c)   increased by $600
(d)   increased by $900

10. A chartered bank has excess reserves of $500 and a required cash reserve ratio of 10%; it grants a loan of $1,000 to a borrower. If the borrower writes a cheque for $1,000, which is deposited in another chartered bank, the first bank will be short of reserves, after the cheque has been cleared, in the amount of
(a) $100
(b) $700
(c) $500
(d) $1,000

11. A chartered bank sells a $1,000 government security to a securities dealer. The dealer pays for the bond in cash, which the bank adds to its vault cash. The money supply has
(a) not been affected
(b) decreased by $1,000
(c) increased by $1,000
(d) increased by $1,000 multiplied by the reciprocal of the cash reserve ratio

12. A chartered bank has deposit liabilities of $100,000, reserves of $37,000, and a required cash reserve ratio of 25%. The amount by which a single chartered bank and the amount by which the banking system can increase loans are, respectively,
(a) $12,000 and $48,000
(b) $17,000 and $68,000
(c) $12,000 and $60,000
(d) $17,000 and $85,000

13. If the required cash reserve ratio were 4%, the value of the monetary multiplier would be
(a) 16
(b) 20
(c) 24
(d) 25

14. The banking system has excess reserves of $700 and makes new loans of $7,000 and is just meeting its reserve requirements. The required cash reserve ratio is
(a) 5%
(b) 6.25%
(c) 8%
(d) 10%

15. The chartered banking system finds that the required cash reserve ratio has changed from 5% to 6.25%, with the result that it is $100 million short of reserves. If it is unable to obtain any additional reserves, it must decrease its money supply by
(a) $100 million
(b) $125 million
(c) $1,600 million
(d) $2,000 million

16. Only one chartered bank in the banking system has excess reserves, and its excess reserves are $100,000. This bank makes a new loan of $80,000 and keeps excess reserves of $20,000. If the required reserve ratio for all banks is 20%, the potential expansion of the money supply because of the loan is
(a) $80,000
(b) $100,000
(c) $400,000
(d) $500,000

17. The money-creating potential of the banking system is reduced when
(a) bankers choose to have excess reserves
(b) borrowers choose to hold none of the funds they have borrowed in currency
(c) the Bank of Canada lowers the required reserve ratio
(d) bankers borrow reserves from the Bank of Canada

18. The excess reserves held by banks tend to
(a) rise during periods of prosperity
(b) fall during periods of recession
(c) rise during periods of recession
(d) fall when interest rates in the economy fall

19. Unless controlled, the money supply will
(a) fall during periods of prosperity
(b) rise during periods of recession
(c) change in a pro-cyclical fashion
(d) change in an anti-cyclical fashion

Use the following balance sheet for the First National Bank in answering the next five questions (20, 21, 22, 23, and 24). Assume the required reserve ratio is 20%.

Assets		Liabilities and Net Worth	
Reserves	$50,000	Demand	
Loans	70,000	deposits	$150,000
Securities	30,000	Capital stock	100,000
Property	100,000		

20. This chartered bank has excess reserves of
(a) $10,000
(b) $20,000
(c) $30,000
(d) $40,000

21. This bank can safely expand its loans by a maximum of
(a) $50,000
(b) $40,000
(c) $30,000
(d) $20,000

22. Using the original bank balance sheet, assume that the bank makes a loan of $10,000 and has a cheque cleared against it for the amount of the loan. Then its reserves and demand deposits will now be
(a) $40,000 and $140,000
(b) $40,000 and $150,000
(c) $30,000 and $150,000
(d) $60,000 and $140,000

23. Using the original bank balance sheet, assume that the bank makes a loan of $15,000 and has a cheque cleared against it for the amount of the loan. Then it will have excess reserves of
(a) $5,000
(b) $10,000
(c) $15,000
(d) $20,000

24. If the original bank balance sheet was for the chartered banking system, rather than a single bank, loans and deposits could have been expanded by a maximum of
(a) $50,000
(b) $100,000
(c) $150,000
(d) $200,000

25. The claims of the owners of the bank against the bank assets is the bank's
(a) net worth
(b) liabilities
(c) balance sheet
(d) fractional reserves

26. The selling of government bonds by chartered banks is most similar to the
(a) making of loans by banks because both actions increase the money supply
(b) making of loans by banks because both actions decrease the money supply
(c) repayment of loans to banks because both actions decrease the money supply
(d) repayment of loans to banks because both actions increase the money supply

Answer the next two questions (27 and 28) on the basis of the following consolidated balance sheet for the chartered banking system. All figures are in billions. Assume that the required reserve ratio is 12.5%.

Assets		Liabilities and Net Worth	
Reserves	$ 40	Demand	
Loans	80	deposits	$200
Securities	100	Capital stock	120
Property	200		

27. The maximum amount by which this chartered banking system can expand the supply of money by lending is
(a) $120 billion
(b) $240 billion
(c) $350 billion
(d) $440 billion

28. If there is a deposit of $20 billion of new currency into chequing accounts in the banking system, excess reserves will increase by
(a) $16.5 billion
(b) $17.0 billion
(c) $17.5 billion
(d) $18.5 billion

29. The formula for the simple money multiplier is given by $m = 1/R$, where R stands for
(a) excess reserves
(b) required reserve ratio
(c) the marginal propensity to save
(d) the interest rate

30. The maximum deposit expansion for the whole banking system is found by multiplying the volume of excess reserves by
(a) the required reserve ratio
(b) 1 minus the required reserve ratio
(c) the money multiplier
(d) the reciprocal of the interest rate

DISCUSSION QUESTIONS

1. List the assets and liabilities found on the simplified balance sheet of a bank.

2. How did the early goldsmiths come to issue paper money and then become bankers? Explain the difference between 100% and a fractional reserve system of banking, and why the latter system is subject to "runs" and requires public regulation.

3. Chartered banks seek both profits and safety. Explain how the balance sheet of the chartered banks reflects the desires of bankers for income and for liquidity.

4. Do the reserves held by chartered banks satisfactorily protect the bank's depositors? Are the reserves of banks needed? Explain your answers.

5. Explain why the granting of a loan by a chartered bank increases the supply of money. Why does the repayment of a loan decrease the supply of money?

6. The owner of a sporting goods store writes a cheque

on his account in a Calgary, Alberta bank and sends it to one of his suppliers, who deposits it in a different bank in Edmonton, Alberta. How does the Edmonton bank obtain payment from the Calgary bank? If the two banks were in Calgary and Halifax, Nova Scotia, is payment any more complicated? How are the reserves of the two banks affected?

7. Why is a single bank only able to loan safely an amount equal to its excess reserves?

8. No one chartered bank ever lends an amount greater than its excess reserves, but the banking system as a whole is able to extend loans and expand the money supply by an amount equal to the system's excess reserves multiplied by the reciprocal of the reserve ratio. Explain why this is possible and how the multiple expansion of deposits (that is, money) takes place.

9. Suppose the following is a simplified balance sheet of the chartered banking system. The cash reserve ratio is 10%.

Assets		Liabilities + Owners' Equity	
Cash reserves	$50	Deposits	$500
Securities	10		
Loans	440		

(a) How much excess reserves does the system have?
(b) Show the effect on the balance sheet of the following transactions, on the assumption that the banking system creates the maximum amount of demand deposits permitted by its reserves.
(1) A customer deposits $10 in cash.
(2) The required reserve ratio drops to 5%.
(3) The banking system sells $5 of securities to the central bank for cash.

10. On the basis of a given amount of excess reserves and a given reserve ratio, a certain expansion of the money supply may be possible. What are two reasons the potential expansion of the money supply may not be fully achieved?

11. Why is there a "need for monetary control" in the Canadian economy?

ANSWERS

Fill-in questions

1. assets, liabilities, net worth

2. liabilities, net worth

3. vault, till

4. fraction

5. create

6. demand, savings, term, notice

7. not changed

8. increased

9. central bank, deposit liabilities, reserve ratio

10. 1994

11. actual reserves, required reserves

12. decreased, increased, decreased, increased

13. excess reserves

14. increases, 10,000

15. decreases, 2,000

16. deposit, central bank; reserves

17. profits, liquidity (safety)

18. monetary multiplier (reciprocal of the reserve ratio), reserves

19. smaller

20. decrease, 120 million

21. currency, excess

22. (a) recession, prosperity; (b) more

Problems and projects

1. (a) A; (b) A; (c) A; (d) L; (e) A; (f) L; (g) A; (h) L

2.

	(a)	(b)	(c)	(d)
Assets:				
Reserves	50	50	160	200
Loans	700	700	700	700
Securities	200	200	200	100
Liabilities and net worth:				
Deposits	850	850	960	900
Capital stock	100	100	100	100

3.

(a)	(1a)	(2a)	(3a)	(4a)
A. Required reserves	$35	$40	$30	$36
B. Excess reserves	15	-5	0	-1
C. New loans — single bank	15	*	0	*

(b)	(1b)	(2b)	(3b)	(4b)
Assets:				
Cash	$ 10	$10	$15	$11
Reserves	40	25	15	25
Loans	115	105	100	125
Securities	50	55	45	69*
Liabilities and net worth:				
Deposits	190	175*	150	180
Capital stock	25	20	25	50

4.   Column 2: 20, 16.67, 16, 12.5, 10, 8.33
Column 3: 1, 1, 1, 1, 1, 1
Column 4: 20, 16.67, 16, 12.5, 10, 8.33

5.

	(1)	(2)	(3)	(4)	(5)	(6)
Assets:						
Reserves	$ 30	$ 30	$ 33	$ 33	$ 24	$ 24
Loans	425	520	425	585	425	405
Securities	100	100	92	92	101	101
Liabilities and net worth:						
Deposits	505	600	500	660	500	480
Capital stock	50	50	50	50	50	50
Advances (loans) from Bank of Canada	0	0	0	0	0	0
Excess reserves	4.75	0	8	0	-1	0
Maximum possible expansion of the money supply	95	0	160	0	-20	0

6.

Bank	(1) Acquired Cash Reserves and Deposits	(2) Required Cash Reserves	(3) Excess Cash Reserves	(4) Amount the Bank Can Lend
Bank A	$1000	$250	$750	$750
Bank B	750	187.50	562.50	562.50
Bank C	562.50	140.63	421.87	421.87
Bank D	421.87	105.47	316.40	316.40
Bank E	316.40	79.10	237.30	237.30
Total for first five banks	3050.77	762.70	2288.07	2288.07
Remaining banks	949.23	237.30	711.93	711.93
Total for system	4000.00	1000.00	3000.00	3000.00

Self-test

1. F;   2. F;   3. T;   4. T;   5. T;   6. F;   7. T;   8. F;
9. T;   10. F;   11. F;   12. T;   13. T;   14. F;   15. F;
16. F; 17. T;   18. F;   19. T;   20. T;   21. T;   22. T;
23. F;   24. T;   25. F;   26. T;   27. T

Multiple-choice

1. (b);   2. (b);   3. (d);   4. (d);   5. (d);   6. (a);
7. (d);   8. (b);   9. (b);   10. (c);   11. (b);   12. (a);
13. (d);   14. (d);   15. (c);   16. (c);   17. (a);   18. (c);
19. (c);   20. (b);   21. (d);   22. (b);   23. (a);   24. (b);
25. (a);   26. (c);   27. (a);   28. (c);   29. (b);   30. (c)

Note for 3.(a) and 3.(b) on page 139.

* If an individual bank is $5 short of reserves, it must either obtain additional reserves of $5 by selling $5 worth of securities, or by getting a $5 advance (very short-term loan) from the Bank of Canada, or by contracting its loans. In (2b) the bank reduced its loans and deposits while in (4b) the bank sold a security for $1 cash.

CHAPTER

12 The Bank of Canada and Monetary Policy

Chapter 12 is the third chapter dealing with money and banking. It explains how the Bank of Canada affects output, income, employment, and the price level in the economy. Central bank policies designed to affect these variables by changing the money supply are called monetary policies. Their goal is full employment without inflation.

You should have little difficulty with this chapter if you have understood the material in Chapter 11. In Chapter 12 there are a number of distinct but interrelated topics covered. The following outline indicates the subject matter found in this chapter.

(a) The central bank and control of the money supply
   1) Functions of the central bank
   2) Techniques used by the central bank to change the money supply
(b) Determination of the rate of interest
   1) Demand for money
      (i) Asset demand
      (ii) Transactions demand
   2) Supply of money
(c) Interest rates and the price of bonds
(d) The effect of monetary policy on interest rates and the equilibrium level of GDP
   1) Aggregate expenditure model
   2) Aggregate demand–aggregate supply model
(e) Effectiveness of monetary policy
(f) Monetary and fiscal policy—a review

As you move through the chapter keep in mind that the economic models introduced in Chapter 8 are being expanded to include a monetary sector and that we are still interested in determining, and changing, the equilibrium level of income. A new factor — monetary policy — is being added to be used in the pursuit of economic stability.

In order to acquire a thorough knowledge of the manner in which each of the Bank of Canada transactions affects reserves, excess reserves, the actual money supply, and the potential money supply, you must study very carefully each of the sets of balance sheets that are used to explain these transactions. On these balance sheets the items to watch are again reserves and deposits! Be sure that you know why each of the balance sheet changes is made and that you are able, on your own, to make the appropriate balance sheet entries to trace through the effects of any transaction.

Following the examination of the functions of the Bank of Canada and the "The Tools of Monetary Policy" there is an explanation of the determination of how the demand for and the supply of money determine the interest rate (in the "money market"); how the interest-rate and the investment-demand schedules determine the level of planned investment in the economy; and how planned investment and the saving schedules together determine the equilibrium GDP. The way in which an expansionary (easy) monetary policy and a contractionary (tight) monetary policy work through this cause–effect chain is illustrated with examples and summarized in Table 12-2 in the textbook (which should be studied).

This explanation of monetary policy makes it clear that the effect of a change in the money supply depends upon just how steep or flat the downsloping demand-for-money and investment-demand curves are. Interest rate changes cause the aggregate expenditure schedule to shift up or down and change the equilibrium level of GDP. The aggregate supply and the aggregate demand curves are also used to show how changes in the money supply affect domestic output and the price level.

The strengths and shortcomings of monetary policy in reducing unemployment (and expanding national output) and in reducing inflation are examined in the next-to-last major section of the chapter. Here you will also encounter the dilemma faced by the Bank of Canada: it cannot simultaneously control both the money supply and the level of interest rates in the economy.

The last section of Chapter 12 is a summary of Chapters 7 through 12. It will restate for you the main outline of the aggregate expenditure theory of employment and the principal public policies that may be used to promote full employment without creating inflation. This section will help you to see that the various principles discussed in the previous chapters are not separate but are, in fact, connected parts of the one theory; and that the public policies discussed in earlier chapters are not really separate policies but are alternative means of achieving the goal of economic stabilization.

This one theory of employment and the alternative means of achieving economic stabilization are summarized for you in Figure 12-5. This is probably the single most important figure in the textbook.

CHECKLIST

When you have studied this chapter, you should be able to:

■ List the principal assets and liabilities of the Bank of Canada.

■ Identify the two main tools of monetary policy; and explain how each may be employed by the central bank to expand and to contract the money supply.

■ Prescribe the specific monetary policies the Bank of Canada utilizes to reduce unemployment, and the specific policies it employs to reduce inflationary pressures in the economy.

■ Identify the two minor selective controls; and explain how each is used to promote economic stability.

■ Explain what the phrase "demand for money" means and list the two reasons for holding money.

■ Describe what determines the equilibrium level of the interest rate.

■ Indicate the relationship that exists between the price of existing bonds and the interest rate.

■ Draw the demand-for-money and the supply-of-money curves and use them to show how a change in the supply of money will affect the interest rate; draw an investment-demand curve to explain the effects of changes in the interest rate on investment spending; and construct a leakages–injections graph to show the effects of a change in planned investment on the equilibrium GDP.

■ Explain, using the aggregate expenditure or aggregate demand–aggregate supply models, the links between a change in the money supply and a change in the equilibrium GDP.

■ Explain the difference between an expansionary (easy) monetary and a contractionary (tight) monetary policy and the tools used by the central bank to implement each one.

■ State precisely how the steepness of the demand-for-money and of the investment-demand curves affects the impact of a change in the money supply on the equilibrium GDP.

■ Use the aggregate demand and aggregate supply curves to show the effects of changes in the money supply on national output and the price level.

■ List three strengths and three shortcomings of monetary policy.

■ State the target (or policy) dilemma confronted by the Bank of Canada; and explain why it faces this dilemma.

■ Summarize the aggregate expenditure model, including a monetary sector, and indicate the policies that may be utilized to promote a full-employment noninflationary GDP.

CHAPTER OUTLINE

1. The objective of monetary policy is full employment without inflation. The Bank of Canada can accomplish this objective by exercising control over the amount of excess reserves held by the chartered banks and thereby influencing the size of the money supply, the rate of interest, and the level of aggregate expenditures.

2. By examining the statement of assets and liabilities of the Bank of Canada, an understanding of the ways in which the central bank can control and influence the reserves of chartered banks and the money supply can be obtained.
(a) The principal assets of the Bank of Canada (in order of size) are securities issued or guaranteed by the Government of Canada, other securities, other assets, and — a very minor item — advances (normally very short-term loans) to the members of the Canadian Payments Association.
(b) Its principal liabilities are its bank notes in circulation, the reserve deposits of the chartered banks, and Government of Canada deposits.

3. The Bank of Canada employs two principal tools (techniques or instruments) to control the reserves of banks and the size of the money supply: open-market operations and switching Government of Canada deposits between the central bank and commercial banks.
(a) It can buy and sell government bonds in the open market.
(1) Buying securities in the open market from either banks or the public increases the reserves of banks.
(2) Selling securities in the open market to either banks

or the public decreases the reserves of banks.

(b) It can switch Government of Canada deposits between itself and the chartered banks; and thus affect the amount of chartered bank reserves.

Less important techniques include the following.

(c) It can change the bank rate. Changes in the bank rate directly affect the cost, and hence, the volume of credit.

(d) It can use moral suasion (or friendly persuasion) to influence the lending policies of the chartered banks.

(e) A tight (easy) money policy involves selling (buying) bonds in the open market, increasing (decreasing) the bank rate, switching government reserves out of (into) the chartered bank.

4. The interest rate is the price paid for the use of money and is determined by the demand for money to hold and the supply of money. The supply of money can be determined by the central bank. The demand for money to hold has two components, a transactions demand and an asset demand. The total demand for money is found by adding the asset demand horizontally to the transactions demand. There is an inverse relation between the quantity demanded of money to hold and the interest rate.

The equilibrium level of the interest rate occurs where the quantity of money people wish to hold equals the quantity of money supplied by the monetary authorities. There is an inverse relation between the price of existing bonds and the interest rate.

5. The mechanisms through which monetary policy affects equilibrium GDP in the aggregate expenditure model are:

(a) In the money market the demand-for and the supply-of-money curves determine the real interest rate; the investment-demand curve and this rate of interest determine planned investment; and planned investment along with the saving curve determine the equilibrium GDP.

(b) If unemployment and deflation is the problem, the Bank of Canada takes policy actions to increase the money supply, causing the interest rate to fall and investment spending to increase, thereby increasing real GDP by a multiple of the increase in investment.

(c) But if inflation is the problem, the Bank of Canada uses its tools to decrease the money supply, causing the interest rate to rise and investment spending to decrease, and thereby reducing inflation.

(d) There are refinements and feedback effects to monetary policy that must be considered:

(1) The steeper the demand-for-money curve and the flatter the investment-demand curve, the greater will be the effect on the equilibrium GDP of a change in the money supply.

(2) Changes in the equilibrium GDP that result from a change in the money supply will alter the demand for money and dampen the effect of the change in the money supply on the GDP.

(e) Stated in terms of the aggregate demand–aggregate supply model: the flatter (steeper) the aggregate supply curve is, the greater (smaller) is the effect of a change in the money supply on real national output and employment and the smaller (greater) is the effect on the price level.

6. Whether monetary policy is effective in promoting full employment without inflation is a debatable question because monetary policy has both strengths and shortcomings in fighting recession and inflation.

(a) Its strengths are that it can be more quickly changed than fiscal policy; it is more isolated from political pressure than fiscal policy; and (some economists believe) it is the key determinant of economic activity and, therefore, more effective than fiscal policy.

(b) Its weaknesses are that it is more effective in fighting inflation than it is in curbing recession; it can be offset by changes in the velocity of money; and it may not have a significant impact on investment spending in the economy.

(c) A most difficult problem for the Bank of Canada is its inability to control both the money supply and the level of interest rates at the same time.

(1) If the Bank of Canada's policy target is the stabilization of interest rates, an increase in the money GDP (and the resulting increase in the demand for money) will require it to increase the money supply. If its policy target is the stabilization of the money supply, an increase in the money GDP (and the demand for money) will force interest rates upward.

(2) Controversy surrounds the issue of which of these two policy targets is preferable. The Bank of Canada switched from stabilizing interest rates to stabilizing the money supply in 1975, and from stabilizing the money supply to a middle-of-the-road policy in late 1982. This flexible policy has been used by the Bank of Canada to deal with the stock market crash of 1987. With the price level remaining relatively stable since 1991, the Bank of Canada has moved aggressively to lower interest rates. However, concern over the external value of the dollar has prevented an orderly progression towards these desired lower rates.

7. In the aggregate expenditure model, the income, employment, output, and prices of an economy are positively related to the level of aggregate expenditures, which has four principal components.

(a)   These four components are consumption spending, which depends upon the stable consumption schedule and the income of the economy; investment spending, which is more unstable; government spending, which depends partly on the level of spending needed to achieve full employment and price stability; and net exports, which are influenced by exchange rates and the levels of domestic and foreign GDP.

(b)   To achieve economic stability, government employs both fiscal and monetary policy; but to be effective, these two types of policy must be coordinated.

IMPORTANT TERMS

bank rate

expansionary (easy) and
   contractionary (tight) monetary policies

feedback effects

monetary policy

money market

moral suasion

open-market operations

prime interest

purchase–resale agreement

sales–repurchase agreement

switching government deposits

target dilemma

transactions, asset, and total demand for money

FILL-IN QUESTIONS

1.   The objective of monetary policy in Canada is to help achieve   and   maintain   a   _____,
_____ level of total output. Responsibility for these monetary policies rests with the
_____ _____ _____ .

2.   The five major functions of the Bank of Canada are to:

(a)   _____

(b)   _____

(c)   _____

(d)   _____

(e)   _____

3.   The two important assets of the Bank of Canada insofar as monetary control is concerned are _____
_____ and
_____ .

4.   The thee major liabilities of the Bank of Canada are
_____ _____ _____,
_____ _____ _____
_____,   and   _____
_____ _____ .

5.   When the Bank of Canada acts as fiscal agent, it means that the central bank holds part of the federal government's _____, helps the government collect _____, and administers the sale and redemption of _____ _____ .

6.   The four tools (or instruments) employed by the monetary authority to control the money supply are
_____ _____, changing
_____ _____ _____,
switching _____ _____
_____ _____, and
_____ _____ .

7.   The Bank of Canada buys and sells government securities in the open market in order to change the amount of new _____ that chartered banks are able to create, and the rate of _____ in the economy.

8.   The most effective major monetary controls are
_____ and
_____ .

9.   The two minor controls are changes in the
_____ _____ and
_____ _____ .

10.   The total demand for money is the sum of: (a) the transactions demand, which depends (directly, inversely) _____ upon the _____; (b) and the asset demand, which depends _____ upon the _____ _____ _____ .

11. Graphically, in an economy in which government neither purchases goods and services nor collects net taxes, and which neither exports nor imports goods and services,
(a) the equilibrium real interest rate is determined by the demand-for- and the supply-of-_____ curves;

(b) this equilibrium interest rate and the _____ curve determine the level of planned investment;
(c) the level of planned investment, using the leakages–injections approach, and the _____ curve determine the equilibrium GDP.
(d) But when the supply-of-money curve increases (shifts to the right), the real interest rate will (increase, decrease) _____, planned investment will _____, and the equilibrium GDP will _____.

12. There is a(n) (inverse, direct) _____ relation between interest rates and the price of existing bonds.

13. If the Bank of Canada were to sell $10 million in government bonds to the public, who paid for them by cheque, and the reserve ratio were 5%, the supply of money would immediately be reduced by $_____, the reserves of the chartered banks would immediately be reduced by $_____, and the excess reserves of the banks would immediately be reduced by $_____. But if these bonds were sold to the chartered banks, the supply of money would immediately be reduced by $_____, the reserves of the banks would immediately be reduced by $_____ , and the excess reserves of the banks would immediately be reduced by $_____.

14. To increase the supply of money, the Bank of Canada should _____ government securities in the open market; to decrease the supply of money, it should _____ securities in the open market.

15. If there were a serious problem with unemployment in the economy, according to the predictions of the aggregate expenditure model, the Bank of Canada should pursue a(n) _____ monetary policy, in which the Bank of Canada would (buy, sell) _____

government bonds as a way of (increasing, decreasing) _____ the money supply, and thereby _____ interest rates. These events would have the effect of _____ investment spending and thus _____ real GDP.

16. To eliminate inflationary pressures in the economy, following the aggregate expenditures model, the monetary authority should seek to (increase, decrease) _____ the reserves of chartered banks; this would tend to _____ the money supply and to _____ the rate of interest; and this, in turn, would cause investment spending, aggregate expenditures, and output to _____. This action by monetary authorities would be considered a _____ monetary policy.

17. The effect of a $1 billion increase or decrease in the money supply upon the equilibrium GDP is greater, the (flatter, steeper) _____ the demand-for-money curve and the _____ the investment-demand curve.

18. An increase in the money supply will shift the aggregate (supply, demand) _____ curve to the (right, left) _____.
The impact on _____ and the _____ _____ depends upon the _____ of the aggregate supply curve.

19. (a) The strengths of monetary policy are that it is more _____, more isolated from _____ _____, and (in the view of some theorists) more _____ than fiscal policy.
(b) The weaknesses of monetary policy are that it is more effective in curbing (recession, inflation) _____ than _____, can be ineffective if the _____ of money changes in the (same, opposite) _____ direction as the money supply, and will not be effective if changes in the interest rate have little or no effect on _____ spending in the economy.

20. The target dilemma faced by the Bank of Canada is that it is (able, unable) _____ to control both the money supply and the level of _____ rates simultaneously.

(a) If it is to stabilize the interest rate, it must (increase, decrease) _____ the money supply when the money GDP rises.

(b) And if it stabilizes the money supply, it must allow the interest rate to _____ when the money GDP rises.

21. In the aggregate expenditure model, the effect of monetary policy on output is transmitted through _____ _____.

22. At different times the Bank of Canada's policy target was the _____ _____, the _____ _____, and more recently the rate of _____.

23. Government seeks to bring about a full-employment noninflationary GDP by employing both _____ and _____ policies.

PROBLEMS AND PROJECTS

1. Below are various items that belong in the balance statement of the Bank of Canada. Place them in their proper place in the blank balance sheet by listing them either on the asset or on the liability side in the order of their dollar importance.

  chartered bank reserves (deposits)
  government of Canada deposits
  securities
  advances (loans) to banks
  Bank of Canada notes

Assets	Liabilities
_____	_____
_____	_____
_____	_____
_____	_____

2. Assume that the consolidated balance sheet below is for all chartered banks. Assume, also, that the required reserve ratio is 5%.

Assets		Liabilities	
Reserves	$ 20	Deposits	$400
Loans	280	Net worth	100
Securities	200		
	$500		$500

(a) To increase the supply of money by $100, the Bank of Canada could _____ securities worth $_____ in the open market; or

(b) shift $_____ of government deposits from the Bank of Canada to the chartered banks; or

(c) reduce the reserve ratio to _____.

(d) To reduce the supply of money by $50, beginning from our original table, the Bank of Canada could _____ securities worth $_____ in the open market; or

(e) increase the reserve ratio to _____.

3. At the top of page 147 are the initial balance sheet of the Bank of Canada and the consolidated balance sheets of the chartered banks. Assume that the cash reserve ratio is 5%. The figures in column (1) show the balance sheets of the Bank of Canada and the chartered banks prior to each of the following three transactions.

Place the new balance sheet figures in the appropriate columns and complete A, B, C, D, and E in the columns. Do not use the figures you place in columns (2) and (3) when you work the next part of the problem: start all parts of the problem with the printed figures in column (1).

(a) The Bank of Canada sells $1 in securities to the public (security dealer), which pays by cheque (column 2).

(b) The Bank of Canada buys $1 in securities from the chartered banks (column 3).

(c) The Government of Canada buys $1 worth of goods from the Canadian manufacturers and pays the manufacturers by cheques drawn on its accounts at the Bank of Canada (column 4).

4. On the left graph on page 147 is the demand-for-money curve that shows the amounts of money consumers and firms wish to hold at various rates of interest (when the money GDP in the economy is given).

(a) Suppose the supply of money is equal to $300.

(1) Draw on this graph the supply-of-money curve.

(2) The equilibrium rate of interest in the economy is _____%.

	(1)	(2)	(3)	(4)
Bank of Canada				
Assets:				
Securities	$ 21	$_____	$_____	$_____
Advances (loans) to chartered banks	0	_____	_____	_____
Liabilities:				
Reserves of chartered banks	10	_____	_____	_____
Government of Canada deposits	2	_____	_____	_____
Bank of Canada notes	9	_____	_____	_____
Chartered Banks				
Assets:				
Reserves	$ 10	_____	_____	_____
Securities	20	_____	_____	_____
Loans	170	_____	_____	_____
Liabilities:				
Deposits	200	_____	_____	_____
Advances (loans) from Bank of Canada	0	_____	_____	_____
A. Required reserves		_____	_____	_____
B. Excess reserves		_____	_____	_____
C. How much has the money supply changed?		_____	_____	_____
D. How much more can the money supply change?		_____	_____	_____
E. What is the total of C and D?		_____	_____	_____

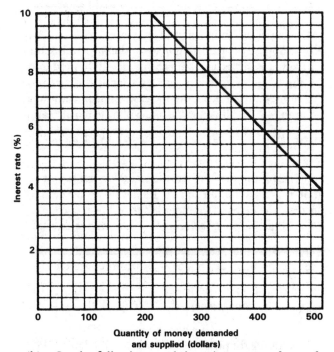

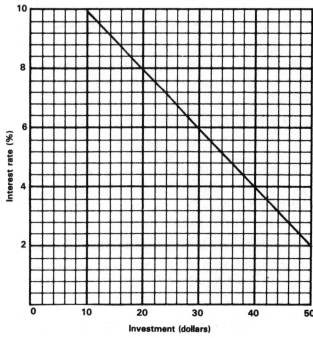

(b) On the following graph is an investment demand curve that shows the amounts of planned investment at various rates of interest.

Given your answer to (2) above, how much will investors plan to spend for capital goods?

(c) On the next graph is the saving curve for an economy in which the only leakage from the GDP is saving. (There are no taxes collected and no imports of goods and services.)

(1) On this graph plot the investment curve when planned investment is the amount given by you in your answer to (b) above.

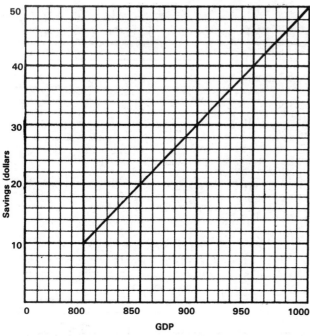

(2) If the only injection into this economy is investment spending (that is, if there is no government spending for and no exports of goods and services), the equilibrium

GDP will be $_____.

(d)   Assume the money supply increases to $400. On the first graph plot the new supply-of-money curve. The new

(1) equilibrium interest rate is _____%;

(2) level of planned investment is $ _____;

(3) equilibrium GDP is $ _____.

(e)   Suppose the full-employment noninflationary GDP in this economy is $875.

(1) At this GDP, saving would be $ _____.

(2) For this GDP to be the equilibrium GDP, investment would have to be equal to $_____.

(3) For investment to be at this level, the rate of interest would have to be _____%.

(4) And for the interest rate to be at this level, the supply of money would have to be equal to $_____.

(f)   In this economy:

(1) the marginal propensity to save is equal to _____ and the multiplier has, therefore, a value equal to _____;

(2) a one percentage point decrease in the interest rate will (increase, decrease) _____ planned

investment by $_____ and will, therefore, (increase, decrease) _____ the equilibrium GDP by $_____;

(3) but for the interest rate to decrease by one percentage point the money supply must (increase, decrease) _____ by $_____.

5.   Columns (1) and (2) in the following table show the money supply and column (3) shows the demand for money. (Dollar figures are in billions and the interest rate is a percentage.)

(1) Supply of Money	(2) Interest Rate	(3) Demand for Money	(4) Demand for Money
$400	0.08	$100	$200
400	.07	200	300
400	.06	300	400
400	.05	400	500
400	.04	500	600
400	.03	600	700
400	.02	700	800

(a)   The equilibrium interest rate is _____%.

(b)   Suppose the Bank of Canada wishes to stabilize the interest rate at this level; but the money GDP produced by the economy increases, and as a result the demand for money in the economy increases to that shown in column (4). The Bank of Canada will have to (increase, decrease) _____ the supply of money to $_____ billion.

(c)   But if the Bank of Canada stabilizes the supply of money at $400 billion and the money GDP increases to increase the demand for money to that shown in column (3) to that shown in column (4), the interest rate will (rise, fall) _____ to _____%.

(d)   If the Bank of Canada stabilizes the interest rate, it must (increase, decrease) _____ the supply of money when the money GDP rises and _____ it when the money GDP falls; and if it holds the supply of money constant, the interest rate will (rise, fall) _____ when the money GDP increases and _____ when the money GDP decreases.

6.   This problem introduces the student to the feedback or circularity that arises with the use of monetary policy. The problem adds a monetary sector to the aggregate

expenditure model.

Suppose the equation for the consumption schedule is given by: $C = 300 + .80$ GDP. Investment is represented by: $I = 100 - 10i$, where the interest rate (i) is given as a whole number instead of as a percentage.(10% is given as 10.)

The equilibrium GDP satisfies: GDP $= C + I$

GDP $= 300 + .80$GDP $+ 100 - 10i$

There is a monetary sector with only an asset demand for money (D_a) given by: $D_a = 400 - 20i$

The supply of money is set by the monetary authority at 300.

(a) The equilibrium interest rate is _____.

(b) The level of investment will be _____.

(c) The equilibrium level of income will be _____.

Now introduce a transactions demand for money (D_t) given by:

$D_t = .05$ GDP

The total demand for money now becomes:

$D_a + D_m = 400-20i + .05$ GDP

The supply of money is still 300.

In (a) and (c) the rate of interest is 5 and GDP equals 1750.

(d) At these values the total demand for money will be _____.

(e) Because the demand for money to hold is (greater than, less than) _____ the supply of money, the public will (buy, sell) _____ bonds.

(f) The interest rate will (rise, fall) _____, investment will (rise, fall) _____, and the equilibrium level of GDP will (rise, fall) _____.

(g) If the monetary authority wished to keep the interest rate at 5 , the money supply would have to be increased to _____.

(h) The monetary authority cannot control both the _____ _____ and the _____ _____.

SELF-TEST

Circle T if the statement is true, F if it is false.

1. The stated objective of monetary policy is to stabilize interest rates. **T F**

2. Under the new Bank Act the chartered banks will only have to maintain reserves against demand deposits and not time or notice deposits. **T F**

3. The Bank of Canada supplies the economy with needed paper currency. **T F**

4. The Bank of Canada holds all of the government's chequing accounts. **T F**

5. Chartered banks' deposits held at the Bank of Canada are counted as an asset by the chartered banks and a liability by the Bank of Canada. **T F**

6. The Bank of Canada is owned by the federal government. **T F**

7. The major asset of the Bank of Canada is Government of Canada securities. **T F**

8. If the Bank of Canada buys $15 in government securities from the public in the open market, the effect will be to increase the excess reserves of chartered banks by $15. **T F**

9. If the Bank of Canada buys $15 in government securities from the chartered banks, the result will be to increase the reserves of the chartered banks by $15. **T F**

10. When the Bank of Canada sells bonds in the open market, the price of these bonds falls. **T F**

11. When chartered banks get an advance (borrow) from the Bank of Canada, they increase their reserves. **T F**

12. If the monetary authority wished to follow a tight money policy, it would seek to reduce the reserves of the chartered banks. **T F**

13. The major tool of monetary policy is changes in the prime rate of interest. **T F**

14. When the central bank moves government deposits from the central bank to the chartered banks , the reserves of the chartered banks will be decreased. **T F**

15. The asset demand for money varies inversely with the rate of interest. **T F**

16. The equilibrium rate of interest is found at the intersection of the demand-for-money and the supply-of-money curves. **T F**

17. An increase in the equilibrium GDP will shift the demand-for-money curve to the left and increase the equilibrium interest rate. **T F**

18. Consumer spending is more sensitive to changes in the rate of interest than is investment demand. **T F**

19. Monetary policy is more effective in fighting depression than it is in curbing inflation. **T F**

20. In an economy in which the GDP is either rising or falling, the Bank of Canada is unable to control both the money supply and interest rates. **T F**

21. An expansionary monetary policy shifts the aggregate demand curve to the right. **T F**

22. It is generally agreed that fiscal policy is more effective than monetary policy in controlling the business cycle because fiscal policy is more flexible. **T F**

23. Through its influence on interest rates, monetary policy affects the level of net exports. **T F**

24. Since 1982 the policy target of the Bank of Canada was simply to control the money supply. **T F**

25. An expansionary monetary policy is one that makes credit cheaper and easier to obtain. **T F**

MULTIPLE-CHOICE

Circle the letter that corresponds to the best answer.

1. The agency directly responsible for monetary policy in Canada is
(a) the Canadian Bankers' Association
(b) the Bank of Canada
(c) the Parliament of Canada
(d) the Department of Finance

2. The largest single asset on the Bank of Canada's balance sheet is
(a) government securities
(b) loans
(c) notes in circulation
(d) chartered banks' deposits

3. All of the following are functions of the Bank of Canada with the exception of
(a) acting as fiscal agent of the government
(b) holding deposits of the chartered banks
(c) regulating the supply of money
(d) determining the prime rate of interest

4. Open-market operations refer to
(a) the buying and selling of government bonds by the Bank of Canada
(b) the buying and selling of government bonds by the chartered banks
(c) the buying and selling of stocks and bonds by the Bank of Canada
(d) the shifting of government deposits to and from the commercial banks by the Bank of Canada.

5. Which of the following controls is being phased out by the end of 1994?
(a) mandated reserve ratio
(b) moral suasion
(c) open-market operations
(d) changing the bank rate

6. Which of the following acts would not have the same general effect upon the economy as the other three?
(a) the Bank of Canada sells bonds in the open market
(b) the Bank of Canada raises the discount rate
(c) the Bank of Canada shifts government deposits into the chartered banks from the central bank
(d) the Bank of Canada raises the reserve ratio

7. Which one of the following is not one of the controls used by the Bank of Canada?
(a) moral suasion
(b) setting tariff rates
(c) setting the bank rate
(d) open-market operations

8. Which of the following are the most important controls used by the Bank of Canada?
(a) changing the reserve ratio and open-market operations
(b) changing the bank rate and open-market operations
(c) shifting government deposits between the central and chartered banks and open-market operations
(d) changing the bank rate and shifting government deposits

9. Assuming the Bank of Canada sells $20 million in government securities to the chartered banks and the reserve ratio is 10%, then the effect will be
(a) to reduce the actual supply of money by $20 million
(b) to reduce the actual supply of money by $2 million
(c) to reduce the potential supply of money by $20 million
(d) to reduce the potential supply of money by $200 million

10. In the aggregate expenditure model chain of cause and effect between changes in the excess reserves of chartered banks and the resulting changes in output and employment in the economy,
(a) an increase in excess reserves will decrease the money supply
(b) a decrease in the money supply will increase the rate of interest
(c) an increase in the rate of interest will increase aggregate expenditures
(d) an increase in aggregate expenditures will decrease output and employment

11. There is an asset demand for money because money is
(a) a medium of exchange
(b) a standard of value
(c) a store of value
(d) a standard of deferred payment

12. The transactions demand for money
(a) varies directly with nominal GDP
(b) varies inversely with nominal GDP
(c) varies directly with the interest rate
(d) varies inversely with the interest rate

13. The total demand for money shows the total amount of money the public will want to hold for transactions and as an asset at each possible
(a) price level
(b) level of nominal GDP
(c) level of employment
(d) interest rate

14. The total demand for money would shift to the left as a result of
(a) an increase in the interest rate
(b) a decline in nominal GDP
(c) a decrease in the interest rate
(d) an increase in nominal GDP

15. The equilibrium rate of interest is determined by
(a) the demand for money to hold and the level of nominal GDP
(b) the transactions demand for money and the supply of money
(c) the total demand for money to hold and the supply of money
(d) the Bank of Canada

16. An increase in the rate of interest would increase
(a) the opportunity cost of holding money
(b) the transactions demand for money
(c) the asset demand for money
(d) the price of bonds

17. Suppose the transactions demand for money is equal to 10% of the nominal GDP, the supply of money is $45 billion, and the asset demand for money is that shown in the following table. If the nominal GDP is $300 billion, the equilibrium interest rate is
(a) 14%
(b) 13%
(c) 12%
(d) 11%

Interest Rate (%)	Asset Demand (billions)
14	$10
13	15
12	20
11	25

18. Using the information in question 17 above, if the nominal GDP remains constant, an increase in the money supply of $5 billion would cause the equilibrium interest rate to
(a) rise to 14%
(b) fall to 11%
(c) remain unchanged
(d) fall to 12%

19. Which one of the following points would be true?
(a) bond prices and the interest rates are directly related
(b) a lower interest rate shifts the aggregate demand curve to the left
(c) the supply of money is directly related to the interest rate
(d) bond prices and interest rates are inversely related

Answer the next two questions on the basis of the following information: bond prices = $10,000; bond fixed annual interest payment = $1000; bond annual rate of interest = 10%.

20. If the price of this bond decreases by $2500, the interest rate in effect will
(a) decrease by 1.1 percentage points
(b) decrease by 1.9 percentage points
(c) increase by 2.6 percentage points
(d) increase by 3.3 percentage points

21. If the price of this bond increases by $2000, the interest rate in effect will
(a) decrease by 1.7 percentage points
(b) decrease by 2.4 percentage points
(c) increase by 1.1 percentage points
(d) increase by 2.9 percentage points

22. When the Bank of Canada decides to buy government bonds, the demand for government bonds will
(a) decrease, bond prices will decrease, and the interest rate will decrease
(b) increase, bond prices will increase, and the interest rate will decrease
(c) increase, bond prices will increase, and the interest rate will increase
(d) decrease, bond prices will increase, and the interest rate will decrease

23. A change in the money supply has the least effect on the equilibrium GDP when
(a) both the demand-for-money and investment-demand curves are steep
(b) both the demand-for-money and investment-demand curves are flat
(c) the demand-for-money curve is flat and the investment-demand curve is steep
(d) the demand-for-money curve is steep and the investment-demand curve is flat

24. An expansionary monetary policy
(a) reduces the supply of money, increases the interest rate, reduces the level of investment, and reduces the equilibrium GDP
(b) increases the money supply, reduces the rate of interest, increases the level of investment, and reduces the equilibrium level of GDP
(c) reduces the money supply, reduces the rate of interest, increases the level of investment, and increases the level of equilibrium GDP
(d) increases the money supply, reduces the interest rate, increases the level of investment, and increases the equilibrium level of GDP.

25. An increase in the money supply is least effective in stimulating aggregate expenditures when the velocity of money
(a) falls as the money supply increases
(b) remains constant
(c) rises as the money supply increases
(d) is equal to 5

26. The Bank of Canada
(a) can stabilize both the interest rate and the money supply
(b) cannot stabilize the interest rate
(c) cannot stabilize the money supply
(d) cannot stabilize both the interest rate and the money supply

27. Which of the following are coordinated policies?
(a) an increase in government expenditures and in the money supply
(b) a decrease in personal tax rates and in the money supply
(c) an increase in transfer payments and a decrease in the money supply
(d) an increase in corporate tax rates and in the money supply

28. The transmission mechanism through which monetary policy affects aggregate demand is primarily through
(a) consumption spending
(b) investment spending
(c) government spending
(d) net exports

DISCUSSION QUESTIONS

1. Define monetary policy and state its basic objective.

2. Describe the five main functions of the Bank of Canada.

3. What are the principal assets and liabilities of the Bank of Canada? Which of these items seems most crucial in its effect on the levels of income, output, employment, and prices in the economy?

4. List the instruments of monetary control possessed by the central bank.

5. Explain how the open-market operations of the Bank of Canada would be used to contract the supply of money. How would they be used to expand the supply of money?

6. What is the difference between the effects of the central bank's buying (selling) government securities in the open market from (to) chartered banks and from (to) investment dealers?

7. Use a simplified balance sheet of the chartered banking system to explain the effect on reserves of switching government deposits between the central bank and the commercial banks.

8. Which of the monetary policy tools available to the Bank of Canada are more effective? Why are they more effective than other tools?

9. What are the two reasons that people wish to hold money? How are these two reasons related to the functions of money?

10. Explain the determinants of the two demands for money. Explain how a change in the size of these determinants will affect the amount of money people wish to hold.

11. Explain how the demand for money to hold and the supply of money determine the interest rate.

12. Describe the relationship between the changes in the interest rate and changes in the price of existing bonds.

13. Using the aggregate expenditure model theory and three graphs, explain what determines (a) the equilibrium interest rate; (b) planned investment; and

(c) the equilibrium GDP. Now employ these three graphs to show the effects of a decrease in the money supply upon the equilibrium GDP.

14. Utilizing your answers to the question above, (a) what determines how large the effect of the decrease in the money supply on the equilibrium GDP will be; and (b) how would the change in the equilibrium GDP affect the demand-for-money curve, the interest rate, planned investment, and the GDP itself?

15. How does a change in the money supply affect the aggregate demand curve? How will a change in the money supply and the resulting shift in the aggregate demand curve affect the real national output and the price level?

16. What are the strengths and shortcomings of monetary policy?

17. Why is monetary policy more effective in controlling inflation than in reducing unemployment?

18. What is the target (or policy) dilemma of the Bank of Canada? Suppose the nominal GDP in the Canadian economy is increasing or decreasing. Why is the Bank of Canada unable to keep both interest rates and the size of the money supply from changing?

19. Distinguish between fiscal and monetary policy and explain how we may use each of them to achieve reasonably full employment and relatively stable prices.

ANSWERS

Fill-in questions

1. full-employment, noninflationary; Bank of Canada

2. (a) hold the deposits of the chartered banks (b) supply the economy with paper currency (c) act as fiscal agent for the government (d) supervise the chartered banks (e) regulate the supply of money

3. Government of Canada securities, advances to the chartered banks

4. chartered bank deposits, Government of Canada deposits, notes in circulation

5. deposits, taxes, government bonds

6. open-market operations, the bank rate, Government of Canada deposits, moral suasion

7. money, interest

8. open-market operations, switching government deposits

9. bank rate, moral suasion

10. (a) directly, nominal GDP (b) inversely, rate of interest

11. (a) money; (b) investment-demand; (c) saving; (d) decrease, increase, increase

12. inverse

13. 10 million, 10 million, 9.5 million; 0, 10 million, 10 million

14. buy; sell

15. expansionary, buy, increasing, decreasing; increasing, increasing

16. decrease, decrease, increase, decrease; contractionary

17. steeper, flatter

18. demand , right; output, price level, shape

19. (a) flexible, political pressure, effective (b) inflation, recession, velocity, opposite, investment

20. unable, interest; (a) increase; (b) increase

21. investment spending

22. interest rate, money supply, inflation

23. fiscal, monetary

Problems and projects

1. Assets: securities, advances (loans) to banks; Liabilities: Bank of Canada notes, bank reserves (deposits), Government of Canada deposits

2. (a) buy,$5; (b) $5.25 (government deposits are not counted as part of the money supply);(c) 4%;(d) sell,$2.50;(e) 5.71%

3.

	(2)	(3)	(4)
Bank of Canada			
Assets:			
Securities	$20	$22	$21
Advances (loans) to chartered banks	0	0	0
Liabilities:			
Reserves of chartered banks	9	11	11
Government of Canada deposits	2	2	1
Bank of Canada notes	9	9	9
Chartered Banks			
Assets:			
Reserves	$ 9	$11	$11
Securities	20	19	20
Loans	170	170	170

3. (continued)

Liabilities:

	199	200	201
Deposits	199	200	201
Advances (loans) from Bank of Canada	0	0	0
A. Required reserves	9.95	10	10.05
B. Excess reserves	-0.95	1	0.95
C. How much has the money supply changed?	-1	0	1
D. How much more can the money supply change?	-19	+20	+19
E. What is the total of C and D?	-20	+20	+20

4. (a) (2) 8; (b) 20; (c) (2) 850; (d) (1) 6, (2) 30, (3) 900; (e) (1) 25, (2) 25, (3) 7, (4) 350; (f) (1) 0.20, 5; (2) increase, 5, increase, 25, (3) increase, 50

5. (a) 5; (b) increase, 500; (c) rise, 6; (d) increase, decrease, rise, fall

6. (a) 5; (b) 50; (c) 1750; (d) 387.50 (e) greater than, sell; (f) rise, fall, fall (g) 387.50; (h) interest rate, money supply

Self-test

1. F; 2. F; 3. T; 4. F; 5. T; 6. T; 7. T; 8. F; 9. T; 10. T; 11. T; 12. T; 13. F; 14. F; 15. T; 16. T; 17. F; 18. F; 19. F; 20. T, 21. T; 22. F; 23. T; 24. F; 25. T

Multiple-choice

1. (b); 2. (a); 3. (d); 4. (a); 5. (a); 6. (c); 7. (b); 8. (c); 9. (d); 10. (b); 11. (c); 12. (a); 13. (d); 14. (b); 15. (c); 16. (a); 17. (b); 18. (d); 19. (d); 20. (d); 21. (a); 22. (b); 23. (c); 24. (d); 25. (a); 26. (d); 27. (a); 28. (b)

CHAPTER

13 The Inflation–Unemployment Relationship: Short-Run Versus Long-run Analysis

The previous six chapters placed special emphasis on the aggregate expenditures model as providing a theoretical foundation for implementing specific policies to ensure a high level of output and employment. Moreover, when generalized into aggregate demand–aggregate supply, the model provided some explanations of rising prices. Beginning in the 1970s some occurrences in the macroeconomy were not readily explainable in terms of the aggregate expenditures model. A number of alternative macro models were then proposed as well as extensions and modifications to the aggregate expenditures model. This chapter provides a discussion of these alternative perspectives of macroeconomic theory and policy by examining the explanations for the simultaneous presence of unemployment and inflation in the Canadian economy. The mainstream views of the relationship between unemployment and inflation during the past three decades as embodied in the Phillips curve are contrasted with new classical economics, with its natural-rate hypothesis and the distinction made between the short-run and long-run aggregate supply curves. The chapter also presents other policy options for dealing with inflation and unemployment and introduces the perspective of supply-side economics.

In the early 1960s most economists believed that it was possible for the Canadian economy to have both full employment and stable prices. This belief was based on the assumption that the price level would not rise until the labour force was fully employed. All that was necessary for full employment without inflation was just the right level of aggregate expenditures. Fiscal and monetary policy could be used to assume that aggregate demand was adequate but not excessive.

But the assumption underlying this simplest aggregate expenditures model was not realistic. The price level can rise before full employment is achieved; and the closer the economy moves to full employment, the greater the rate at which prices rise. This observation became the basis for the concept of an inflation rate–unemployment rate trade-off and its menu of policy choices as described in the supposedly stable Phillips curve. According to the aggregate expenditures model, the reason for inflation before full employment and for the Phillips curve is because some types of labour become fully employed before other types of labour, and possibly also because businesses and unions possess significant market power with which to raise prices and wages.

While this apparent unemployment–inflation rate trade-off created a policy dilemma for economists of the 1960s, the situation and the problem became much more complicated in the 1970s and early 1980s. The problem was stagflation, with rising prices and rising unemployment rates. Stagflation of the period was explained by citing events that produced aggregate supply shocks, decreasing the aggregate supply curve and driving up the price level and reducing real output and employment. The leftward shift in the aggregate supply curve caused the Phillips curve to move to the right, hence the occurrence of both rising prices and unemployment. The events of the 1983-88 period shifted the aggregate supply curve rightward again and the Phillips curve to the left, so the proponents of the aggregate expenditures model claimed.

An alternative explanation of the events of the 1970s and 1980s came from the natural-rate hypothesis of new classical economics. The two variants of this hypothesis were those of adaptive expectations and rational expectations theorists. Both adaptive and rational expectations theorists contend that the downsloping Phillips curve is a figment of an overactive imagination; that it is actually a vertical line; and that government attempts to reduce the unemployment rate below the rate at which the vertical Phillips curve meets the horizontal axis to produce a higher rate of inflation. The major difference between the adaptive expectationists and rational expectationists is that the former believe that expansionary monetary or fiscal policies can bring about a temporary decline in the unemployment rate; the latter argue that such policies do not even reduce unemployment temporarily, and any short-term instability in the macroeconomy is a product of price-level surprises.

New classical economists also distinguish between a short-run and a long-run aggregate supply curve. In the short run, nominal wages are fixed so an increase in the price level increases business profits and real output. In the long run, nominal wages are flexible so business profits and employment return to their original level, making the long-run aggregate supply curve vertical at the potential level of real output. Supporters of the aggregate expenditures model question the speed of these adjustments because of the downward inflexibility of wages and prices and hold that there are opportunities for the use of stabilization policies to reduce the high cost of unemployment or inflation.

The distinction between the short-run and long-run aggregate supply curves requires a reinterpretation of demand-pull and cost-push inflation. Although demand-pull inflation will increase the price level and real output in the short run, once nominal wages increase, the temporary increase in output will be gone; but the price level will be higher at the potential level of output for the economy. Cost-push inflation will increase the price level and decrease real output in the short-run; but again, once nominal wages fall, output and the price level will return to the original level. If policy makers try to counter cost-push inflation by increasing aggregate demand, they may make matters worse by increasing the price level and causing the short-run aggregate supply curve to decrease again.

Other solutions for stagflation have been sought by Canada and other mixed market economies. Discussed in the chapter are market policies and wage–price policies that were used in the 1960s and 1970s to correct aspects of the unemployment and inflation problem. Of more recent appeal, however, was supply-side economics, that gained visibility in the United States during the Reagan administration (1981-89). Supply-side economists pointed to the role of the federal government in causing the slump in productivity and economic growth in the economy during the 1970s. The solutions, which became the program of Reaganomics, were to come from massive reduction in personal and corporate income taxes, reduced government regulation, cuts in social and welfare spending by government, and control over the rate of growth of the money supply. The Laffer curve provided a foundation to the claim that reduced government taxes would not lead to government deficits. Supply-side economics have been criticized for the failure of the large cuts in the tax rates to increase significantly the aggregate supply curve beyond its historical level. The massive levels of government debt accumulated and the stubborn recession, which began in 1989, cast some doubt on the efficacy of supply-side policies.

CHECKLIST

When you have studied this chapter, you should be able to:

■ Explain how the aggregate expenditures model predicted that the economy could achieve both full employment and stable prices; and what was needed to reach these two goals simultaneously.

■ Draw a traditional Phillips curve (after properly labelling the two axes); and explain how to derive this curve by using the aggregate demand–aggregate supply model.

■ State the two basic causes of the inflation shown on the Phillips curve.

■ Explain and use the Phillips curve to illustrate the stabilization policy dilemma.

■ Define stagflation and contrast stagflation with the relationship shown by a Phillips curve.

■ Enumerate the supply-side shocks experienced by the Canadian economy in the 1970s and early 1980s; and use the aggregate demand–aggregate supply model to explain why these shocks led to stagflation.

■ List the events that contributed to stagflation's demise during the 1983-88 period.

■ Describe the Phillips curve from the viewpoint of the aggregate demand–aggregate supply model for the period 1960-88.

■ Explain the natural-rate hypothesis and the two variants of this hypothesis—adaptive expectations and rational expectations.

■ Use the adaptive expectations model to explain the process of inflation and disinflation in the economy.

■ Compare and contrast how adaptive expectations and rational expectations theorists view the Phillips curve.

■ Distinguish the short-run from the long-run aggregate supply curve.

■ Explain the role of stabilization policy if the aggregate supply curve is vertical in the long run.

■ Apply the distinction between the short-run and long-run aggregate supply curve to explain demand-pull and cost-push inflation.

■ State the two kinds of market policies that might be used to combat stagflation.

■ Distinguish between wage–price guideposts and

wage–price controls; explain why they are called income policies.

■ Explain what the advocates of supply-side economics see as the basic causes of stagflation and the policies they would implement to overcome this economic difficulty.

■ Using the Laffer curve explain how tax cuts can be used to overcome the inflation and unemployment problems connected with stagflation.

CHAPTER OUTLINE

1. In the aggregate expenditures model the assumption is made that the aggregate supply curve is horizontal up to the full employment level of output.Increases in expenditure result in increased output up to that point with prices remaining constant. Once the full employment output is reached any further increases in aggregate expenditure result in rising prices.

(a) With this basic model, the economy may realize either unemployment or inflation, but not both problems simultaneously. The stagflation episodes of the 1970s showed this conclusion to be incorrect.

(b) The model can be revised to account for the events of the 1970s by expanding the model into an aggregate demand–aggregate supply model with an upsloping aggregate supply curve and allowing the aggregate supply curve to shift left.

2. If aggregate supply is upsloping, the greater the rate of increase in aggregate demand the greater is the rate of increase in the price level and in real output, and the lower is the rate of unemployment (and vice versa). There is, therefore, an inverse relationship (or trade-off) called the Phillips curve between the inflation rate and the unemployment rate.

(a) There are at least two reasons why inflation occurs before the economy reaches full employment.

(1) Scarcities of some kinds of labour develop before the economy's entire labour force is fully employed; these scarcities increase wage rates, production costs, and prices.

(2) Labour unions and business firms have market power and they raise wage rates and prices as the economy approaches full employment.

(b) While fiscal and monetary policy can be employed to manage aggregate demand and to affect unemployment and the rate of inflation, the nation faces a serious policy dilemma: full employment without inflation and price stability without unemployment are impossible and the nation must choose one of the combinations of inflation and unemployment that lies on the Phillips curve.

(c) Events in the 1960s seem to confirm the inverse relationship between the unemployment and inflation rates.

3. Events of the 1970s and 1980s, however, called into question the stability of the Phillips curve.

(a) In the 1970s and early 1980s the Canadian economy experienced both higher rates of inflation and greater unemployment rates; and this stagflation suggests either that there is no dependable relationship between the inflation and unemployment rates or that the Phillips curve had shifted to the right. This latter occurrence could be explained by a movement to the left of the aggregate supply curve.

(1) During these years six cost or supply-side shocks decreased aggregate supply (moved the aggregate supply curve left) to increase both prices and unemployment in Canada; and the experiences of the Canadian economy suggest that the Phillips curve is not a stable relationship and cannot be used as the basis for economic policy.

(2) The demise of stagflation came in the 1983-88 period because of a variety of factors; but unemployment and inflation moved in the same direction at times, not in the opposite direction implied by the Phillips curve of the 1960s.

(b) The followers of the aggregate demand–aggregate supply model believe that a trade-off between unemployment and inflation does exist. The explanation for the data problems were the supply shocks that produced a rightward shift in the Phillips curve during the 1971-82 period, and changes in the economy that produced a leftward shift during the 1983-88 period.

4. The natural-rate hypothesis questions the existence of a trade-off between inflation and unemployment as indicated by a downsloping Phillips curve and views the economy as stable in the long run at the natural rate of unemployment. The two variants to this hypothesis follow.

(a) The theory of adaptive expectations suggests that an increase in aggregate demand sponsored by government may temporarily reduce unemployment as the price level increases and profits expand; but the actions also set into motion other events.

(1) The increase in the price level reduces the real wages of workers who demand and obtain higher nominal wages. These actions return unemployment to its original level.

(2) Back at the original level, there is now a higher actual and expected rate of inflation for the economy, so the short-run Phillips curve has shifted upward.

(3) The process is repeated when government tries again to reduce unemployment and the rise in the price level

accelerates as the short-run Phillips curve shifts upward. Expansionary policies generate accelerating inflation rather than lower unemployment.

(4) In the long run, the Phillips curve is stable only as a vertical line at the natural rate of unemployment. There is no trade-off between unemployment and inflation.

(b) Rational expectations theory assumes that workers fully anticipate that government policies to reduce unemployment will also be inflationary, and they increase their nominal wage demands to offset the expected inflation. Thus, there will not even be a temporary decline in unemployment, or a short-run Phillips curve.

5. The aggregate supply curve has short-and long-run characteristics and implications for policy.

(a) In the short run, where nominal wages are fixed, the aggregate supply curve is upward sloping: an increase in the price level will increase profits and cause a rise in real output; in contrast, when the price level decreases, profits are reduced and so is real output.

(b) In the long run, where nominal wages are variable, the aggregate supply curve is vertical at the potential level of output: increases in the price level will increase nominal wages and cause a shift to the left in the short-run aggregate supply curve; or declines in the price level reduce nominal wages and shift the short-run aggregate supply curve to the right. But in either case, although the price level changes, output returns to its potential level, so the long-run aggregate supply curve is vertical.

(c) Proponents of new classical economics subscribe to the view that with flexible nominal wages the economy is basically stable at the full-employment level of output in the long run, and thus there is no need for policy actions; recessionary and inflationary gaps will be eliminated by the economy's self-correcting mechanism. Advocates of the generalized aggregate expenditures model contend that nominal wages may be slow to adjust to price level changes and support the use of stabilization policies to reduce unemployment or inflation costs to the economy.

6. Knowledge of the short- and long-run features of aggregate demand and supply provide insights into these types of inflation.

(a) Demand-pull inflation will shift the short-run aggregate demand curve, which increases the price level and causes a temporary increase in real output. But in the long run, nominal wages will increase and the short-run aggregate supply will shift to the left, resulting in an even higher price level with real output returning to its previous level.

(b) Cost-push inflation will shift the short-run aggregate supply curve left.

(1) This action increases the price level and temporarily decreases real output.

(2) The resulting recession will reduce nominal wages shifting the short-run aggregate supply to its original position.

(3) But if government takes actions to counter the cost-push inflation and recession by shifting aggregate demand, the price level will move to an even higher level.

(c) The aggregate supply curve is vertical in the long run.

7. Because of the ineffectiveness of demand-management policies in coping with stagflation, the Canadian policy makers have sought other kinds of policies to prevent decreases in or to increase aggregate supply (to shift the Phillips curve to the left).

(a) Market policies try to eliminate the causes of premature inflation and include:

(1) manpower policies to reduce the scarcities of particular kinds of labour that occur before the labour force is fully employed; and

(2) pro-competition policies to reduce the power of labour unions and business firms to raise wage rates and prices.

(b) Wage–price (or incomes) policies restrict increases in wages and prices by utilizing either guideposts or controls.

(1) Wage–price guideposts are voluntary restraints.

(2) Wage–price controls are mandatory (or legal) restraints that were employed in 1975 to deal with stagflation in the Canadian economy.

(3) Whether to employ wage–price policies has been a vigorously debated issue; the proponents and opponents have based their arguments on the questions of workability and compliance, allocative efficiency, and economic freedom of choice.

(c) Supply-side economists argue that the aggregate expenditure theorists have overemphasized the aggregate demand side and neglected the aggregate supply side in their explanation of the price level and unemployment.

(1) Taxes, they argue, are business costs and increased taxes result in an upward shift in aggregate supply. Reduced taxes, according to the economist, Arthur Laffer, can result in larger tax revenues.

(2) They also argue that taxes and transfer payments reduce the incentives to work, to save, and to invest, and lead to a misallocation of resources, which reduces aggregate supply.

(3) They argue that the increased regulation of industry has adversely affected costs and productivity.

8. From the Canadian economic experiences of the last

two decades have emerged three lessons.
(a)   Macroeconomic instability in the Canadian economy is more and more related to events outside Canada.
(b)   Expectations of inflation lead to inflation and make inflation difficult to control.
(c)   Both aggregate demand and aggregate supply affect output, employment, and the price level of an economy; and both demand-side and supply-side policies have limitations and effects on the other side of a market economy.

IMPORTANT TERMS

adaptive expectations theory
cost-push inflation
demand-pull inflation
incomes policies
inflationary expectations
long-run aggregate supply curve
market policies
natural-rate hypothesis
Phillips curve
rational expectations theory
short-run aggregate supply curve
stagflation
supply shocks
supply-side economics
tax-transfer disincentives
tax wedge
wage–price controls

FILL-IN QUESTIONS

1.   In the simplified aggregate expenditures model the price level of the economy would not increase until the economy reached _____ _____ and inflation was the result of (excess, insufficient) _____ aggregate demand; and the economy can have (either, both) _____ unemployment or/and inflation.

2.   In the aggregate demand–aggregate supply model, when the economy is producing in the upsloping range along the aggregate supply curve,
(a)   an increase in aggregate demand will (increase, decrease) _____ real output and employ-ment and result in _____-_____ inflation;

(b)   a decrease in aggregate supply will _____ real output and employment and result in _____-_____ inflation.

3.   If the aggregate supply curve is upward sloping (and stable):
(a)   the greater the increase in aggregate demand, the (greater, smaller) _____ will be the increase in the price level, the _____ will be the increase in real output, and the _____ will be the unemployment rate; and

(b)   there will be a(n) (direct, inverse) _____ relationship between the rate of inflation and the unemployment rate.

4.   The Phillips curve
(a)   is the relation between the annual rate of increase in the _____ _____ and the _____ rate; and

(b)   has a (positive, negative) _____ slope.

5.   The presence of inflation in the economy before full employment is reached can be explained by 1) _____ _____ imbalances and 2) market power possessed by _____ and _____ _____.

6.   The policy dilemma faced by the Canadian economy is that
(a)   to have full employment it must also have _____, and to have stable prices it must tolerate _____;
(b)   to reduce the unemployment rate the rate of inflation must (increase, decrease) _____; and to reduce the rate of inflation the unemployment rate must _____.

7.   Demand-management policies can be used to (shift the Phillips curve, select a point on the Phillips curve) _____. It is impossible to achieve full employment without _____.

8.   Stagflation refers to a condition of rising _____ and _____ _____.

9. In the 1970s and early 1980s stagflation was caused by a series of _____ _____ .
List the five factors that shifted the aggregate supply curve to the left:

(a) _____

(b) _____

(c) _____

(d) _____

(e) _____

10. The expectation of inflation by workers and employers leads to (higher, lower) _____ wage rates and in turn to a (rise, fall) _____ in production costs, to a(n) (increase, decrease) _____ in aggregate supply, to a (higher, lower) _____ price level, and to a _____ rate of unemployment in the economy.

11. The rising unemployment rates and the sharp inflation following the supply-side shocks can be understood by using the aggregate demand–aggregate supply model.

(a) The shocks (increased, decreased) _____ aggregate supply;

(b) which in turn increased both the _____ level and the _____ rate;

(c) and these two events when they occur simultaneously are called _____ .

12. The result of the supply shocks, according to the aggregate expenditures model defenders, was a movement to the _____ of the Phillips curve.

13. List four factors that contributed to stagflation's demise during the 1983-88 period:

(a) _____

(b) _____

(c) _____

(d) _____

14. There is much debate among economists about the Phillips curve.
(a) The expenditures model advocates contend that during the stagflation of the 1970s, the Phillips curve

shifted (right, left) _____; during the demise of stagflation from 1983-88, the Phillips curve shifted _____ .
(b) Other economists associated with new classical thinking conclude that the downsloping Phillips curve does not _____ in the long run and subscribe to the _____-_____ hypothesis, for which there are two variants — _____ and _____ expectations.
(c) The theory of adaptive expectations suggests that people form their expectations of _____ based on experience and (immediately, gradually) _____ change expectations over time.
With this theory:
(1) the (short-run, long-run) _____ Phillips curve may be downsloping, but the _____ Phillips curve is vertical at the _____;
(2) attempts by government to reduce the unemployment rate bring about a rate of inflation that (increases, decreases) _____ .
(d) The rational expectations theory suggests that
(1) attempts by government to reduce the unemployment rate lead workers to anticipate perfectly the amount of _____ this will cause and to keep their (real, nominal) _____ wages constant to obtain a(n) (increase, decrease) _____ in their _____ wages; and
(2) this brings about (a rise, a fall, no change) _____ in the price level and _____ in the unemployment rate.

15. With the aggregate supply curve:
(a) in the short run, the curve is (upsloping, vertical) _____ and in the long run the curve is _____;
(b) in the short run, nominal wages are (fixed, variable) _____, and in the long run, nominal wages are _____ .
(c) Proponents of new classical economics think that wages and prices are (flexible, inflexible) _____ and that the economy is (stable, unstable) _____

in the long-run at the full-employment level of real output; policy changes by government (will, will not) _____ be anticipated in advance and influence the economy in the short term; in the long run, demand management policies (can, cannot) _____ influence real output and employment but only the _____ _____; only _____ surprises produce temporary changes in real output.

(d)   Modern aggregate expenditure followers accept the distinction between short- and long-run aggregate supply, but contend that wages and prices are (flexible, inflexible) _____ downward, and therefore they advocate (an active, hands-off) _____ policy by government in the short run to reduce the (low, high) _____ cost of inflation and unemployment.

16.   The difference between the shape of the short- and long-run Phillips curve is related to the _____ of the aggregate supply curve. In the short run input prices, especially nominal wages, remain _____ and an increase in prices results in increased real output. The aggregate supply curve is _____ sloping. With a price increase in the long-run, nominal wages _____ as workers seek to recover the loss in real wages, the short-run aggregate supply curve shifts _____, and the level of output _____. The long-run aggregate supply is _____.

17.   If the long-run aggregate supply curve is vertical, the economy would possess a _____-_____ mechanism. The presence of an inflationary gap would exert an _____ pressure on input prices and the short-run aggregate supply curve would shift _____ until the inflationary gap was eliminated. A deflationary gap would lead to a _____ in input prices, a shift to the _____ of aggregate supply, and a move toward the natural rate of _____.

18.   Demand-pull inflation will shift the (short-run, long-run) _____ aggregate demand curve (right, left) _____, which will (decrease, increase) _____ the price level and temporarily _____ real output. As a consequence, the (short-run, long-run) _____ aggregate supply curve will shift left because of a rise in (real, nominal) _____ wages, producing a (lower, higher) _____ price level at the original level of real output.

19.   Cost-push inflation will shift the short-run aggregate supply curve (right, left) _____, thus the price level will (increase, decrease) _____ and real output will temporarily _____. If government takes no actions to counter the cost-push inflation, the resulting recession will _____ nominal wages, and shift the short-run aggregate supply curve back to its original position. Yet, if the government tries to counter the cost-push inflation and recession with an _____ in aggregate demand, the price level will move even higher.

20.   Three kinds of economic policies might be used to deal with stagflation.

(a)   These three policies are _____ policies, _____ policies, and the policies identified with _____ economics.

(b)   If effective, these policies would move the Phillips curve to the (right, left) _____.

21.   Market policies to reduce unemployment include:
(a)   those designed to reduce bottlenecks in labour markets, which are called _____ policies; and
(b)   those aimed at reducing the market power of business firms and labour unions, which are called pro-_____policies.

22.   Wage–price policies

(a)   are sometimes called _____ policies;
(b)   involve either

(1) wage–price (controls, guideposts) _____, which rely upon the voluntary cooperation of labour unions and business firms;

(2) or wage–price _____, which have the force of law to make them effective.

23. It is the view of supply-side economists that
(a) business costs and product prices have increased because
(1) government has raised taxes and these taxes are a

business _____ and a "_____" between the price of a product and the cost of resources;

(2) high marginal tax rates reduce _____ to work, save, invest, and take risks; and

(3) increased government _____ of industry has decreased its productivity;
(b) the remedy for stagflation is a substantial (increase,

decrease) _____ in taxes.

24. The Laffer curve depicts the relationship between

tax rates and _____ _____. In theory, as the tax rates increase from 0%, tax revenues

will (increase, decrease) _____ to some maximum level, after which tax revenues will

_____ as the tax rates increase; or, as tax rates are reduced from 100%, tax revenues will

_____ to some maximum level, after

which tax revenues will _____ as tax revenues decrease.

25. The main supply-side proposition was that the cut in tax rates would significantly shift the (aggregate

demand, aggregate supply) _____ curve

(leftward, rightward) _____ and make the economy grow at a pace greater than historical experience.

The evidence to date (does, does not) _____ appear to support that proposition.

PROBLEMS AND PROJECTS

1. Following is a traditional Phillips curve.
(a) At full employment (a 4% unemployment rate),

the price level would rise by _____ % each year.
(b) If the price level were stable (increasing by 0% a

year), the unemployment rate would be _____ %.

(c) Which of the combinations along the Phillips curve would you choose for the economy? Why would you

select this combination? _____

_____

2. In columns (1) and (2) of the table on page 163 is a portion of an aggregate supply schedule. Column (3) shows the number of full-time workers (in millions) that would have to be employed to produce each of the seven real domestic outputs (in billions) in the aggregate supply schedule. The labour force is 80 million workers, and the

full-employment output of the economy is $_____.
(a) If the aggregate demand schedule were that shown by columns (1) and (4),

(1) the price level would be $_____ and

the real output would be $_____;
(2) the number of workers employed would be

_____, the number of workers unem-

ployed would be _____, and the unem-

ployment rate would be _____ %.
(b) If aggregate demand were to increase to that shown in columns (1) and (5) and aggregate supply remained constant,

(1) the price level would rise to $_____

and the real output would rise to $_____;

(1) Price Level	(2) Real Output Produced	(3) Employment	(4) Real Output Purchased	(5) Real Output Purchased	(6) Real Output Purchased
$3	$ 800	69	$2,300	$2,600	$1,900
4	1,300	70	2,200	2,500	1,800
5	1,700	72	2,100	2,400	1,700
6	2,000	75	2,000	2,300	1,600
7	2,200	78	1,900	2,200	1,500
8	2,300	80	1,800	2,100	1,400
9	2,300	80	1,700	2,000	1,300

(2) employment would increase by _____ workers and the unemployment rate would fall to

_____ % ;

(3) the price level has increased by _____ %.

(c) If aggregate demand were to decrease to that shown in columns (1) and (6) and aggregate supply remained constant,

(1) the price level would fall to $_____

and the real output would fall to $_____ ;

(2) employment would decrease by _____ workers and the unemployment rate would rise to

_____ % ;

(3) the price level has decreased and the rate of inflation has been (positive, negative) _____ .

3. Below is an adaptive expectations model of the short- and long-run Phillips curve.

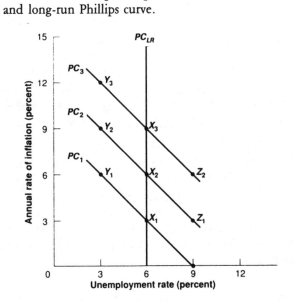

(a) Suppose you begin at point X_1; then an assumption is made that nominal wages are set on the original expectation that a 3% rate of inflation will continue in the economy.

(1) If government invokes expansionary monetary and fiscal policy to reduce the unemployment rate from 6% to 3%, then the actual rate of inflation will move to

_____ %. The higher product prices will lift profits of firms and they will hire more workers; thus in the short run the economy will temporarily move to

point _____ .

(2) If workers then demand and receive higher wages to compensate for the loss of purchasing power from higher than expected inflation, then business profits will fall from previous levels and firms will reduce employment. Therefore, employment will move from point

_____ to point _____ on the graph. The short-run Phillips curve has shifted from

_____ to _____ on the graph.

(3) If the government again tries to stimulate aggregate demand with monetary and fiscal policy to reduce the unemployment rate from 6% to 3%, then prices will rise before nominal wages, and output and employment will

increase, so there will be a move from point _____

to point _____ on the graph.

(4) But when workers get nominal wage increases, profits fall, and employment moves from point _____

at _____ % to point _____

at _____ %. The short-run Phillips curve

has now shifted from _____ to _____ on the graph.

(5) The long-run Phillips curve is the line _____ .

(b) Suppose you begin at point X_3, where the expected and actual rate of inflation is 9% and the unemployment rate is 6%.
(1) If there should be a decline in aggregate demand because of a recession and if the actual rate of inflation should fall to 6%, well below the expected rate of 9%, then business profits will fall and the unemployment rate will decrease to 9% as shown by the movement from point X_3 to point _____.
(2) If firms and workers adjust their expectation to the 6% rate of inflation, then nominal wages will fall, profits will rise, and the economy will move from point _____ to point _____. The short-run Phillips curve has shifted from _____ to _____.
(3) If this process is repeated, the long-run Phillips curve will be traced as line _____.

4. Below is an aggregate demand and aggregate supply model. Assume that the economy is initially in equilibrium at AD_1 and AS_1. The price level will be _____ and the real domestic output will be _____.

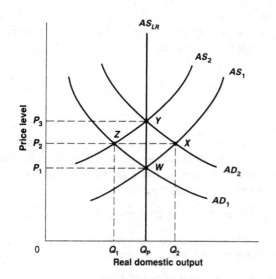

(a) If there is demand-pull inflation, then:
(1) in the short run, the new equilibrium is at point _____, with the price level at _____ and real output at _____;
(2) in the long run, nominal wages will rise so the aggregate supply curve will shift from _____

to _____. The equilibrium will be at point _____ with the price level at _____ and real output at _____; and so the increase in aggregate demand has only moved the economy along its _____ curve.
(b) Now assume that the economy is initially in equilibrium at point W, where AD_1 and AS_1 intersect. If there is cost-push inflation, then:
(1) in the short run, the new equilibrium is at point _____, with the price level at _____ and real output at _____.
(2) If the government tries to counter the cost-push inflation with expansionary monetary and fiscal policy, then aggregate demand will shift from _____ to _____, with the price level becoming _____ and real output _____. But this policy has a trap because the price level has shifted from _____ to _____ and the new level of inflation might shift _____ leftward.
(3) If government does not counter the cost-push inflation, the price level will eventually move to _____ and real output to _____ as the recession reduces nominal wages and shifts the aggregate supply curve from _____ to _____.

SELF-TEST

Circle the T if the statement is true, the F if it is false.
1. In the simplest aggregate expenditures model the aggregate supply curve was horizontal at the prevailing price level until full employment was reached.   **T F**

2. The simplest aggregate expenditures model predicted that the economy could suffer high unemployment and inflation simultaneously.   **T F**

3. The aggregate expenditures model provided a reasonably satisfactory explanation of the macroeconomic behaviour of the Canadian economy between 1930 and 1970, but does not explain the stagflation of the 1970s and early 1980s.   **T F**

4. When aggregate supply is constant, higher rates of inflation are accompanied by higher rates of unemployment.   **T F**

5. According to the conventional Phillips curve the rate of inflation increases as the level of unemployment decreases. **T F**

6. Labour market imbalances and market power are explanations offered to explain the trade-off between unemployment and inflation. **T F**

7. Policies to manage aggregate supply can be used to choose a point on the Phillips curve, but these policies do not improve the "unemployment rate–inflation rate" trade-off reflected in the Phillips curve. **T F**

8. Stagflation refers to a situation in which both the price level and the unemployment rate are rising. **T F**

9. Data points for the whole period 1959-1991 suggest no relation between unemployment and rates of inflation in Canada. **T F**

10. Defenders of the aggregate expenditures model contend that the Phillips curve shifted left during the 1973-82 period and shifted right during the 1983-88 period. **T F**

11. One explanation of stagflation of the 1970s and early 1980s is that it was due to a series of demand shocks over this time period. **T F**

12. Both inflationary expectations and increasing labour productivity shift the aggregate supply curve leftward and cause stagflation. **T F**

13. Expectations of inflation induce workers to demand a higher money wage and their employers to pay them higher wages. **T F**

14. When the nominal wage rate increases at a rate greater than the rate at which the productivity of labour increases, unit labour costs will rise and the aggregate supply curve shifts to the right. **T F**

15. If the nominal wage rate increases by 8 % and the productivity of labour remains constant, unit labour costs will rise. **T F**

16. During the 1983-1989 period unemployment and inflation moved in the direction implied by the Phillips curve. **T F**

17. The natural-rate hypothesis suggests that there is a natural rate of inflation for the economy. **T F**

18. According to the natural-rate hypothesis the economy's natural rate of unemployment can only be achieved with a zero rate of unemployment. **T F**

19. The theory of adaptive expectations indicates that there may be a short-run trade-off between inflation and unemployment, but no long-run trade-off. **T F**

20. From the adaptive expectations perspective, when the actual rate of inflation is higher than expected, the unemployment rate will rise. **T F**

21. According to rational expectations theory economic agents understand how government policies affect the economy and anticipate these impacts in their decision making. **T F**

22. The theory of rational expectations maintains that if workers believe expansionary monetary and fiscal policies will be inflationary and therefore lower their real wages, then the reaction of the workers to these expectations results in higher nominal wages, higher labour costs, and no change in employment in the economy. **T F**

23. Natural-rate theorists conclude that demand-management policies cannot influence real output and employment in the long run, but only the price level. **T F**

24. The long-run aggregate supply curve is, according to rational expectations theory, upsloping at the prevailing price level. **T F**

25. New classical economists hold that price level surprises produce short-run fluctuations in the economy, but in the long run the economy is stable at the full-employment level of output. **T F**

26. The natural-rate hypothesis concludes that, in the long run, demand-management policies cannot influence the price level but can influence the level of real output and employment. **T F**

27. In the short run, the aggregate supply curve is upward sloping because nominal wages are considered variable and rise as prices rise. **T F**

28. The long-run supply curve is vertical at that level of output corresponding to the natural rate of unemployment. **T F**

29. Demand-pull inflation will increase the price level and real output in the short run; but, in the long run, only the price level will increase. **T F**

30. There are two sources of cost-push inflation: increases in nominal wages and increases in taxes. **T F**

31. An inflationary spiral is likely to result from the use of stabilization policies to maintain full employment when the economy is experiencing cost-push inflation. **T F**

32. Of the policies that might be employed to deal with stagflation, the market, wage-price, and supply-side policies are designed to move the Phillips curve to the left.   **T F**

33. Supply-side economists assert that changes in employment, output, and prices can arise on the cost and aggregate supply side.   **T F**

34. The tax "wedge" to which supply-side economists refer is the difference between the price of a product and the cost of economic resources required to produce it.   **T F**

35. If the economy were at point A on the Laffer curve shown below, a decrease in tax rates would increase tax revenues.   **T F**

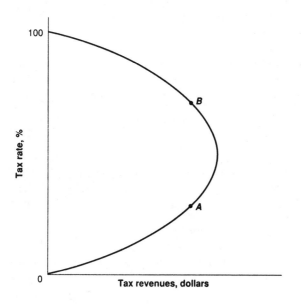

36. The supply-side economists believe that the economy is at a point such as point B on the Laffer curve above, and that a substantial reduction in tax rates would both increase tax revenues and increase incentives to work, invest, innovate, and take risks.   **T F**

MULTIPLE-CHOICE

Circle the letter that corresponds to the best answer.

1. In the aggregate expenditures model it is impossible for the economy to experience
(a) full employment
(b) inflation
(c) unemployment and inflation
(d) full employment and stable prices

2. As long as aggregate supply remains constant and the economy operates along the upward sloping portion of the aggregate supply curve, the greater the increase in aggregate demand,
(a) the greater is the increase in the price level
(b) the greater is the increase in the unemployment rate
(c) the smaller is the increase in real output
(d) the smaller is the increase in employment

3. The conventional Phillips curve
(a) shows the inverse relation between the rate of increase in the price level and the unemployment rate
(b) makes it possible for the economy to achieve full employment and stable prices
(c) indicates that prices do not rise until full employment has been achieved
(d) slopes upward from left to right

4. Labour market adjustments do not eliminate bottleneck problems when there is less than full employment in the economy. Which of the following is not one of the reasons for these labour market imbalances?
(a) Unemployed workers often lack the skills or training needed for a new occupation.
(b) The demand for workers in the markets in which there are labour shortages is inadequate.
(c) There are artificial restrictions that prevent unemployed workers from filling the job openings.
(d) Unemployed workers do not know of the shortages of workers in other labour markets in the economy.

5. If inflation during periods of less than full employment is to be explained by market power, it must be assumed that
(a) only unions possess considerable market power
(b) only employers possess considerable market power
(c) both unions and employers possess considerable market power
(d) neither unions nor employers possess considerable market power

6. The stabilization policy dilemma illustrated by a Phillips curve is the mutual inconsistency of
(a) more employment and price stability
(b) a higher unemployment rate and price stability
(c) inflation and more employment
(d) inflation and a lower unemployment rate

7. Demand-management (monetary and fiscal) policies can be employed to
(a) shift the Phillips curve to the right
(b) shift the Phillips curve to the left
(c) achieve full employment without inflation
(d) choose a point on the Phillips curve

8. Stagflation is characterized by
(a) rising inflation and rising government deficits
(b) rising unemployment and rising government deficits
(c) rising taxes and rising government deficits
(d) rising inflation and rising unemployment

9. Which of the following was one of the supply-side shocks to the Canadian economy during the 1970s and early 1980s?
(a) the imposition of wage and price controls
(b) the appreciation of the dollar
(c) the fall in the price charged by OPEC nations for oil
(d) worldwide agricultural shortfalls

10. If the percentage change in the productivity of labour is 2% and the percentage change in nominal-wage rates is 5%, the percentage change in unit labour costs is
(a) 1%
(b) 3%
(c) 7%
(d) 10%

11. Supply shocks that cause a leftward shift in the aggregate supply curve, aggregate demand remaining constant, will
(a) decrease the price level
(b) decrease the unemployment rate
(c) increase real output
(d) increase both the price level and the unemployment rate

12. Which one of the following would be a factor contributing to the demise of stagflation during the 1983-88 period?
(a) a lessening of foreign competition
(b) a strengthening of the monopoly power of OPEC
(c) a recession brought on largely by a tight monetary policy
(d) an increase in regulation of airline and trucking industries

13. According to the aggregate demand–aggregate supply model, the collapse of the traditional inflation rate-unemployment rate trade-off and the likely shift in the Phillips curve during the later 1980s was the consequence of a
(a) rightward shift in aggregate demand
(b) rightward shift in aggregate supply
(c) leftward shift in aggregate demand
(d) leftward shift in aggregate supply

14. The natural-rate hypothesis suggests that the economy is stable only in the
(a) short run at the natural rate of unemployment
(b) short run at the natural rate of inflation
(c) long run at the natural rate of unemployment
(d) long run at the natural rate of inflation

15. According to the natural-rate hypothesis
(a) the inflation rate is 0 at the natural rate of unemployment
(b) any rate of inflation is compatible with the natural rate of unemployment
(c) a stable Phillips curve does exist, which indicates the long-run trade-off between inflation and unemployment
(d) the long-run Phillips curve is horizontal

16. The theory of adaptive expectations suggests that if increases in nominal wage rates lag behind increases in the price level, and government attempts to reduce unemployment by using fiscal and monetary policies, then employment
(a) and the price level increase in the long run
(b) remains constant and the price level increases in the short run
(c) increases and the price level remains constant in the short run
(d) remains constant and the price level increases in the long run

17. The rational expectations theorists contend that when government attempts to reduce unemployment by using monetary and fiscal policies, unemployment decreases
(a) temporarily and the price level rises
(b) permanently and the price level rises
(c) both temporarily and permanently and the price level rises
(d) neither temporarily nor permanently and the price level rises

18. In the view of natural-rate theorists, the long-run Phillips curve is
(a) horizontal
(b) vertical
(c) upsloping
(d) downsloping

19. Disinflation, or reductions in the rate of inflation, can be explained based on the natural-rate conclusion that when the
(a) actual rate of inflation is lower than the expected rate, the unemployment rate will rise to bring the expected and actual rates into balance
(b) expected rate of inflation is lower than the actual rate, the unemployment rate will rise to bring the expected and actual rates into balance

(c) actual rate of inflation is higher than the expected rate, the unemployment rate will fall to bring the expected and actual rates into balance
(d) expected rate of inflation is higher than the actual rate, the unemployment rate will fall to bring the expected and actual rates into balance

20. The natural-rate theory suggests that the aggregate supply curve
(a) is stable in the short run so long as nominal wages do not increase in the short run in response to the increase in the price level
(b) is unstable in the long run because real wages are continually changing
(c) will shift to the right when the price of capital increases
(d) will shift to the right when nominal wages increase

21. According to new classical thinking, fully anticipated changes in the price level do not change
(a) the level of real output
(b) the level of prices
(c) the inflexibility of wages and prices
(d) the effectiveness of stabilization policy

22. The long-run aggregate supply curve differs from the short-run aggregate supply in that
(a) in the short run an increase in nominal wages causes the aggregate supply to shift to the right, while the aggregate supply is fixed in the long run
(b) in the short run an increase in prices shifts the aggregate supply to the right, while in the long run the aggregate supply will shift to the left
(c) in the short run input prices tend to be fixed so a price increase causes a movement along the aggregate supply;in the long run all prices, including wages, are variable, so a price increase results in a shift to the left of the short-run aggregate supply curve so that the long-run supply is vertical
(d) the short-run aggregate supply curve is horizontal at the prevailing price level, while the long-run aggregate supply is vertical at the rate of output corresponding to the natural rate of unemployment.

23. If the aggregate supply curve is vertical at the full employment rate of output,
(a) demand management policies will not affect the level of output in the short run
(b) there will be no structural unemployment in the long run
(c) inflationary and recessionary gaps will resolve themselves in the long run
(d) there can only be one price level at which full employment is reached

24. In the short run, demand-pull inflation
(a) is caused by a downward shift in the Phillips curve
(b) is the result of a decrease in aggregate demand
(c) produces an increase in real output
(d) creates price level surprises

25. In the long run, demand-pull inflation will
(a) decrease the unemployment rate
(b) decrease the level of nominal wages
(c) increase the level of prices
(d) increase real national output

26. A likely result of treating cost-push inflation by stimulating aggregate demand with monetary and fiscal policies is
(a) an inflationary spiral
(b) a price level surprise
(c) disinflation
(d) a recession

27. Which of the following is not one of the manpower policies that might help relieve the problem of stagflation?
(a) application of anti-monopoly laws to labour unions
(b) removal of discrimination as an obstacle to employment
(c) improvement of the flow of job information between workers without jobs and employers with unfilled positions
(d) expansion of programs that provide job training

28. From the viewpoint of supply-side economists, stagflation is the result of
(a) excessive taxation
(b) government deregulation
(c) a shifting Phillips curve
(d) unanticipated inflation

29. Supply-side economists of the 1980s thought that the American system of taxes reduced
(a) unemployment, but increased inflation
(b) incentives to work, save, and invest
(c) transfer payments to the poor and homeless
(d) the effectiveness of wage–price guideposts for the economy

30. The Laffer curve shows the relationship between
(a) the rate of inflation and the rate of unemployment
(b) the rate of inflation and the rate of employment
(c) the tax rate and the budget deficit
(d) the tax rate and tax revenue

DISCUSSION QUESTIONS

1. Why does the simplest aggregate expenditures model imply that the economy may have either unemployment or inflation but will not experience unemployment and inflation simultaneously?

2. What is a Phillips curve? Explain how a Phillips curve with a negative slope may be derived by holding aggregate supply constant and mentally increasing aggregate demand.

3. What factors, according to the aggregate demand–aggregate supply model, underlie the Phillips curve?

4. What is the stabilization policy dilemma illustrated by the traditional Phillips curve? Does the manipulation of aggregate demand through monetary and fiscal policy move the Phillips curve or cause a movement along the Phillips curve?

5. Were the rates of inflation and of unemployment consistent with the Phillips curve in the 1950s and 1960s? What do these two rates suggest about the curve in the 1970s and early 1980s?

6. What were the supply-side shocks to the Canadian economy during the 1970s and early 1980s? How did these shocks affect aggregate supply and the Phillips curve in Canada?

7. How do expectations of inflation and declines in the growth of labour productivity affect aggregate supply and the Phillips curve?

8. When do increases in nominal-wage rates increase unit labour costs, decrease aggregate supply, and increase the price level in the economy?

9. Describe the factors that contributed to stagflation's demise during the 1983-88 period.

10. Explain the natural-rate hypothesis and briefly describe the two variants of the interpretation of the inflation–unemployment rate data of 1960-1988.

11. What does "adaptive" refer to in the theory of adaptive expectations? Illustrate how this theory is used to explain both inflation and disinflation in the economy.

12. What are the views of the adaptive expectationists on: (a) the effects of expansionary monetary and fiscal policy on employment in the short run and on the short-run Phillips curve; and (b) the long-run Phillips curve? How do they reach these conclusions?

13. How do rational expectationists believe expansionary monetary and fiscal policy affects the price level and employment in the short run and the long run? What assumptions do they make to reach this conclusion?

14. Compare and contrast the theories of rational expectations and adaptive expectations in terms of view on inflationary expectations, the interpretation of the Phillips curve, and the effectiveness of demand-management policies.

15. Identify the basic difference between a short-run and a long-run aggregate supply curve. Explain what happens to aggregate supply when an increase in the price level results in an increase in nominal wages.

16. How do the aggregate demand–aggregate supply model and new classical model view wage and price flexibility in the economy? What implications does each group draw about economic policy for the economy?

17. Explain how the economy corrects for a recessionary or inflationary gap if the long-run aggregate supply curve is vertical.

18. Describe the process of demand-pull inflation in the short run and in the long run. How does demand-pull inflation influence the aggregate supply curve?

19. Define cost-push inflation and describe the two scenarios that provide the basis for its presence in an economy.

20. What are the two kinds of market policies that might be employed to shift the Phillips curve to the left? Within each of these two categories, what specific things might be done to reduce the causes of inflation?

21. Explain (a) what is meant by wage–price policy; (b) why wage–price policy is often called incomes policy; and (c) the difference between wage–price guideposts and wage–price controls.

22. Why do supply-side economists believe the aggregate expenditure model "does not come to grips with stagflation"? Discuss the three ways that supply-side economists contend there are tax and transfer payment disincentives in the economy.

23. Draw a Laffer curve showing the relationship between tax rates and tax revenue. Explain the economic implications of the shape of the Laffer curve according to supply-side economists. Outline three criticisms of the ideas expressed by the Laffer curve.

24. Summarize the major aspects of competing macroeconomic theories and policy perspectives.

ANSWERS

Fill-in questions

1. full employment, excess, either

2. (a) increase, demand-pull; (b) decrease, cost-push

3. (a) greater, greater, smaller; (b) inverse

4. (a) price level, unemployment; (b) negative

5. labour market; labour unions, big business

6. (a) inflation, unemployment; (b) increase, increase

7. select a point on the Phillips curve, inflation

8. inflation, rising unemployment

9. supply shocks; (a) the dramatic rise in the oil prices of OPEC; (b) agricultural shortfalls throughout the world (higher agricultural prices); (c) the devaluation of the dollar; (d) the fall in the rate of growth of labour productivity; (e) inflationary expectations

10. higher, rise, decrease, higher, higher

11. (a) decreased; (b) price, unemployment; (c) stagflation

12. right

13. (any order) (a) recession of 1981-82 with tight monetary policy; (b) intensive foreign competition suppressed some wages and prices; (c) deregulation in some industries depressed wages; (d) a decline in the monopoly power of OPEC

14. (a) right, left; (b) exist, natural-rate, adaptive, rational (either order for last two); (c) inflation, gradually, (1) short-run, long-run, natural rate of unemployment, (2) increases; (d) (1) inflation, real, increase, nominal (2) a rise, no change

15. (a) upsloping, vertical; (b) fixed, variable; (c) flexible, stable, will, cannot, price level, supply; (d) inflexible, active, high

16. stability; fixed; upward; are variable, leftward, declines; vertical

17. self-correcting; upward, left; decrease, right, unemployment

18. short-run, right, increase, increase; short-run, nominal, higher

19. left, increase, decrease; decrease; increase

20. (a) market, wage–price, supply-side; (b) left

21. (a) manpower; (b) competition

22. (a) incomes; (b) (1) guideposts, (2) controls

23. (a) (1) cost, wedge, (2) incentives, (3) regulation; (b) decrease

24. tax revenues; increase, decrease, increase, decrease

25. aggregate supply, rightward; does not

Problems and projects

1. (a) 20; (b) 9; (c) (it's your choice)

2. 2300; (a) (1) 6, 2000, (2) 75, 5, 6.25; (b) (1) 7, 2200, (2) 3, 2.5, (3) 16.67; (c) (1) 5, 1700, (2) 3, 10, (3) negative

3. (a) (1) 6, Y_1, (2) Y_1, X_1; PC_1, PC_2, (3) X_2, Y_2, (4) Y_2, 3, X_3, 6, PC_2, PC_3, (5) PC_{LR}; (b) (1) Z_2, (2) Z_2, X_2; PC_3, PC_2, (3) PC_{LR}

4. P_1, Q_P (a) (1) X, P_2, Q_2, (2) AS_1, AS_2; Y, P_3, Q_P, AS_{LR}; (b) (1) Z, P_2, Q_1, (2) AD_1, AD_2; P_3, Q_P; P_2, P_3, AS_2, (3) P_1, Q_P, AS_2, AS_1

Self-test

1. T; 2. F; 3. T; 4. F; 5. T; 6. T; 7. F;
8. T; 9. T; 10. F; 11. F; 12. F; 13. T; 14. F;
15. T; 16. F; 17. F; 18. F; 19. T; 20. F; 21. T;
22. T; 23. T; 24. F; 25. T; 26. F; 27. F;
28. T; 29. T; 30. F; 31. T; 32. F; 33. T;
34. T; 35. F; 36. T

Multiple-choice

1. (c); 2. (a); 3. (a); 4. (b); 5. (c); 6. (a);
7. (d); 8. (d); 9. (d); 10. (b); 11. (d); 12. (c);
13. (b); 14. (c); 15. (b); 16. (d); 17. (d); 18. (b);
19. (a); 20. (a); 21. (a); 22. (c); 23. (c); 24. (c);
25. (c); 26. (a); 27. (a); 28. (a); 29. (b); 30. (d)

Problems and Controversies in Macroeconomics

CHAPTER

14 The Evolution of Macroeconomics and Recent Controversies

Now that the basic macroeconomic models have been introduced and their predictions set out you are prepared to explore the controversial issues as to the type of economic policy a society should pursue. Chapter 14, therefore, begins a three-chapter section of the text that examines "Problems and Controversies in Macroeconomics." This chapter focuses on alternative views to the aggregate demand–aggregate supply model's position on monetary policy and stabilization policy for the economy. In Chapter 15, the problems with the federal budget deficit and the national debt are examined. Finally, Chapter 16 deals with the topic of economic growth and the long-term performance of the economy.

Economics has always been an arena in which conflicting theories and policies opposed each other. This field of intellectual combat, in major engagements, has seen Adam Smith do battle with the defenders of a regulated economy. It witnessed the opposition of Karl Marx to the orthodox economics of his day. In the 1930s it saw the aggregate expenditures model presented as an alternative to classical macroeconomics. Around these major engagements have been countless minor skirmishes between opposing viewpoints. Out of these major and minor confrontations have emerged, not winners and losers, but the advancement of economic theory and the improvement of economic policy.

Monetarism and (more recently) rational expectations theory are the latest challengers to enter this intellectual arena. The opponent is the reigning champion, the aggregate demand–aggregate supply model, which bested neoclassical economics in the same arena during the 1940s. Monetarists and rational expectation theorists wish to free the economy from what they see as the destabilizing effects of discretionary fiscal and monetary policies. They view the aggregate demand–aggregate supply model as providing a theoretical justification for economic policies that disrupt the working of the market economy and inhibit the market's natural movement towards economic stability.

Chapter 14 examines classical macro theory with its emphasis on market flexibility and its dependence on Say's Law. Next the Keynesian (aggregate expenditures) model is discussed and its policy recommendations contrasted with those that flow from monetarism and rational expectations theory. A good deal of attention is directed towards monetarism. But this chapter is more than a comparison of the attitudes of Keynesians and monetarists, it is also an introduction to the lively debates and controversies that have characterized macroeconomics over the last three decades.

The basic equation of the Keynesians and the equation of exchange of the monetarists say pretty much the same thing. The equation of exchange ($MV = PQ$) is another way of saying that the economy will produce the GDP that is equal to the aggregate quantity of goods and services demanded. The issue is whether the income velocity of money—the V in the equation of exchange—is stable or unstable. If it is stable, as the monetarists contend, then the only kind of policy that can be used to control (to increase or decrease) nominal GDP is monetary policy; fiscal policy cannot expand or contract nominal GDP. But if V is unstable, as the Keynesians argue, then the fiscal policy is the only effective means and monetary policy is an ineffective means of controlling GDP. The issue of whether V is stable or unstable becomes an issue of whether the size of the money supply matters very much or very little. Monetarists argue that the M in the equation of exchange is the only thing that matters, and their Keynesian rivals contend that it doesn't matter very much. But you should see that monetarism is an alternative to Keynesianism; that the economic issue is the stability of V; and that the political issue is, therefore, whether monetary or fiscal policy is more effective. The jury is still hearing the case as to which model better represents reality with new arguments and new insights being presented on a fairly regular basis.

Rational expectations theorists take a more extreme position in the debate over the relative effectiveness of monetary and fiscal policies. Their position is that the economy tends to produce its full-employment output and that neither of the two types of policy —monetary or fiscal—can expand real output and employment in either the short run or the long run: the only effect on the economy of an expansionary monetary or fiscal policy is inflation. They are modern-day (or the new) classical economists who argue that neither the size of the money supply nor the fiscal policies of government has any effect on real output and employment. While this extreme position will be strange to those who have come to believe government can bring about full employment without inflation in the economy, advocates of the rational expectations theory are careful to explain how they reach these conclusions. You should be sure you understand the assumptions they make in order to reach their unusual conclusions before you dismiss their theoretical position.

Economic theory has been changed by the debate among Keynesians, monetarists, and rational expectationists, as has been the case with similar debates over macroeconomics in the past. In particular there is now recognition that "money matters" and that the money supply and monetary policy can have significant effects on the economy. More attention is also being given to the coordination of fiscal and monetary policy, and to the influence of expectations on markets and the economy. These debates have caused economists to reconsider the basic aspects of macroeconomics and have resulted in the incorporation of new ideas into mainstream thinking about the macroeconomy. Table 14-1 in the text provides a good summary of the main conclusions derived from the alternative models.

CHECKLIST

When you have studied this chapter, you should be able to:

■ Explain the two market adjustments that ensured full employment according to the classical economists.

■ State Say's Law and explain how classical economists were able to reason that all saving would be borrowed and spent for capital goods.

■ Define the term "laissez-faire" and present the justification for such a policy as put forth by the classical economists.

■ Present the three reasons why, according to Keynes, the rate of interest may not guarantee the equality of savings and investment; and two reasons why price flexibility may not guarantee full employment.

■ State what determines the equilibrium level of output and employment in the Keynesian theory.

■ Restate and compare the classical and Keynesian models in terms of aggregate demand and aggregate supply curves.

■ Compare the positions of Keynesian and monetarist economics on the competitiveness of a capitalistic economy and its inherent stability and on the role government should play in stabilizing it.

■ Write the equation of exchange, and define each of the four terms in the equation.

■ Show how the basic Keynesian equation is "translated" into the equation of exchange.

■ Explain why the monetarists believe nominal GDP is directly and predictably linked to M.

■ Write a brief scenario that explains what monetarists believe will happen to change the nominal GDP and what will happen to V when M is increased.

■ Construct a scenario that explains what Keynesians believe will happen to the interest rate and to V and nominal GDP if M is increased.

■ State what is meant by a "stable" velocity of money in the classical model.

■ Explain how the assumptions on the velocity of money lead to different outcomes or predictions in the classical and Keynesian models.

■ Explain why Keynesians favour and monetarists reject the use of fiscal policy to stabilize the economy.

■ State the monetary rule of the monetarists, and the two reasons they propose a rule instead of discretionary monetary policy.

■ Use the aggregate demand–aggregate supply models of the Keynesians and the monetarists to compare and contrast the effects of an expansionary monetary or fiscal policy on the real domestic output and the price level.

■ Clarify the debate over the monetarist call for a monetary rule using the aggregate demand–aggregate supply model.

■ State the two basic assumptions of the rational expectations theory; and explain how the advocates of this theory believe firms, workers, and consumers react to the announcement of an expansionary monetary or fiscal policy to frustrate the achievement of the goal of the policy.

■ Use aggregate demand and aggregate supply to show the effects of an expansionary monetary or fiscal policy on real output and the price level in the RET.

■ Write a brief scenario to explain why rational expectations theorists believe discretionary monetary and fiscal policies are ineffective; and state what type of government policy is advocated by these theorists.

■ Present three criticisms of the RET.

■ Outline three of the ideas that have been absorbed from monetarism and RET into contemporary macroeconomics.

CHAPTER OUTLINE

1. There exists a number of competing macroeconomic theories that offer policy prescriptions for achieving economic stability. The debate on the merits of the various models within the economics profession is quite lively with new insights being offered fairly regularly.

2. The classical macro model, the Keynesian (aggregate expenditures) model, monetarism, and the rational expectation theory are treated in this chapter.

3. Neoclassical theory of employment reaches the conclusion that the economy would automatically tend to employ its resources fully and produce a full-employment level of output. This conclusion was based on Say's Law, the role of the interest rate in equalizing planned investment and saving, and the assumption that prices and wages were flexible.

(a) Say's Law stated that the production of goods produced an equal demand for these goods because changes in the rate of interest would ensure that all income not spent (that is income saved) by consumers would be loaned to investors who would spend these borrowed funds for capital goods.

(b) In the presence of an excess supply of goods or labour (unemployment), prices and/or wages would fall until the excesses were eliminated and full employment and maximum output again prevailed in the economy.

(c) Believing that the market economy would automatically ensure a full-employment level of output, the classical economists saw no need for government interference in the operation of the economy.

4. J. M. Keynes, in *The General Theory of Employment, Interest, and Money,* argued that there is nothing automatic about full employment and that an equilibrium level of output could be attained characterized by an inflationary or deflationary gap. According to the Keynesian position,

(a) flexible interest rates do not guarantee the equality of planned investment and saving at the full-employment level of income; and

(b) prices and wages are not flexible downward and, even if wages were flexible downward, the loss of purchasing power would reduce aggregate expenditure and work against the restoration of full employment.

5. Classical and Keynesian models of the economy can be compared with the help of aggregate demand and aggregate supply curves.

(a) In the classical model, the aggregate supply curve is vertical at the economy's full-employment rate of output; and a decrease in aggregate demand will lower the equilibrium price level and have no effect on the real output of (and employment in) the economy.

(b) In the Keynesian model, the aggregate supply curve is horizontal at the current price level; and a decrease in aggregate demand will lower the real output of (and employment in)the economy and have no effect on the equilibrium price level.

(c) In both the classical and Keynesian models, the aggregate demand curve slopes downward; but in the classical model it slopes downward because(with a fixed money supply in the economy) a fall in the price increases the purchasing power of money and enables consumers and business firms to purchase a larger real output.

(d) According to the conclusions of the classical model, an automatic mechanism provides for full employment and government macroeconomic initiatives are unnecessary. According to the Keynesians, fiscal policy is required to eliminate a recessionary gap.

6. Monetarists believe that because markets in a capitalistic economy are competitive the economy would be stable if it were not for government interference, that government intervention destabilizes the economy, and that government should not use either discretionary fiscal or monetary policy to try to stabilize it.

7. In the Keynesian model, the equilibrium output of the economy is the output at which:

$$C_a + I_g + G + X_n = \text{GDP}$$

(a) In the monetarist model the basic equation is the equation of exchange,

$$MV = PQ$$

but because MV (total spending) $= C_a + I_g + G + X_n$, and $PQ = \text{GDP}$, the two equations are different ways of stating the same relationship.

(b) Keynesians assign a secondary role to money because they believe the links in the cause-effect chain are loose ones. Monetarists, believing that V (in the equation of exchange) is constant, find that while a change in M may affect Q in the short run, it will in the long run affect only P. These alternative views of the monetary transmission mechanism are illustrated in Figure 14-3 of the textbook.

8. Whether V in the equation of exchange is stable or

unstable is a critical question; because if it is stable, PQ is closely linked to M, and if it is unstable, the link between PQ and M is loose and uncertain.

(a)   Reasoning that people have a stable desire to hold money relative to holding other assets or to making purchases, monetarists conclude that the quantity of money demanded is a stable percentage of GDP (that GDP/M is constant); that an increase (a decrease) in M will leave firms and households with more (less) money than they wish to have; that they will, therefore, increase (decrease) spending for consumer and capital goods; and that this will cause the GDP and the amount of money they wish to hold for transactions purposes to rise (fall) until their demand for money is equal to M and GDP/M = V.

(b)   But Keynesians argue that consumers and business firms also have an asset demand for money; that this asset demand for money is inversely related to the rate of interest; and that an increase (decrease) in M will decrease (increase) the interest rate, increase (decrease) the amount of money people wish to hold as an asset, lower (raise) V, and leave the effect on GDP uncertain.

(c)   Empirical evidence confirms neither the contention of the monetarist that V is stable nor the contention of the Keynesians that it is variable (or unstable).

9.   Because their theories (their views on the stability of V) differ, Keynesians and monetarists disagree over the effectiveness of fiscal and monetary policies in stabilizing the economy.

(a)   Keynesians favour the use of fiscal policy to stabilize the economy because they believe it is a more powerful stabilizer; but the monetarists argue that the use of fiscal policy is both harmful and ineffective because of the crowding-out effect it has on investment expenditures in the economy.

(b)   Arguing that discretionary changes in M have produced monetary mismanagement and macroeconomic instability, the monetarists have proposed the monetary rule that M be increased at the same annual rate as the potential annual rate of increase in the real GDP.

(c)   In the aggregate demand–aggregate supply model, the monetarists see an aggregate supply curve that is very steep (or vertical) and in which an increase in aggregate demand has little (or no) effect on real domestic output and increases the price level by a relatively large amount. But the Keynesians see an aggregate supply curve that is nearly flat (or horizontal) and in which an increase in aggregate demand has little (or no) effect on the price.

(d)   The debate over the call for a monetary rule by the monetarist is also illustrated in the aggregate demand–aggregate supply model.

(1) From the monetarist perspective, a monetary rule would shift aggregate demand rightward to match a shift in the aggregate supply curve because of economic growth, thus keeping the price level stable.

(2) From the Keynesian view, the loose link between changes in money and aggregate demand mean that a monetary rule might produce too great a shift in aggregate demand (and demand-pull inflation) or too small a shift (and deflation) to match the shift in aggregate supply, and therefore such a rule would contribute to price instability.

10.   The rational expectations theory (RET), developed since the mid-1970s and called the new classical economics, is an alternative to Keynesian economics and to monetarism.

(a)   Economists who advocate the RET make two basic assumptions:

(1) business firms, consumers, and workers understand how the economy works so that they can anticipate the effect on the economy of an economic event or a change in economic policy, and they can use all available information to make decisions in a way to further their own self-interests; and

(2) all markets in the economy are so competitive that equilibrium prices and quantities quickly adjust to these events and changes in public policy.

(b)   From these assumptions the proponents of the RET conclude that the response of the public to the expected inflationary effect of an expansionary monetary (or fiscal) policy will cancel the intended effect on output and employment in the economy.

(c)   In an aggregate demand–aggregate supply model of the RET, the aggregate supply curve is vertical. Any monetary or fiscal policy that increases or decreases aggregate demand affects only the price level and has no effect on real output or employment, real wages, or real interest rates in either the short or the long run.

(d)   Rational expectations theorists argue that discretionary monetary and fiscal policies are ineffective against the business cycle. They would (like the monetarists) replace discretionary policies with rules.

(e)   The appeal of the RET comes from the inability of Keynesian economics to explain and to develop policies to correct stagflation, and from the long-sought connection between micro- and macroeconomics. But RET has been subjected to three basic criticisms.

(1) One criticism is that people are not so well-informed on the workings of the economy and the effect of economic policy on it as the rational expectations theorists assume.

(2) A second criticism is that many markets in the economy are not so competitive as assumed in the RET, and

do not, therefore, adjust their prices as rapidly as assumed.

(3) And the third criticism is that monetary and fiscal policies have worked in the past to expand real output and employment in the economy.

(f)   The controversies and debates in macroeconomics in the past three decades have led to the incorporation of several ideas from monetarism and rational expectations theory into contemporary thinking about macroeconomics. Three examples illustrate this point: changes in the money supply and monetary policy are given more weight than in the past; there is recognition of the need to coordinate fiscal and monetary policy and the dangers of crowding-out of investment activity; and third, more attention is given to the effects of expectations on markets and the economy.

IMPORTANT TERMS

classical theory of employment
crowding-out effect
equation of exchange
Keynesian economics
monetarists
monetary rule
price–wage flexibility
rational expectations theory (RET)
Say's Law
velocity of money

FILL-IN QUESTIONS

1.   Full employment was assured in the classical model by the operation of _____ Law: the equality of planned investment and savings brought about by an equilibrium _____ _____ in the money market and price–wage _____.

2.   According to Say's Law, the production of goods and services creates an equal _____.

3.   Changes in _____, according to the classical economists, ensure that what is not spent on consumer goods is spent on capital goods.

4.   In the classical theory, if saving is greater than investment the rate of interest will (rise, fall) _____;

if investment is greater than saving it will _____; and the rate of interest will move to the level at which

_____ and _____ are equal.

5.   According to the classical theory, if interest rate did not equate saving and investment, and if total output exceeded the level of spending, prices in the output market would tend to (rise, fall) _____ because of competition among business firms. This would make some production unprofitable and temporarily cause _____ in the labour markets; but competition among workers would tend to drive resource prices (upward, downward) _____ and (increase, decrease) _____ their employment. This process would continue until _____ _____.

6.   The classical economists believed the market system contained a _____ ability and that government interference would be _____ to its efficient operation and so a _____ economic policy was desirable.

7.   J. M. Keynes argued that the economy (did, did not) _____ contain a self-correcting mechnism, but an equilibrium could be reached that contained considerable _____ or substantial _____.

8.   According to the Keynesian theory of employment, (a)   saving and investment are done by different _____ and for different _____; (b)   the funds to finance investment come not only from current saving but from the _____ _____ _____ of households and from _____ _____; and (c)   current savings may not be lent to investors in the money market but added to the money _____ of customers or used to retire outstanding bank _____.

9.   Keynes argued that in the modern economy prices and wages (do, do not) _____ fall when there is unemployment; and that wage reduction would lead to (smaller, larger) _____ money incomes, a (fall, rise) _____ in total

spending, a(n) (increase , decrease) _____

in prices, and little or no change in total _____
in the economy.

10.   Reasoning that if a price and wage-rate reduction
would increase the output and employment of an
individual firm, then a general reduction in prices and
wages will increase output and employment in the
economy as a whole is an example of the fallacy of

_____.

11. The aggregate supply curve of the classical

economists is (horizontal, vertical) _____,
and the aggregate supply curve of the Keynesian

economists is _____ up to the full-
employment level of output. For this reason, a decrease
in aggregate demand will have no effect on the price level
and will decrease output in the (classical, Keynesian)

_____ model; but a decrease in aggregate
demand will decrease the price level and have no effect

on output and employment in the _____
model.

12.   The views of the classical and Keynesian economists
also differ on the nature of the aggregate demand curve.
(a)   In the neoclassical way of thinking, the money supply set the basis for aggregate demand. If the price level
falls and the money supply is constant, the purchasing

power of money will (rise, fall) _____
and consumers and business firms will (expand, contract)

_____ their expenditures for goods and
services; aggregate demand will be reasonably stable
if the nation's monetary authorities maintain a

_____.

(b)   From the Keynesian perspective, aggregate demand

is (stable, unstable) _____, even if there
are no changes in the supply of money, in part because

business investment tends to be _____.
Keynesians then believe that the market system is inher-

ently (stable, unstable) _____; advocate

(government intervention, laissez-faire) _____;

and favour (monetary, fiscal) _____

over _____ policy.

13.   Monetarists argue that capitalism is inherently

_____ because most of its markets are

_____, advocate _____
economic policy, and favour the use of (discretionary,

nondiscretionary) _____ (monetary,

fiscal) _____ policy.

14.   The basic equation of the monetarists is

_____ = _____.

(a)   This equation is called the _____

_____ _____.

(b)   Indicate below what each of the four letters in this
equation represents.

(1) M: _____

(2) V: _____

(3) P: _____

(4) Q: _____

15.   The basic equation of the Keynesians is: $C_a + I_g$
$+ G + X_n$ = GDP.

(a) $C_a + I_g + G + X_n$ is _____

_____ and in the equation of exchange is

equal to _____.

(b)   Nominal GDP is equal to _____
in the equation of exchange.

16.   Monetarists argue that
(a)   any increase in M will (increase, decrease)

_____ PQ;
(b)   in the short run any increase in M may (increase,

decrease) _____ both P and Q; but
(c)   in the long run any increase in M will (increase,

decrease) _____ only (P, Q) _____.

17.   In the debate on the stability of V,
(a)   monetarists argue that money is used only as a

_____ _____ _____,

that the only demand for money is the _____
demand, that this demand is a fixed percentage of

_____ _____, and that V

is, therefore, _____;
(b)   Keynesians contend that money is also used as a

_____ _____ _____

and that there is also an _____ demand
for money, that this demand is inversely related to the

_____ _____, and that

V is, therefore, _____.

18. An increase in M,
(a) to the monetarists' way of thinking, will

(1) leave the public with (more, less) _____ money than it wishes to have,

(2) induce the public to (increase, decrease) _____ its spending for consumer and capital goods,

(3) which will result in a(n) _____ in nominal GDP,

(4) until the nominal GDP (or MV) is equal to

_____ times _____;
(b) to the Keynesians' way of thinking, will

(1) result in a(n) _____ in the rate of interest,

(2) which will _____ the demand for money,

(3) and _____ V,
(4) and the effect on nominal GDP will be

_____.

19. It is, in short, the view of the
(a) monetarists that V (in the equation of exchange) is stable and that there is a direct relationship between

_____ and _____;
(b) Keynesians that V is (directly, inversely)

_____ related to the interest rate; that the

interest rate (increases, decreases) _____ when M increases; and that, therefore, M and V are

(directly, inversely) _____ related to each other.

20. The empirical evidence can be used to support either the monetarist or Keynesian viewpoint on the stability of the velocity of money (V).

(a) The fact that there is a (strong, weak) _____ correlation between the money supply and nominal domestic output (PQ) suggests that velocity is (stable,

unstable) _____. This evidence tends to support the (monetarist, Keynesian) _____ position.
(b) Keynesians calculate V by dividing nominal

_____ by M and find that V is (stable,

unstable) _____. A plot of V with the

interest rate also shows a (strong, weak) _____ correlation, which suggests that V is (stable, unstable)

_____.

21. In the debate on the use of fiscal policy
(a) the Keynesians contend that for the purpose of stabilization of the economy, the more effective tool is

_____ policy; but
(b) the monetarists reply that government borrowing to finance a budget deficit will (raise, lower)

_____ the rate of interest and have a

_____ effect on investment spending.

22. Monetarists would have the supply of money increase at the same annual rate as the potential rate of

growth of _____ _____

and this is a rate from _____ to

_____ %.

23. Monetarists proposed the adoption of the "Monetary Rule" because they believe that discretionary monetary policy tends to (stabilize, destabilize)

_____ the economy due to two sources of

monetary mismanagement: 1) _____

and 2) _____.

24. (a) In the Keynesian model of the economy, the aggregate supply curve is relatively (steep, flat)

_____, and an increase in aggregate

demand will have a relatively (large, small) _____

effect on the price level and a relatively _____ effect on the real domestic output.
(b) In the monetarist model, the aggregate supply curve

is relatively _____, and an increase in

aggregate demand will have a relatively _____

effect on price and a relatively _____

effect on real domestic output.

25. In the rational expectations theory,
(a) individuals correctly anticipate the effects of any economic event or a change in public policy on the economy and make decisions based on their anticipations to

maximize their own _____;
(b) the markets in the economy are (noncompetitive,

purely competitive) _____, and prices in

these markets are perfectly (inflexible, flexible)

_____; and that as a result,

(c) an expansionary monetary or fiscal policy will lead the public to expect (inflation, a recession)

_____, and they will react in a way that results in (an increase, a decrease, no change)

_____ in the real output of the economy

and _____ in the price level.

26. The aggregate supply curve in the RET is (vertical,

horizontal) _____, and a change in aggregate demand brings about a change in (the price

level, the real output) _____

and no change in _____ of the economy.

27. Proponents of the RET
(a) contend that discretionary monetary and fiscal poli-

cies may reinforce economic _____ and
(b) like the monetarists, favour (policy rules, discretion-

ary policy) _____.

28. The critics of the RET maintain that people are (less

well, better) _____ informed than assumed in the theory; markets are (more, less)

_____ competitive than assumed in the theory and prices are, therefore, (sticky, flexible)

_____; and monetary and fiscal policies have been employed in the past to (stabilize, destabi-

lize) _____ the economy and to expand

its (real, nominal) _____ output.

29. Some of the ideas from monetarism and rational expectations theory have been incorporated into contemporary macroeconomics. For example, there is more recognition that the money supply and monetary policy

are (important, unimportant) _____ determinants of economic stability, that there needs to

be (more, less) _____ coordination between monetary and fiscal policy, and that

_____ or the reactions of the public affect economic policies that are instituted by society.

PROBLEMS AND PROJECTS

1. You must imagine that you are a monetarist in this problem and assume that V is constant and equal to 4. In the table below is the aggregate supply schedule: the real output Q that producers will offer for sale at seven different price levels P.

P	Q	PQ	MV
$1.00	100	$	$
2.00	110		
3.00	120	_____	_____
4.00	130	_____	_____
5.00	140	_____	_____
6.00	150	_____	_____
7.00	160	_____	_____

(a) Compute and enter in the table above the seven values of PQ.
(b) Assume M is $90. Enter the values of MV on each of the seven lines in the table. The equilibrium

(1) nominal domestic output (PQ or MV) is $____;

(2) price level is $_____;

(3) real domestic output Q is $_____.
(c) When M increases to $175, MV at each price level

is $_____; and the equilibrium

(1) nominal domestic output is $_____;

(2) price level is $_____;

(3) real domestic output is $_____.

2. In this problem, you are a Keynesian. The table below, at the left, shows the amounts of money firms and households wish to have for transactions at different levels of nominal GDP. On the right, the table shows the amounts of money they want to have as assets at different rates of interest.

Nominal GDP	Transactions Demand	Interest Rate	Asset Demand
$ 500	$ 50	7.0%	$ 75
600	60	6.8	80
700	70	6.6	85
800	80	6.4	90
900	90	6.2	95
1,000	100	6.0	100

(a) Suppose the nominal GDP is $500, the interest rate is 7%, and the supply of money is $125.

(1) The amount of money demanded for transactions is

$_____.

(2) The amount of money demanded as an asset is

$_____.

(3) The total amount of money demanded for both purposes is $_____.

(4) The amount of money firms and households wish to have is (greater than, less than, equal to) _____ the amount of money they actually have.

(5) The velocity of money (equal to nominal GDP divided by the supply of money) is _____.

(b)   Assume the Bank of Canada expands the supply of money to $160 by purchasing securities in the open market; and that as a result the rate of interest falls to 6% and the nominal GDP rises to $600.

(1) The amount of money demanded for transactions is now $_____, and the amount demanded as an asset is now $_____.

(2) The total amount of money demanded is $_____, and the amount of money the public wishes to have is _____ the amount of money they actually have.

(3) The velocity of money is _____.

(c)   Suppose the federal government pursues an expansionary fiscal policy that raises the nominal GDP from $600 to $800 and the interest rate from 6% to 6.8%; and the money supply remains at $160.

(1) The transactions demand for money is $_____, the asset demand is $_____, and the total demand is $_____.

(2) The velocity of money is _____.

(d)   The effect of the easy money policy was to (increase, decrease) _____ the velocity of money, and the effect of the expansionary fiscal policy was to _____ it.

3.   On the following graph are three aggregate supply curves: AS_1, AS_2, and AS_3.

(a) AS_1 is the (Keynesian, classical, rational expectations) _____ supply curve; AS_2 is the _____ supply curve, and AS_3 is the _____ supply curve.

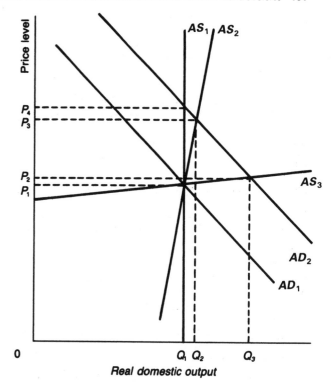

(b)   Regardless of which is the economy's supply curve, if the aggregate demand curve is AD_1, the equilibrium real domestic output is _____ and the equilibrium price level is _____.

(c)   Should aggregate demand increase from AD_1 to AD_2 in the

(1) classical model, the equilibrium real domestic output would (increase, decrease, remain constant) _____ to (at) _____, and the equilibrium price level would (increase, decrease, remain constant) _____ to (at) _____;

(2) Keynesian model, the equilibrium real domestic output would _____ to (at) _____, and the equilibrium price level would _____ to (at) _____;

(3) rational expectations model, the equilibrium real domestic output would _____ to (at) _____, and the equilibrium price level would _____ to (at) _____.

4. Suppose that the economy is presently operating at full employment with a money supply of 40 billion dollars and a velocity of money of 6. Real GDP increases at the rate of 5% per year. The required reserve ratio of the commercial banks is 20%. Given the velocity of money is a constant 6, by how much would the central bank have to reduce the reserve ratio in order to maintain stable prices next year, *ceteris paribus*?

SELF-TEST

Circle T if the statement is true, F if it is false.

1. According to the classical economists, full employment is normal in a market economy. **T F**

2. The classical economists believed that demand management policies were required to overcome economic instability. **T F**

3. Say's Law states that, in a competitive market, price is determined by supply and demand. **T F**

4. In both the classical and Keynesian theories of employment, saving is income not expended for consumer goods and services. **T F**

5. In the classical theory, if saving exceeds investment, a deflationary gap will exist and equilibrium GDP will decline. **T F**

6. In the classical model, an increase in saving will shift the supply of saving curve to the right, lower the interest rate, expand the volume of investment, and preserve the full-employment level of output. **T F**

7. According to the classical model, wage and price flexibility together with interest rate fluctuations would maintain full employment. **T F**

8. In the classical model, involuntary unemployment would equal the natural rate of unemployment in the long run. **T F**

9. The Keynesians view savers and investors as distinct groups in the economy and savings are largely unrelated to the rate of interest. **T F**

10. In the Keynesian model, the volume of investment is determined solely by the rate of interest. **T F**

11. According to the Keynesians, planned investment can be different than the volume of saving and cause fluctuations in output and employment. **T F**

12. The Keynesians doubted the ability of price and

wage flexibility to promote full employment since general wage cuts would lower money incomes and cause a reduction in the demand for goods and services. **T F**

13. A less than full-employment equilibrium is possible in the Keynesian model. **T F**

14. In terms of aggregate demand and aggregate supply, the classical model yielded a horizontal aggregate demand curve and a vertical aggregate supply curve. **T F**

15. The Keynesian model assumptions result in a horizontal aggregate supply and a downward sloping aggregate demand, which is unstable due to the volatility of investment spending. **T F**

16. The monetarists suggest that a competitive market system, free from government interference, would provide substantial economic stability. **T F**

17. The monetarists favour an active monetary policy and a balanced budget as anti-cyclical weapons. **T F**

18. The basic equations of the Keynesians and the monetarists are no more than two different ways of stating the same relationship. **T F**

19. The fundamental equation of monetarism is termed the equation of exchange. **T F**

20. Most monetarists believe that an increase in the money supply will have no effect on real output and employment in either the short run or the long run. **T F**

21. Monetarists argue that V, in the equation of exchange, is stable and that a change in M will bring about a direct and proportional change in P in the long run. **T F**

22. In the Keynesian model, changes in the money supply have a more direct effect on the price and output levels than in the monetarist model. **T F**

23. In the monetarist model, a stable velocity of money means a constant velocity of money. **T F**

24. If the velocity of money is stable, the monetarist model predicts a direct relationship exists between the money supply and nominal GDP. **T F**

25. According to the Keynesians, the velocity of money is unstable so there is no direct relationship between changes in the money supply and nominal GDP. **T F**

26. Because of the stability of the velocity of money, Keynesians conclude that monetary policy is the more

powerful and reliable stabilization device.   **T F**

27. Monetarists believe that fiscal policy is ineffectual because of a severe crowding-out effect.   **T F**

28. Monetarists conclude that discretionary monetary policy has resulted in macroeconomic instability.   **T F**

29. Strict monetarists advocate that the central bank expand the money supply at a rate inversely related to the rate of unemployment.   **T F**

30. Statistical evidence reveals that the velocity of money has remained almost constant from one year to the next.   **T F**

31. Rational expectations theory assumes that both product and resource markets are uncompetitive and that wages and prices are "sticky."   **T F**

32. Rational expectations theory implies that the aggregate supply curve is vertical.   **T F**

33. Rational expectations macroeconomists argue that economic agents understand the workings of the economy and make decisions that further their own self-interests.   **T F**

34. Economists who have advanced the rational expectations theory argue that discretionary fiscal and monetary policy have helped to stabilize the economy.   **T F**

35. Monetarists and Keynesians would agree that expansionary stabilization policies will produce demand-pull inflation with a vertical aggregate supply curve.   **T F**

36. A legacy of new classical economics is that economists and policy makers are more sensitive about how expectations might affect the outcome of a policy change.   **T F**

MULTIPLE-CHOICE

Circle the letter that corresponds to the best answer.

1. The classical economists believed
(a) the price system was capable of providing for full employment of the economy's resources
(b) the money supply determined the velocity of money
(c) monetary and fiscal policy were required to reach full employment
(d) prices were "sticky" in a downward direction

2. In the classical theory of employment, a decline in interest rates will

(a) decrease saving and investment
(b) decrease saving and increase investment
(c) increase saving and decrease investment
(d) increase saving and increase investment

3. The classical theory predicts that an increase in the supply of saving will
(a) lower interest rates and reduce investment
(b) raise interest rates and reduce investment
(c) lower interest rates and expand investment
(d) raise interest rates and expand investment

4. If the rate of interest did not equate saving and investment and total output was greater than total spending, the classical economists argued that competition would tend to force
(a) product and resource prices down
(b) product prices up and resource prices down
(c) product prices up and resource prices up
(d) product prices down and resource prices up

5. Which of the following is not involved in Keynes' criticism of the classical theory of employment?
(a) a reduction in wages will lead only to a reduction in total spending, not to an increase in employment
(b) investment spending is not influenced by the rate of interest
(c) prices and wages are simply not flexible downward in a modern market economy
(d) saving in modern economies depends upon the level of disposable income and is little influenced by the rate of interest

6. Keynesian economists argue that the sources of funds that finance investment are
(a) current saving
(b) the accumulated money balances of households
(c) created by commercial banks
(d) all of the above

7. The Keynesian economists also argue that saving is
(a) used to finance investment expenditure
(b) added to the money balances of savers
(c) used to retire loans made previously by banks
(d) used for all of the above

8. The Keynesian aggregate supply curve
(a) is horizontal up to full employment
(b) slopes upward
(c) is vertical
(d) slopes downward

9. The aggregate supply of the classical model
(a) is horizontal at the prevailing price level
(b) slopes upward
(c) is vertical at the full-employment level

(d) slopes downward

10. According to the classical model,
(a) aggregate demand will determine the level of real domestic output, while aggregate supply determines the price level
(b) the money supply determines the interest rate, which in turn determines the level of investment, which in turn determines the level of real output
(c) aggregate supply will determine the full employment level of output, while aggregate demand will determine the price level
(d) the key to price stability was to control the interest rate in order to prevent changes in investment spending shifting the aggregate demand curve

11. All of the following are parts of the Keynesian model, with the exception that
(a) the aggregate supply is horizontal
(b) the aggregate demand is unstable
(c) saving and planned investment are only equal at the full-employment level of output
(d) active macroeconomic policies by government are necessary to mitigate recessions

12. In the classical theory of employment, a decrease in aggregate demand results in
(a) a decrease in the price level and no change in output
(b) a decrease in both the price level and output
(c) no change in the price level and a decrease in output
(d) no change in either the price level or output

13. A decrease in aggregate demand in the Keynesian model results in
(a) a decrease in both the price level and in output
(b) a decrease in the price level and no change in output
(c) no change in the price level and a decrease in output
(d) no change in either the price level or output

14. Monetarists
(a) argue for the use of discretionary monetary policy
(b) contend that government policies have reduced the stability of the economy
(c) believe a capitalistic economy is inherently unstable
(d) believe the markets in a capitalistic economy are largely noncompetitive

15. Which of the following is not true?
(a) MV is total spending
(b) PQ is the real GDP
(c) MV is nominal GDP
(d) $MV = C_a + I_g + G + X_n$

16. If V (in the equation of exchange) is constant, an increase in M will necessarily increase
(a) P

(b) Q
(c) both P and Q
(d) P times Q

17. Monetarists argue that velocity is stable and that the amount of money that the public will want to hold depends primarily on the level of
(a) nominal GDP
(b) investment
(c) consumption
(d) prices

18. From the monetarist viewpoint, an increase in the supply of money will
(a) raise the rate of interest
(b) increase spending for consumer and capital goods
(c) increase the asset demand for money
(d) decrease the demand for government securities

19. Keynesians argue that
(a) the only demand for money is the asset demand
(b) the only demand for money is the transactions demand
(c) there is no transaction demand for money
(d) there is both a transactions and an asset demand for money

20. From the Keynesian viewpoint, an increase in supply of money will
(a) raise the rate of interest
(b) decrease spending for consumer and capital goods
(c) increase the asset demand for money
(d) decrease the demand for government securities

21. Because money is demanded not only for transactions purposes but also to hold as an asset, Keynesians argue that
(a) the velocity of money is constant
(b) the velocity of money is stable
(c) the velocity of money is predictable
(d) the velocity of money is variable and unpredictable

22. The rule suggested by the monetarists is that the money supply should be increased at the same rate as
(a) the price level
(b) the inverse of the price level
(c) the velocity of money
(d) the potential growth in real GDP

23. In the classical model,
(a) the aggregate supply curve is very steep and an increase in aggregate demand will have little or no effect on the price level
(b) the aggregate supply curve is nearly flat and an increase in aggregate demand will have little or no effect on the price level

(c) the aggregate supply curve is very steep and an increase in aggregate demand will have a large effect on the price level

(d) the aggregate supply curve is nearly flat and an increase in aggregate demand will have a large effect on the price level

24. In the Keynesian model,
(a) the aggregate supply curve is very steep and an increase in aggregate demand will have a large effect on real domestic output
(b) the aggregate supply curve is nearly flat and an increase in aggregate demand will have a large effect on real domestic output
(c) the aggregate supply curve is very steep and an increase in aggregate demand will have little or no effect on real domestic output
(d) the aggregate supply curve is nearly flat and an increase in aggregate demand will have little or no effect on real domestic output

25. In the rational expectations theory,
(a) individuals understand how the economy works and can correctly anticipate the effects of an event or a change in public policy on the economy
(b) the markets in the economy are purely competitive
(c) to maximize their own self-interests, individuals respond to any expansionary fiscal or monetary policy in a way that prevents an increase in real output and fosters an increase in the price level
(d) all of the above are true

26. In the model of the rational expectations theorists, an increase in aggregate demand will
(a) increase the price level and have no real effect on real domestic output
(b) increase real domestic output and have no effect on the price level
(c) increase both the price level and the real domestic output
(d) have none of the above effects

27. To stabilize the economy, rational expectation theorists favour the use of
(a) price controls
(b) discretionary fiscal policy
(c) discretionary monetary policy
(d) policy rules

28. The contention that changes in the money supply cause direct changes in aggregate demand and therefore changes in nominal GDP would be most closely associated with the view of
(a) Keynesians

(b) monetarists
(c) new classical economists
(d) rational expectations economists

29. Proponents of rational expectations argue that people
(a) are not as rational as they are assumed to be by monetarists
(b) tend to forecast the consequences of economic change, which frustrates policy makers
(c) consistently make forecasting errors, which can be exploited by policy makers
(d) do not respond quickly to changes in wages and prices, causing a misallocation of resources in the economy

30. The idea that the Bank of Canada should follow a monetary rule would find the most support from which combination?
(a) Keynesians and monetarists
(b) RET economists and Keynesians
(c) RET economists and monetarists
(d) neoclassical economists and Keynesians

31. A distinguishing feature of the rational expectations in the aggregate demand–aggregate supply model would be an aggregate
(a) demand curve that is downward sloping
(b) demand curve that is vertical
(c) supply curve that is vertical
(d) supply curve that is horizontal

32. Which of the following would be an idea from monetarism or rational expectations that has been absorbed into mainstream macroeconomics?
(a) the importance of government spending, taxation, and fiscal policy
(b) the importance of the money supply and monetary policy
(c) the building of macroeconomic foundations for microeconomics
(d) the emphasis on discretion rather than rules for guiding economic policy

DISCUSSION QUESTIONS

1. According to the classical economists, what level of employment would tend to prevail in an economy? On what two basic assumptions did their analysis of the level of employment rest?

2. What is Say's Law? How were the classical economists able to reason that whatever is saved is spent?

3. In the classical model how did the operation of the

money market, flexible prices and wages, and competition drive the economy toward full employment?

4. On what grounds did J. M. Keynes argue that flexible interest rates would not assure the operation of Say's Law? What were his reasons for asserting that flexible prices and wages would not assure full employment, and what was the classical response to his assertion?

5. What is
(a) the difference between the classical and the Keynesian aggregate supply curve; and
(b) the difference between the effects a decrease in aggregate demand would have on the price level and on the real domestic output in the two models? Why does the classical aggregate demand curve have a negative (downward) slope?

6. What is the basic equation of the Keynesians and the basic equation of the monetarists? Define all terms in both equations and explain how the Keynesian equation can be converted to the monetarist equation.

7. Explain how a change in M in the equation of exchange will, to the monetarist way of thinking, affect (a) P times Q, (b) P and Q in the short run, (c) P and Q in the long run.

8. Explain the differences between the monetarist and Keynesian views on why firms and households demand money (or liquid balances); on what determines the demand for money; and the stability, therefore, of the velocity of money.

9. Suppose firms and households, because of an increase in the money supply, find themselves with more money than they wish to have. What do the monetarists believe they will do with this excess money? What effect will this have on the velocity of money and nominal GDP?

10. Suppose the supply of money increases. What do Keynesians believe will happen to the rate of interest, the amount of money firms and households will wish to hold, planned investment spending, and the nominal GDP?

11. Explain why "a critical theoretical issue involved in the Keynesian-monetarist debate centres on the question of whether the velocity of money, V, is stable."

12. What empirical evidence is there to support the Keynesian contention that V is unstable, or the monetarist contention that it is relatively stable?

13. Why do the Keynesians advocate and the monetarists reject the use of fiscal policy to stabilize the economy?

14. What is the monetary rule? Why do monetarists suggest this rule to replace discretionary monetary policy?

15. How do the aggregate demand–aggregate supply models of the Keynesians and monetarists differ? What effect will an expansionary monetary or fiscal policy have upon real domestic output and price level in each of these models?

16. Explain how and why rational expectations theorists believe firms, workers, and consumers will respond to an expansionary monetary or fiscal policy; and how these responses make the policy ineffective and promote economic instability.

17. How will an expansionary monetary or fiscal policy affect real domestic output and the price level in the rational expectations theorists' aggregate demand–aggregate supply model? Why does it have these effects?

18. What criticisms have been made of the RET by its opponents?

19. What influence have monetarism and rational expectations had on contemporary macroeconomic theory and policy? Give three examples of ideas that have changed contemporary thinking.

ANSWERS

Fill-in questions

1. Say's; interest rate, flexibility

2. demand for these goods and services

3. the rate of interest

4. fall, rise, saving, investment

5. fall; unemployment, downward, increase; all those willing to work at the going wage rate are employed and total planned spending equals total output

6. self-regulating, detrimental, *laissez-faire*

7. did not, unemployment, inflation

8. (a) groups, reasons (b) accumulated money balances, commercial banks (c) balances, loans(debts)

9. do not, smaller, fall, decrease, employment (output)

10. composition

11. vertical, horizontal; Keynesian, classical

12. (a) rise, expand, constant supply of money (b) unstable, unstable; unstable, government intervention, fiscal, monetary

13. stable, competitive, *laissez-faire*, nondiscretionary, monetary

14. $MV = PQ$; (a) equation of exchange; (b) (1) the money supply, (2) the velocity of money, (3) the average price of each unit of physical output, (4) the physical volume of goods and services produced

15. (a) total spending, MV; (b) PQ

16. (a) increase; (b) increase, (c) increase, P

17. (a) medium of exchange, transactions, nominal GDP, stable; (b) store of value, asset, interest rate, unstable

18. (a) (1) more, (2) increase, (3) increase, (4) P, Q; (b) (1) decrease, (2) increase, (3) decrease, (4) uncertain

19. (a) M, PQ; (b) directly, decreases, inversely

20. strong, stable; monetarist; (b) GDP, unstable; strong, unstable

21. (a) fiscal; (b) raise, crowding-out

22. real GDP, 3, 5

23. destabilize; 1) irregular time lags, 2) stabilizing the interest rate is the wrong target

24. (a) flat, small, large; (b) steep, large, small

25. (a) self-interests; (b) purely competitive, flexible; (c) inflation, no change, an increase

26. vertical, the price level, the real output

27. (a) instability; (b) policy rules

28. less well, less, sticky, stabilize, real

29. important, more, expectations

Problems and projects

1. (a) 100, 220, 360, 520, 700, 900, 1120; (b) 360, 360, 360, 360, 360, 360, 360, (1) 360, (2) 3.00, (3) 120; (c) 700, (1) 700, (2) 5.00, (3) 140

2. (a) (1) 50, (2) 75, (3) 125, (4) equals to, (5) 4; (b) (1) 60, 100, (2) 160, equal to, (3) 3.75; (c) (1) 80, 80, 160, (2) 5; (d) decrease, increase

3. (a) rational expectations, classical, Keynesian; (b) Q_1, P_1; (c) (1) increase, Q_2, increase, P_3, (2) increase, Q_3, increase, P_2, (3) remain constant, Q_1, increase, P

4. approximately one percentage point to 19.04%

Self-test

1. T; 2. F; 3. F; 4. T; 5. F; 6. T; 7. T; 8. F; 9. T; 10. F; 11. T; 12. T; 13. T; 14. F; 15. T; 16. T; 17. F; 18. T; 19. T; 20. F; 21. T; 22. F; 23. F; 24. T; 25. T; 26. F; 27. T; 28. T; 29. F; 30. F; 31. F; 32. T; 33. T; 34. F; 35. T; 36. T

Multiple-choice

1. (a); 2. (b); 3. (c); 4. (a); 5. (b); 6. (d); 7. (d); 8. (a); 9. (c); 10. (c); 11. (c); 12. (a); 13. (c); 14. (b); 15. (b); 16. (d); 17. (a); 18. (b); 19. (d); 20. (c); 21. (d); 22. (d); 23. (c); 24. (b); 25. (d); 26. (a); 27. (d); 28. (b); 29. (b); 30. (c); 31. (c); 32. (b)

CHAPTER

15 Budget Deficits and the Public Debt

The federal government can operate with a budget deficit, a budget surplus, or with a balanced budget during a year. On a national accounts basis, 1974 was the last year the government of Canada had a budget surplus. In the past decade, these budget deficits have grown quite large and have caused problems for the Canadian economy. Chapter 15, therefore, looks at the issues surrounding the budget deficits of the 1980s and the related growth of the public debt.

Any budget surplus or deficit affects the size of the federal government (sometimes called the national) debt; surpluses decrease it and deficits increase it. As a consequence of persistent deficits during and since World War II the public debt has increased. The federal government finances the public debt by selling securities (bonds). To those who have purchased these securities the government pays interest each year; and as the size of the debt has increased (and interest rates in the economy have risen) the annual interest payments on the debt have also increased.

These facts are the background for this chapter. After defining a budget deficit and the public debt, the chapter examines three budget philosophies. You should be aware that the philosophy adopted by the federal government has a significant impact on the output of and employment in the economy and on the public debt. A brief explanation of the reasons for the increases in the public debt (wars and recessions) and of the absolute and relative sizes of the debt and the interest payments on the debt is next. Then comes an examination of the economic implications or consequences of the debt. Here you will learn that the debt creates problems for the economy (but these problems do not include bankrupting the federal government or shifting the cost of a war—or of other government programs—to future generations). The problems are four in number. The debt and the payment of interest on it appears: (1) to make the distribution of income in the economy more unequal; (2) to reduce the incentives that induce people and business firms to produce and expand their outputs; (3) to decrease the Canadian standard of living if a part of the debt is owed to foreigners; (4) and to have a crowding-out effect on investment in plant and equipment in Canada.

Crowding out is probably the most serious of these four problems. You should be sure that you understand how crowding out works and how it imposes a burden on future generations by reducing the growth of the nation's capital stock. To understand why it reduces the growth of the capital stock, borrowing to finance an increase in government expenditures is compared with increasing taxes to finance these expenditures. To the extent that deficit financing is obtained abroad there will be reduced crowding out; but an appreciation of the Canadian dollar results, which causes a reduction in net exports.

Recent deficits are of concern because of their relatively large size, the difficulty experienced by the government in reducing their size during a period of cyclical prosperity in the middle 1980s, the high interest cost that interfered with governmental anti-cyclical policies during the last recession, and their role in promoting trade deficits. Be sure you study each link in the chain of events that can lead to the contraction of output and employment as a result of large deficits.

Whether deficit financing imposes a burden on future generations depends upon how it is financed. For the economy as a whole a burden results if output decreases as a result of a deficit. A deficit can result in a redistribution of income but this should not be confused with a reduction of output, which is the real burden of the debt.

There is not any new theory in this chapter, just an application of theory you have previously covered. At the end of the chapter you will learn that debt plays a positive role in a dynamic economy and a budgetary deficit can be used to promote economic stability.

CHECKLIST

When you have studied this chapter, you should be able to:

- Define a budget deficit (and surplus) and the public debt; and explain how the latter is related to the former.
- Explain each of the three budget philosophies.
- State the absolute and relative size of the public debt and of the annual interest charges on this debt; and enumerate the principal causes of the debt.
- Compare the relative size of the public debt of Canada to public debts of other industrialized countries.
- Explain how adjusting the size of the nominal public debt for inflation affects the real size of the debt and the real size of a budget deficit; and why the accounting procedures employed by the federal government do not accurately reflect its financial condition.
- Give three reasons why a large public debt will not bankrupt the government.
- Discuss whether the public debt imposes a burden on future generations; and why the public debt is for the most part also a public credit.
- Enumerate the four real issues related to the public debt.
- Compare the effects of an internal debt with the effects of an external debt on the economy.
- Describe the crowding-out effect of borrowing to finance an increase in government expenditures and the burden this method of financing expenditures places on future generations; compare the burden imposed on future generations by this method of finance with the burden placed on them if the increased expenditures are financed by increased taxation; and qualify in two ways this comparison.
- Explain how the type of goods purchased by government or the stage of the business cycle in which the expenditures are made determines the burden of a current budget deficit on future generations.
- Discuss the four concerns with the deficits and growing public debt in the past decade.
- Trace the effects of borrowing abroad to finance an increase in government expenditure on interest rates, the attractiveness of Canadian securities to foreign investors, the international value of the Canadian dollar, Canadian exports and imports, and Canadian output and employment.
- Explain why increasing debt is necessary in a growing economy if the economy is to remain at full employment, and explain when it is necessary for the public debt to expand.

CHAPTER OUTLINE

1. The budget deficit of the federal government is the amount by which its expenditures exceed its revenues in any year. The public debt at any time is the sum of the federal government's previous annual deficits less any annual surpluses.

2. If the federal government utilizes fiscal policy to combat recession and inflation, its budget is not likely to be balanced in any particular year. Three budgetary philosophies may be adopted by government; and the adoption of any of these philosophies will affect employment, real output, and the price level of the economy.

(a) Proponents of an annually balanced budget would have government expenditures and tax revenues equal in every year. Such a budget is pro-rather than counter-cyclical; but conservative economists favour it to prevent the expansion of the public sector (and the contraction of the private sector) of the economy without the increased payment of taxes by the public.

(b) Those who advocate a cyclically balanced budget propose matching surpluses (in years of prosperity) with deficits (in depression years) to stabilize the economy; but there is no assurance that the surpluses will equal the deficits over the years.

(c) Advocates of functional finance contend that deficits, surpluses, and the size of the debt are of minor importance; and that the goal of full employment without inflation should be achieved regardless of the effects of the necessary fiscal policies upon the budget and the size of the public debt.

3. Any government surplus or deficit automatically affects the size of the public debt.

(a) The Government of Canada's public debt has grown substantially since 1926. This debt is not primarily the result of federal borrowing during wartime; it is primarily the consequence of fiscal policies—government deficits of the past decade.

(b) The total public debt, which includes that of the provincial and local governments and hospitals, currently exceeds $550 billion.

(1) The size of the debt as a percentage of GNP did not grow so rapidly as the absolute size of the debt between 1954 and 1989; but relative to GNP it has increased significantly since the late 1970s.

(2) Since the late 1970s the interest payments on the

debt (because of increases in the size of the debt and higher interest rates in the economy) have also increased significantly; and the interest payments as a percentage of the economy's GNP have grown dramatically.

(3) About 6.4% of the public debt is owed to the Bank of Canada and 93.6% to others; but more importantly, about 23% of it is owed to foreign citizens, firms, and governments.

(4) Because the accounting system used by the federal government records its debts but not its assets, the public debt is not a true picture of its financial position. When adjusted for inflation, the decrease in the real value of its debt can exceed its nominal deficit and result in a real budget surplus.

(5) Among the G-7 countries Canada has the second highest gross debt as a percent of GDP.

4.   The contentions that a large debt will eventually bankrupt the government and that borrowing to finance expenditures passes the cost onto future generations are false.

(a)   The debt cannot bankrupt the government

(1) because the government need not retire (reduce) the debt and can refund (or refinance) it;

(2) because the government has the constitutional authority to levy and collect taxes; and

(3) because the government can always print (or create) money to pay both the principal and the interest on it.

(b)   Deficit financing does not necessarily shift the burden of the debt to future generations.

(1) The debt is largely internally held and the repayment of any portion of the principal and the payment of interest on it does not reduce the wealth or purchasing power of Canadians.

(2) If the increase in government spending is financed by increased personal taxes, the burden of the increased spending is on the present generation whose consumption is reduced; but if it is financed by an increased public debt, the increased borrowing of the federal government will raise interest rates, crowd out investment spending, and future generations will inherit a smaller stock of capital goods.

(3) The burden imposed on future generations is lessened if the increase in government expenditures is for real or human capital or if the economy were initially operating at less than full employment (and it stimulates an increase in investment demand).

(4) Debt held in foreign countries is a burden because both interest and debt repayment require a transfer of real output to other nations.

5.   But the debt does create real and potential problems in the economy.

(a)   The payment of interest on the debt probably increases the extent of income inequality.

(b)   The payment of taxes to finance these interest payments may also reduce the incentives to bear risks, to innovate, to invest, and to save, and so slow economic growth in the economy.

(c)   The portion of the debt that is externally held requires the repayment of principal and the payment of interest to foreign citizens and institutions and transfers a part of the real output of the Canadian economy to them.

6.   Since the mid-1970s the federal government has incurred increasingly large deficits and the public debt has risen.

(a)   This has caused concern because the deficits and the increases in the public debt have grown larger, because interest costs of the debt have risen, and because some of the deficits have taken place in a peacetime economy operating close to full employment.

(b)   These large deficits have produced a cause-and-effect chain of events: they have increased interest rates, and higher interest rates have crowded out real private investment. The increased interest rates have made Canadian securities more attractive to foreigners and the resulting increased foreign investment causes an appreciation of the Canadian dollar, which, in turn, decreases Canadian exports and increases imports. The reduction in net exports has a contractionary effect on Canadian GDP and reduces the expansionary effect of a deficit. However, there is another consideration in that the inflow of foreign funds has lowered interest rates more than would otherwise have been the case, so the crowding-out effect is lessened.

(c)   Despite the problems associated with deficits and the public debt, private and public debt have an important role to play: they absorb the saving done in a growing economy at full employment and sustain the aggregate expenditures of consumers, businesses, and governments at the full-employment level. If consumers and firms do not borrow sufficient amounts, the public debt must be increased to maintain full employment and economic growth in the economy.

7.   A few economists, following the predictions of the Ricardian equivalence theorem, assert that neither a crowding-out effect nor a trade deficit follow from a budget deficit.

IMPORTANT TERMS

annually balanced budget
budget deficit

crowding-out effect
cyclically balanced budget
external debt
functional finance
public debt

FILL-IN QUESTIONS

1. The budget deficit of the federal government in any year is equal to its (expenditures, revenues) _____ less its _____ in that year; and the public debt is equal to the sum of the federal government's past budget _____ less its budget _____.

2. An annually balanced budget is (pro-, counter-) _____ cyclical because governments tend to (raise, lower) _____ taxes and to _____ their purchases of goods and services during a recession (and to do just the opposite during an inflation).

3. A cyclically balanced budget suggests that, to ensure full employment without inflation, the government incur deficits during periods of _____ and surpluses during periods of _____, with the deficits and surpluses equalling each other over the business cycle.

4. Functional finance has as its main goal the achievement of _____, and would regard budget _____ and increases in the _____ _____ as being of secondary importance.

5. The principal causes of the public debt are past _____ and _____ and high _____ _____.

6. The federal public debt is

(a) equal to about $_____ billion and about _____% of the GNP, and the annual interest charges on this debt are about $_____ billion and equal about

_____% of the GNP;

(b) for the most part an (internal, external) _____ debt.

7. (a) About 77% of the public debt is owed to the _____ _____ and to the Bank of _____; and

(b) _____% of this debt is owed to foreigners.

8. The accounting procedures used by the federal government reflect its (assets, debts) _____ but do not reflect its _____. Because inflation (increases, decreases) _____ the real value of the public debt, the nominal budget deficit should be adjusted to take into account the reduction in the real public debt during periods of rising prices.

9. The possibility that the federal government will go bankrupt is a false issue. It need not (reduce, refinance) _____ its debt; it can retire maturing securities by _____ them or by creating _____ and it has the constitutional authority to _____ and _____ taxes.

10. As long as the government expenditures that lead to the increase in the public debt are not financed by borrowing from foreigners, the public debt of Canada is also an _____ of the Canadian people who own government securities.

11. The public debt is a burden on an economy if it is (internally, externally) _____ held. The debt and the payment of interest on it may, however, (increase, decrease) _____ income inequality in the economy; dampen the _____ to work, take risks, save, and invest in the economy; and have a _____ effect on investment.

12. A public debt that is internally held imposes a burden on future generations if the borrowing done to finance an increase in government expenditures (increases, decreases) _____ interest rates, _____ investment spending, and leaves future generations with a smaller stock of _____

goods.

(a) But if the increased government expenditures are financed by an increase in the taxes on personal income, the present generation will have fewer _____ goods and the burden of the increased government expenditures will be on the _____ generation.

(b) These generalizations are subject to two qualifications: The size of the burden of increased government expenditures financed by borrowing on future generations is weakened if the government expenditures finance increases in physical or human _____ or if the economy had been operating at (full, less than full) _____ employment.

13. A government deficit results in a(n) (increased, decreased) _____ interest rate, which causes an (inflow, outflow) _____ of foreign capital. The increased (demand for, supply of) _____ Canadian currency in the foreign exchange market results in a(n) (appreciation, depreciation) _____ of the Canadian dollar, which in turn causes a(n) (increase, decrease) _____ in Canadian exports and a(n) _____ in Canadian imports. The change in net exports has a(n) (expansionary, contractionary) _____ effect on the Canadian GDP.

14. Growing concerns over the budget deficits of the last decade are due to:

(a) _____

(b) _____

(c) _____

(d) _____

15. A few economists disagree with contemporary analysis of the problems caused by government deficits. From their perspective

(a) financing a deficit by borrowing is the same as financing a deficit through a tax increase because of their use of the _____ _____ theorem.

(b) They think that with a budget deficit interest rates (will, will not) _____ increase because private saving will (increase, decrease) _____

in anticipation of higher future taxes, and this saving increase will (increase, offset) _____ the borrowing demands of governments in the credit market.

16. Public and private debts play a positive role if they absorb a sufficient amount of _____ to enable an economy that is (stationary, growing) _____ to remain at _____ _____.

PROBLEMS AND PROJECTS

1. Columns (1) and (2) in the following table are the investment-demand schedule and show planned investment (I) at different rates of interest (i). Assume the marginal propensity to consume in the economy is 0.8 and the marginal propensity to import (MPM) is 0.

(1) i	(2) I	(3) I'
0.08	$115	$125
0.07	140	150
0.06	165	175
0.05	190	200
0.04	215	225

(a) If the federal government were to spend an additional $20 for goods and services, the equilibrium real GDP would (increase, decrease) _____ by $_____.

(b) If the federal government had obtained the additional $20 by

(1) increasing taxes by $20, the equilibrium real GDP would have (increased, decreased) _____ by a total of $_____;

(2) borrowing $20 in the money market and this borrowing had increased the interest rate from 5% to 6%, (i) planned investment spending would have (increased, decreased) _____ by $_____,

(ii) the equilibrium real GDP would have _____ by $_____, and

(iii) the net effect of the increased government spending of the $20 borrowed in the money market would have been to _____ the equilibrium real GDP by $_____.

(c) But if the government deficit-spending had improved business profit expectations and shifted the investment-demand schedule to the one shown in columns (1) and (3) in the table above, the total effect of the increased government spending of the $20 borrowed in the money market would have been to

_____ the equilibrium real GDP by

$_____.

2. This question uses the aggregate expenditures model of the closed economy to illustrate the economic stability effects of a requirement for a balanced budget. The condition met at the equilibrium level of income, as outlined in Chapter 7, is $Y = C + I + G$, where Y is output.

Suppose the consumption (C) schedule is related to disposable income (Y_d) and is given by: $C = 50 + 2/3\ Y_d$.

Assume also that there is a proportional tax system in the economy and taxes equal 25% of income so that: $Y_d = Y - 1/4\ Y$.

(a) In the table below fill in the column indicating disposable income at three income levels. All values are in dollars.

Y	Y_d	C	I	G	Aggregate Expenditure
250	____	____	____	____	____
300	____	____	____	____	____
350	____	____	____	____	____

(b) Given that $I = 25$ and $G = 75$ complete the table .

(c) (1) The equilibrium level of income is _____.

(2) Taxation revenue is _____.

(3) The budget surplus (+) or deficit (−) is _____.

(d) Suppose I drops to 15. Complete the following table.

Y	Y_d	C	I	G	Aggregate Expenditure
250	____	____	____	____	____
280	____	____	____	____	____
300	____	____	____	____	____

(1) The new equilibrium level of income is _____.

(2) The multiplier is _____.

(3) Taxation revenue is _____.

(4) The budget surplus (+) or deficit (−) is _____.

(e) Suppose the rule was made that the budget must be balanced and in this illustration is to be accomplished by reducing government expenditure. Complete the next table, which shows the equilibrium level of income at various levels of government expenditures for the model in this question, with I set at 15.

G	Y	Surplus (+) or Deficit (−)
75	280	_____
70	270	_____
65	260	_____
60	250	_____

(1) The equilibrium level of income at which the budget is balanced is _____.

(2) The requirement of a balanced budget (increased, decreased) _____ the change in equilibrium income brought about initially by a decrease of 10 in investment spending.

(3) The requirement of a balanced budget has (increased, decreased) _____ the multiplier.

3. Inflation reduces the purchasing power of the government debt and some economists argue that the "real" deficit for a year should be calculated by subtracting this decline in purchasing power from the nominal deficit. Given the following information obtain the approximate "real" deficit for 1980 and 1990 by subtracting the loss in purchasing power of the public debt from the nominal budget deficit.

Federal government debt on Jan. 1, 1980 was 70.6 billion; and on Jan. 1, 1990 was 317 billion.

	1980	1990
Price level change	10.77%	3.32%
Nominal deficit (billions)	10.663	29.810
Real deficit	_____	_____

SELF-TEST

Circle T if the statement is true, F if it is false.

1. The budget deficit of the federal government in any year is equal to the amount by which its revenues exceed its expenditures. **T F**

2. A budget surplus increases the public debt, a budget deficit reduces it. **T F**

3. Over the last decade the corporate portion of the public debt has been decreasing and the government portion increasing.   **T F**

4. There is no assurance that a nation can use fiscal policy both to promote full employment and balance its budget cyclically.   **T F**

5. Proponents of functional finance argue that a balanced budget, whether it is balanced annually or over the business cycle, is of minor importance when compared with the objective of full employment without inflation.   **T F**

6. According to the aggregate expenditure model an annually balanced budget would promote economic stability.   **T F**

7. The primary reason for the large increase in the public debt since 1930 is the deficit spending during the years of the Great Depression.   **T F**

8. The federal public debt was about $348 billion in 1991.   **T F**

9. Between 1940 and the present, both the public debt and the interest charges on this debt as percentages of the GDP have decreased.   **T F**

10. About 50% of the public debt is currently held by foreigners.   **T F**

11. Inflation increases the real value of the nominal public debt.   **T F**

12. Selling government securities to foreigners to finance increased expenditures by the federal government imposes a burden on future generations.   **T F**

13. The crowding-out effect of borrowing in the money market to finance an increase in government expenditures is the result of the rise in interest rates in these markets.   **T F**

14. Crowding out shifts the investment demand curve to the left.   **T F**

15. Financing increased government expenditures by increasing personal taxes imposes a burden on future generations.   **T F**

16. Higher interest rates in Canada not only crowd out real investment but make financial investment by foreigners in Canada less attractive.   **T F**

17. The higher interest rates due to a budget deficit attract foreign capital and cause a depreciation of the Canadian dollar.   **T F**

18. Economists who use the Ricardian equivalence

theorem in their analysis believe that federal government deficits have a significant crowding-out effect on investment.   **T F**

19. To maintain full employment in a growing economy it is necessary for the total of public and private debt to increase.   **T F**

20. The federal government could finance a deficit by selling bonds to the Bank of Canada and, through this method, really print money to cover its revenue shortfall.   **T F**

MULTIPLE-CHOICE

Circle the letter that corresponds to the best answer.

1. The Canadian public debt is the sum of all previous
(a) expenditures of the federal government
(b) budget deficits of the federal government
(c) budget deficits less the budget surpluses of the federal government
(d) budget deficits less the budget surpluses of the federal and provincial governments

2. Which of the following would involve reducing government expenditures and increasing tax rates during a depression?
(a) an annually balanced budget policy
(b) functional finance
(c) a cyclically balanced budget policy
(d) a policy employing built-in stability

3. As a percentage of the gross domestic product, the public debt and interest on the debt are respectively about
(a) 47% and 1%
(b) 52% and 6.2%
(c) 55% and 5%
(d) 65% and 6%

4. The annual interest payments on the public debt today are about
(a) $32 billion
(b) $37 billion
(c) $42 billion
(d) $21 billion

5. Since 1980
(a) both the public debt and the interest charges on the debt relative to the GDP have increased
(b) the public debt relative to the GDP has decreased, and the interest charges on the debt relative to the GDP have increased
(c) the public debt relative to the GDP has increased,

and the interest charges on the debt relative to the GDP have decreased
(d) both the public debt and the interest charges on the debt relative to the GDP have decreased

6. Which nation has the larger public debt relative to its GDP in 1992?
(a) Canada
(b) United States
(c) Germany
(d) Italy

7. The accounting procedures used by the federal government record
(a) only its assets
(b) only its debts
(c) both its assets and debts
(d) its net worth

8. Inflation is a tax on
(a) the holders of the public debt and reduces the real size of a budget deficit
(b) the holders of the public debt and expands the real size of a budget deficit
(c) the federal government and reduces the real size of a budget deficit
(d) the federal government and expands the real size of a budget deficit

9. The public debt cannot bankrupt the federal government because the federal government
(a) need not reduce the size of the debt
(b) is able to refinance the debt
(c) can create money to repay the debt and pay the interest on it
(d) all of the above

10. All of the following are used by the government to finance its budget deficit, with the exception of
(a) sale of bonds to the Canadian public
(b) sale of bonds to the Canadian central bank
(c) sale of bonds to foreign investors
(d) sale of common stock to Canadian investors

11. Incurring internal debts to finance a war does not pass the cost of war on to future generations because
(a) the opportunity cost of the war is borne by the generation that fights it
(b) the government need not pay interest on internally held debts
(c) there is never a need for government to refinance the debt
(d) war-time inflation reduces the relative size of the debt

12. Which of the following would be a consequence

of the retirement of the internally held portion of public debt?
(a) a reduction in the nation's productive capacity
(b) a reduction in the nation's standard of living
(c) a redistribution of the nation's wealth among its citizens
(d) an increase in aggregate expenditures in the economy

13. Which of the following is a consequence of the public debt of Canada?
(a) it increases incentives to work and invest
(b) it transfers a portion of the Canadian output of goods and services to foreign nations
(c) it reduces income inequality in Canada
(d) it leads to greater saving at every level of disposable income

14. The crowding-out effect of borrowing in the money market to finance an increase in government expenditures
(a) increases the interest rate and reduces current private investment expenditures
(b) decreases the interest rate and increases private investment expenditures
(c) allows an increase in government and private borrowing
(d) places the burden of the debt on the present generation

15. The crowding-out effect of government borrowing to finance its increased expenditures is reduced
(a) when the economy is operating at less than full employment
(b) when the expenditures expand human capital in the economy
(c) when the government's deficit financing improves the profit expectations of business firms
(d) when any one or more of the above are true

16. Which one of the following is not one of the sources of the recent concern with the deficits of the federal government and the growth of the public debt?
(a) the large increases in the sizes of the deficits and in the public debt
(b) the operation of the economy at full employment
(c) the mounting interest costs of the debt
(d) the fact that large deficits were being incurred during all four phases of the business cycle

17. Suppose the multiplier is 3. Were the amount of saving done at full employment to increase by $20, and were private borrowing to increase by $5, to maintain full employment the public debt would have to increase by
(a) $5

(b) $15

(c) $45

(d) $60

18. The increased demand by foreigners for Canadian bonds that result from higher Canadian interest rates

(a) increase the external debt of Canada and cause the Canadian dollar to depreciate

(b) lower the external debt of Canada and cause the Canadian dollar to appreciate

(c) increase the external debt of Canada and cause the Canadian dollar to appreciate

(d) lower the external debt of Canada and cause the Canadian dollar to depreciate

19. When the Canadian dollar appreciates

(a) Canadian exports tend to increase

(b) Canadian imports tend to increase

(c) Canadian net exports tend to increase

(d) none of the above tend to occur

20. Some modern economists, using the Ricardian equivalence theorem, argue that recent federal deficits have

(a) had desirable effects on the economy because of the fiscal policy stimulus

(b) had little effect on the economy because households respond to budget deficits by increasing their present saving in anticipation of higher future taxes

(c) created a sizable trade imbalance with other nations and contributed to the selling of Canadian assets to foreigners

(d) caused interest rates to rise and crowded out private investment

DISCUSSION QUESTIONS

1. What is the difference between the (federal) budget deficit and the public debt?

2. Explain why an annually balanced budget is not "neutral" and how it can intensify, rather than reduce, the tendencies for GDP to rise and fall.

3. How does a cyclically balanced budget philosophy differ from the philosophy of functional finance? Why do advocates of functional finance argue that budget deficits and a mounting public debt are of secondary importance?

4. How big is the public debt of Canada, absolutely and relatively? How large are the interest charges on the debt, absolutely and relatively? What has happened to the size of the debt and interest charges since 1926, and since 1975? Why have these changes occurred?

5. In what way do the accounting procedures of the federal government misstate its actual financial position (its net worth)? How does inflation affect the real size of the public debt and the real size of the federal government's budget deficits?

6. Why can't the public debt result in the bankruptcy of the federal government?

7. Explain the difference between an internally held and an externally held public debt. If the debt is internally held, government borrowing to finance a war does not pass all the cost of the war on to future generations. Why?

8. How does the public debt and the payment of interest on this debt affect (a) the distribution of income and (b) incentives? Why does the portion of the public debt externally held impose a burden on the economy?

9. How can deficit financing impose a burden on future generations? Why don't increases in government expenditures financed by increased personal taxes impose the same burden on future generations? What will lessen the burden of deficit financing on future generations?

10. What tends to happen to the amount of saving done at full employment as the full-employment GDP grows? Why, in a growing economy, must debt increase in order to maintain full employment and economic growth?

11. What heightened the concern of the public in the early 1980s over budget deficits and the increase in the public debt? How do budget deficits (and the increase in the public debt) affect (a) interest rates; (b) planned domestic investment in real capital and the financial investment of foreigners in Canadian bonds; (c) the external debts of Canada and the international value of the dollar; (d) Canadian exports and imports of goods and services; and (e) employment and real output in the Canadian economy?

12. Explain how an economist, using the Ricardian equivalence theorem, could conclude that a budget deficit would have neither crowding-out nor trade deficit linkages.

ANSWERS

Fill-In Questions

1. expenditures, revenues, deficits, surpluses

2. pro-, raise, lower

3. recession, inflation

4. full employment without inflation, deficits, public debt

5. wars, recessions, interest rates

6. (a) 350, 52, 42, 6.2; (b) internal

7. (a) Canadian public, Canada; (b) 23

8. debts, assets; decreases

9. reduce, refinancing, money, levy, collect

10. asset

11. externally; increase, incentives, crowding-out

12. increases, decreases, capital; (a) consumer, present; (b) capital, less than full

13. increased, inflow; demand for, appreciation, decrease, increase; contractionary

14. (a) their enormous size (b) rising interest costs (c) inappropriate cyclical policy (d) balance of trade problems

15. (a) Ricardian equivalence (b) will not, increase, offset

16. saving, growing, full employment

Problems and projects

1. (a) increase, 100 (b) (1) increased, 20, (2)(i) decreased, 25 (ii) decreased, 125 (iii) decrease, 25 (c) increase, 25

2. (a) Y_d: 187.50, 225, 262.50
(b) C: 175, 200, 225
I: 25, 25, 25
G: 75, 75, 75
Agg. Exp.: 275, 300, 325
(c) (1) 300; (2) 75; (3) 0
(d) Y_d: 187.50, 210, 225
C: 175, 190, 200
I: 15, 15, 15
G: 75, 75, 75
Agg. Exp.: 265, 280, 290
(1) 280, (2) 2, (3) 70, (4) -5
(e) surplus(+)/deficit (-): -5; -2.5; 0; + 2.5
(1) 260 (2) increased, (3) increased

3. 1980: 3.06 billion; 1990: 19.29 billion

Self-test

1. F; 2. F; 3. F; 4. T; 5. T; 6. F; 7. F; 8. T; 9. F; 10. F; 11. F; 12. T; 13. T; 14. F; 15. F; 16. F; 17. F; 18. F; 19. T; 20. T

Multiple-Choice

1. (c); 2. (a); 3. (b); 4. (c); 5. (a); 6. (d); 7. (b); 8. (a); 9. (d); 10. (d); 11. (a); 12. (c); 13. (b); 14. (a); 15. (d); 16. (b); 17. (b); 18. (c); 19. (b); 20. (b)

CHAPTER

16 Economic Growth

Chapter 16 is the last of three chapters that discusses macroeconomic issues and problems of recent concern in Canada. While the previous chapters focused primarily on short-term instability in output and the price level, this chapter looks at the longer-term problem of economic growth—the factor that ultimately determines the living standard that can be provided the citizens of this country.

After briefly defining and pointing out the significance of growth, the text analyses the six factors that make growth possible. The four supply factors increase the output potential of the economy. Whether the economy actually produces its full potential—that is, whether the economy has both full employment and full production—depends upon two other factors: the level of aggregate expenditures (the demand factor) and the efficiency with which the economy reallocates resources (the allocative factor).

To explain the role that the six factors play in determining growth in an economy two familiar models—the production possibilities model and the aggregate demand–aggregate supply model—are utilized. The supply factors shift the production possibilities curve to the right and make possible a higher level of output. In the aggregate supply model a movement to the right of the aggregate supply curve also occurs. It is simply not enough to have the potential to produce, but there must also exist a demand for the product in the market economy. The aggregate demand for the economy's output together with the aggregate supply determine the actual output level. Both the short-run and long-run shifts in aggregate supply combined with shifts in aggregate demand (and the supply and demand factors underlying these shifts) determine the output and price level.

Why has Canada grown economically or why have living standards improved over time? First, because Canada's population and the size of its labour force have grown. Second, and more important, the productivity of the labour force in Canada has increased. The increase

in the productivity of labour is the result of technological advances; the expansion of the stock of capital goods in the Canadian economy; the improved education and training of its labour force; economies of scale; the reallocation of resources; the generous quantities of natural resources with which the Canadian economy was endowed; and its social, cultural, and political environment. But in addition to the increases in the ability of the economy to produce goods and services made possible by the supply and allocative factors, aggregate expenditures expanded sufficiently (though unsteadily) to bring about most of the actual growth made possible by the increases in the quantity and the productivity of labour.

Beginning in the early 1970s, however, the rate at which the productivity of labour in Canada increased was dramatically less than it had been in earlier years. The same slowdown was experienced by the major industrialized countries, but in the important manufacturing sector the Canadian productivity performance lagged behind that of its major competitors. Canada's productivity performance compares favourably with that of other countries over a period of years. It is the more recent slowdown that is the cause of the present concern. This slowdown has a number of causes and, in a more internationally competitive economy, holds the prospect of slower improvements in Canadian living standards. You should be sure you understand the causes, because the solutions to problems require elimination of the causes.

The latter part of Chapter 16 asks an important question— whether economic growth is desirable in the already affluent Canadian economy. The controversy over whether growth should be a social goal with a high priority in Canada has, of course, two sides to it. The case in defence of and the case against growth are both considered. You will have to decide for yourself which case is the stronger and whether the social benefits from growth are worth the costs. Should, as a society, we determine that growth is desirable we must then determine the policy or combination of policies to best achieve this.

Actually, Chapter 16 uses some of the ideas, terms, and theories found in earlier chapters to explain what makes an economy capable of growing (that is, what increases the size of its full-employment or capacity output) and what is necessary if it is actually to grow (that is, if it is to produce all that its expanding capital allows). You also are presented with historical data on the Canadian economy to place economic growth in a long-run perspective. With careful reading you should have little or no trouble with Chapter 16, providing you understood the material in the earlier chapters.

CHECKLIST

When you have studied this chapter, you should be able to:

■ Distinguish between employment theory and growth economics.

■ Define economic growth in two different ways.

■ Explain why economic growth is important to any economy.

■ Use the "rule of 70" to demonstrate how different growth rates affect real domestic output over time.

■ Identify the four supply factors that determine the rate of economic growth.

■ Explain demand and allocative factors that affect economic growth.

■ Use the production possibilities curve to explain how the supply and demand factors affect economic growth.

■ Use the aggregate demand–aggregate supply model to explain how both demand and supply factors interact over time to determine the change in both real output and the price level.

■ Describe the growth record of the Canadian economy in the twentieth century, and its two long-term rates of economic growth.

■ Explain the difference between the productivity of labour and total factor productivity (TFP).

■ State the two fundamental means by which an economy can increase its real GDP, and the relative importance of these two means of increasing the real GDP in Canada since 1961.

■ Enumerate the several sources of the growth of the productivity of labour in Canada, and state their relative importance in the growth of its real national income using Table 16-3.

■ Enumerate the four principal causes and the three principal implications of the slowdown in the rate at which labour productivity has increased in Canada since the early 1970s.

■ Present the case against further economic growth in Canada.

■ Defend further economic growth.

■ Outline the three types of economic policies that might be utilized to stimulate growth in Canada.

CHAPTER OUTLINE

1. While employment theory is concerned with the short run and an economy with a fixed productive capacity, growth economics deals with the long run and changes in productive capacity over time.

(a) Economic growth means an increase in either the total or the per capita real output of an economy. It is measured in terms of the annual percentage rate of growth of either total or per capita real output.

(b) Economic growth is important because it lessens the burden of scarcity: it provides the means of satisfying existing wants more fully and of fulfilling new wants.

(c) One or two percentage point differences in the rate of growth result in substantial differences in annual increases in the economy's output.

2. In general, potential output can increase by increasing the quantity of inputs, or by using inputs more efficiently, or some combination of both. Whether the potential growth will occur depends upon demand factors and the efficient allocation of existing resources.

(a) Supply factors include the quantity and quality of resources (human, natural, capital) and technology.

(b) Demand factors influence the utilization of the inputs and determine whether a full employment output is attained.

(c) Allocative efficiency determines whether maximum output is obtained from the existing stock of resources.

3. Two of the economic models previously introduced can be used in the analysis of economic growth.

(a) (1) In the production possibilities model, economic growth shifts the production possibilities curve outward because of increased supplies of the inputs or increasing input productivity.

(2) Whether the economy operates on the curve depends on demand considerations as well as the efficient allocation of the inputs.

(b) In the aggregate demand–aggregate supply model supply factors that contribute to economic growth shift the vertical supply curve to the right. Since the price level has increased over time, this suggests that the increase in potential output has been accompanied by an even greater increase in aggregate demand.

4.   The growth record of the Canadian economy has been impressive, with real GDP increases averaging more than 4% per year since 1961; but on a per capita basis the growth rate is much less impressive. If the slowdown in per capita real income (which began in the early 1970s) is not reversed, the outlook for continued improvement in Canadian living standards becomes somewhat uncertain. A promising reversal of the decreasing growth rate in productivity was cut short by the 1990-1991 cyclical downturn.

(a)   Economic well-being may be understated by economic growth figures because they do not take into account improvements in product quality or increases in leisure time.

(b)   But growth may have adverse effects on the environment and the quality of life, thus the data may overstate the benefits of growth.

5.   Output can increase due to 1) an increase in resource inputs and/or 2) an improvement in the output per unit of input. In Canada 75% of the increase in real GDP between 1961 and 1989 was due to input increases and 25% due to productivity growth. Factors contributing to the real growth follow.

(a)   (1) The size of Canadian labour input has grown at an annual rate of 2% over the last 30 years. Declines in the rate of population growth were offset by immigration and the increased participation of women in the labour force.

(2) Over the 1961-1989 period the capital to labour ratio grew at an annual rate of 1.7% per year. An increased quantity of capital per worker results in a more productive work force. In addition, technological improvement usually entails investment in new machinery.

(3) Increased investment in human capital (in the education and training of workers) improved worker productivity.

(4) Economies of scale and improved resource allocation also expanded the productivity of workers.

(5) Canada's exploitation of abundant and varied natural resources contributed to its impressive growth record.

(6) A social-cultural-political environment that stressed the desirability of continued improvement in individual economic circumstances provided an environment conducive to economic growth.

(b)   The improvement in the efficiency of input usage is measured by total factor productivity. This measure reflects the growth in output not accounted for by the growth of all the inputs. Total factor productivity is bound up with technological advance—new production

techniques, product innovation, the discovery of new knowledge, and new forms of business organization and managerial techniques. As noted above, 25% of the total growth in real GDP was due to increased input efficiency.

6.   From the early 1970s to the middle 1980s the annual rates of increase in the productivity of labour have slowed down substantially below the levels realized in the three decades following World War II. A reversal of this trend in the later years of the 1980s was cut short by a recession. The slowdown was caused by the slower growth in total factor productivity. Suggested causes have included:

(a)   increased energy prices, which led to the use of less-productive labour intensive techniques

(b)   a slowing of technological progress

(c)   unfavourable intersectoral shifts

(d)   slower improvements in labour quality

(e)   depressed demand induced by the federal government in an effort to control inflation.

7.   The significance of this slowdown is that

(a)   it decreases the rates at which real wage rates and the standard of living can rise;

(b)   it contributes to rising unit labour costs and to inflation in the Canadian economy; and

(c)   it leads to higher prices for Canadian goods in world markets and the loss of these markets to Canadian producers.

8.   Canadians today debate whether economic growth is or is not desirable.

(a)   Those opposed to rapid economic growth contend that

(1) it pollutes the environment;

(2) it is not needed to resolve domestic problems;

(3) it makes people more anxious and insecure; and

(4) while providing more goods and services, it does not result in a better life.

(b)   Those in favour of growth argue that

(1) it results in a higher standard of living and lessens the burden of scarcity;

(2) it is not the cause of pollution;

(3) it is the easiest way to bring about a more equitable distribution of income; and

(4) ending or slowing growth will not improve the quality of life.

9.   To stimulate economic growth in the Canadian economy Keynesians stress policies that would expand aggregate expenditures and constrain government spending and consumption; supply-side economists stress policies that would expand the economy's capacity output by increasing saving, investment, work effort, and risk taking; and others advocate the use of an industrial policy

that would shape the structure and the composition of industry in the economy.

IMPORTANT TERMS

economic growth
industrial policy
labour productivity
supply, demand, and allocative factors in growth
total factor productivity (TFP)

FILL-IN QUESTIONS

1.   Employment theory assumes that the productive capacity of the economy is (fixed, variable) _____, while growth economics is concerned with an economy whose productive capacity (increases, remains constant) _____ over time.

2.   Economic growth can mean an increase in either the _____ or the _____ of an economy.

3.   A rise in output per capita (increases, decreases) _____ the standard of living and _____ the burden of scarcity in the economy.

4.   Assume that an economy has a GDP of $400 billion. If the growth rate is 6%, GDP will increase by $_____ billion a year; but if the rate of growth is only 4%, the annual increase in GDP will be $_____ billion. A two percentage point difference in the growth rate results in a $_____ billion difference in the annual increase in GDP.

5.   Graphically, economic growth can be shown as a _____ shift of the production possibilities curve or as a combined shift to the right of the _____ _____ and _____ _____ curves.

6.   In the production possibilities model, economic growth increases primarily because of (demand, supply) _____ factors, but the economy may not

reach its full potential because there may be less than full _____ or full _____.

7.   The four supply factors in economic growth are:

(a)   _____

(b)   _____

(c)   _____

(d)   _____

The other two factors are the _____ factor and the _____ factor.

8.   The real GDP of any economy in any year is equal to the _____ of labour employed multiplied by the _____ of labour.
(a)   The former is measured by the (number of workers, hours of labour) _____ employed.
(b)   The latter is equal to the real GDP per _____ per _____.

9.   In recent decades a (rising, falling) _____ price level has accompanied economic growth. This suggests that the aggregate (demand, supply) _____ has increased more rapidly than the aggregate _____.

10.   Data on growth in output may understate the improvement in living standards since _____ _____ and increases in _____ _____ are not reflected in the figures.

11.   Any tendency for the rate of growth in productivity to fall can be lessened or overcome by increasing the _____ of workers. The three principal means of doing this are to increase the stock of _____, to improve _____, and to improve the _____ and _____ of the work force.

12.   Expenditures for new capital goods both increase _____ _____ and add to the _____ _____ of the economy; the amount by which investment expenditures expand the latter depend upon the volume of investment expenditures and the _____-_____

_____.

13.   In Canada, since 1946, real GDP has increased about _____ fold, and real per capita GDP has increased about _____ fold.

14.   Since 1961 real GDP has increased on the average about _____% per year, while per capita real output has increased at a rate of about _____% per year.

15.   Technological progress means that we learn how to employ given quantities of resources to obtain greater _____; and, more often than not, this progress requires _____ in new machinery and equipment.

16.   In the 1961-1989 period about _____% of the increase in real output was due to total _____ _____ or getting more output per unit of _____ and _____.

17.   The rate of growth in labour productivity (increased, decreased) _____ in the 1973-1982 period.

(a)   This resulted in a (rise, fall) _____ in the rates at which the standard of _____ and the (money, real) _____ wages of labour have increased, in a (rise, fall) _____ in unit labour costs and (inflation, deflation) _____ in Canada, and the loss of international markets to (Canadian, foreign) _____ producers of goods and services.

(b)   Its causes were probably due to (increased, decreased) _____ energy prices and a reduction in _____ progress, which may have followed a (rise, decline) _____ in R&D spending as a proportion of GDP, slower improvements in labour _____, some lessening of the intersectoral shift of the _____ _____ and depressed _____ induced by the _____ _____.

18.   If there is to be economic growth in a society the social environment must encourage changes in _____, in productive _____, and capital facilities.

19.   Influential economists arguing against the need for growth in Canada believe that growth _____ the environment, does not lead to the solution of _____ _____, breeds _____ and _____, and does not result in the _____ _____.

20.   Those who favour growth for the Canadian economy argue that it is the basic way to raise the standard of _____ and lessen the _____ dilemma, that economic growth does not necessarily result in _____, that growth is the only practical way of obtaining a more _____ distribution of _____, and that limiting growth will not bring about a _____ _____.

21.   To stimulate economic growth in Canada,
(a)   Keynesians stress the (supply, demand) _____-side of growth, favour (high, low) _____ interest rates to expand _____ spending, and would use fiscal policies to (expand, contract) _____ government spending and consumption;
(b)   supply-side economists stress policies that would stimulate _____, _____, _____ _____, and entrepreneurial _____ to expand (aggregate expenditures, capacity output) _____.
(c)   Others stress policies that would shape the _____ and _____ of Canadian industry and are called _____ policy.

PROBLEMS AND PROJECTS

1.   Suppose the real GDP and the population of an economy in six different years were those shown in the following table.

Year	Population (Millions)	Real GDP (Billions of Dollars)	Per Capita Real GDP
1	30	$ 9	$300
2	60	24	$_____
3	90	45	$_____
4	120	66	$_____
5	150	90	$_____
6	180	99	$_____

(a) How large would the real per capita GDP of the economy be in each of the other five years? Put your figures in the above table.
(b) What was the amount of growth in real GDP between year 1 and year 2? $_____
(c) What was the rate of growth in real GDP between year 3 and year 4? _____%

2. The table below shows the quantity of labour (measured in hours) and the productivity of labour (measured in real GDP per hour) in a hypothetical economy in three different years.

Year	Quantity of Labour	Productivity of Labour	Real GDP
1	1,000	$100	$_____
2	1,000	105	$_____
3	1,100	105	$_____

(a) Compute the economy's real GDP in each of the three years and enter them in the table.
(b) Between years 1 and 2, the quantity of labour remained constant; but
(1) the productivity of labour increased by _____%; and
(2) as a consequence, real GDP increased by _____%.
(c) Between years 2 and 3, the productivity of labour remained constant; but
(1) the quantity of labour increased by _____%; and
(2) as a consequence, real GDP increased by _____%.
(d) Between years 1 and 3,
(1) real GDP increased by _____%; and
(2) this rate of increase is approximately equal to the sum of the rates of increase in the _____

and the _____ of labour.

3. The following table gives the average annual percentage change in labour productivity and related measures in Canada and the United States for the 1961-1973 and 1982-1989 periods.

Manufacturing industries	1961-1973		1982-1989	
	Canada	United States	Canada	United States
Real GDP per person-hour	3.9	2.8	1.7	1.7
Real GDP	5.9	4.2	4.6	4.5
Person-hours	1.9	1.4	2.8	2.7
Unit labour cost	3.5	3.3	3.5	2.4
Compensation per person hour	7.6	6.2	5.3	4.1

(a) In comparing the economic performance of the manufacturing sector of the economies of the two countries what conclusions do you arrive at concerning:
(1) productivity growth rates
(2) unit labour costs
(3) relative wage rates
(b) Suppose that in 1961 labour was about 20% more productive in the United States than in Canada. What has happened to that productivity gap in the last thirty years?
(c) If the exchange rate between the U.S. dollar and the Canadian dollar had remained constant over this time period, have Canadian manufacturers, on the whole, become more or less competitive against their U. S. counterparts?

SELF-TEST

Circle T if the statement is true, F if it is false.

1. Growth economics is concerned with an economy in which productive capacity is not fixed. T F

2. The better of the two definitions of economic growth is an increase in the per capita real output of the economy. T F

3. Suppose two economies each have GDPs of $500 billion. If the GDPs grow at annual rates of 3% in the first and 5% in the second economy, the difference in their amounts of growth in one year is $10 billion. T F

4. The potential of an increased productive capacity of an economy will not be completely realized unless there is full employment of resources and full production in the economy. T F

5. Economic growth moves an economy from some

point inside the production possibilities curve to a point on the production possibilities boundary. **T F**

6. An increase in growth will increase the long-run aggregate supply curve and the short-run aggregate supply curve, but decrease the aggregate demand curve. **T F**

7. The demand factor in economic growth refers to the ability of the economy to expand its production as the demand for product grows. **T F**

8. The allocative factor in economic growth refers to the ability of the economy to move resources from one use to another as the productive capacity of the economy grows. **T F**

9. The productivity of labour measures the real output per member of the labour force. **T F**

10. Real GDP has tended to increase more rapidly than per capita GDP in Canada. **T F**

11. Growth and rates-of-growth estimates generally attempt to take account of changes in the quality of goods produced and in the amount of leisure that members of the economy enjoy. **T F**

12. The real GDP of an economy in any year is equal to its input of labour divided by the productivity of labour. **T F**

13. The population of Canada is over five times what it was in 1900. **T F**

14. The growth in real GDP in Canada has increased at a steady, if not overly rapid, rate since 1961. **T F**

15. A decline in the rate of increase of population will bring about a decline in the rate of increase of real GDP. **T F**

16. Total factor productivity measures the change in output not accounted for by changes in the quantity of inputs. **T F**

17. More often than not, technological progress requires the economy to invest in new machinery and equipment. **T F**

18. The Canadian social, cultural, and political environment has, in general, worked to slow Canadian economic growth. **T F**

19. Increased total factor productivity was more important than increased labour inputs in the growth of the Canadian economy between 1961 and 1989. **T F**

20. Since 1961, increased inputs of labour and capital have together accounted for the major part of real GDP growth in Canada. **T F**

21. Canada was unique among industrialized countries in suffering a decrease in productivity growth in the 1970s. **T F**

22. Increases in labour productivity can, at least in the Canadian economy, be taken pretty much for granted, because the rate of increase has been nearly constant for much more than half a century. **T F**

23. By opening larger markets for our products, various free trade agreements will allow the productivity improvements that accompany larger sized plants to be realized in Canada. **T F**

24. Depressed demand had little to do with the Canadian labour productivity slowdown, 1974-84. **T F**

25. The availability of natural resources in Canada has been a significant factor in the growth of the Canadian economy. **T F**

26. Supply-side economists favour increasing taxes to stimulate saving, investment, and economic growth in the economy. **T F**

27. Economic growth lessens the problem of scarcity. **T F**

MULTIPLE-CHOICE

Circle the letter that corresponds to the best answer.

1. Which of the following is not one of the benefits of economic growth to a society?
(a) everyone enjoys a greater real income
(b) the standard of living in that society increases
(c) the burden of scarcity decreases
(d) the society is better able to satisfy new wants

2. If the real output of an economy were to increase from $2,000 billion to $2,100 billion in one year, the rate of growth of real output during that year would be
(a) 0.5%
(b) 5%
(c) 10%
(d) 50%

3. Suppose an economy has a GDP of $700 billion and an annual growth rate of 5%. Over a two-year period, GDP will increase by
(a) $14 billion
(b) $35 billion
(c) $70 billion
(d) $71.75 billion

The labour input in hours worked and the real GDP for a hypothetical economy are given in the table below. Answer questions 4 and 5 on the basis of the data.

Year	Hours Worked (Millions)	Real GDP (Billions)
1980	15	$24
1981	15.6	25
1982	16	27.22

4.   Over the time period real GDP grew at an average annual rate of
(a)   20%
(b)   10%
(c)   6.5%
(d)   12%

5.   Over the time period the rate of growth of labour productivity
(a)   increased at a constant rate
(b)   increased at a decreasing rate
(c)   increased at an increasing rate
(d)   decreased

6.   If the production possibilities curve of an economy moves from *AB* to *CD* on the following graph, it is most likely caused by
(a)   supply factors
(b)   demand factors
(c)   allocative factors
(d)   industrial policy

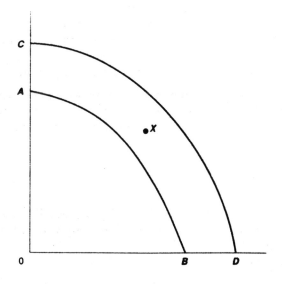

7.   If the production possibilities curve in the diagram above is *CD* and the economy is operating at *X*, the

reasons are most likely to be due to
(a)   supply and environmental factors
(b)   demand and allocative factors
(c)   increased labour productivity
(d)   increased total factor productivity

8.   Which of the following is not a supply factor in economic growth?
(a)   an expansion in purchasing power
(b)   an increase in the economy's stock of capital goods
(c)   more natural resources
(d)   technological improvements

9.   Since 1946, real per capita GDP in Canada has increased about
(a)   fivefold
(b)   sixfold
(c)   tenfold
(d)   twentyfold

10.   From 1961-1991 the total output of the Canadian economy has increased at an average annual rate of about
(a)   4-4.4%
(b)   2-2.5%
(c)   3-3.5%
(d)   5-5.5%

11.   Total output per capita in Canada from 1961-1991 increased at an annual rate of about
(a)   0.8%
(b)   1.7%
(c)   2.8%
(d)   3.8%

12.   The supply of which of the following is the most nearly fixed?
(a)   natural resources
(b)   labour
(c)   capital
(d)   money

13.   About what percentage of the increase in the total output of the Canadian economy between 1961 and 1989 was due to increases in the quantities of capital and labour employed?
(a)   20%
(b)   23%
(c)   54%
(d)   75%

14.   During the 1973-89 period the productivity of labour in Canada increased at an average annual rate of about
(a)   0.8%
(b)   1.0%
(c)   1.5%

(d) 4.0%

15. The decline in the rate at which the productivity of labour increased between 1973 and 1982 in Canada can be attributed to a number of factors. Which of the following is probably not one of these factors?
(a) an increase in the relative prices of Canadian goods in world markets
(b) increased energy prices
(c) slower improvements in labour quality
(d) the decline in research and development expenditures as a percentage of GDP in Canada

16. If the decline in the rate at which the productivity of labour has increased (which is evident for the period 1973-1982 in Canada) should continue, the result will be
(a) a decline in the international value of the Canadian dollar
(b) a decline in the standard of living in Canada
(c) higher inflation rates in Canada
(d) all of the above

17. Which of the following is not one of the consequences when aggregate expenditures increase by less than the productive capacity of the economy?
(a) inflation
(b) a recessionary gap
(c) a slower rate of economic growth
(d) unemployed labour

18. Which of the following is not a part of the case against economic growth?
(a) growth produces pollution
(b) growth impedes the increased production of consumer goods
(c) growth prevents the attainment of a better life
(d) growth is not needed to provide us with the means of solving domestic social problems

19. Which of the following is not a part of the case in defence of economic growth?
(a) growth lessens the unlimited wants–scarce resources problem
(b) growth lessens the extent of anxiety and insecurity
(c) growth need not be accompanied by the pollution of the environment
(d) growth is the only practical way to reduce poverty

20. To promote economic growth, Keynesians would tend to give the most support to
(a) an industrial policy
(b) an easy money policy
(c) constraints on government spending
(d) constraints on consumption spending

21. What type of policy is being suggested by the person who makes this statement: ''What this nation needs is a comprehensive plan developed by government and business to direct economic activity to those opportunities that have the best chance of creating more economic growth for the nation? ''
(a) a demand-side policy
(b) a supply-side policy
(c) an industrial policy
(d) an investment policy

DISCUSSION QUESTIONS

1. How does growth economics differ from the theory of employment (or the theory of national income determination)?

2. What is meant by economic growth? Why should Canadians be concerned with economic growth?

3. How does economic growth affect the production possibilities curve? What demand and allocative assumptions are necessary to achieve maximum productive potential?

4. Describe how economic growth can be illustrated in an aggregate demand–aggregate supply model. What has happened to aggregate demand compared to long-run aggregate supply when the price level and real domestic output both increase?

5. What are the six basic ingredients of economic growth? What is the essential difference between the supply factors and the other two factors? Is there any relationship between the strength of the supply factors and the strength of the demand factor?

6. What is meant by allocative efficiency? Why is this kind of efficiency important if there is to be economic growth?

7. What has been the growth record of the Canadian economy since 1946, and since 1961? Compare recent Canadian growth rates with those in other nations.

8. What is the relationship between the real GDP produced in any year and the quantity of labour employed and the labour productivity?

9. In what units are the quantity of labour and the productivity of labour measured? What are the factors that affect the productivity of labour?

10. What is the relationship between investment and the stock of capital? What is the connection between increases in the capital stock and the rate of economic growth?

11. If the quantity of the labour and capital inputs stayed constant from year to year what productivity measure would indicate how quickly production is growing?

12. What have been the sources of the economic growth that Canada has experienced from 1961-1989?

13. By how much have the annual increases in the productivity of labour declined in Canada in the 1973-1989 period? What were (a) the causes and (b) the consequences of this decline?

14. What are the economic consequences if aggregate demand increases less than productive capacity increases? What are the long-term consequences of this macroeconomic instability?

15. What arguments can be presented on both sides of the question of whether growth in Canada is desirable?

16. What (a) policies do Keynesians advocate to stimulate economic growth; (b) policies do supply-side economists favour to stimulate economic growth; (c) is meant by "industrial policy"?

17. What relationship exists between international competitiveness of Canadian firms and the relative rates of productivity growth in Canada and abroad?

ANSWERS

Fill-in questions

1. fixed, increases

2. total real output (GDP), real output (GDP) per capita

3. increases, reduces

4. 24, 16; 8

5. rightward, aggregate demand, aggregate supply

6. supply, employment, production

7. (a) quantity and quality of natural resources (b) quantity and quality of human resources (c) the supply or stock of capital goods (d) technology; demand, allocative

8. quantity, productivity; (a) hours of labour; (b) worker, hour (either order)

9. rising; demand, supply

10. improved products, leisure time

11. productivity; capital, technology, education, training

12. aggregate expenditures, productive capacity, capital–output ratio

13. ten, five

14. 4.1, 1.7

15. output (production), investment

16. 25, factor productivity, capital, labour

17. decreased, (a) fall, living, real, rise, inflation, foreign (b) increased, technological, decline, quality, labour force, demand, federal government

18. products, techniques

19. pollutes, domestic problems, anxiety, insecurity, good life

20. living, unlimited wants–scarce resources, pollution, equitable, income, better life

21. (a) demand, low, investment, contract; (b) saving, investment, work effort, risk-taking, capacity output; (c) structure, composition, industrial

Problems and projects

1. (a) 400, 500, 550, 600, 550; (b) $15 billion; (c) 46.67%

2. (a) 100,000, 105,000, 115,500; (b) (1) 5, (2) 5; (c) (1) 10, (2) 10; (d) (1) 15.5, (2) quantity, productivity

3. (a) (1) The productivity of labour increased at a faster rate in Canada in the 1961-1989 period and at the same rate in the later period. (2) Unit labour costs increased at a faster rate in Canada in both periods. (3) Wage rates increased at a faster rate in Canada in both periods. (b) The productivity gap closed over the time period due to the more rapid rate of productivity growth in Canada in the earlier period. (c) Canadian manufacturers would have become less competitive due to the greater rate of increase of unit costs.

Self-test

1. T; 2. T; 3. T; 4. T; 5. F; 6. F; 7. F; 8. T; 9. F; 10. T; 11. F; 12. F; 13. T; 14. F; 15. T; 16. T; 17. T; 18. F; 19. F; 20. T; 21. F; 22. F; 23. T; 24. F; 25. T; 26. F; 27. T

Multiple-choice

1. (a); 2. (b); 3. (d); 4. (c); 5. (c); 6. (a); 7. (b); 8. (a); 9. (a); 10. (a); 11. (b); 12. (a); 13. (d); 14. (c); 15. (a); 16. (d); 17. (a); 18. (b); 19. (b); 20. (a); 21. (c)

International Economics and the World Economy

PART 5

CHAPTER

17 International Trade: Comparative Advantage and Protectionism

This is the first of three chapters dealing with international trade and finance. International trade is a subject that is becoming more familiar to Canadians following a vigorous national debate on the merits of the Free Trade Agreement with the United States and the proposed North American Free Trade Agreement between Canada, the United States, and Mexico. Many of the terms, concepts, and ideas encountered in these chapters will be unfamiliar; but most of this material is fairly straightforward and the theoretical foundation of free trade not overly difficult to grasp if you will take some pains to examine it. The ideas and concepts employed are new, but they are not especially complex.

At the beginning, it is essential to recognize that international trade is important to Canada. Canada's merchandise exports and imports were, respectively, $138 and $135 billion in 1991. In relative terms, some other nations have merchandise exports and imports that are larger percentages of their GDPs, but the Canadian percentage of about 25% is not trivial, and when services are included the proportion of GDP devoted to exports increases to almost 30%. It is equally important for you to understand from the beginning that international trade differs from the trade that goes on within nations. Different nations use different monies, not just one money; resources are less mobile internationally than they are intranationally; and governments interfere even more with foreign than they do with domestic trade.

But while foreign trade differs from domestic trade in these three ways, nations trade for the same basic reason that people within a nation trade—to take advantage of the benefits of specialization. Nations specialize in and export those goods and services that they can produce with a comparative advantage. A comparative advantage means that the opportunity cost of producing a particular good or service is lower in that nation than in another nation. Nations produce and export those goods and services in which they have a comparative advantage. In this way, all nations are able to obtain

products that are produced as inexpensively as possible. Put another way, when nations specialize in those products in which they have a comparative advantage, the world as a whole can obtain more goods and services from its resources; and each of the nations of the world can enjoy a standard of living higher than it would have if it did not specialize and export and import.

But regardless of the advantages of specialization and trade among nations, people in Canada and throughout the world have for well over 200 years debated whether free trade or protection was the better policy for their nation. Economists took part in this debate and, with few exceptions, argued for free trade and against protection. Those who favour free trade contend that free trade benefits both the nation and the world as a whole. "Free traders" argue that tariffs, import quotas, and other barriers to international trade prevent or reduce specialization and decrease both a nation's and the world's production and standard of living.

But nations have erected and continue to erect barriers to trade with other nations. The questions upon which the latter part of this chapter focuses attention are: (1) what motivates nations to impose tariffs and to limit the quantities of goods imported from abroad; (2) what effects does protection have upon a nation's own prosperity and upon the prosperity of the world; and (3) what kinds of arguments do those who favour protection employ to support their position — on what grounds do they base their contention that their nation will benefit from the erection of barriers that reduce imports from foreign nations?

The chapter's final major section covers three topics: (1) a review of Canadian trade policy over the past century; (2) the Canada–U.S. Free Trade Agreement (FTA); and (3) a brief overview of the proposed North America Free Trade Zone. In 1934 a series of gradual but substantial tariff reductions began that have continued right up to the present under the General Agreement on Tariffs and Trade (GATT). There has also been economic integration among nations that reduces restrictions on their trade flows with one another. The European Economic Community, or Common Market, and the proposed North America free trade zone are examples of economic structures that reduce impediments to trade. However, protectionism is not dead—far from it—and a discussion of the causes and costs of the rebirth of protectionism conclude this chapter.

CHECKLIST

When you have studied this chapter, you should be able to:

- Explain the importance of international trade to the Canadian economy as a whole and list the major exports and imports of Canada.

- Enumerate the three features of international trade that distinguish it from the trade that takes place within a nation.

- State the two economic circumstances that make it desirable for nations to specialize and trade.

- Explain the basic concept of comparative advantage.

- Compute, when you are given the necessary figures, the opportunity cost of producing two commodities in two countries; determine which nation has the comparative advantage in the production of each commodity; calculate the range in which the terms of trade will be found; and explain the gains to each nation and to the world from specialization and trade.

- Construct a numerical example to illustrate the case where trade will not take place between two countries.

- Assuming constant opportunity costs, use production possibilities diagrams to illustrate the possible gains from trade for two countries.

- Explain how the model's predictions on trade and production patterns will change if the constant cost assumption is changed to increasing opportunity costs.

- Restate the case for free trade.

- Identify the four principal types of artificial barriers to international trade and the four motives for erecting these barriers.

- Explain the economic effects of a protective tariff on resource allocation, the price of the commodity, the total production of the commodity, and the outputs of foreign and domestic producers of the commodity.

- Identify the gainers and losers from trade restrictions.

- Analyse the economic effects of an import quota and compare them with the economic effects of a tariff.

- Enumerate the arguments used to support the case for protection and find the weakness in each of these arguments.

- Describe the National Policy and its effects on the structure of Canadian industry.

- Contrast Canada's desire for access for her upgraded raw materials with the other developed nations' desires for access to Canada's raw materials; and contrast the resulting divergent policies.

- Explain the features and the economic significance of the Canada–U.S. Free Trade Agreement.

- Give arguments for and against free trade between Canada and the United States.

- Identify the North America Free Trade Agreement (NAFTA).

- List the interrelated factors that explain the rebirth of protectionism in Canada and especially in the United States; and present examples of this rebirth.

CHAPTER OUTLINE

1.   Trade between nations is large enough and unique enough to warrant special attention.

(a)   For Canada,

(1) the country's merchandise imports and exports are both about 25% of its GDP and both were close to $138 billion a year in 1991;

(2) this trade provides both important capital goods and markets for raw materials;

(3) although once described as "hewers of wood and drawers of water," only 22% of Canadian merchandise exports are now classified as "crude materials and food";

(4) over 75% of Canada's trade, both exports and imports, is with the United States; about 13% is with Japan and the Common Market (including the United Kingdom); and the balance, about 12%, is with the rest of the world.

(b)   International trade has three characteristics that distinguish it from domestic trade: resources are less mobile, the nations use different currencies (or money), and the trade is subjected to more government interference.

2.   Specialization and trade between nations are advantageous because the world's resources are not evenly distributed and the efficient production of different commodities necessitates different methods and combinations of resources.

3.   The basis for trade is the principle of comparative

advantage, which states that total output will be greatest when each good is produced in the country where its opportunity cost is lowest. A simple hypothetical example illustrates comparative advantage and the gains from trade.

(a) Suppose the world is composed of only two nations, each of which is capable of producing two different commodities and in which the production possibilities curves are different straight lines (the opportunity cost of producing a particular good is constant but differs between the two countries).

(b) With different opportunity cost ratios, each nation will have a comparative (cost) advantage in the production of one of the two commodities; and if the world is to use its resources economically, each nation must specialize in the production of the commodity whose opportunity cost is least. In this way the world experiences the smallest loss of alternative goods when the decision is reached to produce and consume a particular output combination.

(c) The ratio at which one product is traded for another—the terms of trade—lies between the opportunity cost ratios of the two nations.

(d) Each nation can share in the gains from this trade because specialization permits a greater total output from the same resources and a better allocation of the world's resources.

(e) If cost ratios in the two nations are not constant, specialization may not be complete.

(f) If opportunity cost ratios do not differ, then no basis for mutually beneficial trade exists.

(g) The basic argument for free trade among nations is that it leads to a better allocation of resources and a higher standard of living in the world; but it also increases competition and deters monopoly in these nations.

4. Nations, however, retard international trade by imposing tariffs, import quotas, a variety of nontariff barriers, and voluntary export restrictions.

(a) Special-interest groups within nations benefit from protection and persuade their governments to erect trade barriers; but the costs to consumers of this protection exceed the benefits to the economy. Demand and supply diagrams can be used to readily indicate the effects of trade barriers.

(b) The imposition of a tariff on a good imported from abroad has both direct and indirect effects on an economy.

(1) The tariff increases the domestic price of the good, reduces its domestic consumption, expands its domestic production, decreases foreign production, and transfers income from domestic consumers to government.

(2) It also reduces the income of foreign producers and the ability of foreign nations to purchase goods and services in the nation imposing the tariff, causes the contraction of relatively efficient industries in that nation, decreases world trade, and lowers the real output of goods and services.

5. The arguments for protectionism are many, but they often are of questionable validity.

(a) The military self-sufficiency argument can be challenged because it is difficult to determine which industry is "vital" to national defence and must be protected. It would be more efficient economically to provide a direct subsidy to military producers rather than impose a tariff.

(b) Trade barriers do not necessarily increase domestic employment because:

(1) imports may eliminate some jobs, but create others; therefore, imports may only change the composition of employment, not the overall level of employment;

(2) the exports of one nation become the imports of another; tariff barriers can be viewed as "beggar thy neighbour" policies;

(3) there is likely to be retaliation from other nations from the imposition of trade barriers that will reduce national output and employment; and,

(4) they create a less efficient allocation of resources by shielding protected domestic industries from the rigours of competition.

(c) Using tariff barriers to permit diversification for stability in an economy is not necessary for advanced economies such as Canada and there may be economic costs to diversification in less-developed nations.

(d) It is alleged that infant industries need protection until they are sufficiently large to compete. But the argument may not apply to developed economies: it is difficult to select which industries will prosper; protectionism tends to persist long after it is needed; and direct subsidies may be more economically efficient. The need for a "breathing spell" is also questionable for some industries because it may not improve efficiency and may make the industry more dependent on protection.

(e) A variation on the infant-industry argument suggests that trade barriers protect home producers from foreign competition, allowing the firm to grow more rapidly and achieve greater economies of scale than foreign competitors. The protected firm can then dominate world markets because of lower costs. Comparative advantage can be acquired by strategic economic policies rather than depending solely on a country's resource allocation.

(f) Sometimes protection is sought against the "dumping" of excess foreign goods on Canadian markets. Dumping is a legitimate concern and is restricted under Canadian trade law; but to use dumping as an excuse for widespread tariff protection is unjustified and the number of documented cases is few. If foreign companies are more efficient (low cost) producers, what may appear to be dumping may actually be comparative advantage at work.

(g)   Protection is sometimes sought because of the cheap foreign labour argument. It should be realized that nations gain from trade based on comparative advantage, and without trade living standards will be lower.

(h)   In summary, most of the protectionist arguments are fallacious or based on half-truths. The only points that have some validity, under certain conditions, are the infant-industry and military-sufficiency arguments, but both are subject to abuse. The historical evidence suggests that free trade promotes and protectionism deters prosperity and economic growth in the world.

6.   From Sir John A. Macdonald's National Policy of 1879 to 1989 Canada had been a high-tariff country, with harmful effects to its industrial structure. Over time the country slowly reduced tariffs, and in 1989 embarked on a free trade venture with the United States (and quite probably with Mexico beginning in 1994).

(a)   Since 1934, tariff rates have been substantially reduced. Many nations, including Canada, have signed the 1947 General Agreement on Tariffs and Trade in an attempt to eliminate trade barriers. Successive rounds of negotiations have reduced the barriers to trade, with the present Uruguay Round possibly concluding on a successful note sometime in 1993.

(b)   The European Common Market has sought the economic integration of Western Europe, and the Common Market nations have achieved considerable integration and have increased their growth rates; but their success has created problems for nonmember nations.

(c)   Canada has entered into a trade agreement with the United States that will see the elimination of a wide range of trade restrictions and tariffs over the next number of years. The result is not free trade but freer trade. If the proposed agreement with Mexico and the United States is ratified by the three countries, a North American free trade area will be realized, with the prospect of a Western Hemisphere free trade area in the future.

(d)   Some of the elements of the Free Trade Agreement with the United States are still to be settled and, with economic self-interest a factor on the part of both participants, some hard bargaining is inevitable.

(e)   In recent years pressures for protection from goods produced abroad have reemerged in Canada. There are several interrelated causes of these pressures for protection.

(1) Freer trade has produced the predicted winners and losers, and those firms and workers that have been adversely affected have called for restoration of protection.

(2) With the movement towards fewer world-wide trade barriers, increased foreign competition is being felt by more firms and their work forces.

(3) Newly industrialized nations have become fierce competitors, especially in some manufacturing industries in which Canadian firms thought themselves immune from foreign competition and were slow to react to a changing economic environment.

IMPORTANT TERMS

absolute advantage
Canada–U.S. Free Trade Agreement (FTA)
comparative advantage
cost ratio
dumping
economic integration
European Community (EC or Common Market)
export subsidies
gains from trade
General Agreement on Tariffs and Trade (GATT)
import quotas
labour- (land-, capital-,) intensive commodity
most-favoured-nation clause
National Policy
nontariff barriers (NTBs)
revenue and protective tariffs
strategic trade policy
terms of trade
trading possibilities line
voluntary export restrictions (VERs)

FILL-IN QUESTIONS

1.   The merchandise imports and exports of Canada in 1991 each amount to about _____ % of the economy's GDP or about $_____ billion.

2.   Ranked in order of their importance, the four

principal exports of Canada are _____,
_____,
_____, and
_____;
the four most important imports are _____,
_____,
_____,
and _____.

3. Special attention is devoted to international trade
because resources are (more, less) _____
mobile between nations than within a nation; because
each nation employs a different _____;
and because international trade is subject to (more, fewer)
_____ political interferences and controls
than domestic trade.

4. Nations tend to trade among themselves because the
distribution of economic resources among them is (even,
uneven) _____ and because the efficient
production of various goods and services necessitates (the
same, different) _____ technologies or
combinations of resources.

5. The nations of the world tend to specialize in and
export those goods in the production of which they have
a _____ _____, and to
import those goods in the production of which they do
not have a _____ _____.

6. Given two nations, each of which can produce the
same two goods, the principle of comparative advantage
states that total output can be increased if each country
produces that good with the _____
_____ _____ and trades
with the second country for the other good.

7. If the opportunity cost of 1 kilogram of bananas in
country X is 4 Panama hats, while in country Y, the
opportunity cost of 1 kilogram of bananas is 3 Panama
hats:

(a) hats are relatively (more, less) _____
expensive in country X and bananas relatively
_____ expensive;

(b) hats are relatively _____ expensive in
country Y and bananas relatively _____
expensive;
(c) X has a comparative advantage and should specialize in the production of _____ and Y has
a comparative advantage and should specialize in the
production of _____.
(d) When X and Y specialize and trade, the terms of
trade will be somewhere between _____
and _____ hats for each kilogram of
bananas; and will depend upon _____.
(e) When the actual terms of trade turn out to be 3½
hats for 1 kilogram of bananas, the cost of obtaining
(1) 1 Panama hat has been decreased from _____
to _____ kilograms of bananas in Y;
(2) 1 kilogram of bananas has been decreased from
_____ to _____ Panama
hats in X.
(f) This international specialization will not be complete if the cost of producing either good (increases,
decreases, remains constant) _____ as a
nation produces more of it.

8. The basic argument for free trade is that it results
in a better _____ of resources and a higher
_____ of living.

9. The barriers to international trade include
_____, _____ quotas, the
_____ barriers, and _____
_____ restrictions.

10. Nations erect barriers to international trade to
benefit the economic positions of _____-
_____ groups even though these barriers
(increase, decrease) _____ economic efficiency and trade among nations, and the benefits to a
nation are (greater, less) _____ than the
costs to it.

11. When Canada imposes a tariff on a good that is
imported from abroad,
(a) the price of that good in Canada will (increase,
decrease) _____;
(b) the total purchases of the good in Canada will
_____;

(c) the output of

(1) Canadian producers of the good will _____;

(2) foreign producers of the good will _____;

(d) the ability of foreigners to buy goods and services in Canada will _____, and, as a result, output and employment in Canadian industries that sell goods and services abroad will _____.

12. While a tariff generates revenue for the Canadian _____, an import quota transfers that revenue to _____ _____.

13. List the five arguments that protectionists employ to justify trade barriers.

(a) _____

(b) _____

(c) _____

(d) _____

(e) _____
The only two arguments containing any reasonable justification for protection are the _____ and the _____ arguments.

14. Canada became a high-tariff country in 1879 as a result of the _____ _____.
Since 1988 Canada has promoted free trade by taking an active role in _____ negotiations, by completing the _____ _____ _____ with the United States, and by negotiating a proposed trade treaty — the _____ _____ _____ _____ _____ — with Mexico and the United States.

15. The specific aims of the European Common Market were the abolition of _____ among member nations, the establishment of common tariffs on goods imported from _____ nations, the free movement of _____ and _____ among member nations, and common policies with respect to other matters.

16. Under terms of the Free Trade Agreement all trade restrictions will be eliminated over a _____ year period. Though all tariffs will be abolished between the two countries by _____, trade will not be completely free because of a multitude of _____.

17. The four exclusions from the FTA are:

(a) _____

(b) _____

(c) _____

(d) _____

18. What are the three interrelated factors that have resulted in the recent resurgence of pressures for the protection of Canadian industries?

(a) _____

(b) _____

(c) _____

19. When foreign firms undersell Canadian firms on the Canadian market, they are sometimes accused of _____, a practice of selling abroad at less than the _____ _____ _____.

PROBLEMS AND PROJECTS

1. Assume there is only one input-labour hours. In England it takes 5 labour hours to produce a unit of cloth and 3.5 labour hours to produce 1 unit of wine. There are a total of 50 labour hours available in the English economy.

In Canada it takes 2.5 labour hours to produce 1 unit of cloth and 2 labour hours to produce 1 unit of wine. There are a total of 30 labour hours available in Canada.

(a) Construct the production possibilities schedule for cloth and wine in England and Canada.

(b) Canada has an absolute advantage in the production of _____.

(c) Canada has a comparative advantage in the production of _____.

(d) If trade takes place, Canada should produce _____, export _____, and import _____.

(e) Suppose that the number of labour hours available in England increases to 100. Canada now has the absolute advantage in the production of

_____.

(f) Canada now has a comparative advantage in the production of _____.

(g) If trade takes place, Canada should produce

_____, export _____,

and import _____.

(h) Moral of the problem: Trade is based upon

_____ advantage and not _____

advantage.

2. At the top of the next column are the production possibilities curves for two nations: Canada and Chile. Suppose these two nations do not currently engage in international trade or specialization, and suppose that points A and a show the combinations of wheat and copper they now produce and consume.

(a) The straightness of the two curves indicates that the cost ratios in the two nations are (changing, constant)

_____.

(b) Examination of the two curves reveals that the cost ratio in

(1) Canada is _____ million tonnes of

wheat for _____ million kilograms of copper.

(2) Chile is _____ million tonnes of

wheat for _____ million kilograms of copper.

(c) If these two nations were to specialize and trade wheat for copper,

(1) Canada would specialize in the production of wheat

because _____;

(2) Chile would specialize in the production of copper

because _____.

(d) The terms of trade, if specialization and trade occur, will be greater than 2 and less than 4 million tonnes of wheat for 1 million kilograms of copper because

_____.

(e) Assume the terms of trade turn out to be 3 million tonnes of wheat for 1 million kilograms of copper. Draw in the trading possibilities curve for Canada and Chile.

(f) With these trading possibilities curves, suppose Canada decides to consume 5 million tonnes of wheat

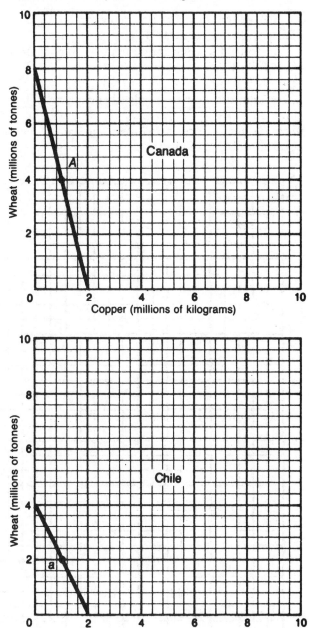

and 1 million kilograms of copper, while Chile decides to consume 3 million tonnes of wheat and 1 million kilograms of copper. The gains from trade to

(1) Canada are _____ million tonnes of

wheat and _____ million kilograms of copper.

(2) Chile are _____ million tonnes of

wheat and _____ million kilograms of copper.

3. This question requires that you construct a graph similar to that in Figure 17-3.

The demand schedule for oil in the country of Breton is given by:

$Q_d = 304 - .5P$

The domestic or home supply schedule is given by:

$Q_b = 3P$

where P is the price per barrel of oil and both Q_d and Q_b refer to barrels of oil.

(a)   The world price of oil is $38 per barrel and foreign producers will fill any demand not taken up by Breton production at that price. (Transportation costs are assumed equal to 0.) Obtain, in barrels,

(1) quantity demanded of oil in Breton

(2) Breton production of oil

(3) Breton imports of oil

(b)   Using the graph below construct a diagram to illustrate part (a).

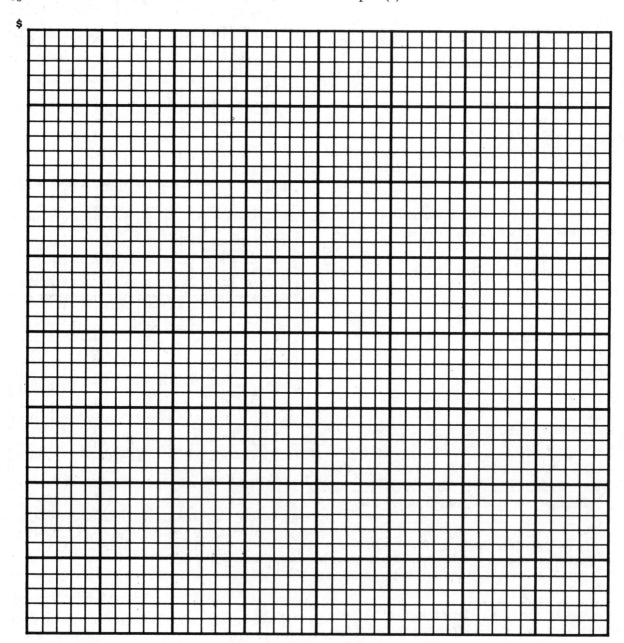

$

0   Q

(c)   Suppose the government sets a tariff of $10 per barrel of imported oil. Foreign producers will now supply all the oil not met by Breton producers at $48 per barrel. Obtain, in barrels,
(1) Breton demand
(2) Breton production
(3) Breton imports
(4) Breton tariff revenue
(d)   Place this new information in the chart you constructed in part (b).
(e)   Instead of a tariff of $10 the government has decided to put in place an import quota that would result in the same price of $48 per barrel in Breton.
(1) At what level (barrels) should the import quota be set?
(2) What happens to the tariff revenue that the government previously collected?

4.   The following table shows the quantities of woollen gloves demanded (D) in Canada at several different prices (P). Also shown in the table are the quantities of woollen gloves that would be supplied by Canadian producers (S_c) and the quantities that would be supplied by foreign producers (S_f) at the nine different prices. This problem is similar to problem 3 except the supply curve for imports is upward sloping and the results that you arrived at in 3 will be somewhat modified because of this change in the model's assumptions.
(a)   Compute and enter in the table the total quantities that would be supplied (S_t) by Canadian and foreign producers at each of the prices.

P	D	S_c	S_f	S_t	S_{1f}	S_{1t}
$2.60	450	275	475	___	___	___
2.40	500	250	450	___	___	___
2.20	550	225	425	___	___	___
2.00	600	200	400	___	___	___
1.80	650	175	375	___	___	___
1.60	700	150	350	___	___	___
1.40	750	125	325	___	___	___
1.20	800	0	300	___	___	___
1.00	850	0	0	___	___	___

(b)   If the market for woollen gloves in Canada is a competitive one, the equilibrium prices for woollen gloves is $_____ and the equilibrium quantity is _____.
(c)   Suppose now that the Canadian government imposes an 80 cents ($0.80) per pair of gloves tariff on all gloves imported into Canada from abroad. Compute and enter into the table the quantities that would be supplied (S_{1f}) by foreign producers at the nine different

prices. (Hint: If foreign producers were willing to supply 300 pairs at a price of $1.20 when there was no tariff, they are now willing to supply 300 pairs at $2.00, the $0.80 per pair tariff plus the $1.20 they will receive for themselves. The quantities supplied at each of the other prices may be found in a similar fashion.)
(d)   Compute and enter into the table the total quantities that would now be supplied (S_{1t}) by Canadian and foreign producers at each of the nine prices.
(e)   As a result of the imposition of the tariff, the equilibrium price has risen to $ _____ and the equilibrium quantity has fallen to _____.
(f)   The number of pairs sold by
(1) Canadian producers has (increased, decreased) _____ by _____;
(2) foreign producers has (increased, decreased) _____ by _____.
(g)   The total revenues (after the payment of the tariff) of
(1) Canadian producers—who do not pay the tariff—have (increased, decreased) _____ by $_____;
(2) foreign producers—on whose products the tariff is paid by Canadian consumers—have (increased, decreased) _____ by $_____.
(h)   The total amount spent by Canadian buyers of woollen gloves has _____ by $ _____.
(i)   The tariff revenue of the Canadian government has _____ by $_____.
(j)   The total number of dollars earned by foreigners has _____ by $ _____; and, as a result, the total foreign demand for goods and services produced in Canada will _____ by $_____.

SELF-TEST

Circle T if the statement is true, F if it is false.

1.   Merchandise exports in Canada account for about 35% of GDP.   **T F**

2.   Canada's exports are heavily weighted toward raw materials, and imports toward end products.   **T F**

3. Merchandise export trade with the United States accounts for approximately 75% of total Canadian merchandise exports. **T F**

4. International trade is a substitute for the international mobility of resources. **T F**

5. International trade allows countries to realize the advantages of specialization. **T F**

Use the following production possibilities tables to answer questions 6, 7, 8, 9, 10 below and to answer multiple-choice questions 8 and 9.

	Adanac Production-Possibilities Table					
Product	Production Alternatives					
	A	B	C	D	E	F
Butter	0	4	8	12	16	20
Cloth	40	32	24	16	8	0

	Zatelba Production Possibilities Table					
Product	Production Alternatives					
	A	B	C	D	E	F
Butter	0	12	24	36	48	60
Cloth	60	48	36	24	12	0

6. In Adanac the opportunity cost of 1 unit of cloth is 1/4 unit of butter. **T F**

7. In Adanac the opportunity cost of butter is constant. **T F**

8. In Zatelba the opportunity cost of one unit of cloth is 1 unit of butter. **T F**

9. Adanac has the comparative advantage in the production of cloth. **T F**

10. The best terms of trade for Adanac would be 1 butter for 1 cloth. **T F**

11. With specialization and trade, the trading possibilities curve of both nations would move to the right of their production possibilities curve. **T F**

12. Increasing production costs tends to prevent specialization among trading nations from being complete. **T F**

13. Trade among nations tends to bring about a more efficient use of the world's resources and a greater world output of goods and services. **T F**

14. Free trade among nations tends to increase monopoly and lessen competition in these nations. **T F**

15. A tariff on coffee in Canada is an example of a protective tariff. **T F**

16. The imposition of a tariff on a good imported from abroad will lower the price of the good and raise the quantity of it bought and sold. **T F**

17. When a tariff is placed on a Canadian import, there are groups in Canada who gain and other groups in Canada who lose. **T F**

18. To advocate tariffs that would protect domestic producers of goods and materials essential to national defence is to substitute a political-military objective for the economic objective of efficiently allocating resources. **T F**

19. An increase in a nation's imports will, other things remaining constant, expand aggregate expenditures, real output, and employment in that nation. **T F**

20. An import quota specifies the minimum price that can be charged for an imported good. **T F**

21. The economic impact of tariffs and import quotas is similar. **T F**

22. One-crop economies may be able to make themselves more stable and diversified by imposing tariffs on goods imported from abroad; but these tariffs are apt also to lower the standard of living in these economies. **T F**

23. The only argument for tariffs that has, in the appropriate circumstances, any economic justification is the increase-domestic-employment argument. **T F**

24. If Canada concludes a trade agreement with and lowers the tariff rates on goods imported from another nation, the lower tariff rates are then charged on those goods when they are imported from other nations in the world with which Canada has trade agreements containing a most-favoured-nation clause. **T F**

25. The members of the European Economic Community have had rapid economic growth since they formed the Common Market in 1958. **T F**

26. The economic integration of nations creates larger markets for firms within the nations that integrate, and makes it possible for these firms and their customers to benefit from the economies of large-scale (mass) production. **T F**

27. The cost of protecting Canadian firms and employees from foreign competition is the rise in the prices of products produced in Canada, and this cost almost always exceeds its benefits. **T F**

28. The Canada–U.S. Free Trade Agreement (FTA) is an example of the gains to be obtained from voluntary export restrictions. **T F**

29. The FTA will not reduce all tariffs between the U.S. and Canada to zero by 1999. **T F**

30. There are no industries excluded in the FTA. **T F**

31. The FTA will probably result in the restructuring of Canadian manufacturing industries. **T F**

32. Under the FTA, Canada will be able to impose an export tax on oil and natural gas. **T F**

33. New trading rules and regulations were set out in the Canada–U.S. Free Trade Agreement to cover any trade disputes arising out of the agreement. **T F**

34. The proposed North America Free Trade Agreement includes Central American nations. **T F**

MULTIPLE-CHOICE

Circle the letter that corresponds to the best answer.

1. In 1990, the merchandise exports of Canada amounted to approximately what percentage of Canada's GDP?
(a) 15%
(b) 28%
(c) 10%
(d) 25%

2. To which of the following does the largest percentage of the Canadian exports of merchandise go?
(a) European Community (excluding the United Kingdom)
(b) U.S.A.
(c) Japan
(d) United Kingdom

3. From which does the largest percentage of the Canadian imports of merchandise come?
(a) European Community (excluding the United Kingdom)
(b) U.S.A.
(c) Japan
(d) United Kingdom

4. The second most important Canadian export market is
(a) European Economic Community (including the United Kingdom)

(b) Japan
(c) Latin America
(d) United States

5. International trade is a special and separate area of economic study because
(a) international trade involves the movement of goods over greater distances than trade within a nation
(b) resources are more mobile internationally than domestically
(c) countries engaged in international trade use different monies
(d) international trade is based on comparative advantage

6. Nations would not need to engage in trade if
(a) all products were produced from the same combinations of resources
(b) world resources were evenly distributed among nations
(c) world resources were perfectly mobile
(d) all of the above

7. Country A has a comparative advantage over country B in the production of good G
(a) when good G is produced in both countries and wages are lower in country A
(b) when country A has an absolute advantage in the production of good G
(c) when the opportunity cost of good G is lower in country A than in country B
(d) when the opportunity cost of good G is lower in country B than in country A

8. Suppose that country B has a comparative advantage over country A in the production of good G. It can be concluded that
(a) country B has an absolute advantage in the production of good G
(b) the production of good G in country B uses less resources than in country A
(c) the opportunity cost of producing good G is less in country B than in country A
(d) inputs are more efficient in country B than in country A

Use the tables preceding true-false question 6 to answer the following three questions.

9. If Adanac and Zatelba engage in trade, the terms of trade will be
(a) between 1 and 2 units of butter for 1 unit of cloth
(b) between 1/2 and 1 unit of butter for 1 unit of cloth
(c) between 3 and 4 units of butter for 1 unit of cloth

(d)   between 1/8 and 1/4 unit of butter for 1 unit of cloth.

10.   If Adanac and Zatelba, in the absence of trade between them, both produced combination D, the gains from trade would be
(a)   6 units of cloth
(b)   8 units of butter
(c)   12 units of cloth
(d)   12 units of butter

11.   If, after trade commenced, the exchange ratio was 1 cloth for 1/2 butter, the gains from trade would
(a)   all go to Adanac
(b)   all go to Zatelba
(c)   be equally distributed between Adanac and Zatelba
(d)   be captured by the larger of the two countries

12.   The terms of trade
(a)   are given by the reciprocal of the foreign exchange rate
(b)   measure the number of units of imports obtained per unit of export
(c)   are given by the reciprocal of the foreign trade multiplier
(d)   improve whenever the exchange rate depreciates

13.   If two countries produce and trade two goods according to the principle of comparative advantage,
(a)   both countries can produce at a point to the right of their production possibilities curves
(b)   at least one country will produce at a point to the right of its production possibilities curve
(c)   at least one country will consume quantities of the two goods superior to that attainable on their domestic production possibilities curve
(d)   all of the above

14.   Changing the assumption of constant costs to one of increasing costs in the trade model results in
(a)   the principle of comparative advantage no longer holding
(b)   only one of two trading partners gaining from trade
(c)   after trade, production specialization being less complete than in the constant cost model
(d)   trade flows being greater than in the constant cost model

15.   Which one of the following is characteristic of tariffs?
(a)   they prevent the importation of goods from abroad
(b)   they specify the maximum amounts of specific commodities that may be imported during a given period of time
(c)   they often protect domestic producers from foreign

competition
(d)   they enable nations to reduce their exports and increase their imports during periods of depression

16.   The motive for the erection by a nation of barriers to the importation of goods and services from abroad is to
(a)   improve economic efficiency in that nation
(b)   protect and benefit special-interest groups in that nation
(c)   reduce the prices of the goods and services produced in that nation
(d)   expand the export of goods and services to foreign nations

17.   When the tariff is imposed on a good imported from abroad,
(a)   the demand for the good increases
(b)   the demand for the good decreases
(c)   the supply of the good increases
(d)   the supply of the good decreases

18.   Tariffs lead to
(a)   the contraction of relatively efficient industries
(b)   an overallocation of resources to relatively efficient industries
(c)   an increase in the foreign demand for domestically produced goods
(d)   an underallocation of resources to relatively inefficient industries

19.   Which one of the following arguments for protection is the least fallacious and most pertinent in modern industrial countries today?
(a)   the military self-sufficiency argument
(b)   the increase-domestic-employment argument
(c)   the cheap foreign labour argument
(d)   the infant-industry argument

20.   Which of the following is the likely result of Canada employing tariffs to protect its high wages and standard of living from cheap foreign labour?
(a)   an increase in Canadian exports
(b)   a rise in the Canadian real GDP
(c)   a decrease in the average productivity of Canadian workers
(d)   a decrease in the quantities of resources employed by industries producing the goods on which tariffs have been levied

21.   Which of the following is a likely result of imposing tariffs to increase domestic employment?
(a)   a short-run increase in domestic employment
(b)   retaliatory increases in the tariff rates of foreign nations
(c)   a long-run decline in exports

(d) all of the above

22. The infant-industry argument for tariffs
(a) is especially pertinent to the advanced industrial nations
(b) generally results in tariffs that are removed after the infant industry has matured
(c) makes it rather easy to determine which infant industries will become mature industries with comparative advantages in producing their goods
(d) might better be replaced by an argument for outright subsidies for infant industries

Answer the next four questions (23, 24, 25, and 26) on the basis of the following diagram, where S_d and D_d are the domestic supply and demand for a product and P_w is the world price of that product.

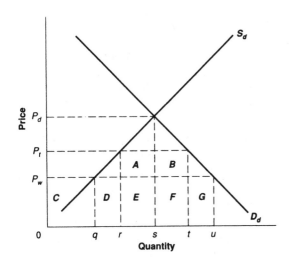

23. In a closed economy (without international trade), the equilibrium price would be
(a) $0P_d$; but in an open economy, the equilibrium price will be $0P_t$
(b) $0P_d$; but in an open economy, the equilibrium price will be $0P_w$
(c) $0P_w$; but in an open economy, the equilibrium price will be $0P_d$
(d) $0P_w$; but in an open economy, the equilibrium price will be $0P_t$

24. If there were free trade in this economy and no tariffs, the total revenue going to the foreign producers is represented by
(a) area C
(b) areas A and B combined
(c) areas A, B, E, and F combined
(d) areas D, E, F, and G combined

25. If a per unit tariff was imposed in the amount of P_wP_t, then domestic producers would supply
(a) $0q$ units and foreign producers would supply qu units
(b) $0s$ units and foreign producers would supply su units
(c) $0r$ units and foreign producers would supply rt units
(d) $0t$ units and foreign producers would supply tu units

26. Given a per unit tariff in the amount of P_wP_t, the amount of the tariff revenue paid by consumers of this product is represented by
(a) area A
(b) area B
(c) areas A and B combined
(d) areas D, E, F, and G combined

27. Under the National Policy introduced in 1879,
(a) Canada entered into a free trade agreement with the United States
(b) Canada became a member of GATT
(c) Canada declared free trade in natural resource products
(d) Canada imposed high tariffs to protect the manufacturing sector

28. Which of the following is not characteristic of the General Agreement on Tariffs and Trade? Nations signing the agreement were committed to
(a) the elimination of import quotas
(b) the reciprocal reduction of tariffs by negotiation
(c) the nondiscriminatory treatment of all trading nations
(d) the establishment of a world customs union

29. The European Common Market
(a) is designed to eliminate tariffs and import quotas among its members
(b) aims to allow the free movement of capital and labour within the member nations
(c) imposes common tariffs on goods imported into the member nations from outside the Common Market area
(d) does all of the above

30. The Canada–U.S. Free Trade Agreement will result in
(a) complete free trade
(b) freer trade
(c) less trade between Canada and the U.S.
(d) none of the above

31. Which of the following is excluded from the FTA?
(a) agricultural marketing boards
(b) iron and steel

(c) oil and gas

(d) textiles

32. Under the FTA, Canada and the U.S. have agreed to

(a) reduce nontariff barriers

(b) increase nontariff barriers

(c) make product standards, testing, and approval processes different in their respective countries

(d) make mergers illegal

33. The FTA will result in

(a) the deindustrialization of Canada

(b) less competitive Canadian industries

(c) more monopoly power in the Canadian economy

(d) a restructuring of some Canadian industries, which will require reallocation of inputs

34. The term *dumping* refers to

(a) selling an imported good in Canada at a price less than the price in the home market

(b) selling an imported good in Canada at a price that is less than the price in the home market plus the transportation cost to Canada

(c) selling an imported good in Canada at a price less than the cost of producing it

(d) selling an imported good in Canada that was produced in a foreign government-owned establishment

35. Pressures for the protection of Canadian industries have increased in recent years because of

(a) previous decreases in the barriers to trade

(b) recession and unemployment in Canada

(c) increased competition from imported products

(d) all of the above

DISCUSSION QUESTIONS

1. In relative and absolute terms, how important is international trade to Canada? What are the principal exports and imports of the Canadian economy?

2. Which nations are the principal "trading partners" of Canada? How much of this trade is with the developed nations of the world, and how much of it is with the underdeveloped nations?

3. Are the Canadian economy's exports of merchandise to the following greater or less than its imports of merchandise from them? (a) Japan; (b) the United Kingdom; (c) European Economic Community (less U.K.); and (d) the rest of the world.

4. In what ways is international trade different from the trade that takes place within a nation?

5. Why do nations specialize in certain products and export their surplus production of these goods at the same time that they are importing other goods? Why do they not use the resources employed to produce the surpluses they export to produce the goods they import?

6. What two facts—one dealing with the distribution of the world's resources and the other related to the technology of producing different products—are the basis for trade among nations?

7. Explain (a) the theory or principle of comparative advantage; (b) what is meant by and what determines the terms of trade; (c) the gains from the trade.

8. What is the "case for free trade"?

9. What motivates nations to erect barriers to the importation of goods from abroad, and what types of barriers do they erect?

10. Suppose Canada were to increase the tariff on radios imported from Germany (and other foreign countries). What would be the effect of this tariff-rate increase on

(a) the price of radios in Canada;

(b) the total number of radios sold in Canada during a year;

(c) the number of radios produced by and employment in the German radio industry;

(d) production by and employment in the Canadian radio industry;

(e) German income obtained by selling radios in Canada;

(f) the German demand for goods produced in Canada;

(g) the production of and employment in those Canadian industries that now export goods to Germany;

(h) the standards of living in Canada and in Germany;

(i) the allocation of resources in the Canadian economy;

(j) the allocation of the world's resources?

11. What is the "case for protection"? How valid and pertinent to Canada is each of the basic arguments for protection?

12. Is comparative advantage dependent solely on a country's resource endowment?

13. What were the three cardinal principles contained in the General Agreement on Tariffs and Trade?

14. What were the four main goals of the European Economic Community?

15. Identify the groups that would benefit from and would be hurt by a tariff on the importation of cars into Canada.

16. What economic factors led Canada to seek a greater integration of its economy with those of the United States and Mexico?

17. According to a Government of Canada release, ''the NAFTA represents both a response and a challenge to the changing nature of international business.'' What are the changes that the quotation is referring to and in what way is the NAFTA (a) a response and (b) a challenge?

ANSWERS

Fill-in questions

1. 25, 138

2. transportation equipment, wood and paper, other end products, nonferrous metals; other end products, transportation equipment, industrial machinery, chemicals

3. less, money (currency), more

4. uneven, different

5. comparative advantage, comparative advantage

6. lowest opportunity cost

7. (a) less, more; (b) more, less; (c) hats, bananas; (d) 3, 4, world demand and supply for hats and bananas; (e) (1) 1/3, 2/7; (2) 4, 3½; (f) increases

8. allocation, standard

9. tariffs, import, nontariff, voluntary export

10. special-interest, decrease, less

11. (a) increase; (b) decrease; (c) (1) increase, (2) decrease; (d) decrease, decrease

12. government, foreign producers

13. (a) military self-sufficiency; (b) infant industry; (c) increase domestic employment; (d) diversification for stability; (e) cheap foreign labour; military self-sufficiency, infant-industry

14. National Policy: GATT, Free Trade Agreement, North American Free Trade Agreement

15. tariffs and import quotas, nonmember, capital, labour

16. ten, 1999, exceptions

17. (a) agricultural marketing boards; (b) cultural industries; (c) social insurance programs; (d) regional development programs (any order)

18. (a) the freer trade that resulted from past reduc-

tions in trade barriers; (b) the increased competition from abroad that resulted from a more open economy; (c) the increased competitiveness of foreign products that resulted from lower labour costs and prices abroad;

19. dumping, cost of production

Problems and projects

1. (a)

England		Canada	
Cloth	Wine	Cloth	Wine
10	0	12	0
9	1.43	11	1.25
8	2.86	10	2.50
7	4.29	9	3.75
6	5.71	8	5.00
5	7.14	7	6.25
4	8.57	6	7.50
3	10.00	5	8.75
2	11.43	4	10.00
1	12.86	3	11.25
0	14.29	2	12.50
		1	13.75
		0	15.00

(b) both goods
(c) cloth
(d) cloth, cloth, wine
(e) neither good
(f) cloth
(g) cloth, cloth, wine
(h) comparative, absolute

2. (a) constant; (b) (1) 8, 2, (2) 4, 2; (c) (1) it has a comparative advantage in producing wheat (its cost of producing wheat is less than Chile's), (2) it has a comparative advantage in producing copper (its cost of producing copper is less than Canada's); (d) one of the two nations would be unwilling to trade if the terms of trade were outside this range; (f) (1) 1, 0, (2) 1, 0

3. (a) (1) 285; (2) 114; (3) 171 (c) (1) 280; (2) 144; (3) 136; (4) 1360 (e) (1) 136 (2) The tariff revenue is taken by foreign producers.

4. (a) 750, 700, 650, 600, 550, 500, 450, 300, 0; (b) $2.00, 600; (c) 375, 350, 325, 300, 0, 0, 0, 0, 0; (d) 650, 600, 550, 500, 175, 150, 125, 0, 0; (e) $2.20, 550; (f) (1) increased, 25, (2) decreased, 75; (g) (1) increased, $95, (2) decreased, $345; (h) increased, $10; (i) increased, $260; (j) decreased, $345, decrease, $345

Self-test

1. F; **2.** F; **3.** T; **4.** T; **5.** T; **6.** F; **7.** T; **8.** T; **9.** T; **10.** T; **11.** T; **12.** T; **13.** T; **14.** F; **15.** F;

16. F;   **17.** T;   **18.** T;   **19.** F;   **20.** F;   **21.** F;
22. T;   **23.** F;   **24.** T;   **25.** T;   **26.** T;   **27.** T;
28. F;   **29.** T;   **30.** F;   **31.** T;   **32.** F;   **33.** F;   **34.** F

Multiple-Choice

1. (d);   **2.** (b);   **3.** (b);   **4.** (a);   **5.** (c);   **6.** (d);

7. (c);   **8.** (c);   **9.** (b);   **10.** (d);   **11.** (b);   **12.** (b);
13. (c);   **14.** (c);   **15.** (c);   **16.** (b);   **17.** (d);   **18.** (a);
19. (a);   **20.** (c);   **21.** (d);   **22.** (d);   **23.** (b);
24. (d);   **25.** (c);   **26.** (c);   **27.** (d);   **28.** (d);   **29.** (d);
30. (b);   **31.** (a);   **32.** (a);   **33.** (d);   **34.** (c);   **35.** (d)

CHAPTER

18 Exchange Rates and the Balance of Payments

In the last chapter you learned why nations engage in international trade and why they erect barriers to trade with other nations. In Chapter 18 you will learn: (1) how nations using different monies (or currencies) are able to trade with each other; (2) how transactions with non-residents are recorded in the balance of payments accounts; (3) how to interpret various balance of payments accounts and terminology; (4) what is meant by a "favourable" or "unfavourable" balance of trade; (4) how the relative value of different national currencies are determined; and (5) a brief outline of different exchange rate systems that trading nations have used in the present century.

Countries use different currencies, and the means they employ to overcome the difficulties that result from the use of different monies is fairly simple. When the residents of a nation (its consumers, business firms, or governments) wish to buy goods or services or real or financial assets from, make loans or gifts to, or pay interest and dividends to the residents of other nations, they buy some of the money used in that nation. They pay for the foreign money with some of their own money. In other words, they exchange their own money for foreign money. And when the residents of a nation sell goods or services or real or financial assets to, receive loans or gifts from, or are paid dividends or interest by the residents of foreign nations and obtain foreign money, they sell this foreign money—often called foreign exchange—in return for some of their own money. That is, they exchange foreign money for their own money. The markets in which one money is sold and is paid for with another money are called foreign-exchange markets. The price that is paid (in one money) for a unit of another money is called the foreign-exchange rate (or the rate of exchange). And, in Canada at present, the foreign-exchange rate for any foreign currency is determined by the demand for and the supply of that foreign currency. It is sometimes difficult to think about the "price" of a unit of money, even when that money is a unit of for-

eign currency. At the beginning of the study of foreign exchange rates, it is helpful to look upon a unit of foreign currency as no different than a bushel of wheat whose price is determined by the forces of demand and supply in a market economy.

As you know from Chapter 17, nations buy and sell large quantities of goods and services across national boundaries. But the residents of these nations also buy and sell such financial assets as stocks and bonds and such real assets as land and capital goods in other nations; and the governments and individuals in one nation make gifts (remittances) in other nations. At the end of a year, nations summarize their foreign transactions with the rest of the world. This summary is called the nation's balance of international payments: a record of how it obtained foreign money during the year and what it did with this foreign money. Of course, all foreign money obtained was used for some purpose—it did not evaporate—and consequently the balance of payments always balances. However, various sections of the balance of payments need not balance and the student must be aware of the various definitions and usages in this area. The balance of international payments is an extremely important and useful device for understanding the amounts and kinds of international transactions in which the residents of a nation engage. But it also enables us to understand the meaning of a balance of payments imbalance (a deficit or a surplus), the causes of these imbalances, and their economic implications.

Probably the most difficult section of this chapter is concerned with balance of payments deficits and surpluses. A balance of payments deficit (surplus) is found when the receipts of foreign money are less (greater) than the payments of foreign money and the nation's official international reserves are reduced (expanded). You should pay particular attention to the way in which a system of flexible exchange rates and the way in which a system of fixed exchange rates will correct balance of payments deficits and surpluses; and note the advantages and disadvantages of these two alternative methods of eliminating imbalances. Be sure that you understand what is meant by the depreciation and appreciation of a currency in the foreign-exchange market and the effect of both on the price, in domestic currency, of traded goods.

As examples of these two types of exchange-rate systems you will find in the final section of the chapter an examination of the gold standard, the Bretton Woods system, and the managed floating exchange rate system. In the first two systems exchange rates are fixed; and, in the third system, exchange rates are fixed in the short run (to obtain the advantages of fixed exchange rates) and flexible in the long run (to enable nations to correct balance of payments deficits and surpluses).

One last word for you. This chapter is filled with new terms. Some of these are just special words used in international economics for concepts with which you are already familiar. Be very sure to learn what all of the new terms mean. It will simplify your comprehension of this chapter and enable you to understand more readily the macroeconomic problems that can occur in an open economy, which are discussed in Chapter 19.

CHECKLIST

When you have studied this chapter, you should be able to:

- Explain how Canadian exports create a demand for Canadian dollars and generate a supply of foreign exchange; and how Canadian imports create a demand for foreign exchange and generate a supply of Canadian dollars.

- Define "foreign exchange," "foreign-exchange market," and "foreign-exchange rate." When a participant in the foreign-exchange market demands Canadian dollars, identify what exactly is offered in exchange or payment for them.

- Be able to translate the Canadian dollar price of a unit of foreign currency into the foreign currency price of a Canadian dollar.

- Explain how a nation's exports, in a sense, finance its imports.

- Define each of the balances found in the balance of international payments; and distinguish between a surplus and deficit in each of the balances.

- Explain how a nation finances a payments deficit and what it does with a payments surplus.

- Show how a nation can export more goods and services than it imports and still have a balance of payments deficit; and how it can have a trade deficit

and still have a balance of payments surplus.

- Explain the relationship between the current- and capital-account balances, and between the balance of payments and changes in the official international reserves of a nation.

- From the viewpoint of the Canadian economy, identify the different participants in the foreign-exchange market who demand U.S. dollars; identify the participants in the same foreign-exchange market who supply U.S. dollars.

- Explain, from a Canadian viewpoint, why the demand for U.S. dollars in the foreign-exchange market is downward sloping and the supply of U.S. dollars is upward sloping.

- Construct a numerical example to illustrate a depreciation of the Canadian dollar relative to the U.S. dollar; and show the effect on the Canadian price of imports from the United States and the U.S. dollar price of Canadian exports.

- Provide an explanation of how flexible (floating) exchange rates function to eliminate payments deficits and surpluses; and enumerate the three disadvantages of this method of correcting imbalances.

- Identify the five principal determinants of the demand for and supply of a particular foreign money; and explain how a change in each of these determinants would affect the rate of exchange for that foreign money.

- Enumerate the four means by which a nation may defend a fixed (or "pegged") foreign-exchange rate.

- Explain how a nation with a payments deficit might employ its international reserves to prevent a fall in the international value of its currency.

- List the three conditions a nation had to fulfil if it was to be on the gold standard; explain how gold flows operated to reduce payments deficits and surpluses; and identify its two advantages and its two basic drawbacks.

- Explain how the Bretton Woods system stabilized exchange rates and attempted to provide for orderly changes in exchange rates to eliminate payments imbalances.

- Describe how the United States severed the link between gold and the international value of the dollar in 1971, which led to the floating of the dollar and brought to an end the old Bretton Woods system.

- Explain what is meant by a system of managed floating exchange rates; and enumerate its virtues and shortcomings.

CHAPTER OUTLINE

1. Trade between two nations differs from domestic trade because the nations use different monies; but this problem is resolved by the existence of foreign-exchange markets in which the money used by one nation can be purchased and paid for with the money of the other nation.

(a) Canadian exports create a demand for dollars and generate a supply of foreign money in the foreign-exchange markets; increase the money supply in Canada and decrease foreign money supplies; and earn monies that can be used to pay for Canadian imports.

(b) Canadian imports create a supply of dollars and generate a demand for foreign money in foreign-exchange markets; decrease the money supply in Canada and increase foreign money supplies; and use monies obtained by exporting.

2. The balance of international payments for a nation is an annual record of all its transactions with the other nations in the world; and it records all the payments received from and made to the rest of the world.

(a) The current-account section of a nation's balance of payments statement records its trade in goods and services.

(1) The balance on goods and services, called the balance of trade, is equal to the value of the export of goods and services less the value of the import of goods and services; and

(2) the balance on current account is equal to the balance on goods and services plus the nonmerchandise balance (balance on investment income and transfers).

(3) For 1991 Canada had a current-account deficit of \$29.2 billion. Canada had to obtain this amount either from reserves or foreign investors to finance the excess of current-account expenditures of foreign currencies over earnings of foreign currencies.

(b) The capital account section of a nation's balance of international payments records its sales of real and financial assets (which bring in foreign money) and its purchases of real and financial assets from foreign owners (which uses up foreign money). The nation has a capital-account surplus (deficit) if its sales are greater (less) than its purchases of real and financial assets.

(c) The current and capital accounts in a nation's international balance of payments are interrelated. A nation with a current-account deficit can finance the deficit by borrowing or selling assets abroad (with a capital-account surplus), and a nation with a current-account surplus can lend or buy assets abroad (incur a capital-account deficit)

(d) The official reserves of Canada, held in the Exchange Fund Account, increase when the country has a net surplus on its current and capital accounts and decreases when the country has a net deficit on these accounts. By placing the changes in reserves in the capital account, as in Table 18-1, the nation's total outpayments and inpayments are made to equal each other (or the balance of payments are made to balance).

(e) Whenever the balance of payments is said to be in surplus or deficit, this refers to the net surplus or deficit before the changes in reserves have been included. A nation is said to have a balance of payments surplus (deficit) when the current- and capital-account balance is positive (negative) and the official reserves increase (decrease).

(f) The merchandise deficit of a nation implies its producers are losing their competitiveness in foreign markets, but it is beneficial to consumers in that nation who receive more goods (imports) from abroad than they must pay for (export). A balance of payments deficit is undesirable to the extent that the nation's official international reserves are limited and require the nation to take painful macroeconomic adjustments to correct it.

3. The kinds of adjustments a nation with a balance of payments deficit or surplus must make to correct the imbalance depends upon whether exchange rates are flexible (floating) or fixed.

(a) If foreign-exchange rates float freely, the demand for and the supply of foreign exchange determine foreign-exchange rates; and the exchange rate for any foreign money is the rate at which the quantity of that money demanded is equal to the quantity of it supplied.

(1) A change in the demand for or supply of a foreign money will cause the exchange rate for that money to rise or fall; and when there is a rise (fall) in the price paid in dollars for a foreign money, it is said that the dollar has depreciated (appreciated) and that the foreign money has appreciated (depreciated).

A Helpful Hint

The application of the terms *depreciate* and *appreciate* to foreign exchange confuses many students. Here are some hints that will help reduce the confusion.

1. Depreciate means decrease; and appreciate means increase.

2. What decreases when Country A's currency depreciates and increases when its currency appreciates is the quantity of Country B's currency that can be purchased for one unit of Country A's currency.

3. When the exchange rate for B's currency

(a) *rises*, the quantity of B's currency that can be purchased from one unit of A's currency decreases (just as a rise in the price of cigars decreases the number of cigars that can be bought for a dollar) and A's currency has depreciated;

(b) *falls*, the quantity of B's currency that can be purchased for one unit of A's currency increases (just as a fall in the price of cigars increases the number of cigars that can be bought for a dollar) and A's currency has appreciated.

(2) Changes in the demand for or supply of a foreign currency are largely the result of changes in tastes, relative income changes, relative price changes, changes in relative real interest rates, and speculation.

(3) Floating exchange rates provide an automatic adjustment mechanism for balance of payments deficits or surpluses. When a nation has a payments deficit (surplus), foreign-exchange rates will rise (fall). This will make foreign goods and services more (less) expensive, decrease (increase) imports, make a nation's goods and services less (more) expensive for foreigners to buy, and increase (decrease) its exports. These adjustments in foreign-exchange rates and in imports and exports correct the nation's payments deficit (surplus).

(4) But flexible exchange rates increase the uncertainties faced by exporters, importers, and investors (and reduce international trade); change the terms of trade; and destabilize economies (by creating inflation or unemployment).

(b) When nations fix (or "peg") foreign-exchange rates, the governments of these nations must intervene in the foreign-exchange markets to prevent shortages and surpluses of foreign monies.

(1) One way for a nation to stabilize foreign-exchange rates is for its government to sell (buy) a foreign money in exchange for its own money (or gold) when there is a shortage (surplus) of the foreign money.

(2) A nation with a payments deficit might also discourage imports by imposing tariffs, import quotas, and special taxes; and encourage exports by subsidizing them.

(3) To eliminate a payments deficit, a nation might require exporters who earn foreign exchange to sell it to the government. The government would then ration the available foreign exchange among importers and make the value of imports equal to the value of exports.

(4) Another way for a nation to stabilize foreign-exchange rates is to employ fiscal and monetary policies to reduce its national income and price level and to raise interest rates relative to those in other nations; and, thereby, reduce the demand for and increase the supply of the different foreign monies.

4. The nations of the world in their recent history have employed three different exchange-rate systems.

(a) Between 1879 and 1934 (with the exception of the World War I years) the operation of the gold standard kept foreign-exchange rates relatively stable.

(1) A nation was on the gold standard when it:

(i) defined its monetary unit in terms of a certain quantity of gold;

(ii) maintained a fixed relationship between its stock of gold and its money supply; and

(iii) allowed gold to be exported and imported without restrictions.

(2) Foreign-exchange rates between nations on the gold standard would fluctuate only within a narrow range (determined by the cost of packing, insuring, and shipping gold from country to country); and if a foreign-exchange rate rose (fell) to the upper (lower) limit of the range, gold would flow out of (into) a nation.

(3) But if a nation has a balance of payments deficit (surplus) and gold flowed out of (into) the country, its money supply would decrease (increase). This would raise (lower) interest rates and reduce (expand) aggregate demand, domestic output, employment, and prices in that country; and the balance of payments deficit (surplus) would be eliminated.

(4) The gold standard resulted in nearly stable foreign-exchange rates (which by reducing uncertainty stimulated international trade), and automatically corrected balance of payments deficits and surpluses. But it required that nations accept such unpleasant adjustments as recession and inflation to eliminate their balance of payments deficits and surpluses.

(5) During the worldwide Great Depression of the 1930s, nations decided that remaining on the gold standard threatened their recoveries from the depression; and the devaluations of their currencies (to expand exports and reduce imports) led to the breakdown and abandonment of the gold standard.

(b) From the end of World War II until 1971, the Bretton Woods System, committed to the adjustable-peg system of exchange rates and managed by the International Monetary Fund (IMF), kept foreign-exchange rates relatively stable.

(1) The adjustable-peg system required the United States to sell gold to other member nations at a fixed price and the other members of the IMF to define their monetary units in terms of either gold or U.S. dollars (which established fixed exchange rates among the currencies of all member nations). It also required the other member nations to keep the exchange rates for their currencies from rising by selling foreign currencies, selling gold, or borrowing on a short-term basis from the IMF.

(2) The system also provided for orderly changes in exchange rates to correct a fundamental imbalance (per-

sistent and sizable balance of payments deficits) by allowing a nation to devalue its currency (increase its defined gold or dollar equivalent).

(3) The other nations of the world used gold and U.S. dollars as their international monetary reserves in the Bretton Woods System. For these reserves to grow, the United States had to continue to have balance of payments deficits; but to continue the convertibility of dollars into gold it had to reduce the deficits. Faced with this dilemma, the United States in 1971 suspended the convertibility of the dollar, brought an end to the Bretton Woods System of fixed exchange rates, and allowed the exchange rates for the U.S. dollar and the other currencies to float.

(c) Exchange rates today are managed by individual nations to avoid short-term fluctuations and they are allowed to float in the long term to correct balance of payments deficits and surpluses. This new system of managed floating exchange rates is favoured by some and criticized by others.

(1) Its proponents contend that this system has not led to any decrease in world trade and has enabled the world to adjust to severe economic shocks.

(2) Its critics argue that it has resulted in volatile exchange rates and has not reduced balance of payments deficits and surpluses; that it reinforces inflationary pressures in a nation; and that it is a ''nonsystem'' that a nation may employ to achieve its own domestic economic goals.

5. Since 1971, with the exception of four years, Canada's current account has had a negative balance, which has been offset by an inflow of foreign investment capital.

IMPORTANT TERMS

balance of payments
balance of payments deficit and surplus
balance of trade
Bretton Woods System
capital account
currency appreciation and depreciation
current account
current-account balance
devaluation
direct investment
exchange controls
fixed exchange rates
flexible (floating) exchange rates

foreign-exchange markets
G-7 nations
gold export and import points
gold standard
International Monetary Fund (IMF)
managed floating exchange rates
nonmerchandise balance
official international (foreign-exchange) reserves
portfolio investment
purchasing power parity
rate of exchange
statistical discrepancy
transfers

FILL-IN QUESTIONS

1.   The rate of exchange for the French franc is the number of (francs, dollars) _____ that a Canadian must pay to obtain one (franc, dollar) _____ .

2.   When the rate of exchange for the Saudi Arabian riyal is 34 Canadian cents, the rate of exchange for the Canadian dollar is _____ riyals.

3.   Canadian
(a) exports create a (demand for, supply of) _____ foreign money, generate a _____ dollars, (increase, decrease) _____ the money supply in Canada, and _____ money supplies abroad;

(b) imports create a _____ foreign money, generate a _____ dollars, _____ the money supply in Canada, and _____ money supplies abroad.

4.   In addition to the demand for foreign exchange by Canadian firms that wish to import goods from foreign countries, Canadians also demand foreign money to purchase _____ and _____ and _____ services abroad and to pay _____ and _____ on foreign investments in Canada.

5.   The balance of payments of a nation records all pay-

ments its residents make to and receive from residents in _____ .

(a) Any transaction that earns foreign exchange for that nation is a (debit, credit) _____ and is shown with a (+ , -) _____ sign.

(b) A transaction that uses up foreign exchange is a _____ and is shown with _____ sign.

6. When a nation has a

(a) balance of trade deficit, its exports of _____ and _____ are (greater, less) _____ than its imports of _____ and _____ .

(b) balance of trade surplus, its exports of _____ and _____ are _____ than its imports of goods and services;

(c) current-account deficit, its balance on goods and services plus its net _____ income and net _____ is (positive, negative) _____ .

7. The capital account records the capital inflows and capital outflows of a nation.

(a) The capital inflows are the expenditures made (in that nation, abroad) _____ for _____ and _____ assets by residents of (that nation, other nations) _____ ; and the capital outflows are the expenditures made _____ by residents of _____ for _____ and _____ assets.

(b) A nation has a capital-account surplus when its capital-account inflows are (greater, less) _____ than its outflows.

8. A nation:

(a) may finance a current-account deficit by (buying, selling) _____ assets or by (borrowing, lending) _____ abroad; and

(b) may use a current-account surplus to (buy, sell) _____ assets or to (borrow, lend) _____ abroad.

9. Canada generally has had a merchandise-account (surplus, deficit) _____ and a current-account _____ in its balance of payments in the last 20 years.

10. (a) The official international reserves of a nation are the quantities of (foreign monies, its own money) _____ owned by its _____ bank.

(b) In Canada these reserves are held in the _____ _____ Account.

(c) When the entry on line 9(a) in Table 18-1 in the text has a + (plus) sign, this means the Bank of Canada, on behalf of the government, has put (up, down) _____ward pressure on the Canadian dollar by (buying, selling) _____ U.S. dollars (for, out of) _____ the Exchange Fund Account.

(d) Thus a + (plus) sign on line 9(a) in text Table 18-1 means Canada has had a balance of payments (surplus, deficit) _____ ; and a – (minus) sign means Canada has had a payments _____ .

11. If foreign-exchange rates float freely (that is, the central bank is not supporting the value of the currency: line 9(a) in text Table 18-1 has a value of 0) and a nation is tending towards a balance of payments deficit,

(a) that nation's money in the foreign-exchange markets will (appreciate, depreciate) _____ and foreign monies will _____ .

(b) As a result of these changes in foreign-exchange rates, the nation's imports will (increase, decrease) _____ , its exports will _____ , and the size of its deficit will _____ .

12. When a nation's currency appreciates, it takes (more, less) _____ units of foreign currency to buy a unit of the nation's currency.

13. If the Canadian dollar appreciates relative to the U.S. dollar, then the U.S. dollar must _____ relative to the Canadian dollar.

14. What effect (depreciation or appreciation) would each of the following have upon the value of the Canadian dollar in U.S. dollar terms (other things equal)?

(a) A rise in real interest rates in Canada: _____

(b) A rise in the national income of Canada:

_____

(c) An increase in the price level in the United States:

_____

(d) The expectation in the United States that inflation will be more rapid in Canada than in the United States:

_____

(e) The belief of speculators that the Canadian dollar will appreciate against the U.S. dollar: _____

15. The demand for U.S. dollars, in the foreign-exchange market, is downsloping because as the U.S. dollar becomes less expensive American goods become

_____ in Canadian dollars, and therefore Canadians will increase their purchases of these goods and services.

16. In general, the higher a nation's price level, the

_____ is the amount of its currency that can be obtained for a unit of foreign currency.

17. The _____ _____ _____ theory holds that exchange rates adjust to reflect differences in price levels in various countries.

18. Supporters of a freely fluctuating exchange rate system argue that the exchange rates _____ adjust to eliminate balance of payments _____

or _____.

19. There are three disadvantages of freely floating foreign-exchange rates: the risks and uncertainties associated with flexible rates tend to (expand, diminish)

_____ trade between nations; when a nation's currency depreciates, its terms of trade with other nations are (worsened, bettered) _____; and fluctuating exports and imports can destabilize an

economy and result in _____ or

_____ in that economy.

20. To fix or "peg" the rate of exchange for the German mark when
(a) the exchange rate for the mark is rising, Canada

would (buy, sell) _____ marks in exchange for dollars;
(b) the exchange rate for the mark is falling, Canada would _____ marks in exchange for dollars.

21. A nation with a balance of payments deficit
(a) might attempt to eliminate the deficit by (taxing, subsidizing) _____ imports or by

_____ exports;
(b) might employ exchange controls and ration foreign exchange among those who wish to (export, import)

_____ goods and services and require all

those who _____ goods and services to sell

the foreign exchange they earn to the _____.

22. A nation is on the gold standard when it defines

its money in terms of _____, maintains a

fixed relationship between its _____

supply and gold _____, and allows gold

to be freely _____ from and _____ into the nation.

23. When the nations of the world were on the gold standard,
(a) exchange rates were relatively (stable, unstable)

_____;

(b) but when a nation had a payments deficit

(1) gold flowed (into, out of) _____ the nation;
(2) its money supply and price level (increased, decreased) _____, and its interest rates

_____; and

(3) its payments deficit (rose, fell) _____,

and it experienced (inflation, recession) _____.

24. The Bretton Woods system was established to bring

about (flexible, fixed) _____ exchange rates; and, to accomplish this, it employed the

_____ system of exchange rates. Under the Bretton Woods system,
(a) a member nation defined its monetary unit in terms

of _____ or _____;
(b) each member nation stabilized the exchange rate for its currency and prevented it from rising by (buying,

selling) _____ foreign currency, which it

obtained from its _____

fund, by (buying, selling) _____ gold, or

by (borrowing from, lending to) _____ the International Monetary Fund;

(c)   a nation with a deeply rooted payments deficit could

(devalue, revalue) _____ its currency;

(d)   official international reserves included both

_____ and _____; and

(e)   it was hoped that exchange rates in the short run

would be (stable, flexible) _____ enough to promote international trade and in the long run would

be _____ enough to correct balance of payments imbalances.

25.   The system of exchange rates that has developed

since 1971 has been labelled a system of _____

_____ exchange rates. This means that individual nations will

(a)   in the short term, buy and sell foreign exchange

to keep exchange rates _____;

(b)   in the long term, allow exchange rates to rise or fall

to correct payments _____.

PROBLEMS AND PROJECTS

1.   Assume a Canadian exporter sells $3 million worth of wheat to an import firm in Colombia. If the rate of exchange for the Colombian peso is $0.02 (two cents), the wheat has a total value of 150 million pesos.

(a)   There are two ways the import firm in Colombia may pay for the wheat. It might write a cheque for 150 million pesos drawn on its bank in Bogota and send it to the Canadian exporter.

(1) The Canadian exporter would then sell the cheque to its bank branch in Vancouver and its demand deposit

there would increase by $_____ million.

(2) This Vancouver bank branch sells the cheque for 150 million pesos to its main branch, that is, the head office branch of the bank that keeps an account in the Bogota bank.

(a)   The Vancouver bank branch's account in the main

branch increases by _____ million

(dollars, pesos) _____; and

(b)   the main branch's account in the Bogota bank

increases by _____ million (pesos, dollars)

_____.

(b)   The second way for the importer to pay for the

wheat is to buy from its bank in Bogota a draft on a Canadian bank for $3 million, pay for this draft by writing a cheque for 150 million pesos drawn on the Bogota bank, and send the cheque to the Canadian exporter.

(1) The Canadian exporter would then deposit the draft in its account in the Vancouver bank branch and its demand deposit account there would increase by

$_____ million.

(2) The Vancouver bank branch collects the amount of the draft from the Canadian bank on which it is drawn through the Vancouver clearing house.

(a)   The account at the Bank of Canada of the bank of which the Vancouver branch forms a part increases by

$_____ million; and

(b)   the account of the bank on which the draft was

drawn decreases by $_____ million.

(c)   Regardless of the method employed by the Colombian importer to pay for the wheat,

(1) the export of the wheat created a (demand for,

supply of) _____ dollars and a

_____ pesos;

(2) the number of dollars owned by the Canadian

exporter has (increased, decreased) _____ and the number of pesos owned by the Colombian

importer has _____.

2.   Use the 1990 Canadian balance of payment data given on page 235 to complete the table, which is similar to Table 18-1 of the text. Data is in billions of dollars.

3.   Below are the supply and demand schedules for the British pound.

Quantity of Pounds Supplied	Price $	Quantity of Pounds Demanded
400	5.00	100
360	4.50	200
300	4.00	300
286	3.50	400
267	3.00	500
240	2.50	620
200	2.00	788

(a)   If the exchange rates are flexible,

(1) what will be the rate of exchange for the pound?

$_____

(2) what will be the rate of exchange for the dollar?

£_____

	Receipts (exports) +	Payments (imports) −	Balance
CURRENT ACCOUNT			
(1) Merchandise	$146.0	$135.2	_____
(2) Services (invisibles)			
(a) travel (tourism)	7.4	12.0	_____
(b) freight and shipping	5.3	5.4	_____
(c) business services	7.9	10.9	_____
(d) government services	.8	1.3	_____
Total services	_____	_____	_____
(3) Total goods and services (balance of trade)	_____	_____	_____
(4) Investment income	8.7	32.9	_____
(5) Transfers			
(a) inheritance and immigrants' funds	8.1	1.4	_____
(b) personal and institutional remittances	.9	1.0	_____
(c) official contributions		2.7	_____
(d) withholding tax	1.6	.2	_____
(e) Total transfers	_____	_____	_____
(6) Total current account	_____	_____	_____
CAPITAL ACCOUNT			
(7) Direct Investment (excluding reinvested earnings)			+ 4.3
(8) Portfolio securities (a) bonds			+ 13.4
(b) stocks			− 2.8
(9) Government of Canada assets			
(a) official international reserves			− .65
(b) loans and subscriptions			− 1.4
(10) Allocation of special drawing rights			0.0
(11) Other capital movements			+ 8.2
(12) Total capital account, net flow			_____
(13) Statistical discrepancy			_____

(3) how many pounds will be purchased in the market?

_____

(4) how many dollars will be purchased in the market?

_____

(b) If the Government of Canada wished to fix or "peg" the price of the pound at $5.00, it would have

to (buy, sell) _____ (how many)

_____ pounds for $_____.

4. (a) Suppose the foreign exchange rate between the yen and Canadian dollar was: 1 yen = Cdn. $0.010285 and the exchange rate between the Canadian dollar and U.S. dollar was: U.S. $1.00 = Cdn. $1.2748. On the basis of this information we can expect 1 yen to cost U.S.

$_____.

(b) Suppose that the exchange rate was actually 1 yen = U.S. $0.0090 and you possess 10,000 Canadian dollars. Show that by buying and selling foreign currencies you could increase the number of Canadian dollars you hold.

5. The exchange rate between the Canadian dollar and the U.S. dollar is freely fluctuating and determined by the demand for and supply of U.S. dollars in the foreign exchange market. What effect, if any, is each of the following events likely to have on the exchange rate, other things being equal?

Place your answer in the space provided in the table on page 236 by placing an "X" in the appropriate column. The answer for (a) is included as a guide.

(a) Canadian corporations make large payments to American bondholders.

(b) The rate of inflation in Canada increases relative to the U.S. inflation rate.

(c)   The Bank of Canada purchases Canadian dollars with U.S. dollars on behalf of the Exchange Fund Account.

(d)   The United States economy enters the recovery stage of the business cycle, while the Canadian economy remains mired in recession.

(e)   The province of Ontario finances its deficit by borrowing in New York.

(f)   Interest rates fall in Canada and remain constant in the United States.

(g)   Falling unit labour costs in Canada increase the competitiveness of Canadian exports in the U.S. market.

(h)   An American-owned firm in Canada earns profits that are reinvested in Canada.

(i)   Speculators anticipate a depreciation of the Canadian dollar relative to the U.S. dollar.

(j)   The demand by Americans for Canadian-produced whiskey diminishes sharply.

	Canadian $ appreciates	Canadian $ depreciates	No effect
(a)		X	
(b)			
(c)			
(d)			
(e)			
(f)			
(g)			
(h)			
(i)			
(j)			

SELF-TEST

Circle T if the statement is true, F if it is false.

1.   The importation of goods by Canadians from abroad creates a supply of dollars in the foreign-exchange market.   **T F**

2.   Canadian exports expand foreign money supplies and reduce the supply of money in Canada.   **T F**

3.   The balance of international payments of Canada records all the payments its residents receive from and make to the residents of foreign nations.   **T F**

4.   Exports are shown with a plus sign (+), and imports are shown with a minus sign (–), in the balance of international payments of a nation.   **T F**

5.   When a Canadian province sells bonds in Europe, the inflow of money shows up in the Canadian balance of payments in the capital account with a minus (–) sign attached.   **T F**

6.   If a nation's exports of goods, services, and transfers are less than its imports of goods, services, and transfers, the nation's balance of international payments will show a balance is due from other nations in the current account.   **T F**

7.   A country will have a positive balance of trade whenever the value of exported goods is greater than the value of imported goods.   **T F**

8.   An example of direct investment would be the purchase by a resident of Germany of a Province of Ontario bond.   **T F**

9.   By including changes in official reserves and loans and subscriptions as part of the capital account, the sum of Canada's current- and capital-account balances and the statistical discrepancy always equals zero.   **T F**

10.   Canada normally has a merchandise trade surplus and an overall current-account deficit.   **T F**

11.   Any nation with a balance of payments deficit will lose official international reserves.   **T F**

12.   A foreign exchange rate is the price, in Canadian dollars, of a unit of foreign currency.   **T F**

13.   Suppose that Canadian $1.20 = U.S. $1.00. It must also be true that U.S. $0.80 = Canadian $1.00.   **T F**

14.   The Canadian dollar has depreciated, relative to a foreign currency, whenever it takes more Canadian dollars to purchase a unit of the foreign currency.   **T F**

15.   The Canadian dollar has depreciated relative to the U.S. dollar whenever it takes less U.S. dollars to purchase a Canadian dollar.   **T F**

16.   Whenever the Canadian dollar depreciates relative to the U. S. dollar, the Canadian dollar price of American imports will rise.   **T F**

17.   In a system of floating exchange rates, the foreign exchange rate is set by the central bank.   **T F**

18.   The quantity demanded of U.S. dollars is downward sloping because Canadians purchase greater quantities of American goods and require larger quantities of U.S. dollars as the U.S. dollar becomes less expensive in Canadian dollar terms.   **T F**

19. When the Bank of Canada buys U.S. dollars for the Exchange Fund Account, it is putting upward pressure on the international value of the Canadian dollar. **T F**

20. Financing government deficits by borrowing abroad causes the Canadian dollar to depreciate. **T F**

21. If a nation has a balance of payments deficit and exchange rates are flexible, the price of that nation's money in the foreign-exchange markets will fall, and this will reduce its imports and increase its exports. **T F**

22. An increase in the number of dollars earned as dividends by Japanese investors in Canadian corporations will increase the demand for dollars and the supply of yen, and the price of the dollar will appreciate in Japan. **T F**

23. Were Canada's terms of trade with Venezuela to worsen, Venezuela would obtain a greater quantity of Canadian goods and services for every barrel of oil it exported to Canada. **T F**

24. To increase its official international reserves (foreign-exchange reserves), a nation must have a balance of payments surplus. **T F**

25. If Canada wishes to fix (or "peg") the value of the Canadian dollar in terms of the U.S. dollar, the Bank of Canada must sell U.S. dollars (in exchange for Canadian dollars) when the Canadian dollar is tending to depreciate. **T F**

26. The expectations of speculators in Canada that the exchange rate for the Japanese yen will fall in the future will increase the supply of yen in the foreign-exchange market and decrease the exchange rate for the yen. **T F**

27. A nation using exchange controls to eliminate a payments surplus might devalue its currency. **T F**

28. If country A defined its money as worth 100 grains of gold and country B defined its money as worth 20 grains of gold, then (ignoring packing, insuring, and shipping charges) 5 units of country A's money would be worth 1 unit of country B's money. **T F**

29. When nations were on the gold standard, foreign-exchange rates fluctuated only within limits determined by the cost of moving gold from one nation to another. **T F**

30. If a nation maintains an exchange stabilization fund, it would purchase its own money with gold or foreign monies when the value of its money falls in foreign-exchange markets. **T F**

31. In the Bretton Woods system, a nation could not devalue its currency by more than 10% without the permission of the International Monetary Fund. **T F**

32. One of the basic shortcomings of the Bretton Woods system was its inability to bring about the changes in exchange rates needed to correct persistent payments deficits and surpluses. **T F**

33. Using the managed floating system of exchange rates, a nation with a persistent balance of payments surplus should allow the value of its currency in foreign-exchange markets to decrease. **T F**

34. A fall in the exchange rate for a nation's currency tends to increase its exports and to decrease its imports. **T F**

MULTIPLE-CHOICE

Circle the letter that corresponds to the best answer.

1. If a Canadian could buy 25,000 British pounds for $100,000, the rate of exchange for the pound would be
(a) $40
(b) $25
(c) $4
(d) $0.25

2. There is an increased demand for foreign currency (increased supply of Canadian dollars) when Canadians
(a) pay for goods and services imported from foreign countries
(b) make payments of interest and dividends to foreign countries on their investments in Canada
(c) make real and financial investments in foreign countries
(d) do all of the above

3. A nation's balance of trade is equal to its
(a) exports less its imports of merchandise (goods)
(b) exports less its imports of goods and services
(c) exports less its imports of goods and services plus its net investment income and transfers
(d) exports less its imports of goods, services, and capital

4. A nation's balance on the current account is equal to its
(a) exports less its imports of merchandise (goods)
(b) exports less its imports of goods and services
(c) exports less its imports of goods and services plus its net investment income and net transfers
(d) exports less its imports of goods, services, and capital

5. Investment income in Canada's balance of payments is

(a) highly positive and includes interest and dividends
(b) highly negative and includes interest and dividends
(c) positive and includes interest only
(d) negative and includes interest only
(e) positive and includes dividends only

6. Capital flows into Canada include the purchase by foreign residents of
(a) a factory building owned by Canadians
(b) shares of stock owned by Canadians
(c) bonds owned by Canadians
(d) an apartment building owned by Canadians
(e) all of the above

7. A Canadian current-account deficit may be financed by
(a) borrowing abroad
(b) selling real assets to foreigners
(c) selling financial assets to foreigners
(d) any of the above

8. Traditionally, Canada has had
(a) a positive balance on merchandise trade
(b) a deficit on current account
(c) a capital inflow from abroad
(d) all of the above

9. Given the change in reserves is zero, if Canada has a capital-account surplus, it must also have a
(a) current-account surplus
(b) current-account deficit
(c) balance of payments surplus
(d) balance of payments deficit

10. A nation may be able to correct or eliminate a persistent (long-term) balance of payments deficit by
(a) lowering the barriers on imported goods
(b) reducing the international value of its currency
(c) expanding its national income
(d) reducing its official international reserves

11. If exchange rates float freely, the exchange rate for any currency is determined by
(a) the demand for it
(b) the supply of it
(c) the demand for and the supply of it
(d) the official reserves that ''back'' it

12. Under a floating exchange rate system, an increase in Canadian interest rates relative to U. S. interest will
(a) appreciate the Canadian dollar relative to the U.S. dollar
(b) depreciate the Canadian dollar relative to the U.S. dollar
(c) raise the price of U.S. goods in Canadian dollars

(d) appreciate the U.S. dollar relative to the Canadian dollar

13. If a Canadian province finances a deficit by borrowing abroad,
(a) Canadian interest rates will rise
(b) the Canadian dollar will depreciate
(c) the Canadian dollar will appreciate
(d) there will be an outflow of capital from Canada

14. If a nation had a balance of payments surplus and exchange rates floated freely,
(a) the foreign-exchange rate for its currency would rise, its exports would increase, and its imports would decrease
(b) the foreign-exchange rate for its currency would rise, its exports would decrease, and its imports would increase
(c) the foreign-exchange rate for its currency would fall, its exports would increase, and its imports would decrease
(d) the foreign-exchange rate for its currency would fall, its exports would decrease, and its imports would increase

15. Assuming exchange rates are flexible, which of the following would increase the Canadian dollar price of the Swedish krona?
(a) a rate of inflation greater in Sweden than in Canada
(b) real interest-rate increases greater in Sweden than in Canada
(c) national income increases greater in Sweden than in Canada
(d) expectations that the price of the krona will be lower in the future

16. Which of the following would be one of the results associated with the use of freely floating foreign-exchange rates to correct a nation's balance of payments surplus?
(a) the nation's terms of trade with other nations would be worsened
(b) importers in the nation who had made contracts for the future delivery of goods would find that they had to pay a higher price than expected for the goods
(c) if the nation were at full employment, the decrease in exports and the increase in imports would be inflationary
(d) exporters in the nation would find their sales abroad had decreased

17. Disadvantages of a floating exchange rate system include all of the following except
(a) uncertainty over future exchange rates
(b) instability in the macroeconomy caused by changing exchange rates
(c) decline in the terms of trade that accompany a currency depreciation
(d) an automatic adjustment mechanism for balance of payments problems

18. The use of exchange controls to eliminate a nation's balance of payments deficit results in
(a) decreasing the nation's imports
(b) decreasing the nation's exports
(c) decreasing the nation's price level
(d) decreasing the nation's income

19. A nation with a balance of payments surplus might attempt to eliminate this surplus by employing
(a) import quotas
(b) higher tariffs
(c) subsidies on items the nation exports
(d) none of the above

20. Which one of the following conditions did a nation not have to fulfil if it was to be one under the gold standard?
(a) use only gold as a medium of exchange
(b) maintain a fixed relationship between its gold stock and its money supply
(c) allow gold to be freely exported from and imported into the nation
(d) define its monetary unit in terms of a fixed quantity of gold

21. If the nations of the world were on the gold standard and one nation had a balance of payments surplus,
(a) foreign-exchange rates in that nation would rise toward the gold import point
(b) gold would tend to be imported into that country
(c) the level of prices in that country would tend to fall
(d) employment and output in that country would tend to fall

22. Under the gold standard, a nation with a balance of payments deficit would experience all but one of the following. Which one?
(a) gold would flow out of the nation
(b) the nation's money supply would contract
(c) interest rates in the nation would fall
(d) real domestic output, employment, and prices in the nation would decline

23. Which of the following was the principal disadvantage of the gold standard?
(a) unstable foreign-exchange rates
(b) persistent payments imbalances
(c) the uncertainties and decreased trade that resulted from the depreciation of gold
(d) the domestic macroeconomic adjustments experienced by a nation with a payments deficit or surplus

24. All but one of the following were elements in the adjustable-peg system of foreign-exchange rates. Which one?

(a) each nation defined its monetary unit in terms of gold or dollars
(b) nations bought and sold their own currencies to stabilize exchange rates
(c) nations were allowed to devalue their currencies when faced with persistent payments deficits
(d) the deposit by all nations of their international reserves with the IMF

25. The objective of the adjustable-peg system was exchange rates that were
(a) adjustable in the short run and fixed in the long run
(b) adjustable in both the short and long run
(c) fixed in both the short and long run
(d) fixed in the short run, adjustable in the long run

26. The dilemma created by the U.S. payments deficits was that
(a) to maintain the status of the dollar as an acceptable international monetary reserve the deficit had to be reduced, and to increase these reserves the deficits had to be continued
(b) to maintain the status of the dollar the deficit had to be continued, and to increase reserves the deficit had to be eliminated
(c) to maintain the status of the dollar the deficit had to be increased, and to expand reserves the deficit had to be reduced
(d) to maintain the status of the dollar the deficit had to be reduced, and to expand reserves the deficit had to be reduced

27. "Floating" the U.S. dollar means
(a) the value of the dollar is to be determined by the demand for and the supply of the dollar
(b) the dollar price of gold is to be increased
(c) the price of the dollar is to be set by international agreement
(d) the gold content of the dollar is to be reduced

28. A system of managed floating exchange rates
(a) allows nations to stabilize exchange rates in the short term
(b) requires nations to stabilize exchange rates in the long term
(c) entails stable exchange rates in both the short and long term
(d) none of the above

29. Floating exchange rates
(a) tend to correct payments imbalances
(b) reduce the uncertainties and risks associated with international trade
(c) increase the world's need for official international reserves

(d)   tend to expand the volume of world trade

30.   If 1 Japanese yen sold for Cdn. $0.010285 on Dec. 12 and sold for Cdn. $0.010384 on Dec. 15 then:

(a)   the yen has depreciated relative to the Canadian dollar

(b)   the yen has appreciated relative to the Canadian dollar

(c)   the Canadian dollar has appreciated relative to the yen

(d)   none of the above

DISCUSSION QUESTIONS

1.   What is foreign exchange and the foreign-exchange rate? Who are the demanders and suppliers of a particular foreign exchange, say, the French franc? Why is a buyer (demander) in the foreign-exchange markets always a seller (supplier) also?

2.   What is meant when it is said that "a nation's exports pay for its imports"? Do nations always pay for all their imports with exports?

3.   What is a balance of international payments? What are the principal sections of a nation's balance of payments? What are the three kinds of exports and imports listed in it?

4.   How does a nation finance a balance of payments deficit and what does it do with a balance of payments surplus?

5.   Is it good or bad for a nation to have a balance of payments deficit or surplus?

6.   What is the difference between direct and portfolio investment?

7.   In a floating exchange rate system the exchange rate is determined by the forces of supply and demand. Use the balance of payments as given in Table 18-1 to enumerate the demanders and suppliers of foreign currencies.

8.   What types of events cause the exchange rate for a foreign currency to appreciate or depreciate? How will each of these events affect the exchange rate for a foreign money and for a nation's own money?

9.   How can freely floating foreign-exchange rates eliminate balance of payments deficits and surpluses? What are the problems associated with this method of correcting payments imbalances?

10.   Describe the effect on the Canadian dollar price of foreign goods when the Canadian dollar depreciates.

11.   How may a nation employ its foreign-exchange reserves to fix or "peg" foreign-exchange rates? Be precise. How does a nation obtain or acquire these official international reserves?

12.   What kinds of trade controls may nations with payments deficits employ to eliminate their deficits?

13.   How can foreign-exchange controls be used to overcome a payments deficit? Why do such exchange controls necessarily involve the rationing of foreign exchange? What effect do these controls have upon prices, output, and employment in nations that use them?

14.   If foreign-exchange rates are fixed, what kind of domestic macroeconomic adjustments are required to eliminate a payments deficit? To eliminate a payments surplus?

15.   When was a nation on the gold standard? How did the international gold standard correct payments imbalances? What were the disadvantages of this method of eliminating payments deficits and surpluses?

16.   Why does the operation of the international gold standard ensure relatively stable foreign-exchange rates, that is, rates that fluctuate only within very narrow limits? What are the limits, and what are the advantages, of stable exchange rates?

17.   What is the "critical difference" between the adjustment necessary to correct payments deficits and surpluses under the gold standard and those necessary when exchange rates are flexible? How did this difference lead to the demise of the gold standard during the 1930s?

18.   Explain (a) why the International Monetary Fund was established, and what the objectives of the adjustable-peg (or Bretton Woods) system were; (b) what the adjustable-peg system was, and the basic means it employed to stabilize exchange rates in the short run; and (c) when and how the system was to adjust exchange rates in the long run.

19.   What did nations use as official international reserves under the Bretton Woods system? Why was the dollar used by nations as an international money, and how could they acquire additional dollars?

20.   Explain the dilemma created by the need for expanding official international reserves and for maintaining the status of the U.S. dollar.

21.   Explain what is meant by a managed floating system of foreign-exchange rates. When are exchange rates managed, and when are they allowed to float?

22.   Explain the arguments of the proponents and the critics of the managed floating system.

ANSWERS

Fill-in questions

1.   dollars, franc

2.   2.94

3.   (a) supply of, demand for, increase, decrease; (b) demand for, supply of, decrease, increase

4.   tourism, freight, shipping (either order), interest, dividends (either order)

5.   the other nations of the world; (a) credit, +; (b) debit, −

6.   (a) goods, services, less, goods, services (b) goods, services, greater; (c) investment, transfers, negative

7.   (a) in that nation, real, financial, other nations, in other nations, that nation, real, financial (either order); (b) greater

8.   (a) selling, borrowing; (b) buy, lend

9.   surplus, deficit

10.   (a) foreign monies, central; (b) Exchange Fund; (c) up, selling, out of; (d) deficit, surplus

11.   (a) depreciate, appreciate; (b) decrease, increase, decrease

12.   more

13.   depreciate

14.   (a) appreciation; (b) depreciation; (c) appreciation; (d) depreciation; (e) appreciation

15.   cheaper

16.   greater

17.   purchasing power parity

18.   automatically, surpluses, deficits

19.   diminish, worsened, recession, inflation (either order)

20.   (a) sell; (b) buy

21.   (a) taxing, subsidizing; (b) import, export, government

22.   gold, money, stock, exported, imported

23.   (a) stable; (b) (1) out of, (2) decreased, rose, (3) fell, recession

24. fixed, adjustable-peg; (a) gold, U.S. dollars (either order); (b) selling, exchange-stabilization, selling, borrowing from; (c) devalue; (d) gold, U.S. dollars (either order); (e) stable, flexible

25.   managed floating; (a) stable; (b) imbalances

Problems and projects

1.   (a) (1) 3, (2) (a) 3, dollars, (b) 150, pesos; (b) (1) 3, (2) (a) 3, (b) 3; (c) (1) demand for, supply of, (2) increased, decreased

2.   Answers are in billions of dollars (1) +10.8 (2) (a) −4.6, (b) −.1, (c) −3.0, (d) −.5; Total services: 21.4, −29.6, −8.2 (3) 167.4, −164.8, +2.6 (4) −24.2 (5) (a) +6.7, (b) −.1, (c) −2.7, (d) +1.4 (e) 10.6, −5.3, +5.3 (6) 186.7, −203, −16.3 (12) +21.05 (13) −4.75

3.   (a) (1) 4.00, (2) ¼, (3) 300, (4) 1200; (b) buy, 300, 1500; (c) sell, 380, 950

4.   (a) U.S. $0.008068 (b) (1) buy yen with Cdn. $10,000 (2) buy U.S. dollars with yen (3) buy Cdn. dollars with U.S. dollars (4) end with Can. $11,155.27

5.

	Canadian $ appreciates	Canadian $ depreciates	No effect
(a)		X	
(b)		X	
(c)	X		
(d)	X		
(e)	X		
(f)		X	
(g)	X		
(h)			X
(i)		X	
(j)		X	

Self-test

1. T; 2. F; 3. T; 4. T; 5. F; 6. F; 7. F; 8. F; 9. T; 10. T; 11. T; 12. T; 13. F; 14. T; 15. T; 16. T; 17. F; 18. T; 19. F; 20. F; 21. T; 22. F; 23. T; 24. T; 25. T; 26. T; 27. F; 28. F; 29. T; 30. T; 31. T; 32. T; 33. F; 34. T

Multiple-choice

1. (c); 2. (d); 3. (b); 4. (c); 5. (b); 6. (e); 7. (d); 8. (d); 9. (b); 10. (b); 11. (c); 12. (a); 13. (c); 14. (b); 15. (b); 16. (d); 17. (d); 18. (a); 19. (d); 20. (a); 21. (b); 22. (c); 23. (d); 24. (d); 25. (d); 26. (a); 27. (a); 28. (a); 29. (a); 30. (b)

CHAPTER

19 Macroeconomic Policy in an Open Economy

In an open economy policies designed to stabilize the domestic economy can have an effect on the exchange rate, imports and exports, and the balance of payments. If policy makers have a balance of payments objective in addition to domestic stability, they may find that the goals are incompatible. This chapter sets out two goals: full employment with price stability (internal balance) and a zero balance on current account (external balance). Then it investigates the effect on these goals of monetary and fiscal actions designed to offset inflationary or deflationary gaps. The internal balance takes precedence over a balance on current account.

This chapter utilizes the aggregate expenditure model of Chapters 7 and 8. Exports depend upon the level of foreign income, and imports vary directly with the level of domestic income. Exchange rates are first set fixed and different monetary and fiscal actions are implemented to investigate their effects on the level of income and on exports and imports. In this model the *ceteris paribus* assumption is used, and the central bank maintains a fixed exchange rate without affecting any other economic aggregate. Two different levels of employment (unemployment, inflation) are considered along with a current-account surplus and deficit. This yields four possible models, each with a fixed exchange rate, in which monetary or fiscal policy is changed and the effects on the internal and external balance noted.

Fluctuating exchange rates replace the fixed rates in the next model. Both monetary and fiscal policy changes result in an interest rate change in the domestic economy which, in turn, causes a capital inflow or outflow. The foreign exchange rate will change resulting in a change in net exports, which can reinforce or offset the effect of the original policy change. Expansionary fiscal policy is weakened while expansionary monetary policy is strengthened by the induced capital flows.

The effect of domestic macroeconomic policies on a country's balance of payments objective are set out in Table 19-1 for the fixed exchange rate case and Tables 19-2 and 19-3 for fluctuating exchange rates. Be sure that you follow the economic reasoning that leads to the predictions of both models.

CHECKLIST

When you have studied this chapter you should be able to:

- Identify the assumed domestic (or internal) and international (or external) goals of the Canadian economy; and state which goal is assumed to have the higher priority.

- Assuming fixed exchange rates, describe the effects on the domestic economy and on net exports of an expansionary fiscal and monetary policy.

- Assuming fixed exchange rates, describe the effects on the domestic economy and net exports of contractionary fiscal and monetary policy.

- Using the results from the above, explain the effect on the internal and external balance of monetary and fiscal policies when the initial conditions are: 1) inflation and a trade deficit; 2) unemployment and a trade deficit; 3) inflation and a trade surplus; and 4) unemployment and a trade surplus.

- Identify the macroeconomic circumstances in which tariffs and/or currency revaluation and devaluation can be used to reach an internal and external balance when a trade-off between the two exists.

- Assuming fluctuating exchange rates, describe the induced effect on the exchange rate and net exports of expansionary and contractionary fiscal and monetary policy.

- Provide an explanation of why the net exports effect weakens the effects of fiscal policy.

- Explain how exchange rate changes strengthen domestic monetary policy.

- Describe the economic process through which an

expansionary monetary policy is compatible with correcting a current-account deficit, while a contractionary monetary policy conflicts with correcting a current-account deficit.

CHAPTER OUTLINE

1. A nation is assumed to have as goals the achievement of full employment output with low inflation for the domestic economy and a balance of 0 in its current account. The first goal is sometimes termed an internal balance and the latter goal an external balance. The two goals are not always compatible and it may require more than one policy change to achieve both simultaneously.

2. Expanding the aggregate expenditures model by adding fixed exchange rates and later fluctuating exchange rates provides a model that provides predictions as to the effect of fiscal and monetary changes on the internal and external balance. The internal balance is assumed to be of higher priority than a zero balance in the current account.

(a)   It is assumed that the foreign exchange rate is fixed and that the central bank provides the necessary foreign exchange, *ceteris paribus*.

(1) Stimulative fiscal or monetary policy increases the level of output, which, in turn, increases imports and reduces the level of net exports.

(a) The use of stimulative monetary or fiscal policy is compatible with the objective of overcoming unemployment and a current-account surplus.

(b) The goals of internal and external balance are incompatible if stimulative monetary or fiscal policy is applied in an economy suffering from unemployment and a current-account deficit.

(2) Contractionary fiscal or monetary policy reduces the level of output, reduces imports, and increases net exports.

(a) The goals of internal and external balance are compatible if contractionary fiscal or monetary policy is applied in an economy characterized by inflation and a current-account deficit.

(b) The use of contractionary fiscal or monetary policy will not achieve both internal and external balance if applied in an economy suffering from inflation and with a surplus on current account.

(3) Cases (1)(b) and 2(b) illustrate instances where the achievement of an internal balance, which was assumed to have priority, conflicts with the goal set out for the international trade sector. One resolution of the conflict is to change one other policy measure so as to alter the composition of the aggregate expenditures. For example, a revaluation (increase in the external value) of the

domestic currency would aid in achieving a balanced current account in (2)(b); while the imposition of tariffs would reduce the current-account deficit in (1)(b).

(b)   With flexible exchange rates the application of monetary and fiscal policy changes the domestic rate of interest, which, in turn, results in a capital inflow or outflow as investors seek higher returns. The inflow or outflow of capital results in a change in the exchange rate, which causes a change in the level of net exports.

(1)(a) An expansionary fiscal policy can increase domestic interest rates and results in a capital inflow and an appreciation of the domestic currency. The appreciation of the currency results in reduced exports and increased imports so that net exports decline and the original stimulus is weakened.

(b) A contractionary fiscal policy may reduce interest rates, cause a capital outflow, depreciate the domestic currency, and expand net exports. Again fiscal policy is weakened.

(2)(a) An expansionary monetary policy reduces interest rates, causes a capital outflow, depreciates the domestic currency, and increases net exports. This policy works to overcome both unemployment and a balance of payments deficit.

(b) A contractionary monetary policy raises interest rates, causes a capital inflow, appreciates the domestic currency, and reduces net exports. Twin goals of alleviating inflation and a current-account deficit would not be met by using a tight money policy.

(3) When the exchange rates are flexible, an expansionary (easy) money policy will be more effective than fiscal policy in reducing unemployment and a current-account deficit because it lowers interest rates and the international value of its currency, expands exports, and reduces imports.

3. A tight money policy designed to achieve specific domestic objectives can have unwanted repercussions. For example, a tight money policy used to combat domestic inflation can lead to the appreciation of the domestic currency and a reduction in net exports. To domestic producers, foreign markets can no longer be profitably serviced and financial difficulties result. Circumstances can sometimes result in difficult trade-offs in an open economy.

IMPORTANT TERMS

devaluation
external and internal balance
net export effect
policy conflict

FILL-IN QUESTIONS

1.   The internal goal of the economy is assumed to be the achievement of _____ _____ with low _____; while the external goal is a balance of _____ in the _____ _____.

2.   The (internal, external) _____ goal is considered to be of higher priority, which means that the effect of macroeconomic policies to stabilize output on the _____ _____ is investigated.

3.   If imports are directly related to domestic income then policies that change the level of income will also change the level of net _____. The goals of changing both incomes and net exports in a particular direction may not be _____.

4.   Assuming a fixed exchange rate model:
(a)   An increase in government expenditure will increase _____ _____ which, in turn, increases (exports, imports) _____. The increase in _____ would (increase, decrease) _____ a current-account surplus or _____ a current-account deficit.
(b)   An expansion of the money supply is termed an _____ or _____ _____ policy. An increase in the money supply will _____ the domestic _____ _____, increase the level of investment and increase _____ _____. Imports would _____, so net exports would _____, and there would be a _____ in the current-account surplus or an _____ in the current-account deficit.
(c)   If a country was experiencing unemployment and a current-account surplus, an expansionary monetary or fiscal policy would (improve, worsen) _____ the internal balance and _____ the

external balance.
(d)   If a country was experiencing unemployment and a current- account deficit, an expansionary monetary or fiscal policy would _____ the internal balance and _____ the external balance.
(e)   In 4(c) an external and internal balance are (compatible, conflicting) _____, while in 4(e) they are _____. Expansionary macro policies are compatible with a current-account _____, but are in conflict with eliminating a current-account _____.

5.   Assuming a fluctuating exchange rate model,
(a)   An increase in government expenditures will tend to increase the domestic interest rate. As interest rates rise there will occur a capital (inflow, outflow) _____ as investors seek out the higher return. There will be an increased (demand for, supply of) _____ domestic currency on the foreign exchange market so the foreign price of a unit of domestic currency will (increase, decrease) _____. The domestic currency (appreciates, depreciates) _____. Exports become (cheaper, dearer) _____ in foreign currency and imports become _____ in domestic currency. Net exports will (increase, decrease) _____. The _____ in net exports will _____ aggregate demand and (strengthen, weaken) _____ the effect of expansionary fiscal policy.
(b)   An increase in the money supply will reduce _____ _____, increase _____ spending, and increase the equilibrium level of income. As interest rates fall there will be an (outflow, inflow) _____ of capital in search of the relatively (higher, lower) _____ rates abroad. This results in a (greater, less) _____ demand for foreign currency and a(n) (increased, decreased) _____ price of foreign currency. The domestic currency will (appreciate, depreciate) _____, which makes domestic goods

(cheaper, dearer) _____ in foreign currency and foreign goods _____ in domestic currency. Exports of goods and services will (increase, decrease) _____ and imports of goods and services _____. Net exports _____ and the net export effect (reinforces, diminishes) _____ the effect of the expansionary monetary policy.

(c) An expansionary monetary policy would overcome the problem of unemployment combined with a current-account _____. A contractionary monetary policy would lessen inflationary pressures, but would conflict with the goal of correcting a current-account _____.

PROBLEMS AND PROJECTS

1. Assume

(a) the Canadian economy has fully employed its labour force, is experiencing inflation, and has a current-account deficit.

(1) To reduce the inflationary pressures in the economy requires a(n) (expansionary, contractionary) _____ fiscal policy or a(n) (tight, easy) _____ monetary policy.

(2) If these measures are successful in curbing inflation without reducing employment, the economy's

  (a) exports will tend to (increase, decrease) _____,

  (b) imports will tend to _____, and

  (c) the trade deficit of the Canadian economy will tend to (increase, decrease) _____.

(3) The measures undertaken to reduce inflation in Canada worked to (reduce, widen) _____ the trade deficits.

(4) But if the economy had begun with a trade surplus, the fiscal and monetary measures taken to fight inflation would have (widened, narrowed) _____ the trade surplus.

(b) the Canadian economy has a relatively large portion (say 10%) of its labour force unemployed, is experiencing a recession, and has a current-account deficit.

(1) To reduce unemployment and increase the economy's real output requires a(n) _____

fiscal policy or a(n) _____ monetary policy.

(2) If these measures are successful in expanding employment and output in the economy,

  (a) exports will tend to _____,

  (b) imports will tend to _____, and

  (c) the trade deficit of the Canadian economy will tend to _____.

(3) The measures taken to reduce unemployment in Canada worked to (reduce, widen) _____ the trade deficit.

(4) But if the economy had begun with a payments surplus, the fiscal and monetary policies employed to fight recession would have (widened, narrowed) _____ the surplus.

2. Suppose the monetary authority uses changes in the interest rate as the primary method to influence other macroeconomic magnitudes. Indicate the short-term effect on the internal balance and external balance of an *increase* in interest rates under the following conditions. "Deficit" and "surplus" refer to the current account. Place "improve" or "worsen" to indicate a movement toward and away from internal and external balance. Assume fixed exchange rates.

Economic condition	Effect on Internal balance	External balance
(a) Recession and deficit	_____	_____
(b) Inflation and deficit	_____	_____
(c) Recession and surplus	_____	_____
(d) Inflation and surplus	_____	_____

SELF-TEST

Circle T if the statement is true, F if it is false.

1. The external goal of an economy is assumed to be a zero balance in its balance of payments.   **T F**

2. Achieving full employment and a current account balance of zero can be conflicting goals.   **T F**

3. The external (or international) goal of Canada can be reasonably assumed to have a higher priority than its internal (or domestic) goal.   **T F**

4. As the incomes of Canadians rise, they buy more goods and services produced in Canada and more goods

and services produced abroad. **T F**

5. Under fixed exchange rates a restrictive fiscal policy will diminish an export surplus, while a restrictive monetary policy will increase an export surplus. **T F**

6. In the fixed exchange rate model, the policies used by a country to eliminate unemployment are compatible with the elimination of that country's current-account deficit. **T F**

7. In the fixed exchange rate model, the policies used by a country to reduce inflation conflict with the elimination of a current-account surplus. **T F**

8. In the fixed exchange rate model, there always exists a monetary or fiscal policy which, operating alone, can lead to both internal and external balance. **T F**

9. In a currency devaluation the government increases the international price of the domestic currency. **T F**

10. Tariff reductions and the revaluation of its currency would (if there were no retaliation) enable a nation to reduce both its rate of inflation and a current-account surplus. **T F**

11. A fall in the exchange rate for a nation's currency tends to increase its exports and decrease its imports. **T F**

12. A rise in the exchange rate for its currency will help to lessen a nation's unemployment and reduce its current-account deficit. **T F**

13. In the fluctuating exchange rate model, a decrease in the domestic money supply will reduce the interest rate and cause a depreciation of the exchange rate. **T F**

14. An easy money policy, in the fluctuating exchange rate model, will result in a decrease in net exports. **T F**

15. An expansionary fiscal policy tends to increase interest rates in the economy. **T F**

16. Exchange rate changes in response to interest rate changes in the floating exchange rate model strengthen fiscal policy. **T F**

17. In the fluctuating exchange rate model, expansionary fiscal policy will achieve the goals of increased employment and the elimination of a current-account deficit. **T F**

18. An easy monetary policy is more effective in reducing unemployment and a current-account deficit than an expansionary fiscal policy in the fluctuating exchange rate model. **T F**

19. Exchange rate changes in response to interest rate changes in the floating exchange rate model strengthen monetary policy. **T F**

20. In the fluctuating exchange rate model, an expansionary monetary policy will reduce a trade surplus. **T F**

21. Under flexible exchange rates an open market purchase by the central bank will improve a deficit on current account. **T F**

22. Anti-inflationary macro policies are compatible with correcting a trade deficit. **T F**

23. There can be a trade-off between the use of monetary policy to affect the current-account balance and to achieve domestic macroeconomic stability. **T F**

MULTIPLE-CHOICE

Circle the letter that corresponds to the best answer.

1. The domestic (or internal) goal of the Canadian economy is
(a) full employment
(b) a relatively stable price level
(c) full employment with little or no inflation
(d) a zero-account balance

2. The international (or external) goal of Canada is
(a) full employment with little or no inflation
(b) a current-account surplus
(c) a current-account deficit
(d) a zero current-account balance

3. Which of the following policies are compatible?
(a) those designed to eliminate inflation and a current-account deficit
(b) those utilized to eliminate unemployment and a trade surplus
(c) both of the above
(d) neither of the above

4. In the fixed exchange rate model which of the following policies conflict?
(a) those designed to reduce unemployment and a trade deficit
(b) those designed to reduce inflation and a trade surplus
(c) both of the above
(d) neither of the above

5. A revaluation of a country's currency would
(a) reduce the domestic price of foreign goods
(b) reduce the domestic price of domestic goods

(c) increase the domestic price of foreign goods
(d) reduce the price in foreign currency of domestic goods

6. Which of the following would (if there were no retaliation) enable a nation to reduce both unemployment and a current-account deficit?
(a) a reduction in its tariffs and the devaluation of its currency
(b) a reduction in its tariffs and the revaluation of its currency
(c) an increase in its tariffs and the devaluation of its currency
(d) an increase in its tariffs and the revaluation of its currency

7. Increasing aggregate demand in the fixed exchange rate model would lead to external and internal balance in an economy characterized by
(a) unemployment and a current-account deficit
(b) inflation and a current-account deficit
(c) unemployment and a current-account surplus
(d) inflation and a current-account surplus

8. In the case of inflation and a current-account deficit under fixed exchange rates, there should be applied
(a) expansionary fiscal and monetary policy
(b) expansionary fiscal and a tight monetary policy
(c) contractionary fiscal and monetary policy
(d) contractionary fiscal and an easy monetary policy

9. An easy money policy will
(a) expand output and employment and increase interest rates in the economy
(b) expand output and employment and decrease interest rates in the economy
(c) contract output and employment and increase interest rates in the economy
(d) contract output and employment and decrease interest rates in the economy

10. With floating exchange rates an expansionary fiscal policy will cause
(a) a depreciation of the domestic currency
(b) an appreciation of the domestic currency
(c) no change in the international value of the domestic currency
(d) any of the above

11. Which of the following would occur in an open economy with a fluctuating exchange rate as the result of an increase in the money supply?
(a) a decrease in the level of income
(b) a depreciation of the exchange rate
(c) a decrease in exports

(d) an appreciation of the exchange rate

12. Given an increase in government expenditure in an open economy with a fluctuating exchange rate, there will occur
(a) an increase in exports
(b) a decrease in interest rates
(c) an increase in imports
(d) a depreciation of the exchange rate

DISCUSSION QUESTIONS

1. What domestic and international goals is the economy assumed to have? Which of these goals is assumed to have a higher priority?

2. Explain why the policies employed by a nation to reduce unemployment or inflation conflict with achieving an external balance.

3. Suppose contractionary fiscal policy is being used to overcome inflation in an economy with a balance of payments surplus. Outline the effects of such a policy on the external balance. What would you recommend as to tariff levels in order to reach an external balance?

4. In what circumstances would the revaluation of a currency promote reaching both an internal and external balance?

5. Explain how the crowding out of net exports tends to weaken expansionary fiscal policy in the presence of fluctuating exchange rates.

6. Why is there an absence of a crowding-out effect of net exports with expansionary monetary policy in the fluctuating exchange rate model.

7. What is the difference between a devaluation and a depreciation of a currency?

ANSWERS

Fill-in questions

1. full employment, inflation, zero, current account

2. internal, current account

3. exports; compatible

4. (a) equilibrium output, imports; imports, decrease, increase; (b) expansionary, easy money; reduce, interest rate, equilibrium output; increase, decrease, reduction, increase (c) improve, improve (d) improve, worsen (e) compatible, conflicting; surplus, deficit

5. (a) inflow; demand for, increase; appreciates; dearer, cheaper; decrease; decrease, decrease, weaken (b) interest rate, investment; outflow, higher; greater, increased; depreciate, cheaper, dearer; increase, decrease; increase, reinforces (c) deficit, deficit

Problems and projects

1. (a) (1) contractionary, tight, (2) (a) increase, (b) decrease, (c) decrease, (3) reduce, (4) widened; (b) (1) expansionary, easy, (2) (a) decrease, (b) increase, (c) increase, (3) widen, (4) narrowed

2. (a) worsen   improve
    (b) improve   improve
    (c) worsen   worsen
    (d) improve   worsen

Self-test

1. F; **2.** T; **3.** F; **4.** T; **5.** F; **6.** F; **7.** T; **8.** F; **9.** F; **10.** T; **11.** T; **12.** F; **13.** F; **14.** F; **15.** T; **16.** F; **17.** F; **18.** T; **19.** T; **20.** F; **21.** T; **22.** T; **23.** T

Multiple-Choice

1. (c); **2.** (d); **3.** (c); **4.** (c); **5.** (c); **6.** (c); **7.** (c); **8.** (c); **9.** (b); **10.** (b); **11.** (b); **12.** (c)

20 Growth and the Less-Developed Countries

This chapter looks at the problem of raising the standard of living faced by the less-developed nations of the world. Economic growth, both in these less-developed nations and in the developed or the industrially advanced nations, requires that the nation's resources and technological knowledge be expanded. Application of this principle in the less-developed nations, however, faces a set of obstacles quite different from those that limit economic growth in Canada. The emphasis in this chapter is on the obstacles to economic growth in the poor and less-developed nations of the world. You should concentrate your attention on these obstacles. You will then understand why increasing the quantity and quality of resources and improving technology is especially difficult in the world's less-developed countries.

The existence of these special obstacles does not mean that increases in the living standards of the less-developed nations are impossible. Table 20-1 does show that the annual growth rate in per capita GNP in the less-developed countries did exceed that in the industrially advanced countries in the 1965–1989 period. Newly industrialized countries have achieved a very high growth rate, but at the same time some countries in the less-developed category have experienced declining per capita output. In order to achieve sustained growth the less-developed nations are going to have to do things that did not need to be done in Canada (or in the other industrial nations) in order to grow. Governments of countries with low per capita incomes will have to take an active role in establishing an environment that will promote growth and limit public sector problems for economic development. For some countries dramatic changes in social practices and institutions will be required. If these things are not done, improvements in living standards will be, at best, very slow and probably will not occur.

No matter how successful the less-developed nations are in eliminating these obstacles they probably will still not be able to grow very rapidly without the help of the developed nations. There seem to be at least two reasons why the developed nations will offer the less-developed ones some amount of assistance. The citizens of the more advanced nations feel some moral obligation to aid the less fortunate peoples of the world; and they may feel it is in their own self-interest to aid the poor of the world.

The debts of less-developed countries have risen significantly in the past two decades. In fact, in 1991 the external debt of less-developed nations that was owed to foreign governments and financial institutions was equal to about 26% of the combined gross national products of the less-developed nations. The causes of this debt crisis are due in part to the events of the 1970s and early 1980s. During this period, less-developed nations had to pay more for imported oil, incurred high borrowing costs because of higher interest rates, and faced reduced net export earnings because of the appreciation of the dollar. In recent years, to reduce the debt burdens these nations have been forced to enact restrictive domestic programs that often have adverse effects on net export earnings and economic growth. There are two proposed solutions to the debt crisis, but, as you will learn, each proposal has some adverse secondary effects.

Less-developed nations have (on the whole) grown during the past twenty-five years; but the rate at which they have grown was not much larger than the rate at which the developed nations have grown. This has meant (because the GDPs per capita in the former nations were initially so much smaller) that the gap between the two groups has widened over this period of time. For this and other reasons less-developed countries have become increasingly dissatisfied with their relationships with the advanced industrial nations; and they have argued for the establishment of a New International Economic Order. Here you should look at these relationships from the viewpoint of the less-developed nations that are not oil exporters. To understand the proposals they have made you must understand why they feel their relationships with the developed nations benefit mostly the developed nations and largely hurt the less-developed nations.

CHECKLIST

When you have studied this chapter, you should be able to:

■ Distinguish between industrially advanced and less-developed countries and describe the economic characteristics of the two groups.

■ Explain why the gap between the standards of living in less-developed countries and the industrially advanced countries have widened and calculate differences when given a simple example.

■ Enumerate the human implications of the poverty in the less-developed nations.

■ Identify the four factors that make growth in real GDP possible.

■ Identify the three specific problems related to human resources that plague the less-developed nations; and the problems rapid population growth can create in these nations.

■ Describe the conditions of unemployment and underemployment in less-developed countries.

■ State reasons for low labour productivity in less-developed countries.

■ Present three reasons for the emphasis on capital formation in the less-developed nations; explain the obstacles to saving and the obstacles to investment in these nations.

■ Describe the "circle of poverty" in which many of the less-developed countries are caught.

■ Explain why transferring the technologies used in the industrially advanced nations to the less-developed ones may not be a realistic method of improving the technology of the latter nations.

■ Enumerate several of the socio-cultural and institutional factors that inhibit growth in the less-developed nations.

■ List five reasons why governments in the less-developed nations will have to play a crucial role if rapid growth rates in per capita income are to be achieved.

■ Describe the problems with the public sector in fostering economic development.

■ Identify the three ways in which the industrially advanced nations may help the less-developed nations to grow economically.

■ Explain the causes and consequences of the debt crisis in less-developed countries; evaluate the proposed solutions.

■ State the six proposals made by less-developed nations that would, if implemented, result in a New International Economic Order; and the arguments made by them in support of these proposals.

CHAPTER OUTLINE

1. There is considerable inequality in income among nations.

(a)   Nations can be classified into two major groups.

(1) The 19 industrially advanced countries (IACs), which are characterized by high per capita incomes, large stocks of capital goods, advanced technology for production, and a highly educated work force. These nations include Canada, the United States, Japan, and nations in Western Europe, Australia, and New Zealand.

(2) The remaining 97 nations, termed less-developed countries (LDCs), which are poor, not industrialized, are heavily dependent on agriculture, have high population growth, and have low rates of literacy. People in these nations comprise about three-fourths of the world's population. Of this group, there are 56 middle-income LDCs with average annual per capita income of $2040 and 41 low-income LDCs with per capita income averaging $330.

(b)   The newly industrialized nations such as Hong Kong, South Korea, Taiwan, and Singapore, have experienced high rates of economic growth in the 1980s; while many other LDCs have experienced a decrease in GDP per capita. If the growth rates were the same for high and low-income nations, the gap in per capita income would widen because the income base is higher.

(c)   Compared with the developed nations, LDCs have not only lower per capita incomes but also lower life expectancies, higher infant mortality, lower literacy rates, less food per person, and fewer nonhuman sources of energy.

2. Economic growth requires that the quantity and quality of economic resources be increased and that technological knowledge be expanded; but there are many obstacles to such a program in LDCs.

(a)   Many (but not all) LDCs possess inadequate natural resources and the farm products that LDCs typically export are subject to significant price variation.

(b)   Many LDCs are over-populated, there is substantial unemployment and underemployment of labour, and labour productivity is low.

(c)   LDCs are short of capital goods and these nations

find it difficult to accumulate capital because of low savings potential, the flight of capital to IACs, and the absence of investors and incentives to invest.

(d) Technological knowledge is primitive in LDCs. Although they might adopt the technologies of the advanced nations, those technologies are not always appropriate to the resource endowments of the LDCs and they must therefore develop their own technologies.

(e) In addition, it is difficult for LDCs to alter the social, cultural, and institutional environment in the process of promoting economic growth.

3. In summary, LDCs save little and, therefore, invest little in real and human capital because they are poor; and because they do not invest, their outputs per capita remain low and they remain poor. Even if this vicious circle were to be broken, a rapid increase in population would leave the standard of living unchanged.

4. There are differing views about the role that government plays in fostering economic growth in LDCs.

(a) The positive view holds that, in the initial stages of economic development, government action is needed to help overcome such obstacles as the lack of law and order, entrepreneurship, and infrastructure. Government policies may also assist capital formation and be helpful in resolving social and institutional problems.

(b) There are also problems and disadvantages with government involvement in promoting growth from such factors as bureaucratic impediments, corruption, bad administration, and the importance of political objectives over economic goals. The use of central planning restricts competition and individual incentives, which are ingredients in the growth process.

5. Industrially advanced nations of the world can help the poor nations develop in a number of ways.

(a) They can lower the barriers that prevent the LDCs from selling their products in the developed nations.

(b) Loans and grants from governments and international organizations also enable the LDCs to accumulate capital.

(c) The flow of private capital from industrially advanced nations helps the LDCs increase their productive capacities and per capita outputs.

6. There is a crisis because of the large external debts of LDCs.

(a) The debts that LDCs owe to foreign governments and foreign financial institutions have increased significantly over the two decades, and are roughly equal to 26% of the total amount of the gross domestic products of LDCs. But for some countries they are much larger.

(b) The causes of the debt crisis rest with world events during the 1970s and early 1980s.

(1) Higher prices for imported oil during the 1970s and early 1980s forced LDCs to borrow to cover current-account deficits.

(2) Canada and other industrially advanced nations imposed tight monetary policies in the early 1980s to restrain inflation, but this policy raised interest rates and costs for LDC borrowing and brought on recession to industrially advanced nations. The result was reduced imports from LDCs.

(3) The appreciation in the international value of the Canadian and U.S. dollars during the 1981–85 period forced LDCs to pay more for imported manufactured goods from North America and to receive less in return for their exports.

(4) Severe debt problems in Mexico in 1982 signalled problems with LDC loans in the financial community and resulted in reduced loans from private sources. Increasing federal budget deficits in the United States during most of the 1980s absorbed more private capital that might otherwise be lent to LDCs.

(c) In recent years, the International Monetary Fund worked with nations on an individual basis to resolve debt problems. In return for debt rescheduling, LDCs often must impose austerity measures and use net export earning to pay for debt retirement, but these conditions have reduced economic development funds, retarded economic growth, and lowered capital income.

(d) The conditions of the 1970s and 1980s that contributed to the LDC debt crisis have reversed and the problem has eased somewhat. For the future, the two basic solutions focus on (a) continuation of country-by-country negotiations, which may require too many years to solve the problem; and (b) debt forgiveness by industrially advanced countries, which might have an adverse effect on private lending.

7. Because they have not grown as rapidly as they had hoped and are dissatisfied with their relationship with industrially advanced nations, the LDCs have urged the creation of a New International Economic Order that would involve six controversial features: changing the rules of the game in world economic institutions, preferential tariff treatment, less exploitation by and dependence on foreign corporations, improved terms of trade for LDC products, debt relief, and increased foreign aid from governments in industrially advanced nations.

IMPORTANT TERMS

brain drain
capital flight

capital-saving and capital-using technological advance
capricious universe view
industrially advanced countries (IACs)
infrastructure
land reform
less-developed countries (LDCs)
neocolonialism
New International Economic Order (NIEO)
nonfinancial investment
preferential tariff treatment
stabilization fund
terms of trade
the will to develop
unemployment and underemployment
vicious circle of poverty
World Bank

FILL-IN QUESTIONS

1. There is income inequality among nations.
(a) Industrially advanced countries (IACs) have (high, low) _____ per capita incomes, while there are less-developed nations (LDCs) that have _____ per capita incomes. The sharp contrast in income is shown in Table 20-2 with Japan having the highest per capita GNP in 1990 of U.S. $_____ and Mozambique the lowest at U.S. $_____.
(b) Among the LDCs, there is a group of 56 nations that are classified as (middle, low) _____-income LDCs with per capita GNP of $_____, and 41 nations that are classified as _____ income LDCs with per capita GNP of $_____.
(c) Singapore, Hong Kong, South Korea, and Taiwan are considered _____ _____ nations and had annual rates of economic growth in real GNP from 1960–89 of _____ to _____%. Many LDCs have experienced _____ real per capita GNP in the 1980s.
(d) IACs have a (higher, lower) _____ starting base for per capita income than LDCs, so the same percentage growth rate for both IACs and LDCs

means an increase in the _____ income gap.
(e) Also, low per capita income in LDCs means that life _____, adult _____, daily _____ supply, and _____ consumption are (higher, lower) _____, and infant mortality is _____.

2. (a) The industrially advanced countries have developed _____ economies based on large stocks of _____ goods, advanced production _____ and _____-_____ labour forces.
(b) The economies of the less-developed countries tend to have _____ industries, a large portion of the work force in the _____ industry, _____ population growth, _____ labour productivity, dated production _____, a small stock of capital _____, and exports consisting mainly of _____ _____ or _____ _____.

3. The process for economic growth is the same for IACs and LDCs. It involves more _____ use of existing resources and also increasing supplies of _____ _____, _____ _____, _____ _____, and improving its _____.

4. The distribution of natural resources among LDCs is (even, uneven) _____; many LDCs lack vital natural resources. Although _____ nations have been able to use oil resources for economic growth, much of the natural resources in LDCs are owned or controlled by companies in _____. Exports of products from LDCs are subject to _____ fluctuations.

5. (a) In terms of human resources, many LDCs have population growth rates of about _____%

compared to _____ % for IACs; given the growth rate for LDCs, "rule of 70" would suggest that the population of LDCs will double in about

_____ years. Production increases are sometimes accompanied by a population increase due to

an unchanged birth rate and a _____ mortality rate. Rapid population growth can cause per capita GNP to (increase, decrease) _____ .

(b)   Rapid population growth can have an adverse effect on the transition to a modern economy because

(1) reduced _____ restricts the accumulation of _____ ,

(2) a growing population requires more investment to maintain the existing _____ to labour ratio,

(3) a growing population may lead to the overexploitation of _____ natural resources, and

(4) the rapid growth of cities through migration can lead to massive _____ problems.

(c)   There is both _____ and

_____ among workers in LDCs.

(d)   Labour _____ is also very low in most LDCs, in part because these nations have not been

able to invest in _____ _____ .

The so-called _____ _____ contributes to the decline in skill level and productivity as the best-trained workers leave LDCs to work in IACs.

6.   Capital accumulation is critical to the development of LDCs.

(a)   If there were more capital goods, this would improve _____ _____ and help boost per capita GNP. An increase in capital goods is necessary because the _____ of arable land is limited. The process of capital formation is "cumulative," investment increases the (population, output, natural resources) _____ of the economy, and this in turn makes it possible for the economy to save more and invest more in capital goods.

(b)   The formation of domestic capital requires that a nation _____ and invest. The former is difficult in LDCs because of a low _____

_____ , and the latter is difficult because

of a lack of _____ and of _____ to invest. There is also the problem of _____

_____ where savings are transferred to IACs.

(c)   Many LDCs do not have much public capital goods, or the _____ , necessary for productive _____ investment.

(d)   Nonfinancial (or in-kind) investment involves the transfer of surplus labour from (agriculture, industry) _____ to the improvement of agricultural facilities or the _____ .

7.   The technologies used in the advanced industrial nations might be borrowed by and used in the underdeveloped nations; but

(a)   the technologies used in the advance nations are based upon a labour force that is (skilled, unskilled) _____ , labour that is relatively (abundant, scarce) _____ , and capital that is relatively _____ , and their technologies tend to be (labour, capital) _____ -using. While

(b)   the technologies required in the LDCs must be based on a labour force that is _____ , labour that is relatively _____ , and capital that is relatively _____ , and their technologies need to be _____ -using.

(c)   If technological advances make it possible to replace a worn-out plow (costing $10 when new) with a new $5 plow, the technological advance is capital- (saving, using)

_____ .

8.   The "will to develop" in LDCs involves a willingness to change the _____ and _____ arrangements of the nation.

9.   In most LDCs saving is small because the _____ per capita is small. Because saving is small, _____ in real and human capital is also small. And for this reason the _____ of labour and _____ per capita remain small.

10.   List five reasons why the role of government in

fostering economic development will need to be large in the LDCs, especially during the early stages of development.

(a) _____

(b) _____

(c) _____

(d) _____

(e) _____

11. There can also be _____

_____ _____ with government's role in the economy of LDCs because government

_____ can impede social and economic change, central planners give too much emphasis to

_____ objectives rather than economic objectives, and there can be _____ and

_____ in government. Central planning models also restrict _____ and individual

_____, which are factors in economic development.

12. The three major ways in which industrially advanced nations can assist economic development in the

LDCs are _____,

_____, and

_____.

13. The LDC debt crisis arose from the large (internal, external) _____ debts that have accumulated over the past two decades. In 1992, these debts were about $_____ billion and equal to about

_____ % of the total of the gross national products of LDCs.

14. The causes of the LDC debt crisis are due to world events during the 1970s and early 1980s.

(a) Oil prices (increased, decreased) _____

during the 1970s and this event _____ the borrowing needs of LDCs to pay for imported oil.

(b) In the early 1980s, the IACs had a (tight, easy)

_____ monetary policy that (increased, decreased) _____ real interest rates and

_____ the cost to LDCs of servicing

debts. The recession of the early 1980s in the IACs also

_____ the exports of farm products from LDCs to the industrialized nations.

(c) Over the 1981–84 period, the international value of the U.S. and Canadian dollars (appreciated, depreciated) _____, which meant that

LDCs had to pay (more, less) _____ for

imports and receive _____ in return for exports.

(d) The debt crisis in _____ in 1982 shook confidence in LDCs and reduced private

_____ by banks and financial institutions. The increasing United States' federal budget

_____ during the early 1980s also absorbed more private capital.

15. The economic consequence of the LDC debt crisis has been that creditor nations and the International

Monetary Fund have _____ debts to reduce the annual burden of interest and principal repayments. In return, LDCs have had to implement domes-

tic _____ programs that tend to reduce

the _____ of living and transfer

_____ _____ earnings to debt repayment and away from investment. Some experts have also worried that the LDCs' debts are a threat to

the _____ and _____

systems of the _____.

16. One solution to the LDC debt crisis is to negotiate (separately with, with the group of) _____

indebted nations; but the problem is that it will take too

many _____ and thwart _____

_____ in those LDCs. Another solution is

to _____ the debts, but this action might have an adverse effect on private lending and encourage

further _____.

17. In pressing for the establishment of a New International Economic Order, the LDCs have argued (among other things) that:

(a) because LDC nations had no part in their formation and because they are ''stacked'' against them, there

should be a change in the _____ by which

international trade, finance, and investment are conducted;

(b) the IACs, to deprive LDCs of their export markets, have erected barriers to _____ and the LDCs should be accorded preferential _____ _____;

(c) the dealings of the LDCs with corporations in the advanced nations have led to the greater part of the benefits from the _____ of their natural resources going to others and to the increased _____ of LDCs on world markets;

(d) there has been, as a result of the higher prices charged for manufactured goods by corporations in the IACs, a shift against them in the _____ of _____ and that these might be improved by the establishment of _____ funds and by _____;

(e) except for the oil-exporting countries, the size of their _____ abroad has increased and these should either be _____ or _____;

(f) the foreign aid that they have received has been _____ and should be increased to _____% of the GNP of the IACs, have no _____ attached to it, and should be provided on a long-term and _____ basis.

PROBLEMS AND PROJECTS

1. Suppose that the real GDP per capita in the average industrially advanced nation is $8000 per year and in the average less-developed nation is $500 per year.
(a) The gap between their standards of living is $_____ per year.
(b) If GNP per capita were to grow at a rate of 5% during a year in both the industrially advanced and the less-developed nations,
(1) the standard of living in the industrially advanced nations would rise to $_____ a year;
(2) the standard of living in the less-developed nations would rise to $_____ a year; and

(3) the gap between their standards of living would (narrow, widen) _____ to $_____ a year.

2. Suppose that the real GDP per capita in Adanac is $8000 and growing at the rate of 2% per year. In the country of Selaw real GDP per capita is $3600. How many years will it take for the real incomes per capita to be equal in both countries if the growth rate in per capita income in Selaw is: (a) 4%; (b) 6%; (c) 8%?

3. While economic conditions are not identical in all less-developed nations, there are certain conditions common to or typical of most of them. In the spaces after each of the following characteristics, indicate briefly the nature of this characteristic in most less-developed nations.
(a) Standard of living (per capital income).

_____

(b) Average life expectancy. _____
(c) Extent of unemployment. _____
(d) Literacy. _____
(e) Technology. _____
(f) Percentage of the population engaged in agriculture. _____
(g) Size of the population relative to the land and capital available. _____
(h) The birth and death rates. _____
(i) Quality of the labour force. _____
(j) Amount of capital equipment relative to the labour force. _____
(k) Level of saving. _____
(l) Incentive to invest. _____
(m) Amount of basic social capital. _____
(n) Extent of industrialization. _____
(o) Size and quality of the entrepreneurial class and the supervisory class. _____
(p) Per capita public expenditures for education and per capita energy consumption. _____
(q) Per capita consumption of food. _____
(r) Disease and malnutrition. _____

4. Suppose that it takes a minimum of 5 units of food to keep a person alive for a year, that the population can

double itself every 10 years, and that the food supply can increase every 10 years by an amount equal to what it was in the beginning (year 0).

(a)   Assume that both the population and the food supply grow at these rates. Complete the following table by computing the size of the population and the food supply in years 10 through 60.

Year	Food supply	Population
0	200	20
10	——————	——————
20	——————	——————
30	——————	——————
40	——————	——————
50	——————	——————
60	——————	——————

(b)   What happens to the relationship between the food supply and the population in the 30th year?

(c)   What would actually prevent the population from growing at this rate following the 30th year?

(d)   Assuming that the actual population growth in the years following the 30th does not outrun the food supply, what would be the size of the population in:

(1) Year 40: _____

(2) Year 50: _____

(3) Year 60: _____

(e)   Explain why the standard of living failed to increase in the years following the 30th, even though the food supply increased by 75% between years 30 and 60.

SELF-TEST

Circle the T if the statement is true, the F if it is false.

1.   About three-fourths of the world's population lives in 97 less-developed countries.   **T F**

2.   The annual per capita GNP growth rate in the industrially advanced countries was about twice that recorded in the less-developed countries during the 1965–1989 period.   **T F**

3.   Per capita GNP was about U.S. $20,470 in Canada and U.S. $180 in Bangladesh in 1990.   **T F**

4.   The difference between the per capita incomes in the less-developed nations and the per capita incomes in the developed nations has decreased over the past years.   **T F**

5.   Economic growth in both industrially advanced and less-developed nations requires using resources more efficiently or increasing the supplies of these resources.**T F**

6.   It is impossible to achieve a high standard of living with a small supply of natural resources.   **T F**

7.   Nations with large populations are less developed.   **T F**

8.   A factor preventing the elimination of unemployment in the less-developed nations is the small number of job openings available in the cities.   **T F**

9.   Saving in LDCs is a smaller percentage of national output than in IACs, and this is the chief reason total saving in LDCs is small.   **T F**

10.   Before private investment can be increased in under-developed nations it is necessary to reduce the amount of investment in infrastructure.   **T F**

11.   Technological advances in LDCs will be made rapidly because they do not require pushing forward the frontiers of technological knowledge, and the technologies used in IACs can be easily transferred to the less-developed ones.   **T F**

12.   When technological advances are capital-saving, it is possible for an economy to increase its productivity without any net investment in capital goods.   **T F**

13.   Labour-saving and capital-using technologies are typically appropriate to LDCs.   **T F**

14.   Emancipation from custom and tradition is often the fundamental prerequisite of economic development.   **T F**

15.   The policies of the governments of less-developed nations have often tended to reduce the incentives of foreigners to invest in the less-developed nations.   **T F**

16.   Governments always play a positive role in the economic development of LDCs.   **T F**

17.   LDCs will not need foreign aid if the developed nations will reduce tariffs and import quotas on the goods that the under-developed nations export.   **T F**

18.   Capital flight harms domestic growth by diverting savings out of the country.   **T F**

19.   Capital flight can take the form of underinvoicing of exports and overinvoicing of imports.   **T F**

20.   An increase in the output and employment of Canada works to the advantage of the less-developed nations because it provides the less-developed nations

with larger markets for their exports. **T F**

21. Foreign aid from the IACs to the less-developed nations has consistently exceeded 1% of their GNP. **T F**

22. Many in LDCs believe that the public and private aid extended by the IACs to the LDCs is designed to increase profits in the former and to exploit the latter countries. **T F**

23. In 1992 the total external debts of LDCs was equal to about 26% of the total of the gross national products of LDCs. **T F**

24. During the 1970s and early 1980s, higher prices on imported oil, a fall in the export earnings of LDCs, an appreciation of the Canadian and U.S. dollars, and a decrease in private lending all contributed to create the LDC debt crisis. **T F**

25. The simplest solution to the LDC debt crisis and the one with fewest repercussions would be to have the creditors in IACs forgive the debts of LDCs. **T F**

26. Were a fund to be established to stabilize the price of a commodity such as copper, the fund would be used to purchase the commodity when its price fell. **T F**

27. Preferential tariff treatment for LDCs means that the IACs would set their tariffs on commodities imported from LDCs below those established for the same commodities imported from IACs. **T F**

28. One of the proposals associated with the establishment of a New International Economic Order is that the aid from IACs to LDCs be automatic, have no "strings" attached to it, and equal at least 1% of the GNPs of the IACs. **T F**

MULTIPLE-CHOICE

Circle the letter that corresponds to the best answer.

1. Which of the following would be considered an LDC?
(a) China
(b) Kuwait
(c) Taiwan
(d) New Zealand

2. If per capita income is $600 a year in an LDC and per capita income is $12,000 in an IAC, then a 2% growth rate increases the absolute income gap by
(a) $120
(b) $228

(c) $240
(d) $252

3. When the average annual rate of growth in per capita GNP in an LDC is 1%, approximately how many years will it take for the standard of living to double?
(a) 27 years
(b) 35 years
(c) 57 years
(d) 70 years

4. Which of the following is high in the less-developed nations?
(a) life expectancy
(b) infant mortality
(c) literacy
(d) per capita energy consumption

5. Which of the following is an obstacle to economic growth in less-developed nations?
(a) the supply of natural resources
(b) the size and quality of the labour force
(c) the supply of capital equipment
(d) all of the above

6. The less-developed countries are characterized by all of the following, with the exception of
(a) high proportion of the labour force in agriculture
(b) dated production techniques
(c) high unemployment
(d) high capital to labour ratio

7. An increase in the total output of consumer goods in a less-developed nation may not increase the average standard of living because
(a) of diminishing returns
(b) it may provoke an increase in the population
(c) of disguised unemployment
(d) the skill level of the labour force is low

8. Which of the following best describes the unemployment found in the less-developed nations?
(a) the result of cyclical fluctuations in aggregate demand
(b) the agricultural workers who have migrated from rural to urban areas and failed to find employment in the cities
(c) the workers in excess of the optimum population
(d) workers whose productivity is subject to diminishing returns

9. Which of the following is not a reason for placing special emphasis on capital accumulation in less-developed nations?
(a) the inflexible supply of arable land

(b)   the low productivity of workers

(c)   the low marginal contribution of capital equipment

(d)   the possibility that capital accumulation will be ''cumulative''

10.   Which of the following is not a factor limiting saving in less-developed nations?

(a)   the output of the economy is too low to permit a large volume of saving

(b)   those who do save do not make their saving available to their own economies

(c)   the highly unequal distribution of income

(d)   the low marginal contribution of capital equipment to production

11.   When citizens of LDCs transfer savings or invest savings in IACs, it is referred to as

(a)   brain drain

(b)   capital flight

(c)   savings potential

(d)   in-kind investment

12.   Which of the following is not an obstacle to capital formation (investment) in less-developed nations?

(a)   the absence of strong incentives to invest

(b)   the lack of basic social capital

(c)   the absence of a large entrepreneurial class

(d)   the lack of capital-saving changes in technology

13.   Which of the following is an example of infrastructure?

(a)   a steel plant

(b)   an electric-power plant

(c)   a farm

(d)   a deposit in a financial institution

14.   Which of the following is not a factor leading to low productivity in the less-developed nations?

(a)   low investment in human capital

(b)   low marginal propensity to consume

(c)   the absence of an entrepreneurial class

(d)   low levels of physical capital per worker

15.   Which of the following seems to demand attention and be one of the institutional changes required in most less-developed nations?

(a)   adoption of birth control

(b)   development of strong labour unions

(c)   increase in the nation's public capital

(d)   land reform

16.   Assume the total real output of an LDC increases from $100 billion to $115.5 billion, while its population expands from 200 million to 210 million people. Real income per capita has, as a result, increased by

(a) $50

(b) $100

(c) $150

(d) $200

17.   The role of government in the early stages of economic development will probably be a major one for several reasons. Which one of the following is not one of these reasons?

(a)   only government can provide a larger amount of the needed infrastructure

(b)   the absence of private entrepreneurs to accumulate capital and take risks

(c)   the necessity of creating new money to finance capital accumulation

(d)   the slowness and uncertainty of the market system in fostering development

18.   The technology used in IAC countries may not be appropriate for less-developed countries due to

(a)   a higher rate of population growth in the less-developed countries

(b)   lower per capita income in the less-developed countries

(c)   higher per capita energy consumption in the IACs

(d)   differences in factor endowments in the IACs and the less-developed countries

19.   In recent years, many LDCs have come to recognize that

(a)   competition and economic incentives for individuals are necessary for economic development

(b)   there are few disadvantages from government involvement in the development process

(c)   private capital is not required for economic development

(d)   the World Bank serves as an institutional barrier to economic growth

20.   An event that occurred during the 1970s or early 1980s that contributed to the LDC debt crisis was

(a)   a sharp decline in the price of oil charged by OPEC nations

(b)   a depreciation in the international value of the U.S dollar

(c)   a tight monetary policy and recession in the IAC

(d)   a rise in net export earnings of the LDC

21.   To raise funds to pay interest and principal on external debt, LDCs have had to put into place domestic economics that tend to

(a)   decrease imports, increase exports, and lower the standard of living

(b)   increase imports, decrease exports, and lower the

standard of living

(c) decrease imports, decrease exports, and lower the standard of living

(d) increase imports, decrease exports, and raise the standard of living

22. The terms of trade for a nation exporting tin worsen whenever

(a) the price of tin rises

(b) the price of tin falls

(c) the price of tin rises and the prices of imported goods decline

(d) the price of tin falls and the prices of imported goods rise

23. Which one of the following is not one of the proposals included in the New International Economic Order for which LDCs have argued?

(a) a change in the rules by which international financial institutions are governed

(b) the elimination of OPEC

(c) the renegotiation and cancellation of the debts of LDCs to the IACs

(d) abandonment of the neo-colonial policies of the IACs

24. The list of institutions directing financial resources to the less-developed countries include all but

(a) the World Bank

(b) the Canadian International Development Agency

(c) the Bank of Canada

(d) the International Finance Corporation

DISCUSSION QUESTIONS

1. What is the degree of income inequality among nations of the world? Classify nations into two groups and describe this inequality. What further division can be made among poor nations? How does the overall level of GNP per capita and the rates of GNP growth compare among rich nations and poor nations?

2. What are the "human implications" of poverty found in LDCs? (Use the socioeconomic indicators found in Table 20-2 of the text to contrast the quality of life in IACs and LDCs.)

3. Describe the basic avenues of economic growth. Do these avenues differ for IACs and LDCs?

4. How would you describe the natural resource situation for LDCs? In what ways do price fluctuations affect LDC exports? Is a weak natural resource base an obstacle to economic growth?

5. Describe the implications of the high rate of growth in population and its effects on the standard of living. Can the standard of living be raised by merely increasing the output of consumer goods in LDCs? What is the meaning of the cliché, "the rich get richer and the poor get children," and how does it apply to LDCs?

6. What obstacles do the human resources of LDCs place in the path of economic development? What is the distinction between unemployment and underemployment and how do the concepts apply to LDCs? What are the reasons for the low level of labour productivity in LDCs? How does "brain drain" affect LDCs?

7. What reasons exist for placing special emphasis on capital accumulation as a means of promoting economic growth in LDCs?

8. Why is domestic capital accumulation difficult in LDCs? Answer both in terms of the saving side and the investment side of capital accumulation. Is there "capital flight" from LDCs?

9. In addition to the obstacles that limit domestic investment, what other obstacles tend to limit the flow of foreign capital into LDCs? What role does infrastructure play in capital formation?

10. How might the LDCs improve their technology without engaging in slow and expensive research? Why might this be an inappropriate method of improving the technology used in the LDCs?

11. What is meant by the "will to develop"? How is it related to social and institutional change in LDCs?

12. Explain the "vicious circle" of poverty found in the LDCs. How does population growth make an escape from this vicious circle difficult?

13. Why is the role of government expected to be a positive one in the early phases of development in LDCs? What have been the problems with the involvement of government in economic development?

14. How can Canada help LDCs? What types of aid can be offered? How is it possible for Canada to assist LDCs without spending a penny on "foreign aid"? Is this type of aid sufficient to ensure rapid and substantial development in LDCs?

15. Discuss the World Bank in terms of its purposes, characteristics, sources of funds, promotion of private capital flows, and success. What are its affiliates and their purposes?

16. Describe the dimensions of the LDC debt crisis.

What were the causes of the crisis? Explain the economic consequences for LDCs and IACs of the debt crisis. Are there any solutions?

17. Explain the principal proposals that constitute the program of the LDCs for the establishment of a New International Economic Order. Explain the arguments made by the LDCs to support each of these proposals.

ANSWERS

Fill-in questions

1. (a) high, low; 23,810, 80. (b) middle, 2040, low, 330 (c) new industrialized, 6, 7; declining; (d) higher, absolute; (e) expectancies, literacy, calorie, energy, lower, higher

2. (a) market, capital, technologies, well-educated (b) few, agricultural, rapid, low, technology, equipment, agricultural commodities, raw materials

3. efficient, natural resources, human resources, capital goods, technology

4. uneven, OPEC, IACs; price

5. (a) 2, 0.7, 35; declining; decrease; (b) (1) savings, capital, (2) capital (3) limited, (4) urban (c) unemployment and underemployment; (d) productivity, human capital, brain drain

6. (a) labour productivity, supply, output; (b) save; saving potential, investors, incentives, capital flight; (c) infrastructure, private; (d) agriculture, infrastructure

7. (a) skilled, scarce, abundant, capital; (b) unskilled, abundant, scarce, labour (c) saving

8. institutions, social

9. income; investment; productivity, output (income)

10. (a) the existence of widespread banditry and inter-tribal warfare in many LDCs; (b) the absence of a sizable and vigorous entrepreneurial class; (c) the great need for social goods and services; (d) government action may be the only means of promoting saving and investment; (e) government can more effectively deal with the social–institutional obstacles to growth

11. public sector problems, bureaucracy, political, maladministration, corruption; competition, incentives

12. by expanding trade with the LDCs (lowering the barriers to trade), private flows of capital, foreign aid (public loans and grants)

13. external, 1530, 26

14. (a) increased, increased; (b) tight, increased, increased; decreased; (c) appreciated, more, less; (d) Mexico, lending; deficits

15. rescheduled; austerity, standard, net export; banking, financial, IACs

16. separately with, decades (years), economic growth; forgive, defaults

17. (a) rules; (b) trade, tariff treatments; (c) exploitation, dependence; (d) terms, trade, stabilization, indexing; (e) debts, cancelled, rescheduled; (f) insufficient, 0.7, strings, automatic

Problems and projects

1. (a) 7500; (b) (1) 8400, (2) 525, (3) widen, 7875

2. (a) 41–42 years; (b) 20–21 years; (c) 13–14 years

3. (a) low; (b) short; (c) widespread; (d) low; (e) primitive; (f) large; (g) large; (h) high; (i) poor; (j) small (k) low; (l) absent; (m) small; (n) small; (o) small and poor; (p) small; (q) low; (r) common

4. (a) Food supply: 400, 600, 800, 1000, 1200, 1400; Population: 40, 80, 160, 320, 640, 1280; (b) The food supply is just able to support the population. (c) The inability of the food supply to support a population growing at this rate. (d) (1) 200, (2) 240, (3) 280; (e) The population increased as rapidly as the food supply.

Self-test

1. T; **2.** F; **3.** T; **4.** F; **5.** T; **6.** F; **7.** F; **8.** T; **9.** F; **10.** F; **11.** F; **12.** T; **13.** F; **14.** T; **15.** T; **16.** F; **17.** F; **18.** T; **19.** T; **20.** T; **21.** F; **22.** T; **23.** T; **24.** T; **25.** F; **26.** T; **27.** T; **28.** T

Multiple-choice

1. (a); **2.** (b); **3.** (d); **4.** (b); **5.** (d); **6.** (d); **7.** (b); **8.** (b); **9.** (c); **10.** (d); **11.** (b); **12.** (d); **13.** (b); **14.** (b); **15.** (d); **16.** (a); **17.** (c); **18.** (d); **19.** (a); **20.** (c); **21.** (a); **22.** (d); **23.** (b); **24.** (c)

Glossary

Ability-to-pay principle — The belief that those who have the greater income (or wealth) should be taxed absolutely and relatively more than those who have less.

Abstraction — Elimination of irrelevant and non-economic facts to obtain an economic principle.

Actual budget — The amount spent by the federal government (to purchase goods and services and for transfer payments) less the amount of tax revenue collected by it in any (fiscal) year; and which can *not* reliably be used to determine whether it is pursuing an expansionary or contractionary fiscal policy. Compare with the Cyclically-adjusted budget (*see*).

Actual cash reserve — The amount a bank has as Vault cash and on deposit at the Bank of Canada.

Actual deficit — The size of the federal government's Budget deficit (*see*) or surplus actually measured or recorded in any given year.

Actual investment — The amount that business Firms do invest; equal to Planned investment plus Unplanned investment.

Adaptive expectations theory — The idea that people determine their expectations about future events (for example, inflation) on the basis of past and present events (rates of inflation) and only change their expectations as events unfold.

Adjustable pegs — The device utilized in the Bretton Woods system (*see*) to change Exchange rates in an orderly way to eliminate persistent Payments deficits and surpluses; each nation defined its monetary unit in terms of (pegged it to) gold or the U.S. dollar, kept the Rate of exchange for its money stable in the short run, and changed (adjusted) it in the long run when faced with International disequilibrium.

Adverse selection problem — A problem that arises when information known to one party to a contract is not known to the other party, causing the latter to incur major costs. Example: Individuals who have the poorest health are more likely to buy health insurance.

Aggregate demand — A schedule or curve that shows the total quantity of goods and services demanded (purchased) at different price levels.

Aggregate demand–aggregate supply model — The macroeconomic model that uses Aggregate demand and Aggregate supply (*see both*) to determine and explain the Price level and the real Domestic output.

Aggregate expenditures — The total amount spent for final goods and services in the economy.

Aggregate expenditures–domestic output approach — Determination of the Equilibrium gross domestic product (*see*) by finding the real GDP at which Aggregate expenditures are equal to the real Domestic output.

Aggregate expenditures schedule — A schedule or curve that shows the total amount spent for final goods and services at different levels of real GDP.

Aggregate supply — A schedule or curve that shows the total quantity of goods and services supplied (produced) at different price levels.

Aggregation — Treating individual units or data as one unit or number. For example, all prices of individual goods and services are combined into a Price level, or all units of output are aggregated into Real GDP.

Agricultural Stabilization Board — The federal agency established in 1958 to support the following commodities at not less than 90% of their average price over the previous five years, with adjustments according to production costs: cattle, hogs, and sheep; industrial milk and cream; and oats and barley not produced on the Prairies [where the Canadian Wheat Board (*see*) has jurisdiction].

Allocative efficiency — The apportionment of resources among firms and industries to obtain the production of the products most wanted by society (consumers): the output of each product at which its Marginal cost and Price are equal.

Allocative factor — The ability of an economy to reallocate resources to achieve the Economic growth that the Supply factors (*see*) make possible.

Annually balanced budget — The equality of government expenditures and tax collections during a year.

Anticipated inflation — Inflation (*see*) at a rate that was equal to the rate expected in that period of time.

Anti-combines — (*See* Combines Investigation Act.)

Anti-Inflation Board — The federal agency established in 1975 (and disbanded in 1979) to administer the government's inflation control program.

Applied economics — (*See* Policy economics.)

Appreciation — An increase in the international price of a currency caused by market forces; not caused by the central bank; the opposite of Depreciation.

Arbitration — The designation of a neutral third party to render a decision in a dispute by which both parties (the employer and the labour union) agree in advance to abide.

Asset — Anything with a monetary value owned by a firm or an individual.

Asset demand for money — The amount of money people want to hold as a Store of value (the amount of their financial assets they wish to have in the form of Money); and which varies inversely with the Rate of interest.

Authoritarian capitalism — An economic system (method of organization) in which property resources are privately owned and government extensively directs and controls the economy.

Authoritarian socialism — (*See* Command economy.)

Average fixed cost — The total Fixed cost (*see*) of a Firm divided by its output (the quantity of product produced).

Average product — The total output produced per unit of a resource employed (total product divided by the quantity of a resource employed).

Average propensity to consume — Fraction of Disposable income that households spend for consumer goods and services; consumption divided by Disposable income.

Average propensity to save — Fraction of Disposable income that households save; Saving divided by Disposable income.

Average revenue — Total revenue from the sale of a product divided by the quantity of the product sold (demanded); equal to the price at which the product is sold so long as all units of the product are sold at the same price.

Average tax rate — Total tax paid divided by total (taxable) income; the tax rate on total (taxable) income.

Average (total) cost — The Total cost of a Firm divided by its output (the quantity of product produced); equal to Average fixed cost (*see*) plus Average variable cost (*see*).

Average variable cost — The total Variable cost (*see*) of a Firm divided by its output (the quantity of product produced).

Balanced budget multiplier — The effect of equal increases (decreases) in government spending for goods and services and in taxes is to increase (decrease) the Equilibrium gross domestic product.

Balance of (international) payments — The annual statement of a nation's international economic dealings showing the Current account (*see*) balance and the Capital account (*see*) balance, the latter including the balance in Official international reserves (*see*).

Balance of payments deficit — When the balance in Official international reserves (*see*) is *positive*.

Balance of payments effect — The inflow of foreign funds that usually accompanies a takeover or the establishment of a new foreign-controlled firm, and the resulting Transfer effect (*see*) outflow of interest and dividends abroad.

Balance of payments surplus — When the balance in Official international reserves (*see*) is *negative*.

Balance of trade — The addition of the balances on goods (merchandise) and services in the Current account (*see*) of the Balance of payments (*see*).

Balance on the capital account — The Capital inflows (*see*) of a nation less its Capital outflows (*see*), both of which include Official international reserves (*see*).

Balance on current account — The exports of goods (merchandise) and services of a nation less its imports of goods (merchandise) and services plus its Net investment income from nonresidents (*see*) and its Net transfers.

Balance on goods and services — The Balance of trade (*see*).

Balance sheet — A statement of the Assets (*see*), Liabilities (*see*), and Net worth (*see*) of a Firm or individual at some given time.

Bank Rate — The interest rate that the Bank of Canada charges on advances (*normally* very short-term loans) made to the chartered banks and other members of the Canadian Payments Association (*see*), equivalent to Discount rate in the United States.

Bankers' bank — The bank that accepts the deposits of and makes loans to chartered banks: the Bank of Canada.

Barrier to entry — Anything that artificially prevents the entry of Firms into an industry.

Barter — The exchange of one good or service for another good or service.

Base year — The year with which prices in other years are compared when a Price index (*see*) is constructed.

Beggar-my-neighbour policy — A government policy that expands a nation's exports or reduces its imports and thereby lessens its Balance-of-payments deficit and increases its rates of employment and economic growth by reducing the exports or expanding imports and worsening the Balance-of-payments position, employment, and economic growth in other nations.

Benefit-cost analysis — Deciding whether to employ resources and the quantity of resources to employ for a project or program (for the production of a good or service) by comparing the marginal benefits with the marginal costs.

Benefit-loss rate — The percentage of any increase in earned income by which subsidy benefits in a Negative income tax (*see*) plan are reduced.

Benefits-received principle — The belief that those who receive the benefits of goods and services provided by government should pay the taxes required to finance them.

Bid rigging — The illegal action of oligopolists who agree either that one or more will not bid on a request for bids or tenders or, alternatively, agree on what bids they will make, and forbidden under the Competition Act (*see*).

Big business — A business Firm that either produces a large percentage of the total output of an industry, is large (in terms of number of employees or stockholders, sales, assets, or profits) compared with other Firms in the economy, or both.

Bilateral monopoly — A market in which there is a single seller (Monopoly) and a single buyer (Monopsony).

Board of Transport Commissioners — The federal agency established by the Railway Act of 1903 to regulate freight rates; superseded by the Canadian Transport Commission (*see*) in 1967.

Brain drain — The emigration of highly educated, highly skilled workers from a country.

Break-even income (1) — The level of Disposable income at which Households plan to consume (spend) all of their income (for consumer goods and services) and to save none of it.

Break-even income (2) — The level of earned income at which Negative income tax (*see*) is reduced to zero and at which normal (positive) income tax applies on further increases in earned income.

Break-even point — Any output that a (competitive) Firm might produce at which its Total cost and Total revenue would be equal; an output at which it has neither a profit nor a loss.

Bretton Woods system — The international monetary system developed after World War II in which Adjustable pegs (*see*) were employed, the International Monetary Fund (*see*) helped to stabilize Foreign exchange rates, and gold and the Key currencies (*see*) were used as Official international reserves (*see*).

Budget deficit — The amount by which the expenditures of the federal government exceed its revenues in any year.

Budget line — A curve that shows the different combinations of two products a consumer can purchase with a given money income.

Budget restraint — The limit imposed upon the ability of an individual consumer to obtain goods and services by the size of the consumer's income (and by the prices that must be paid for the goods and services).

Built-in stability — The effect of Nondiscretionary fiscal policy (*see*) upon the economy; when Net taxes vary directly with the Gross domestic product, the fall (rise) in Net taxes during a recession (inflation) helps to eliminate unemployment (inflationary pressures).

Business cycle — Recurrent ups and downs over a period of years in the level of economic activity.

Business monopoly — A market situation in which a single firm or small number of firms dominate the output of an industry.

Canada Assistance Plan — The federal Act under which the federal government makes funds available to the provinces for their programs of assistance to disabled, handicapped, unemployed (who are not entitled to unemployment insurance benefits), and other needy persons.

Canada Deposit Insurance Corporation — Federal Crown Corporation that, for a fee payable by the chartered banks and federally-chartered trust companies, insures their customers' deposits up to a limit of $60,000 per customer per bank or trust company.

Canada Labour Code — The federal law of 1970 that consolidated previous legislation regulating employment practices, labour standards, and so on, in the federal jurisdiction.

Canada Pension Plan — The compulsory, contributory, earnings-related federal pension plan that covers most employed members of the labour force between the ages of 18 and 65, and payable at the latter age; it came into effect in 1965; there is transferability between the Plan and the Quebec Pension Plan, which applies to the people of that province.

Canada-United States Free Trade Agreement (FTA) — An accord, which came into effect on January 1, 1989, to eliminate all Tariffs (*see*) between the two countries over the following ten years.

Canadian Congress of Labour (CCL) — The Federation of Industrial unions (*see*) formed in 1940 and affiliated with the Congress of Industrial Organizations (*see*); amalgamated into Canadian Labour Congress (*see*) in 1956.

Canadian International Development Agency (CIDA) — The federal agency responsible for the operation and administration of Canada's international development assistance programs of approximately $2.5 billion a year.

Canadian Labour Congress (CLC) — The largest federation of Labour unions (*see*) in Canada, with 3 million members in international and national unions; founded in 1956 on the amalgamation of the Canadian Congress of Labour (*see*) and the Trades and Labour Congress of Canada (*see*).

Canadian Payments Association — The federal agency set up in 1982 to provide for Cheque clearing (*see*).

Canadian Transport Commission — The federal agency set up in 1967 to prevent abuse of monopoly power in the telecommunications and land, water, and air transport industries; on its creation, it took over the Board of Transport Commissioners (*see*), the Air Transport Board, and the Maritime Commission.

Canadian Wheat Board — Federal Crown Corporation established in 1935, which does not own or operate grain-handling facilities but has complete control over the way western wheat is marketed and the price at which it is sold. The Board also acquired complete control of the supplies of all Prairie coarse grains in 1949.

Capacity-creating aspect of investment — The effect of investment spending on the productive capacity (the ability to produce goods and services) of an economy.

Capital — Man-made resources used to produce goods and services; goods that do not directly satisfy human wants; capital goods.

Capital account — That part of the Balance of payments (*see*) that records the net inflows and outflows of liquid capital (money) for direct and portfolio investments at home and abroad, and includes the balance in Official international reserves (*see*).

Capital account deficit — A negative Balance on the capital account (*see*).

Capital account surplus — A positive Balance on the capital account (*see*).

Capital consumption allowances — Estimate of the amount of Capital worn out or used up (consumed) in producing the gross domestic product; depreciation.

Capital flight — The transfer of savings from less developed to industrially advanced countries to avoid government expropriation, taxation, and high rates of inflation or to realize better investment opportunities.

Capital gain — The gain realized when securities or properties are sold for a price greater than the price paid for them.

Capital goods — (*See* Capital.)

Capital inflow — The expenditures made by the residents of foreign nations to purchase equity, shares, and bonds from the residents of a nation.

Capital-intensive commodity — A product that requires a relatively large amount of Capital to produce.

Capital outflow — The expenditures made by the residents of a nation to purchase equity, shares, and bonds from the residents of foreign nations.

Capital-output ratio — The ratio of the stock of Capital to the productive (output) capacity of the economy; and the ratio of a change in the stock of Capital (net investment) to the resulting change in productive capacity.

Capital-saving technological advance — An improvement in technology that permits a greater quantity of a product to be produced with a given amount of Capital (or the same amount of the product to be produced with a smaller amount of Capital).

Capital-using technological advance — An improvement in technology that requires the use of a greater amount of Capital to produce a given quantity of a product.

Cartel — A formal written or oral agreement among Firms to set the price of the product and the outputs of the individual firms or to divide the market for the product geographically.

Cash (primary) reserve — The weighted average of the 10% of their demand (current and personal chequing) account deposits and the 3% of their notice account deposits that the Chartered banks (*see*) must hold as Vault cash (*see*) or on deposit with the Bank of Canada. In August 1989 the average required cash reserve ratio was 4.03%. It is expected that when a Bank Act is passed the reserve requirement will be abolished.

Causation — A cause-and-effect relationship; one or several events bring about or result in another event.

Ceiling price — (*See* Price ceiling.)

Central bank — The bank whose chief function is the control of the nation's money supply: the Bank of Canada.

Central economic planning — Determination of the objectives of the economy and the direction of its resources to the attainment of these objectives by the national government.

Ceteris paribus assumption — (*See* "other things being equal" assumption.)

Change in amount consumed — Increase or decrease in consumption spending that results from an increase or decrease in Disposable income, the Consumption schedule (curve) remaining unchanged; movement from one line (point) to another on the same Consumption schedule (curve).

Change in amount saved — Increase or decrease in Saving that results from an increase or decrease in

Disposable income, the Saving schedule (curve) remaining unchanged; movement from one line (point) to another on the same Saving schedule (curve).

Change in the consumption schedule — An increase or decrease in consumption at each level of Disposable income caused by changes in the Nonincome determinants of consumption and saving (*see*); an upward or downward movement of the Consumption schedule.

Change in the saving schedule — An increase or decrease in Saving at each level of Disposable income caused by changes in the Nonincome determinants of consumption and saving (*see*); an upward or downward movement of the Saving schedule.

Chartered bank — One of the 66 multibranched, Privately owned, commercial, financial intermediaries that have received charters by Act of Parliament and that alone, with Quebec Savings Banks, may call themselves "banks"; and which accept Demand deposits (*see*).

Chartered banking system — All chartered banks as a group.

Checkoff — The deduction by an employer of union dues from the pay of workers and the transfer of the amount deducted to a labour union.

Chequable deposit — Any deposit in a Chartered bank or other financial intermediary (trust company, credit union, etc.) against which a cheque may be written and which deposit, if it is in a bank, is thus part of the M1 (*see*) money supply.

Cheque clearing — The process by which funds are transferred from the chequing accounts of the writers of cheques to the chequing accounts of the recipients of the cheques; also called the "collection" of cheques.

Chequing account — A Demand deposit (*see*) in a chartered bank.

Circuit velocity of money — (*See* Income velocity of money.)

Circular flow of income — The flow of resources from Households to Firms and of products from Firms to Households accompanied in an economy using money by flows of money from Households to Firms and from Firms to Households.

Civilian labour force — Persons fifteen years of age and older who are not residents of the Yukon or the Northwest Territories, who are not in institutions or the armed forces, and who are employed for a wage or salary, seeking such employment, or self-employed for gain.

Classical theory — The Classical theory of employment (*see*).

Classical theory of employment — The macroeconomic generalizations accepted by most economists before the 1930s that led to the conclusion that a capitalistic economy would employ its resources fully.

Closed economy — An economy that neither exports nor imports goods and services.

Close-down case — The circumstance in which a Firm would experience a loss greater than its total fixed cost if it were to produce any output greater than zero; alternatively, a situation in which a firm would cease to operate when the price at which it can sell its product is less than its Average variable cost.

Coase theorem — The idea that Externality problems may be resolved through private negotiations of the affected parties.

Coincidence of wants — The item (good or service) that one trader wishes to obtain is the same item another trader desires to give up and the item the second trader wishes to acquire is the same item the first trader desires to surrender.

COLA — (*See* Cost-of-living adjustment.)

Collection of cheques — (*See* Cheque clearing.)

Collective bargaining — The negotiation of work agreements between Labour unions (*see*) and their employers.

Collective voice — The function a union performs for its members as a group when it communicates their problems and grievances to management and presses management for a satisfactory resolution to them.

Collusion — A situation in which Firms act together and in agreement (collude) to set the price of the product and the output each firm will produce or to determine the geographic area in which each firm will sell.

Collusive oligopoly — Occurs when the few firms composing an oligopolistic industry reach an explicit or unspoken agreement to fix prices, divide a market, or otherwise restrict competition; may take the form of a Cartel (*see*), Gentleman's agreement (*see*), or Price leadership (*see*).

Combined tax-transfer system — The percentage of income collected as taxes less the percentage of income received as transfer payments in different income classes.

Combines Investigation Act — The federal Act, first passed in 1910, whose avowed aim is to prevent agreements to lessen competition unduly; amended and renamed the Competition Act in June 1986.

Command economy — An economic system (method of organization) in which property resources are publicly owned and Central economic planning (*see*) is used to direct and coordinate economic activities.

Commercial bank — (*See* Chartered bank.)

Communism — (*See* Command economy.)

Company union — An organization of employees that is dominated by the employer (the company) and does not engage in genuine collective bargaining with the employer.

Comparable worth doctrine — The belief that women should receive the same salaries (wages) as men when the levels of skill, effort, and responsibility in their different jobs are the same.

Comparative advantage — A lower relative or Comparative cost (*see*) than another producer.

Comparative cost — The amount the production of one product must be reduced to increase the production of another product; Opportunity cost (*see*).

Competing goods — (*See* Substitute goods.)

Competition — The presence in a market of a large number of independent buyers and sellers and the freedom of buyers and sellers to enter and to leave the market.

Competition Act — The Act that amended the Combines Investigation Act (*see*) in June 1986 and, in so doing, renamed it the Competition Act.

Competitive industry's short-run supply curve — The horizontal summation of the short-run supply curves of the Firms in purely competitive industry (*see* Pure competition); a curve that shows the total quantities that will be offered for sale at various prices by the Firms in an industry in the Short run (*see*).

Competitive industry's short-run supply schedule — The summation of the short-run supply schedules of the Firms in a purely competitive industry (*see* Pure competition); a schedule that shows the total quantities that will be offered for sale at various prices by the Firms in an industry in the Short run (*see*).

Competitive labour market — A market in which a large number of (noncolluding) firms demand a particular type of labour from a large number of nonunionized workers.

Complementary goods — Goods or services for which there is an inverse relationship between the price of one and the demand for the other; when the price of one falls (rises) the demand for the other increases (decreases).

Complex multiplier — The Multiplier (*see*) when changes in the Gross domestic product change Net taxes and Imports, as well as Saving.

Concentration ratio — The percentage of the total sales of an industry made by the four (or some other number) largest sellers (Firms) in the industry.

Conditional grant — A transfer to a province by the federal government for a Shared-cost program whereby the federal government undertakes to pay part of the costs (usually half) of programs run by the provinces in accordance with federally set standards; such grants are mostly for health, post-secondary education, and general welfare [mostly under the Canada Assistance Plan (*see*)].

Confederation of National Trade Unions (CNTU) — The Labour union (*see*) federation that represents approximately 20% of Quebec's union members; established in 1921 as the Federation of Catholic Workers of Canada, it was later renamed the Canadian and Catholic Confederation of Labour; it adopted its present name and became nonconfessional in 1956.

Conglomerate combination — A group of Plants (*see*) owned by a single Firm and engaged at one or more stages in the production of different products (of products that do not compete with each other).

Conglomerate merger — The merger of a Firm in one Industry with a Firm in another industry (with a Firm that is neither supplier, customer, nor competitor).

Congress of Industrial Organizations (CIO) — The organization of affiliated Industrial unions formed in the United States in 1936.

Constant-cost industry — An Industry in which the expansion of the Industry by the entry of new Firms has no effect upon the prices the Firms in the industry pay for resources and no effect, therefore, upon their cost schedules (curves).

Consumer goods — Goods and services that satisfy human wants directly.

Consumer sovereignty — Determination by consumers of the types and quantities of goods and services that are produced from the scarce resources of the economy.

Consumption schedule — Schedule that shows the amounts Households plan to spend for Consumer goods at different levels of Disposable income.

Contractionary fiscal policy — A decrease in Aggregate demand brought about by a decrease in Government expenditures for goods and services, an increase in Net taxes, or some combination of the two.

Contractionary monetary policy — Contracting, or restricting the growth of, the nation's Money supply (*see*).

Corporation — A legal entity ("person") chartered by the federal or a provincial government, and distinct and separate from the individuals who own it.

Corporate income tax — A tax levied on the net income (profit) of Corporations.

Correlation — Systematic and dependable association between two sets of data (two kinds of events).

Cost-of-living adjustment (COLA) — An increase in the incomes (wages) of workers that is automatically received by them when there is inflation in the economy and guaranteed by a clause in their labour contracts with their employer.

Cost-plus pricing — A procedure used by (oligopolistic) firms to determine the price they will charge for a product and in which a percentage markup is added to the estimated average cost of producing the product.

Cost-push inflation — Inflation that results from a decrease in Aggregate supply (from higher wage rates and raw material prices) and that is accompanied by decreases in real output and employment (by increases in the Unemployment rate).

Cost ratio — The ratio of the decrease in the production of one product to the increase in the production of another product when resources are shifted from the production of the first to the production of the second product; the amount the production of one product decreases when the production of a second product increases by one unit.

Craft union — A labour union that limits its membership to workers with a particular skill (craft).

Credit — An accounting notation that the value of an asset (such as the foreign money owned by the residents of a nation) has increased.

Credit union — An association of persons who often have a common tie (such as being employees of the same Firm or members of the same Labour union) that sells shares to (accepts deposits from) its members and makes loans to them.

Creeping inflation — A slow rate of inflation; a 2 to 4% annual rise in the price level.

Crop restriction — A method of increasing farm revenue when demand for the product is inelastic. Usually done through a Farm products marketing board (*see*) allotting quotas.

Cross elasticity of demand — The ratio of the percentage change in Quantity demanded of one good to the percentage change in the price of some other good. A negative coefficient indicates the two products are Substitute goods; a positive coefficient indicates Complementary goods.

Crowding model of occupational discrimination — A model of labour markets that assumes Occupational discrimination (*see*) against women and minorities has kept them out of many occupations and forced them into a limited number of other occupations in which the large Supply of labour (relative to the Demand) results in lower wages and incomes.

Crowding-out effect — The rise in interest rates and the resulting decrease in planned investment spending in the economy caused by increased borrowing in the money market by the federal government.

Currency — Coins and Paper money.

Currency appreciation — (*See* Exchange rate appreciation.)

Currency depreciation — (*See* Exchange rate depreciation.)

Current account — That part of the Balance of payments (*see*) that records the total current receipts for merchandise exports, services, investment income from nonresidents, and transfers and the total current payments for merchandise imports, services, investment income to nonresidents, and transfers.

Current account deficit — A negative Balance on current account (*see*).

Current account surplus — A positive Balance on current account (*see*).

Customary economy — (*See* Traditional economy.)

Cyclically-adjusted budget — What the budget balance would be for the total government sector if the economy were operating at an average or cyclically-adjusted level of activity.

Cyclically-adjusted deficit — The budget deficit that would have occurred even though the economy was operating at an average or cyclically-adjusted level of activity.

Cyclically balanced budget — The equality of Government expenditures for goods and services and Net taxes collections over the course of a Business cycle; deficits incurred during periods of recession are offset by surpluses obtained during periods of prosperity (inflation).

Cyclical unemployment — Unemployment caused by insufficient Aggregate expenditures.

Debit — An accounting notation that the value of an asset (such as the foreign money owned by the residents of a nation) has decreased.

Declining economy — An economy in which Net investment (*see*) is less than zero (Gross investment is less than Depreciation).

Declining industry — An industry in which Economic profits are negative (losses are incurred) and which will, therefore, decrease its output as Firms leave the industry.

Decrease in demand — A decrease in the Quantity demanded of a good or service at every price; a shift of the Demand curve to the left.

Decrease in supply — A decrease in the Quantity supplied of a good or service at every price; a shift of the Supply curve to the left.

Deduction — Reasoning from assumption to conclusions; a method of reasoning that tests a hypothesis (an assumption) by comparing the conclusions to which it leads with economic facts.

Deficiency payments — A method of Price support (*see*) whereby the government pays a subsidy to producers when the market price is below the minimum price demand suitable by the government.

Deflating — Finding the Real gross domestic product (*see*) by decreasing the dollar value of the Gross domestic product produced in a year in which prices were higher than in the Base year (*see*).

Deflation — A fall in the general (average) level of prices in the economy.

Demand — A Demand schedule or a Demand curve (*see* both).

Demand curve — A curve that shows the amounts of a good or service buyers wish to purchase at various prices during some period of time.

Demand deposit — A deposit in a Chartered bank against which cheques may be written for immediate payment; bank-created money.

Demand factor — The increase in the level of Aggregate expenditures that brings about the Economic growth made possible by an increase in the productive potential of the economy.

Demand management — The use of Fiscal policy (*see*) and Monetary policy (*see*) to increase or decrease Aggregate expenditures.

Demand-pull inflation — Inflation that is the result of an increase in Aggregate demand.

Demand schedule — A schedule that shows the amounts of a good or service buyers wish to purchase at various prices during some period of time.

Dependent variable — A variable that changes as a consequence of a change in some other (independent) variable; the "effect" or outcome.

Deposit multiplier — (*See* Monetary multiplier.)

Depository institution — A Firm that accepts the deposits of Money of the public (businesses and persons); Chartered banks and other Financial intermediaries (*see*).

Depreciation (1) — (*See* Capital consumption allowances.)

Depreciation (2) — A decrease in the international price of a currency caused by market forces; not caused by the central bank; the opposite of Appreciation.

Derived demand — The demand for a good or service that is dependent upon or related to the demand for some other good or service; the demand for a resource that depends upon the demand for the products it can be used to produce.

Descriptive economics — The gathering or collection of relevant economic facts (data).

Determinants of aggregate demand — Factors such as consumption, investment, government, and net export spending that, if they change, will shift the aggregate demand curve.

Determinants of aggregate supply — Factors such as input prices, productivity, and the legal-institutional environment that, if they change, will shift the aggregate supply curve.

Determinants of demand — Factors other than its price that determine the quantities demanded of a good or service.

Determinants of supply — Factors other than its price that determine the quantities supplied of a good or service.

Devaluation — A decrease in the defined value of a currency brought about by the central bank; the opposite of Revaluation.

DI — (*See* Disposable income.)

Differentiated oligopoly — An Oligopoly in which the firms produce a Differentiated product (*see*).

Differentiated product — A product that differs physically or in some other way from the similar products produced by other Firms; a product that is similar to but not identical with and, therefore, not a perfect substitute for other products; a product such that buyers are not indifferent to the seller from whom they purchase it so long as the price charged by all sellers is the same.

Dilemma of regulation — When a Regulatory agency (*see*) must establish the maximum price a monopolist may charge, it finds that if it sets the price at the Socially optimum price (*see*), this price is below Average cost (and either bankrupts the Firm or requires that it be subsidized); and if it sets the price at the Fair-return price (*see*), it has failed to eliminate the underallocation of resources that is the consequence of unregulated monopoly.

Direct investment — Investment by nonresidents in a firm they thereby establish or control or come to control through the investment. (*See also* Portfolio investment.)

Directing function of prices — (*See* Guiding function of prices.)

Directly related — Two sets of economic data that change in the same direction; when one variable increases (decreases) the other increases (decreases).

Direct relationship — The relationship between two variables that change in the same direction, for example, product price and quantity supplied.

Discouraged workers — Workers who have left the Civilian labour force (*see*) because they have not been able to find employment.

Discretionary fiscal policy — Deliberate changes in taxes (tax rates) and government spending (spending for goods and services and transfer payment programs) by Parliament for the purpose of achieving a full-employment, noninflationary Gross domestic product and economic growth.

Diseconomies of scale — The forces that increase the Average cost of producing a product as the Firm expands the size of its Plant (its output) in the Long run (*see*).

Disinflation — A reduction in the rate of Inflation (*see*).

Disposable income — Personal income (*see*) less Personal taxes (*see*); income available for Personal consumption expenditures (*see*) and Personal saving (*see*).

Dissaving — Spending for consumer goods and services in excess of Disposable income; the amount by which Personal consumption expenditures (*see*) exceed Disposable income.

Dividend tax credit — A federal government method of reducing the Double taxation (*see*) of corporation income.

Division of labour — Dividing the work required to produce a product into a number of different tasks that are performed by different workers; Specialization (*see*) of workers.

Dollar votes — The "votes" consumers and entrepreneurs in effect cast for the production of the different kinds of consumer and capital goods, respectively, when they purchase them in the markets of the economy.

Domestic economic goal — Assumed to be full employment with little or no inflation.

Domestic income — (*See* Net domestic income.)

Domestic output — Gross domestic product (*see*).

Double counting — Including the value of Intermediate goods (*see*) in the Gross domestic product; counting the same good or service more than once.

Double taxation — Taxation of both corporation net income (profits) and the dividends paid from this net income when they become the Personal income of households.

Dumping — The sale of products below cost in a foreign country.

Duopoly — A market in which there are only two sellers; an Industry in which there are two firms.

Durable good — A consumer good with an expected life (use) of one year or more.

Dynamic progress — The development over time of more efficient (less costly) techniques of producing existing products and of improved products; technological progress.

Earnings — The money income received by a worker; equal to the Wage (rate) multiplied by the quantity of labour supplied (the amount of time worked) by the worker.

Easy money policy — Central bank expanding the Money supply with a view to decreasing interest rates.

Economic analysis — Deriving Economic principles (*see*) from relevant economic facts.

Economic cost — A payment that must be made to obtain and retain the services of a resource; the income a Firm must provide to a resource supplier to attract the resource away from an alternative use; equal to the quantity of other products that cannot be produced when resources are employed to produce a particular product.

Economic efficiency — The relationship between the input of scarce resources and the resulting output of a good or service; production of an output with a given dollar-and-cents value with the smallest total expenditure for resources; obtaining the largest total production of a good or service with resources of a given dollar-and-cents value.

Economic growth — (1) An increase in the Production possibilities schedule or curve that results from an increase in resource supplies or an improvement in Technology; (2) an increase either in real output (Gross domestic product) or in real output per capita.

Economic integration — Cooperation among and the complete or partial unification of the economies of different nations; the elimination of the barriers to trade among these nations; the bringing together of the markets in each of the separate economies to form one large (a common) market.

Economic law — (*See* Economic principle.)

Economic model — A simplified picture of reality; an abstract generalization.

Economic perspective — A viewpoint that envisions individuals and institutions making rational or purposeful decisions based upon a consideration of the benefits and costs associated with one's actions.

Economic policy — Course of action that will correct or avoid a problem.

Economic principle — Generalization of the economic behaviour of individuals and institutions.

Economic profit — The total receipts (revenue) of a firm less all its Economic costs; also called "pure profit" and "above normal profit."

Economic regulation — (*See* Industrial regulation.)

Economic rent — The price paid for the use of land and other natural resources, the supply of which is fixed (perfectly inelastic).

Economics — Social science concerned with using scarce resources to obtain the maximum satisfaction of the unlimited human wants of society.

Economic theory — Deriving Economic principles (*see*) from relevant economic facts; an Economic principle (*see*).

Economies of scale — The forces that reduce the Average cost of producing a product as the Firm expands the size of its Plant (its output) in the Long run (*see*); the economies of mass production.

Economizing problem — Society's human wants are unlimited but the resources available to produce the goods and services that satisfy wants are limited (scarce); the inability of any economy to produce unlimited quantities of goods and services.

EC — European Community — formerly European Economic Community (EEC); (*see* European Common Market).

Efficient allocation of resources — The allocation of the resources of an economy among the production of different products that leads to the maximum satisfaction of the wants of consumers.

Elastic demand — The Elasticity coefficient (*see*) is greater than one; the percentage change in Quantity demanded is greater than the percentage change in price.

Elasticity coefficient — The number obtained when the percentage change in quantity demanded (or supplied) is divided by the percentage change in the price of the commodity.

Elasticity formula — The price elasticity of demand (supply) is equal to

$$\frac{\text{Percentage change in quantity}}{\text{percentage change in price}}$$

which is equal to

$$\frac{\text{change in quantity demanded (supplied)}}{\text{original quantity demanded (supplied)}}$$

$$\text{divided by} \frac{\text{change in price}}{\text{original price}}$$

Elastic supply — The Elasticity coefficient (*see*) is greater than one; the percentage change in Quantity supplied is greater than the percentage change in price.

Emission fees — Special fees that might be levied against those who discharge pollutants into the environment.

Employment rate — The percentage of the Civilian labour force (*see*) employed at any time.

End products — Finished commodities that have attained their final degree of processing, such as commodities used directly for consumption, and machinery.

Entrepreneurial ability — The human resource that combines the other resources to produce a product, makes nonroutine decisions, innovates, and bears risks.

Equality vs. efficiency trade-off — The decrease in Economic efficiency (*see*) that appears to accompany a decrease in Income inequality (*see*); the presumption that an increase in Income inequality is required to increase Economic efficiency.

Equalization payment — An Unconditional grant (*see*) made by the federal government to the seven less wealthy provinces in an attempt to equalize incomes and opportunities across Canada.

Equalizing differences — The differences in the Wages received by workers in different jobs that compensate for nonmonetary differences in the jobs.

Equation of exchange — $MV = PQ$; in which M is the Money supply (*see*), V is the Income velocity of money (*see*), P is the Price level, and Q is the physical volume of final goods and services produced.

Equilibrium domestic output — The real domestic output at which the Aggregate demand curve intersects the Aggregate supply curve.

Equilibrium GDP — The Gross domestic product at which the total quantity of final goods and services produced (the domestic output) is equal to the total quantity of final goods and services purchased (Aggregate expenditures); and at which Leakages (*see*) and Injections (*see*) are equal.

Equilibrium position — The point at which the Budget line (*see*) is tangent to an Indifference curve (*see*) in the indifference curve approach to the theory of consumer behaviour.

Equilibrium price — The price in a competitive market at which the Quantity demanded (*see*) and the Quantity supplied (*see*) are equal; at which there is neither a shortage nor a surplus; and at which there is no tendency for price to rise or fall.

Equilibrium price level — The Price level at which the Aggregate demand curve intersects the Aggregate supply curve.

Equilibrium quantity — The Quantity demanded (*see*) and Quantity supplied (*see*) at the Equilibrium price (*see*) in a competitive market.

Equilibrium real domestic output — The real domestic output that is determined by the equality (intersection) of aggregate demand and aggregate supply; equilibrium GDP.

European Common Market — The association of now twelve Western European nations (with Turkey as an associate member) initiated in 1958 to abolish gradually the Tariffs and Import quotas among them, to establish common Tariffs for goods imported from outside the member nations, to allow the eventual free movement of labour and capital among them, and to create other common economic policies.

European Community — formerly European Economic Community — (*See* European Common Market.)

Excess cash reserve — The amount by which a Chartered bank's Actual cash reserves (*see*) exceeds its Required cash reserve (*see*); Actual cash reserve minus Required cash reserve.

Exchange control — (*See* Foreign exchange control.)

Exchange Fund Account — The account operated by the Bank of Canada on the government's behalf wherein are held Canada's Official international reserves (*see*).

Exchange rate — The Rate of exchange (*see*).

Exchange rate appreciation — An increase in the value of a nation's money in foreign exchange markets caused by free market forces; a decrease in the Rates of exchange for foreign monies.

Exchange rate depreciation — A decrease in the value of a nation's money in foreign exchange markets caused by free market forces; an increase in the Rates of exchange for foreign monies.

Exchange rate determinant — Any factor other than the Rate of exchange (*see*) that determines the demand for and the supply of a currency in the Foreign exchange market (*see*).

Excise tax — A tax levied on the expenditure for a specific product or on the quantity of the product purchased.

Exclusion principle — The exclusion of those who do not pay for a product from the benefits of the product.

Exclusive dealing and tied selling — The illegal action whereby a supplier sells a product only on condition that the buyer acquire other products from the same seller and not from competitors; and forbidden under the Competition Act (*see*).

Exclusive unionism — The policies employed by a Labour union to restrict the supply of labour by excluding potential members in order to increase the Wages received by its members; the policies typically employed by a Craft union (*see*).

Exhaustive expenditure — An expenditure by government that results directly in the employment of economic resources and in the absorption by government of the goods and services these resources produce; Government purchase (*see*).

Exit mechanism — Leaving a job and searching for another one in order to improve the conditions under which a worker is employed.

Expanding economy — An economy in which Net investment (*see*) is greater than zero (Gross investment is greater than Depreciation).

Expanding industry — An industry in which Economic profits are obtained by the firms in the industry and which will, therefore, increase its output as new firms enter the industry.

Expansionary fiscal policy — An increase in Aggregate demand brought about by an increase in Government expenditures for goods and services, a decrease in Net taxes, or some combination of the two.

Expectations — What consumers, business Firms, and others believe will happen or what conditions will be in the future.

Expected rate of net profits — Annual profits a firm anticipates it will obtain by purchasing Capital (by investing) expressed as a percentage of the price (cost) of the Capital.

Expenditure approach — The method that adds all the expenditures made for Final goods and services to measure the Gross domestic product.

Expenditures-output approach — (*See* Aggregate expenditures–domestic output approach.)

Explicit cost — The monetary payment a Firm must make to an outsider to obtain a resource.

Exports — Goods and services produced in a given nation and sold to customers in other nations.

Export subsidies — Government payments that reduce the price of a product to foreign buyers.

Export transaction — A sale of a good or service that increases the amount of foreign money (or of their own money) held by the citizens, firms, and governments of a nation.

External benefit — (*See* Spillover benefit.)

External cost — (*See* Spillover cost.)

External debt — Debt (*see*) owed to foreign citizens, firms, and institutions.

External economies of scale — The reduction in a Firm's cost of producing and marketing that results from the expansion of (the output of or the number of Firms in) the Industry of which the Firm is a member.

Externality — (*See* Spillover.)

Externally held public debt — Public debt (*see*) owed to (Canadian government securities owned by) foreign citizens, firms, and institutions.

Face value — The dollar or cents value stamped on a coin.

Factors of production — Economic resources: Land, Capital, Labour, and Entrepreneurial ability.

Fair-return price — The price of a product that enables its producer to obtain a Normal profit (*see*), and that is equal to the Average cost of producing it.

Fallacy of composition — Incorrectly reasoning that what is true for the individual (or part) is therefore necessarily true for the group (or whole).

Fallacy of limited decisions — The false notion that there are a limited number of economic decisions to be made so that, if government makes more decisions, there will be fewer private decisions to render.

Farm problem — The relatively low income of farmers (compared with incomes in the nonagricultural sectors of the economy) and the tendency for the prices farmers receive and their incomes to fluctuate sharply from year to year.

Farm products marketing boards — The federal and provincial boards, numbering more than 100, that set marketing regulations for commodities ranging from asparagus to turkeys. The boards have the power to allocate quotas, set prices, issue licences, collect fees, and require that the commodity be marketed through them.

Featherbedding — Payment by an employer to a worker for work not actually performed.

Feedback effects — The effects a change in the money supply will have (because it affects the interest rate, planned investment, and the equilibrium GDP) on the demand for money, which is itself directly related to the GDP.

Feedback mechanism — A change in human behaviour that is the result of an actual or predicted undesirable event, and that has the effect of preventing the recurrence or occurrence of the event.

Female participation rate — The percentage of the female population of working age in the Civilian labour force (*see*).

Fewness — A relatively small number of sellers (or buyers) of a good or service.

Fiat money — Anything that is Money because government has decreed it to be Money.

Final goods — Goods that have been purchased for final use and not for resale or further processing or manufacturing (during the year).

Financial capital — (*See* Money capital.)

Financial intermediary — A Chartered bank or other financial institution (trust or mortgage loan company, credit union, *caisse populaire*), which uses the funds (savings) deposited with it to make loans (for consumption or investment).

Financing exports and imports — The use of Foreign exchange markets by exporters and importers to receive and make payments for goods and services they sell and buy in foreign nations.

Firm — An organization that employs resources to produce a good or service for profit and owns and operates one or more Plants (*see*).

(The) firm's short-run supply curve — A curve that shows the quantities of a product a Firm in a purely competitive industry (*see* Pure competition) will offer to sell at various prices in the Short-run (*see*); the portion of the Firm's short-run Marginal cost (*see*) curve that lies above in Average variable cost curve.

Fiscal policy — Changes in government spending and tax collections for the purpose of achieving a full-employment and noninflationary Gross domestic product.

Five fundamental economic questions — The five questions every economy must answer: what to produce, how to produce, how to divide the total output, how to maintain Full employment, and how to assure Economic flexibility (*see*).

Fixed cost — Any cost that in total does not change when the Firm changes its output; the cost of Fixed resources (*see*).

Fixed exchange rate — A Rate of exchange that is prevented from rising or falling by the intervention of government.

Fixed resource — Any resource employed by a Firm the quantity of which the firm cannot change.

Flat-rate income tax — A tax that taxes all incomes at the same rate.

Flexible exchange rate — A Rate of exchange that is determined by the demand for and supply of the foreign money and is free to rise or fall without government interference.

Floating exchange rate — (*See* Flexible exchange rate.)

Floor price — A price set by government that is above the Equilibrium price.

Food and Drugs Act — The federal law enacted in 1920 as outgrowth of legislation dating back to 1875; subsequently amended, the Act and its Regulations now provide for controls over all foods, drugs, cosmetics, and medical devices sold in Canada.

Foreign competition — (*See* Import competition.)

Foreign exchange — (*See* Official international reserves.)

Foreign exchange control — The control a government may exercise over the quantity of foreign money demanded by its citizens and business firms and over the Rates of exchange in order to limit its outpayments to its inpayments (to eliminate a Payments deficit) (*see*).

Foreign exchange market — A market in which the money (currency) used by one nation is used to purchase (is exchanged for) the money used by another nation.

Foreign exchange rate — (*See* Rate of exchange.)

Foreign-trade effect — The inverse relationship between the Net exports (*see*) of an economy and its Price level (*see*) relative to foreign Price levels.

Foreign investment — (*See* Direct investment and Portfolio investment.)

Foreign Investment Review Agency (FIRA) — (*See* Investment Canada.)

45° line — A curve along which the value of the GDP (measured horizontally) is equal to the value of Aggregate expenditures (measured vertically).

Fractional reserve — A Reserve ratio (*see*) that is less than 100% of the deposit liabilities of a Chartered bank.

Freedom of choice — Freedom of owners of property resources and money to employ or dispose of these resources as they see fit, of workers to enter any line of work for which they are qualified, and of consumers to spend their incomes in a manner they deem to be appropriate (best for them).

Freedom of enterprise — Freedom of business Firms to employ economic resources, to use these resources to produce products of the firm's own choosing, and to sell these products in markets of their choice.

Freely floating exchange rates — Rates of exchange (*see*) that are not controlled and that may, therefore, rise and fall; and that are determined by the demand for and the supply of foreign monies.

Free-rider problem — The inability of those who might provide the economy with an economically desirable and indivisible good or service to obtain payment from those who benefit from the good or service because the Exclusion principle (*see*) cannot be applied to it.

Free trade — The absence of artificial (government imposed) barriers to trade among individuals and firms in different nations.

Frictional unemployment — Unemployment caused by workers voluntarily changing jobs and by temporary layoffs; unemployed workers between jobs.

Fringe benefits — The rewards other than Wages that employees receive from their employers and that include pensions, medical and dental insurance, paid vacations, and sick leaves.

Full employment — (1) Using all available economic resources to produce goods and services; (2) when the Unemployment rate is equal to the Full-employment unemployment rate and there is Frictional and Structural but no Cyclical unemployment (and the Real output of the economy is equal to its Potential real output).

Full-employment unemployment rate — The Unemployment rate (*see*) at which there is no Cyclical unemployment (*see*) of the Civilian labour force (*see*) and, because some Frictional and Structural unemployment is unavoidable, equal to from 4% to 6%.

Full production — The maximum amount of goods and services that can be produced from the employed resources of an economy; the absence of Underemployment (*see*).

Functional distribution of income — The manner in which the economy's (the national) income is divided among those who perform different functions (provide the economy with different kinds of resources); the division of Net domestic income (*see*) into wages and salaries, corporation profits, farmers' income, unincorporated business income, interest, and rent.

Functional finance — Use of Fiscal policy to achieve a full-employment, noninflationary Gross domestic product without regard to the effect on the Public debt (*see*).

Game theory — A theory that compares the behaviour of participants in games of strategy, such as poker and chess, with that of a small group of mutually interdependent firms (an Oligopoly).

GATT — (*See* General Agreement on Tariffs and Trade.)

GDP — (*See* Gross domestic product.)

GDP deflator — The Price index (*see*) for all final goods and services used to adjust nominal GDP to derive real GDP.

GDP gap — Potential Real gross domestic product less actual Real gross domestic product.

General Agreement on Tariffs and Trade — The international agreement reached in 1947 by twenty-three nations (including Canada) — and now numbering ninety-six — in which each nation agreed to give equal and nondiscriminatory treatment to the other nations, to reduce tariff rates by multinational negotiations, and to eliminate import quotas.

General equilibrium analysis — A study of the Price system as a whole; of the interrelations among equilibrium prices, outputs, and employments in all the different markets of the economy.

Generalization — Statistical or probability statement; statement of the nature of the relation between two or more sets of facts.

Gentlemen's agreement — An informal understanding on the price to be charged among the firms in an Oligopoly (*see*).

GNP — (*See* Gross national product.)

Gold export point — The Rate of exchange for a foreign money above which — when nations participate in the International gold standard (*see*) — the foreign money will not be purchased and gold will be sent (exported) to the foreign country to make payments there.

Gold flow — The movement of gold into or out of a nation.

Gold import point — The Rate of exchange for a foreign money below which — when nations participate in the International gold standard (*see*) — a nation's own money will not be purchased and gold will be sent (imported) into that country by foreigners to make payments there.

Gold standard — (*See* International gold standard.)

Government current purchases of goods and services — The expenditures of all governments in the economy for Final goods (*see*) and services, less investment goods.

Government purchase — Disbursement of money by government for which government receives a currently produced good or service in return.

Government transfer payment — Disbursement of money (or goods and services) by government for which government receives no currently produced good or service in return.

Gross capital information — (*See* Gross investment.)

Gross domestic product — The total market value of all Final goods (*see*) and services produced in the economy during a year.

Gross investment — Expenditures by business *and by government* for newly produced Capital goods (*see*) — machinery, equipment, tools, and buildings — and for additions to inventories.

Gross national product — Gross domestic product (*see*) plus Net investment income from nonresidents (*see*) (which is always negative in Canada).

Guaranteed annual income — The minimum income a family (or individual) would receive if a Negative income tax (*see*) were to be adopted.

Guaranteed Income Supplement — A 1966 amendment to the Old Age Security Act (*see*) provides for the payment of a full supplement to pensioners with no other income and a partial supplement to those with other, but still low, income.

Guiding function of prices — The ability of price changes to bring about changes in the quantities of products and resources demanded and supplied; (*See* Incentive function of price).

Herfindahl index — A measure of the concentration and competitiveness of an industry; calculated as the sum of the squared market shares of the individual firms.

Homogeneous oligopoly — An Oligopoly (*see*) in which the firms produce a Standardized product (*see*).

Horizontal axis — The "left-right" or "west-east" axis on a graph or grid.

Horizontal combination — A group of Plants (*see*) in the same stage of production and owned by a single Firm (*see*).

Horizontal merger — The merger of one or more Firms producing the same product into a single Firm.

Household — An economic unit (of one or more persons) that provides the economy with resources and uses the money paid to it for these resources to purchase goods and services that satisfy human wants.

Human capital investment — Any action taken to increase the productivity (by improving the skills and abilities) of workers; expenditures made to improve the education, health, or mobility of workers.

Hyperinflation — A very rapid rise in the price level.

IMF — (*See* International Monetary Fund.)

Immobility — The inability or unwillingness of a worker or another resource to move from one geographic area of occupation to another or from a lower-paying to a higher-paying job.

Imperfect competition — All markets except Pure competition (*see*); Monopoly, Monopsony, Monopolistic competition, Monopsonistic competition, Oligopoly, and Oligopsony (*see all*).

Implicit cost — The monetary income a Firm sacrifices when it employs a resource it owns to produce a product rather than supplying the resource in the market; equal to what the resource could have earned in the best-paying alternative employment.

Import competition — Competition that domestic firms encounter from the products and services of foreign suppliers.

Import quota — A limit imposed by a nation on the maximum quantity of a good that may be imported from abroad during some period of time.

Imports — Spending by individuals, Firms, and governments of an economy for goods and services produced in foreign nations.

Import transaction — The purchase of a good or service that decreases the amount of foreign money (or of their own money) held by the citizens, firms, and governments of a nation.

Incentive function of price — The inducement that an increase (a decrease) in the price of a commodity offers to sellers of the commodity to make more (less) of it available; and the inducement an increase (decrease) in price offers to buyers to purchase smaller (larger) quantities; the Guiding function of prices (*see*).

Inclusive unionism — A union that attempts to include all workers employed in an industry as members.

Income approach — The method that adds all the incomes generated by the production of Final goods and services to measure the Gross domestic product.

Income effect — The effect a change in the price of a product has upon the Real income (purchasing power) of a consumer and the resulting effect upon the quantity of that product the consumer would purchase after the consequences of the Substitution effect (*see*) have been taken into account (eliminated).

Income elasticity of demand — The ratio of the percentage change in the Quantity demanded of a good to the percentage change in income; it measures the responsiveness of consumer purchases to income changes.

Income inequality — The unequal distribution of an economy's total income among persons or families in the economy.

Income-maintenance system — The programs designed to eliminate poverty and to reduce the unequal distribution of income.

Incomes policy — Government policy that affects the Money incomes individuals (the wages workers) receive and the prices they pay for goods and services and thereby affects their Real incomes (*see* Wage-price policy.)

Income velocity of money — (*See* Velocity of money.)

Increase in demand — An increase in the Quantity demanded of a good or service at every price; a shift in the Demand curve to the right.

Increase in supply — An increase in the Quantity supplied of a good or service at every price; a shift in the Supply curve to the right.

Increasing-cost industry — An industry in which the expansion of the Industry through the entry of new Firms increases the prices the Firms in the industry must pay for resources and, therefore, increases their cost schedules (moves their cost curves upward).

Increasing returns — An increase in the Marginal product (*see*) of a resource as successive units of the resource are employed.

Independent goods — Goods or services such that there is no relationship between the price of one and the demand for the other; when the price of one rises or falls the demand for the other remains constant.

Independent variable — The variable that causes a change in some other (dependent) variable.

Indifference curve — A curve that shows the different combinations of two products that give a consumer the same satisfaction or Utility (*see*).

Indifference map — A series of indifference curves (*see*), each of which represents a different level of Utility; and which together are the preferences of the consumer.

Indirect taxes — Such taxes as Sales, Excise, and business Property taxes (*see all*), licence fees, and Tariffs (*see*), which Firms treat as costs of producing a product and pass on (in whole or in part) to buyers of the product by charging them higher prices.

Individual demand — The Demand schedule (*see*) or Demand curve (*see*) of a single buyer of a good or service.

Individual supply — The Supply schedule (*see*) or Supply curve (*see*) of a single seller of a good or service.

Induction — A method of reasoning that proceeds from facts to Generalization (*see*).

Industrial Disputes Investigation Act — The 1907 law that marked the beginning of federal labour legislation; it required disputes in the federal jurisdiction to be submitted to a Board of Conciliation and Investigation; replaced by Canada Labour Code (*see*).

Industrial policy — Any policy in which government takes a direct and active role in shaping the structure and composition of industry to promote economic growth.

Industrial regulation — The older and more traditional type of regulation in which government is concerned with the prices charged and the services provided the public in specific industries; in contrast to Social regulation (*see*).

Industrial union — A Labour union that accepts as members all workers employed in a particular industry (or by a particular firm), and that contains largely unskilled or semiskilled workers.

Industrially advanced countries (IACs) — Countries such as Canada, the United States, Japan and the nations of western Europe that have developed Market economies based upon large stocks of technologically advanced capital goods and skilled labour forces.

Industry — The group of (one or more) Firms that produces identical or similar products.

Inelastic demand — The Elasticity coefficient (*see*) is less than one; the percentage change in price is greater than the percentage change in Quantity demanded.

Inelastic supply — The Elasticity coefficient (*see*) is less than one; the percentage change in price is greater than the percentage change in Quantity supplied.

Inferior good — A good or service of which consumers purchase less (more) at every price when their incomes increase (decrease).

Inflating — Finding the Real gross domestic product (*see*) by increasing the dollar value of the Gross domestic product produced in a year in which prices are lower than they were in the Base year (*see*).

Inflation — A rise in the general (average) level of prices in the economy.

Inflationary expectations — The belief of workers, business Firms, and consumers that there will be substantial inflation in the future.

Inflationary gap — The amount by which the Aggregate expenditures schedule (curve) must decrease (shift downward) to decrease the nominal GDP to the full-employment noninflationary level.

Inflationary recession — (*See* Stagflation.)

Infrastructure — For the economy, the capital goods usually provided by the Public sector for the use of its citizens and Firms (*e.g.*, highways, bridges, transit systems, waste-water treatment facilities, municipal water systems, and airports). For the Firm, the services and facilities it must have to produce its products, which would be too costly for it to provide for itself, and which are provided by governments or other Firms (*e.g.*, water, electricity, waste treatment, transportation, research, engineering, finance, and banking).

Injection — An addition of spending to the income-expenditure stream: Investment, Government current purchases of goods and services, and Exports.

Injunction — An order from a court of law that directs a person or organization not to perform a certain act because the act would do irreparable damage to some other person or persons; a restraining order.

In-kind investment — Nonfinancial investment (*see*).

In-kind transfer — The distribution by government of goods and services to individuals and for which the government receives no currently produced good or service in return; a Government transfer payment (*see*) made in goods or services rather than in money.

Innovation — The introduction of a new product, the use of a new method of production, or the employment of a new form of business organization.

Inpayments — The receipts of (its own or foreign) money that the individuals, Firms, and governments of one nation obtain from the sale of goods, services, and investment income, from remittances, government loans and grants, and (liquid) capital inflows from abroad.

Input-output analysis — Using an Input-output table (*see*) to examine interdependencies among different parts (sectors and industries) of the economy and to make economic forecasts and plans.

Input-output table — A table that lists (along the left side) the producing sectors and (along the top) the consuming or using sectors of the economy and that shows quantitatively in each of its rows how the output of a producing sector was distributed among consuming sectors and quantitatively in each of its columns the producing sectors from which a consuming sector obtained its inputs during some period of time (a year).

Insurable risk — An event, the average occurrence of which can be estimated with considerable accuracy, that would result in a loss that can be avoided by purchasing insurance.

Interest — The payment made for the use of money (of borrowed funds).

Interest income — Income of those who supply the economy with Capital (*see*).

Interest rate — The rate of Interest (*see*).

Interest-rate effect — The tendency for increases (decreases) in the Price level to increase (decrease) the demand for money; raise (lower) interest rates; and, as a result, to reduce (expand) total spending in the economy.

Intergovernmental grant — A transfer payment from the federal government to a provincial government or from a provincial to a local government. (*See* Conditional grant and Unconditional grant.)

Interindustry competition — Competition or rivalry between the products produced by Firms in one industry (*see*) and the products produced by Firms in another Industry (or in other Industries).

Interlocking directorate — A situation in which one or more of the members of the board of directors of one Corporation are also on the board of directors of another Corporation; and which is illegal in the United States — but not in Canada — when it tends to reduce competition among the Corporations.

Intermediate goods — Goods that are purchased for resale or further processing or manufacturing during the year.

Internal economic goal — (*See* Domestic economic goal.)

Internal economies — The reduction in the cost of producing or marketing a product that results from an increase in output of the Firm (*see* Economies of (large) scale).

Internally held public debt — Public debt (*see*) owed to (Government of Canada securities owned by) Canadian residents, Firms, and institutions.

International Bank for Reconstruction and Development — (*See* World Bank.)

International economic goal — Assumed to be a current-account balance of zero.

International gold standard — An international monetary system employed in the nineteenth and early twentieth centuries in which each nation defined its money in terms of a quantity of gold, maintained a fixed relationship between its gold stock and money supply, and allowed the free importation and exportation of gold.

International Monetary Fund (IMF) — The international association of nations that was formed after World War II to make loans of foreign monies to nations with temporary Payments deficits (*see*) and to administer the Adjustable pegs (*see*); and which today creates Special Drawing Rights (*see*).

International monetary reserves — The foreign monies — in Canada mostly U.S. dollars — and such other assets as gold and Special Drawing Rights (*see*) that a nation may use to settle a Payments deficit (*see*).

International value of the dollar — The price that must be paid in foreign currency (money) to obtain one Canadian dollar.

Intrinsic value — The value in the market of the metal in a coin.

Inverse relationship — The relationship between two variables that change in opposite directions, for example, product price and quantity demanded.

Investment — Spending for (the production and accumulation of) Capital goods (*see*) and additions to inventories.

Investment Canada — (formerly Foreign Investment Review Agency — FIRA) The federal agency with the professed aim of screening, for benefit to Canada, the setting up in Canada of new firms by nonresidents or the taking over of existing Canadian firms by nonresidents.

Investment curve — A curve that shows the amounts firms plan to invest (along the vertical axis) at different income (Gross domestic product) levels (along the horizontal axis).

Investment-demand curve — A curve that shows real Rates of interest (along the vertical axis) and the amount of Investment (along the horizontal axis) at each Rate of interest.

Investment-demand schedule — Schedule that shows real Rates of interest and the amount of Investment at each Rate of interest.

Investment in human capital — (*See* Human capital investment.)

Investment schedule — A schedule that shows the amounts Firms plan to invest at different income (Gross domestic product) levels.

Invisible hand — The tendency of Firms and resource suppliers seeking to further their self-interests in competitive markets that furthers the best interest of society as a whole (the maximum satisfaction of wants).

Jurisdictional strike — Withholding from an employer the labour services of its members by a Labour union that is engaged in a dispute with another Labour union over which union is to perform a specific kind of work for the employer.

Keynesian economics — The macroeconomic generalizations that are today accepted by most (but not all) economists and that lead to the conclusion that a capitalistic economy does not tend to employ its resources fully and that Fiscal policy (*see*) and Monetary policy (*see*) can be used to promote Full employment (*see*).

Keynesianism — The philosophical, ideological, and analytical views of the prevailing majority of western economists; and their employment theory and stabilization policies.

Keynesian theory — Keynesian economics.

Kinked demand curve — The demand curve a Noncollusive oligopolist (*see*) sees for its output, and which is based on the assumption that rivals will follow a price decrease and will not follow a price increase.

Labour — The physical and mental talents (efforts) of people that can be used to produce goods and services.

Labour force — (*See* Civilian labour force.)

Labour-intensive commodity — A product that requires a relatively large amount of Labour to produce.

Labour productivity — Total output divided by the quantity of labour employed to produce the output; the Average product (*see*) of labour or output per worker per hour or per year.

Labour union — A group of workers organized to advance the interests of the group (to increase wages, shorten the hours worked, improve working conditions, and so on).

Laffer curve — A curve that shows the relationship between tax rates and the tax revenues of government and on which there is a tax rate (between 0 and 100%) at which tax revenues are at a maximum.

Laissez-faire capitalism — (*See* Pure capitalism.)

Land — Natural resources ("free gifts of nature") that can be used to produce goods and services.

Land-intensive commodity — A product that requires a relatively large amount of Land to produce.

Law of conservation of matter and energy — The notion that matter can be changed to other matter or into energy but cannot disappear; all production inputs are ultimately transformed into an equal amount of finished product, energy, and waste (pollution).

Law of demand — The inverse relationship between the price and the Quantity demanded (*see*) of a good or service during some period of time.

Law of diminishing marginal utility — As a consumer increases the consumption of a good or service, the Marginal utility (*see*) obtained from each additional unit of the good or service decreases.

Law of diminishing returns — When successive equal increments of a Variable resource (*see*) are added to the Fixed resources (*see*), beyond some level of employment, the Marginal product (*see*) of the Variable resource will decrease.

Law of increasing opportunity cost — As the amount of a product produced is increased, the Opportunity cost (*see*) — the Marginal cost (*see*) — of producing an additional unit of the product increases.

Law of supply — The direct relationship between the price and the Quantity supplied (*see*) of a good or service during some period of time.

Leakage — (1) a withdrawal of potential spending from the income-expenditures stream: Saving (*see*), tax payment, and Imports (*see*); (2) a withdrawal that reduces the lending potential of the Chartered banking system.

Leakages–injections approach — Determination of the Equilibrium gross domestic product (*see*) by finding the Gross domestic product at which Leakages (*see*) are equal to Injections (*see*).

Least-cost combination rule (of resources) — The quantity of each resource a Firm must employ if it is to produce any output at the lowest total cost; the combination in which the ratio of the Marginal product (*see*) of a resource to its Marginal resource cost (*see*) (to its price if the resource is employed in a competitive market) is the same for all resources employed.

Legal cartel theory of regulation — The hypothesis that industries want to be regulated so that they may form legal Cartels (*see*) and that government officials (the government) provide the regulation in return for their political and financial support.

Legal tender — Anything that government has decreed must be accepted in payment of a debt.

Lending potential of an individual chartered bank — The amount by which a single Chartered bank can safely increase the Money supply by making new loans to (or buying securities from) the public; equal to the Chartered bank's Excess cash reserve (*see*).

Lending potential of the banking system — The amount by which the Chartered banking system (*see*) can increase the Money supply by making new loans to (or buying securities from) the public; equal to the Excess cash reserve (*see*) of the Chartered banking system multiplied by the Money multiplier (*see*).

Less-developed countries (LDCs) — Many countries of Africa, Asia, and Latin America that are characterized by a lack of capital goods, primitive production technologies, low literacy rates, high unemployment, rapid population growth, and labour forces heavily committed to agriculture.

Liability — A debt with a monetary value; an amount owed by a Firm or an individual.

Limited liability — Restriction of the maximum that may be lost to a predetermined amount; the maximum amount that may be lost by the owners (stockholders) of a Corporation is the amount they paid for their shares of stock.

Liquidity — Money or things that can be quickly and easily converted into Money with little or no loss of purchasing power.

Liquidity preference theory of interest — The theory in which the demand for Liquidity (the quantity of Money firms and households wish to possess) and the supply of Liquidity (the quantity of Money available) determine the equilibrium Rate of interest in the economy.

Loaded terminology — Terms that arouse emotions and elicit approval or disapproval.

Loanable funds theory of interest — The concept that the supply of and demand for loanable funds determines the equilibrium rate of interest.

Log-rolling — The trading of votes by legislators to secure favourable outcomes on decisions to provide public goods and services.

Long run — A period of time long enough to enable producers of a product to change the quantities of all the resources they employ; in which all resources and costs are variable and no resources or costs are fixed.

Long-run aggregate supply curve — The aggregate supply curve associated with a time period in which input prices (especially nominal wages) are fully responsive to changes in the price level.

Long-run competitive equilibrium — The price at which the Firms in Pure competition (*see*) neither obtain Economic profit nor suffer losses in the Long run and the total quantity demanded and supplied at that price are equal; a price equal to the minimum long-run average cost of producing the product.

Long-run farm problem — The tendency for the prices of agricultural products and the incomes of farmers to decline relative to prices and incomes in the rest of the economy.

Long-run supply — A schedule or curve that shows the prices at which a Purely competitive industry will make various quantities of the product available in the Long run.

Lorenz curve — A curve that can be used to show the distribution of income in an economy; and when used for this purpose, the cumulated percentage of families (income receivers) is measured along the horizontal axis and the cumulated percentage of income is measured along the vertical axis.

Loss-minimizing case — The circumstances that result in a loss that is less than its Total fixed cost when a competitive Firm produces the output at which total loss is a minimum: when the price at which the firm can sell its product is less than Average total but greater than Average variable cost.

Lump-sum tax — A tax that is a constant amount (the tax revenue of government is the same) at all levels of GDP.

M1 — The narrowly defined Money supply; the Currency (coins and Paper money) and Demand deposits in chartered banks (*see*) not owned by the federal government or banks.

M2 — Includes, in addition to M1, Canadian dollar personal savings deposits and nonpersonal notice deposits at chartered banks.

M2 + — Includes, in addition to M2, deposits at trust and mortgage loan companies, and deposits and shares at *caisses populaires* and credit unions.

M3 — Includes, in addition to M2, Canadian dollar nonpersonal fixed term deposits plus all foreign currency deposits of Canadian residents booked at chartered banks in Canada.

Macroeconomics — The part of economics concerned with the economy as a whole; with such major aggregates as the households, business, international trade, and governmental sectors and with totals for the economy.

Managed floating exchange rate — An Exchange rate that is allowed to change (float) to eliminate persistent Payments deficits and surpluses and is controlled (managed) to eliminate day-to-day fluctuations.

Marginal cost — The extra (additional) cost of producing one more unit of output; equal to the change in Total cost divided by the change in output (and in the short run to the change in total Variable cost divided by the change in output).

Marginal labour cost — The amount by which the total cost of employing Labour increases when a Firm employs one additional unit of Labour (the quantity of other resources employed remaining constant); equal to the change in the total cost of Labour divided by the change in the quantity of Labour employed.

Marginal product — The additional output produced when one additional unit of a resource is employed (the quantity of all other resources employed remaining constant); equal to the change in total product divided by the change in the quantity of a resource employed.

Marginal productivity theory of income distribution — The contention that the distribution of income is equitable when each unit of each resource receives a money payment equal to its marginal contribution to the firm's revenue (its Marginal revenue product).

Marginal propensity to consume — Fraction of any change in Disposable income spent for Consumer goods; equal to the change in consumption divided by the change in Disposable income.

Marginal propensity to import — The fraction of any change in income (Gross domestic product) spent for imported goods and services; equal to the change in Imports (*see*) divided by the change in income.

Marginal propensity to save — Fraction of any change in Disposable income that households save; equal to change in Saving (*see*) divided by the change in Disposable income.

Marginal rate of substitution — The rate (at the margin) at which a consumer is prepared to substitute one good or service for another and remain equally satisfied (have the same total Utility); and equal to the slope of an Indifference curve (*see*).

Marginal resource cost — The amount by which the total cost of employing a resource increases when a Firm employs one additional unit of the resource (the quantity of all other resources employed remaining constant); equal to the change in the total cost of the resource divided by the change in the quantity of the resource employed.

Marginal revenue — The change in the Total revenue of the Firm that results from the sale of one additional unit of its product; equal to the change in Total revenue divided by the change in the quantity of the product sold (demanded).

Marginal-revenue–marginal-cost approach — The method that finds the total output at which Economic profit (*see*) is a maximum (or losses a minimum) by comparing the Marginal revenue (*see*) and the Marginal cost (*see*) of additional units of output.

Marginal revenue product — The change in the Total revenue of the Firm when it employs one additional unit of a resource (the quantity of all other resources employed remaining constant); equal to the change in Total revenue divided by the change in the quantity of the resource employed.

Marginal tax rate — The fraction of additional (taxable) income that must be paid in taxes.

Marginal utility — The extra Utility (*see*) a consumer obtains from the consumption of one additional unit of a good or service; equal to the change in total Utility divided by the change in the quantity consumed.

Market — Any institution or mechanism that brings together the buyers (demanders) and sellers (suppliers) of a particular good or service.

Market demand — (*See* Total demand.)

Market economy — An economy in which only the private decisions of consumers, resource suppliers, and business Firms determine how resources are allocated; the Market system (*see*).

Market failure — The failure of a market to bring about the allocation of resources that best satisfies the wants of society (that maximizes the satisfaction of wants). In particular, the over- or underallocation of resources to the production of a particular good or service (because of Spillovers) and no allocation of resources to the production of Public (social) goods (*see*).

Market for externality rights — A market in which the Perfectly inelastic supply (*see*) of the right to pollute the environment and the demand for the right to pollute would determine the price a polluter would have to pay for the right.

Market period — A period of time in which producers of a product are unable to change the quantity produced in response to a change in its price; in which there is Perfect inelasticity of supply (*see*); and in which all resources are Fixed resources (*see*).

Market policies — Government policies designed to reduce the market power of labour unions and large business firms and to reduce or eliminate imbalances and bottlenecks in labour markets.

Market socialism — An economic system (method of organization) in which property resources are publicly owned and markets and prices are used to direct and coordinate economic activities.

Market system — All the product and resource markets of the economy and the relationships among them; a method that allows the prices determined in these markets to allocate the economy's Scarce resources and to communicate and coordinate the decisions made by consumers, business firms, and resource suppliers.

Median-voter model — The view that under majority rule the median (middle) voter will be in the dominant position to determine the outcome of an election.

Medium of exchange — Money (*see*); a convenient means of exchanging goods and services without engaging in Barter (*see*); what sellers generally accept and buyers generally use to pay for a good or service.

Microeconomics — The part of economics concerned with such individual units within the economy as Industries, Firms, and Households, and with individual markets, particular prices, and specific goods and services.

Minimum wage — The lowest Wage (rate) employers may legally pay for an hour of Labour.

Mixed capitalism — An economy in which both government and private decisions determine how resources are allocated.

Monetarism — An alternative to Keynesianism (*see*); the philosophical, ideological, and analytical views of a minority of North American economists; and their employment theory and stabilization policy, which stress the role of money.

Monetary control instruments — Techniques the Bank of Canada employs to change the size of the nation's Money supply (*see*); Open-market operations (*see*), a change in the Bank Rate (*see*), and Switching Government of Canada deposits (*see*).

Money multiplier — The multiple of its Excess cash reserve (*see*) by which the Chartered banking system (*see*) can expand deposits and the Money supply by making new loans (or buying securities); equal to one divided by the Cash reserve ratio (*see*).

Monetary policy — Changing the Money supply (*see*) in order to assist the economy to achieve a full-employment, noninflationary level of total output.

Monetary rule — The rule suggested by the Monetarists (*see*): the Money supply should be expanded each year at the same annual rate as the potential rate of growth of the Real gross domestic product; the supply of money should be increased steadily at from 3 to 5% per year.

Money — Any item that is generally acceptable to sellers in exchange for goods and services.

Money capital — Money available to purchase Capital goods (*see*).

Money income — (*See* Nominal income.)

Money interest rate — The Nominal interest rate (*see*).

Money market — The market in which the demand for and the supply of money determine the interest rate (or the level of interest rates) in the economy.

Money supply — Narrowly defined: M1 (*see*); more broadly defined: M2, M3, and M2+ (*see*).

Money wage — The amount of money received by a worker per unit of time (hour, day, and so on).

Money wage rate — (*See* Money wage.)

Monopolistic competition — A market in which many Firms sell a Differentiated product (*see*), into which entry is relatively easy, in which the Firm has some control over the price at which the product it produces is sold, and in which there is considerable Nonprice competition (*see*).

Monopoly — (1) A market in which the number of sellers is so few that each seller is able to influence the total supply and the price of the good or service; (2) a major industry in which a small number of Firms control all or a large portion of its output. (*See also* Pure Monopoly.)

Monopsony — A market in which there is only one buyer of the good or service.

Moral hazard problem — The possibility that individuals or institutions will change their behavior in unanticipated ways as the result of a contract or agreement. Example: A bank whose deposits are insured against loss may make riskier loans and investments.

Moral suasion — The statements, pronouncements, and appeals made by the Bank of Canada that are intended to influence the lending policies of Chartered banks.

Most-favoured-nation clause — A clause in a trade agreement between Canada and another nation that provides that the other nation's Imports into Canada will be subjected to the lowest tariff rates levied then or later on any other nation's Imports into Canada.

MR = MC rule — A Firm will maximize its Economic profit (or minimize its losses) by producing the output at which Marginal revenue (*see*) and Marginal cost (*see*) are equal — provided the price at which it can sell its product is equal to or greater than Average variable cost (*see*).

MRP = MRC rule — To maximize Economic profit (or minimize losses), a Firm should employ the quantity of a resource at which its Marginal revenue product (*see*) is equal to its Marginal resource cost (*see*).

Multiplier — The ratio of the change in the Equilibrium GDP to the change in Investment (*see*), or to the change in any other component in the Aggregate-expenditures schedule or to the change in Net taxes; the number by which a change in any component in the Aggregate-expenditures schedule or in Net taxes must be multiplied to find the resulting change in the Equilibrium GDP.

Multiplier effect — The effect upon the Equilibrium gross domestic product of a change in the Aggregate-expenditures schedule (caused by a change in the Consumption schedule, Investment, Net taxes, Government current purchases of goods and services, or Net exports).

Mutual interdependence — Situation in which a change in price (or in some other policy) by one Firm will affect the sales and profits of another Firm (or other Firms) and any Firm that makes such a change can expect the other Firm(s) to react in an unpredictable (uncertain) way.

Mutually exclusive goals — Goals that conflict and cannot be achieved simultaneously.

National income — Total income earned by resource suppliers for their contributions to the production of the Gross national product (*see*); equal to the Gross national product minus the Nonincome charges (*see*).

National income accounting — The techniques employed to measure (estimate) the overall production of the economy and other related totals for the nation as a whole.

National Policy — Sir John A. Macdonald's 1879 policy of high tariff protection for Canadian (Ontario and Quebec) secondary manufacturers.

Natural monopoly — An industry in which the Economies of scale (*see*) are so great that the product can be produced by one Firm at an average cost that is lower than it would be if it were produced by more than one Firm.

Natural rate hypothesis — Contends that the economy is stable in the long run at the natural rate of unemployment; views the long-run Phillips curve (*see*) as being vertical at the natural rate of unemployment.

Natural rate of unemployment — (*See* Full-employment unemployment rate.)

Near-money — Financial assets, the most important of which are savings, term, and notice deposits in Chartered banks, trust companies, credit unions, and other savings institutions, that can be readily converted into Money.

Negative income tax — The proposal to subsidize families and individuals with money payments when their incomes fall below a Guaranteed (annual) income (*see*); the negative tax would decrease as earned income increases (*see* Benefit-loss rate).

Negative relationship — (*See* Inverse relationship.)

Net capital movement — The difference between the real and financial investments and loans made by individuals and Firms of one nation in the other nations of the world and the investments and loans made by individuals and Firms from other nations in a nation.

Net domestic income — The sum of the incomes earned through the production of the Gross domestic product (*see*).

Net exports effect — The notion that the impact of a change in monetary policy will be strengthened by the consequent change in Net exports (*see*). For example a contractionary (expansionary) monetary policy will increase (decrease) domestic interest rates, thereby increasing (decreasing) the foreign demand for dollars. As a result, the dollar appreciates (depreciates) and causes Canadian net exports to decrease (increase).

Net exports — Exports (*see*) minus Imports (*see*).

Net investment — Gross investment (*see*) less Capital consumption allowances (*see*); the addition to the nation's stock of Capital during a year.

Net investment income — The interest and dividend income received by the residents of a nation from residents of other nations less the interest and dividend payments made by the residents of that nation to the residents of other nations. In Canada, always a negative quantity.

Net national income — National income (*see*).

Net national product — Gross national product (*see*) less that part of the output needed to replace the Capital goods worn out in producing the output (Capital consumption allowances [*see*]).

Net taxes — The taxes collected by government less Government transfer payments (*see*).

Net transfers — The personal and government transfer payments made to residents of foreign nations less the personal and government transfer payments received from residents of foreign nations.

Net Worth — The total Assets (*see*) less the total Liabilities (*see*) of a Firm or an individual; the claims of the owners of a firm against its total Assets.

New classical economics — The theory that, although unanticipated price level changes may create macroeconomic instability in the short run, the economy is stable at the full-employment level of domestic output in the long run because of price and wage flexibility.

New International Economic Order — A series of proposals made by the Third World (*see*) for basic changes in its relationships with the advanced industrialized nations that would accelerate the growth of and redistribute world income to the Third World.

NIEO — New International Economic Order (*see*).

NIT — (*See* Negative income tax.)

New perspective view of advertising — Envisions advertising as a low-cost source of consumer information that increases competition by making consumers more aware of substitute products.

NNP — (*See* Net national product.)

Nominal gross domestic output (GDP) — The GDP (*see*) measured in terms of the price level at the time of measurement (unadjusted for changes in price level).

Nominal income — The number of dollars received by an individual or group during some period of time; the money income.

Nominal interest rate — The rate of interest expressed in dollars of current value (not adjusted for inflation).

Nominal wage rate — The Money wage (*see*).

Noncollusive oligopoly — An Oligopoly (*see*) in which the Firms do not act together and in agreement to determine the price of the product and the output each Firm will produce or to determine the geographic area in which each Firm will sell.

Noncompeting groups — Groups of workers in the economy that do not compete with each other for employment because the skill and training of the workers in one group are substantially different from those of the workers in other groups.

Nondiscretionary fiscal policy — The increases (decreases) in Net taxes (*see*) that occur without Parliamentary action when the Gross domestic product rises (falls) and that tend to stabilize the economy.

Nondurable good — A Consumer good (*see*) such as food, beverages, and tobacco.

Nonexhaustive expenditure — An expenditure by government that does not result directly in the employment of economic resources or the production of goods and services; *see* Government transfer payment.

Nonfinancial investment — An investment that does not require households to save a part of their money incomes; but that uses surplus (unproductive) labour to build Capital goods.

Nonincome charges — Capital consumption allowances (*see*) and Indirect taxes (*see*).

Nonincome determinants of consumption and saving — All influences on consumption spending and saving other than the level of Disposable income.

Noninterest determinants of investment — All influences on the level of investment spending other than the rate of interest.

Noninvestment transaction — An expenditure for stocks, bonds, or second-hand Capital goods.

Nonmarket transactions — The production of goods and services not included in the measurement of the Gross domestic product because the goods and services are not bought and sold.

Nonmerchandise balance — The addition of the balances on services, investment income, and transfers in the Current account (*see*) of the Balance of payments (*see*).

Nonprice competition — The means other than decreasing the prices of their products that Firms employ to attempt to increase the sale of their products; and that includes Quality competition (*see*), advertising, and sales promotion activities.

Nonprice determinant of demand — Factors other than its price that determine the quantities demanded of a good or service.

Nonprice determinant of supply — Factors other than its price that determine the quantities supplied of a good or service.

Nonprice level determinants of aggregate demand — Factors such as consumption, investment, government, and net export spending that, if they change, will shift the aggregate demand curve.

Nonprice level determinants of aggregate supply — Factors such as input prices, productivity, and the legal-institutional environment that, if they change, will shift the aggregate supply curve.

Nonproduction transaction — The purchase and sale of any item that is not a currently produced good or service.

Nontariff barriers (NTBs) — All barriers other than Tariffs (*see*) that nations erect to impede trade among nations; Import quotas (*see*), licensing requirements, unreasonable product-quality standards, unnecessary red tape in customs procedures, and so on.

Nonunion shop — A place of employment at which none of the employees are members of a Labour union (and at which the employer attempts to hire only workers who are not apt to join a union).

Normal good — A good or service of which consumers will purchase more (less) at every price when their incomes increase (decrease).

Normal profit — Payment that must be made by a Firm to obtain and retain Entrepreneurial ability (*see*); the minimum payment (income) Entrepreneurial ability must (expect to) receive to induce it to perform the entrepreneurial functions for a Firm; an Implicit cost (*see*).

Normative economics — That part of economics that pertains to value judgments about what the economy should be like; concerned with economic goals and policies.

Notice, term, and savings deposit — A deposit in a Chartered bank against which cheques may or may not be written but for which the bank has the right to demand notice of withdrawal.

NTBs — (*See* Nontariff barriers.)

Occupational discrimination — The form of discrimination that excludes women from certain occupations and the higher wages paid workers in these occupations.

Occupational licensing — The laws of provincial governments that require a worker to obtain a licence from a provincial board (by satisfying certain specified requirements) before engaging in a particular occupation.

Offers to purchase — A method of Price support (*see*) whereby the government buys the surplus created when it sets the minimum price above the Equilibrium price (*see*).

Official international reserves — The International monetary assets (*see*) owned by the federal government and held in its behalf by the Bank of Canada in the Exchange Fund Account.

Official reserves — Official international reserves (*see*).

Okun's law — The generalization that any one percentage point rise in the Unemployment rate above the Full-employment unemployment rate will increase the GDP gap by 2.5% of the Potential output (GDP) of the economy.

Old Age Security Act — The 1951 federal Act, as subsequently amended, by which a Pension is payable to every person aged 65 and older provided the person has resided in Canada for ten years immediately preceding the approval of an application for pension; in addition a Guaranteed Income Supplement (*see*) may be paid; the Pension is payable in addition to the Canada Pension (*see*).

Oligopoly — A market in which a few Firms sell either a Standardized or Differentiated product, into which entry is difficult, in which the Firm's control over the price at which it sells its product is limited by Mutual interdependence (*see*) (except when there is collusion among firms), and in which there is typically a great deal of Nonprice competition (*see*).

Oligopsony — A market in which there are a few buyers.

OPEC — An acronym for the Organization of Petroleum Exporting Countries (*see*).

Open economy — An economy that both exports and imports goods and services.

Open-economy multiplier — The Multiplier (*see*) in an economy in which some part of any increase in the income (Gross domestic product) of the economy is used to purchase additional goods and services from abroad; and which is equal to the reciprocal of the sum of the Marginal propensity to save (*see*) and the Marginal propensity to import (*see*).

Open-market operations — The buying and selling of Government of Canada securities by the Bank of Canada.

Open shop — A place of employment at which the employer may hire either Labour union members or workers who are not (and need not become) members of the union.

Opportunity cost — The amount of other products that must be forgone or sacrificed to produce a unit of a product.

Optimal amount of externality reduction — That reduction of pollution or other negative externality where society's marginal benefit and marginal cost of reducing the externality are equal.

Optimal distribution of income — The distribution of income that would result in the greatest possible (maximum) satisfaction of consumer wants (Utility) in the economy.

Optimal social price — The price of a product that results in the most efficient allocation of an economy's resources and that is equal to the Marginal cost (*see*) of the last unit of the product produced.

Organization of Petroleum Exporting Countries — The cartel formed in 1960 by thirteen oil-producing countries to control the price at which they sell crude oil to foreign importers and the quantity of oil exported by its members.

"Other things being equal" assumption — Assuming that the factors other than those being considered are constant.

Outpayments — The expenditures of (its own or foreign) money that the individuals, Firms, and governments of one nation make to purchase goods, services, and investment income, for Remittances, for government loans and grants, and (liquid) capital outflows abroad.

Output effect — The impact a change in the price of a resource has upon the output a Firm finds it most profitable to produce and the resulting effect upon the quantity of the resource (and the quantities of other resources) employed by the Firm after the consequences of the Substitution effect (*see*) have been taken into account (eliminated).

Paper-money — Pieces of paper used as a Medium of exchange (*see*); in Canada, Bank of Canada notes.

Paradox of thrift — The attempt of society to save more results in the same amount or less Saving.

Paradox of voting — A situation wherein voting by majority rule fails to provide a consistent ranking of society's preferences for public goods or services.

Partial equilibrium analysis — The study of equilibrium prices and equilibrium outputs or employments in a particular market that assumes prices, outputs, and employments in the other markets of the economy remain unchanged.

Partnership — An unincorporated business Firm owned and operated by two or more persons.

Patent laws — The federal laws that grant to inventors and innovators the exclusive right to produce and sell a new product or machine for a period of seventeen years.

Payments deficit — (*See* Balance of payments deficit.)

Payments surplus — (*See* Balance of payments surplus.)

Peak pricing — Setting the price charged for the use of a facility (the User charge [*see*]) or for a good or service at a higher level when the demand for the use of the facility or for the good or service is greater and at a lower level when the demand for it is less.

Perfect elastic demand — A change in the Quantity demanded requires no change in the price of the commodity; buyers will purchase as much of a commodity as is available at a constant price.

Perfect elastic supply — A change in the Quantity supplied requires no change in the price of the commodity; sellers will make available as much of the commodity as buyers will purchase at a constant price.

Perfect inelastic demand — A change in price results in no change in the Quantity demanded of a commodity; the Quantity demanded is the same at all prices.

Perfect inelastic supply — A change in price results in no change in the Quantity supplied of a commodity; the Quantity supplied is the same at all prices.

Personal consumption expenditures — The expenditures of Households for Durable, semidurable, and nondurable consumer goods and for services.

Personal distribution of income — The manner in which the economy's Personal or Disposable income is divided among different income classes or different households.

Personal income — The income, part of which is earned and the remainder of which is unearned, available to resource suppliers and others before the payment of Personal taxes (*see*).

Personal income tax — A tax levied on the taxable income of individuals (households and unincorporated firms).

Personal saving — The Personal income of households less Personal taxes (*see*) and Personal consumption expenditures (*see*); Disposable income less Personal consumption expenditures; that part of Disposable income not spent for Consumer goods (*see*).

Phillips curve — A curve that shows the relationship between the Unemployment rate (*see*) (on the horizontal axis) and the annual rate of increase in the Price level (on the vertical axis).

Planned economy — An economy in which only government determines how resources are allocated.

Planned investment — The amount that business firms plan or intend to invest.

Plant — A physical establishment (Land and Capital) that performs one or more of the functions in the production (fabrication and distribution) of goods and services.

P = MC rule — A Firm in Pure competition (*see*) will maximize its Economic profit (*see*) or minimize its losses by producing the output at which the price of the product is equal to Marginal cost (*see*), provided that price is equal to or greater than Average variable cost (*see*) in the short run and equal to or greater than Average (total) cost (*see*) in the long run.

Policy economics — The formulation of courses of action to bring about desired results or to prevent undesired occurrences (to control economic events).

Political business cycle — The tendency of Parliament to destabilize the economy by reducing taxes and increasing government expenditures before

elections and to raise taxes and lower expenditures after the elections.

Portfolio investment — The buying of bonds and shares by nonresidents, the number of shares bought being insufficient to attain control of the firm. (*See also* Direct Investment.)

Positive economics — The analysis of facts or data for the purpose of establishing scientific generalizations about economic behaviour; compare Normative economics.

Positive relationship — The relationship between two variables that change in the same direction, for example, product price and quantity supplied.

***Post hoc, ergo propter hoc* fallacy** — Incorrectly reasoning that when one event precedes another, the first event necessarily is the cause of the second.

Potential competition — The possibility that new competitors will be induced to enter an industry if firms at present in that industry are realizing large economic profits.

Potential output — The real output (GDP) an economy is able to produce when it fully employs its available resources.

Poverty — An existence in which the basic needs of an individual or family exceed the means available to satisfy them.

Poverty rate — The percentage of the population with incomes below the official poverty income levels established by Statistics Canada.

Predatory pricing — A general, illegal policy of selling at prices unreasonably low with a view to eliminating competition; forbidden under the Competition Act (*see*).

Premature inflation — Inflation (*see*) that occurs before the economy has reached Full employment (*see*).

Price — The quantity of money (or of other goods and services) paid and received for a unit of a good or service.

Price ceiling — A government-fixed maximum price for a good or service.

Price-decreasing effect — The effect in a competitive market of a decrease in Demand or an Increase in Supply upon the Equilibrium price (*see*).

Price discrimination — The selling of a product (at a given time) to different buyers at different prices when the price differences are not justified by differences in the cost of producing the product for the different buyers; an illegal trade practice under the Competition Act (*see*) when it consists in giving a trade purchaser an unfair advantage over its competitors by selling to it at a lower price.

Price elasticity of demand — The ratio of the percentage change in Quantity demanded of a commodity to the percentage change in its price, the responsiveness or sensitivity of the quantity of a commodity buyers demand to a change in the price of the commodity.

Price elasticity of supply — The ratio of the percentage change in the Quantity supplied of a commodity to the percentage change in its price; the responsiveness or sensitivity of the quantity sellers of a commodity supply to a change in the price of the commodity.

Price guidepost — The price charged by an Industry for its product should increase by no more than the increase in the Unit labour cost (*see*) of producing the product.

Price-increasing effect — The effect in a competitive market of an increase in Demand or a decrease in Supply upon the Equilibrium price (*see*).

Price index — An index number that shows how the average price of a "market basket" of goods changes through time. A price index is used to change nominal output (income) into real output (income).

Price leadership — An informal method that the Firms in an Oligopoly (*see*) may employ to set the price of the product they produce: one firm (the leader) is the first to announce a change in price and the other firms (the followers) quickly announce identical (or similar) changes in price.

Price level — The weighted average of the Prices paid for the final goods and services produced in the economy.

Price level surprises — Unanticipated changes in the price level.

Price-maker — A seller (or buyer) of a commodity that is able to affect the price at which the commodity sells by changing the amount it sells (buys).

Price support — The minimum price government allows sellers to receive for a good or service; a price that is the established or maintained minimum price.

Price-taker — A seller (or buyer) of a commodity that is unable to affect the price at which a commodity sells by changing the amount it sells (or buys).

Price-wage flexibility — Changes in the prices of products and in the Wages paid to workers; the ability of prices and Wages to rise or to fall.

Price war — Successive and continued decreases in the prices charged by the firms in an oligopolistic industry by which each firm hopes to increase its sales and revenues and from which firms seldom benefit.

Primary reserve — (*See* Cash reserve.)

Prime rate — The interest rate the Chartered banks (*see*) charge on demand note loans to their best corporate customers.

Principal–agent problem — A conflict of interest that occurs when agents (workers) pursue their own objectives to the detriment of the principal's (employer's) goals.

Private good — A good or service to which the Exclusion principle (*see*) is applicable; and that is provided by privately owned firms to those who are willing to pay for it.

Private property — The right of private persons and Firms to obtain, own, control, employ, dispose of, and bequeath Land, Capital, and other Assets.

Private sector — The Households and business Firms of the economy.

Product differentiation — Physical or other differences between the products produced by different Firms that result in individual buyers preferring (so long as the price charged by all sellers is the same) the product of one Firm to the Products of the other Firms.

Production possibilities curve (frontier) — A curve that shows the different combinations of two goods or services that can be produced in a Full-employment (*see*), Full-production (*see*) economy in which the available supplies of resources and technology are constant.

Production possibilities table — A table that shows the different combinations of two goods or services that can be produced in a Full-employment (*see*), Full-production (*see*) economy in which the available supplies of resources and technology are constant.

Productive efficiency — The production of a good in the least-costly way: employing the minimum quantity of resources needed to produce a given output and producing the output at which Average total cost is a minimum.

Productivity — A measure of average output or real output per unit of input. For example, the productivity of labour may be determined by dividing hours of work into real output.

Productivity slowdown — The recent decline in the rate at which Labour productivity (*see*) in Canada has increased.

Product market — A market in which Households buy and Firms sell the products they have produced.

Profit — (*See*) Economic profit and Normal profit; without an adjective preceding it, the income of those who supply the economy with Entrepreneurial ability (*see*) or Normal profit.

Profit-maximizing case — The circumstances that result in an Economic profit (*see*) for a (competitive) Firm when it produces the output at which Economic profit is a maximum: when the price at which the Firm can sell its product is greater than the Average (total) cost of producing it.

Profit-maximizing rule (combination of resources) — The quantity of each resource a Firm must employ if its Economic profit (*see*) is to be a maximum or its losses a minimum; the combination in which the Marginal revenue product (*see*) of each resource is equal to its Marginal resource cost (*see*) (to its price if the resource is employed in a competitive market).

Program for the Advancement of Industrial Technology — A federal program of providing financial assistance, normally 50%, for the development of new or improved products and processes incorporating advanced technology.

Progressive tax — A tax such that the tax rate increases as the taxpayer's income increases and decreases as income decreases.

Property tax — A tax on the value of property (Capital, Land, stocks and bonds, and other Assets) owned by Firms and Households.

Proportional tax — A tax such that the tax rate remains constant as the taxpayer's income increases and decreases.

Proprietors' income — The net income of the owners of unincorporated Firms (proprietorships and partnerships); the sum of the accrued net income of farm operators from farm production plus the net income of nonfarm unincorporated business, including rent.

Prosperous industry — (*See* Expanding industry.)

Protective tariff — A Tariff (*see*) designed to protect domestic producers of a good from the competition of foreign producers.

Public assistance programs — Programs that pay benefits to those who are unable to earn income (because of permanent handicaps or because they are dependent children), that are financed by general tax revenues, and that are viewed as public charity (rather than earned rights).

Public choice theory — Generalizations that describe how government (the Public sector) makes decisions for the use of economic resources.

Public debt — The amount owed by the Government of Canada to the owners of its securities and equal to the sum of its past Budget deficits (less its Budget surpluses).

Public finance — The branch of economics that analyses government revenues and expenditures.

Public good — A good or service to which the Exclusion principle (*see*) is not applicable; and that is provided by government if it yields substantial benefits to society.

Public interest theory of regulation — The presumption that the purpose of the regulation of an Industry is to protect the public (consumers) from the abuse of the power possessed by Natural monopolies (*see*).

Public sector — The part of the economy that contains all its governments; government.

Public-sector failure — The failure of the Public sector (government) to resolve socioeconomic problems because it performs its functions in an economically inefficient fashion.

Public utility — A Firm that produces an essential good or service, that has obtained from a government the right to be the sole supplier of the good or service in an area, and that is regulated by that government to prevent the abuse of its monopoly power.

Purchasing power parity — The idea that exchange rates between nations equate the purchasing power of various currencies; exchange rates between any two nations adjust to reflect the price level differences between the countries.

Pure capitalism — An economic system (method or organization) in which property resources are privately owned and markets and prices are used to direct and coordinate economic activities.

Pure competition — (1) A market in which a very large number of Firms sells a Standardized product (*see*), into which entry is very easy, in which the individual seller has no control over the price at which the product sells, and in which there is no Nonprice competition (*see*); (2) a market in which there is a very large number of buyers.

Pure monopoly — A market in which one Firm sells a unique product (one for which there are no close substitutes), into which entry is blocked, in which the Firm has considerable control over the price at which the product sells, and in which Nonprice competition (*see*) may or may not be found.

Pure profit — (*See* Economic profit.)

***Pure* rate of interest** — (*See The* Rate of interest.)

Quantity-decreasing effect — The effect in a competitive market of a decrease in Demand or a decrease in Supply upon the Equilibrium quantity (*see*).

Quantity demanded — The amount of a good or service buyers wish (or a buyer wishes) to purchase at a particular price during some period of time.

Quantity-increasing effect — The effect in a competitive market of an increase in Demand or an increase in Supply upon the Equilibrium quantity (*see*).

Quantity supplied — The amount of a good or service sellers offer (or a seller offers) to sell at a particular price during some period of time.

Quasi-public good — A good or service to which the Exclusion principle (*see*) could be applied, but which has such a large Spillover benefit (*see*) that government sponsors its production to prevent an underallocation of resources.

R&D — Research and development; activities undertaken to bring about Technological progress.

Random shock — An event that has a significant effect on an economy but that was unexpected and is not likely to occur again.

Rate of exchange — The price paid in one's own money to acquire one unit of a foreign money; the rate at which the money of one nation is exchanged for the money of another nation.

Rate of interest — Price paid for the use of Money or for the use of Capital; interest rate.

Rational — An adjective that describes the behaviour of an individual who consistently does those things that will enable the achievement of the declared objective of the individual; and that describes the behaviour of a consumer who uses money income to buy the collection of goods and services that yields the maximum amount of Utility (*see*).

Rational expectations theory — The hypothesis that business firms and households expect monetary and fiscal policies to have certain effects upon the economy and, in pursuit of their own self-interests, take actions that make these policies ineffective.

Rationing function of price — The ability of price in a competitive market to equalize Quantity demanded and Quantity supplied and to eliminate shortages and surpluses by rising or falling.

Reaganomics — The policies of the United States Reagan Administration based on Supply-side economics (*see*) and intended to reduce inflation and the Unemployment rate (Stagflation).

Real-balances effect — (*See* Wealth effect.)

Real capital — (*See* Capital.)

Real domestic output (GDP) — The GDP (*see*) measured in terms of a constant price level (adjusted for changes in the price level).

Real gross domestic product — Gross domestic product (*see*) adjusted for changes in the price level; Gross domestic product in a year divided by the GDP deflator (*see*) for that year.

Real income — The amount of goods and services an individual or group can purchase with his, her, or its Nominal income during some period of time; Nominal income adjusted for changes in the Price level.

Real interest rate — The rate of interest expressed in dollars of constant value (adjusted for inflation); and equal to the Nominal interest rate (*see*) less the rate of inflation.

Real rate of interest — The Real interest rate (*see*).

Real wage — The amount of goods and services a worker can purchase with his or her Money wage (*see*); the purchasing power of the Money wage; the Money wage adjusted for changes in the Price level.

Real wage rate — (*See* Real wage.)

Recessionary gap — The amount by which the Aggregate expenditures schedule (curve) must increase (shift upward) to increase the GDP to the full-employment noninflationary level.

Reciprocal selling — The practice in which one Firm agrees to buy a product from a second Firm, and the second Firm agrees, in return, to buy another product from the first Firm.

Reciprocal Trade Agreements Act of 1934 (U.S.) — The federal Act that gave the U.S. President the authority to negotiate agreements with other nations and lower American tariff rates by up to 50% if the other nations would reduce tariff rates on American goods, and which incorporated Most-favoured-nation clauses (*see*) in the agreements reached with these nations.

Refinancing the public debt — Paying owners of maturing Government of Canada securities with money obtained by selling new securities or with new securities.

Regional Development Incentives Act — The federal Act of 1970 designed to create jobs in Canada's slow growth, or "designated" areas.

Regressive tax — A tax such that the tax rate decreases (increases) as the taxpayer's income increases (decreases).

Regulatory agency — An agency (commission or board) established by the federal or a provincial government to control for the benefit of the public the prices charged and the services offered (output produced) by a Natural monopoly (*see*).

Remittance — A gift or grant; a payment for which no good or service is received in return; the funds sent by workers who have legally or illegally entered a foreign nation to their families in the nations from which they have migrated.

Rental income — Income received by those who supply the economy with Land (*see*).

Rent-seeking behaviour — The pursuit through government of a transfer of income or wealth to a resource supplier, business, or consumer at someone else's or society's expense.

Required reserve — [*See* Cash (primary) reserve and Secondary reserve.]

Reserve ratio — [*See* Cash (primary) reserve and Secondary reserve.]

Reserves — [*See* (1) Official international reserves; (2) Cash (primary) reserves and Secondary reserves.]

Resource market — A market in which Households sell and Firms buy the services of resources.

Retiring the public debt — Reducing the size of the Public debt (*see*) by paying money to owners of maturing Government of Canada securities.

Revaluation — An increase in the defined value of a currency brought about by the central bank; the opposite of Devaluation.

Revenue sharing — The distribution by the federal government of some of its tax revenues to provincial governments.

Revenue tariff — A Tariff (*see*) designed to produce income for the (federal) government.

Ricardian equivalence theorem — The idea that an increase in the public debt will have little or no effect on real output and employment because taxpayers will save more in anticipation of future higher taxes to pay the higher interest expense on the debt.

Roundabout production — The construction and use of Capital (*see*) to aid in the production of Consumer goods (*see*).

Rule of 70 — A method by which the number of years it will take for the price level (the increasing variable) to double can be calculated; divide 70 by the annual rate of inflation (the rate of increase).

Sales tax — A tax levied on expenditures for a broad group of products.

Saving — Disposable income not spent for Consumer goods (*see*); not spending for consumption; equal to Disposable income minus Personal consumption expenditures (*see*).

Savings account — A deposit in a financial institution (*see*) that is interest-earning and that can normally be withdrawn by the depositor at any time (though the institution may legally require notice for withdrawal).

Saving schedule — Schedule that shows the amounts Households plan to save (plan not to spend for Consumer goods, *see*) at different levels of Disposable income.

Say's Law — The (discredited) macroeconomic generalization that the production of goods and services (supply) creates an equal demand for these goods and services.

Scarce resources — The fixed (limited) quantities of Land, Capital, Labour, and Entrepreneurial ability (*see all*) that are never sufficient to satisfy the wants of human beings because their wants are unlimited.

Schumpeter-Galbraith view (of oligopoly) — The belief shared by these two economists that large oligopolistic firms are necessary if there is to be a rapid rate of technological progress (because only this kind of firm has both the means and the incentive to introduce technological changes).

SDRs — (*See* Special Drawing Rights.)

Seasonal variation — An increase or decrease during a single year in the level of economic activity caused by a change in the season.

Secondary reserve — The Chartered bank cash in excess of cash reserve requirements, Government of Canada Treasury bills of one year or less, and day-to-day loans to investment dealers who have lines of credit with the Bank of Canada.

Secular trend — The expansion or contraction in the level of economic activity over a long period of years.

Selective controls — The minor techniques used by the Bank of Canada to change the availability of credit: changing the Secondary reserve ratio and Moral suasion (*see both*).

Self-interest — What each Firm, property owner, worker, and consumer believes is best for itself and seeks to obtain.

Semidurable goods — A Consumer good (*see*), other than a Nondurable (*see*), with a life expectancy of less than a year, for example, clothing.

Seniority — The length of time a worker has been employed by an employer relative to the lengths of time the employer's other workers have been employed; the principle that is used to determine which workers will be laid off when there is insufficient work for them all, and which will be rehired when more work becomes available.

Separation of ownership and control — Difference between the group that owns the Corporation (the stockholders) and the group that manages it (the directors and officers) and between the interests (goals) of the two groups.

Service — That which is intangible (invisible) and for which a consumer, firm, or government is willing to exchange something of value.

Shared-cost programs — (*See* Conditional grant.)

Shortage — The result of a price ceiling: a maximum price set by government below the Equilibrium price (*see*).

Short run — A period of time in which producers of a product are able to change the quantity of some but not all of the resources they employ; in which some resources — the Plant (*see*) — are Fixed resources (*see*) and some are Variable resources (*see*); in which some costs are Fixed costs (*see*) and some are Variable costs (*see*); a period of time too brief to allow a Firm (*see*) to vary its plant capacity but long enough to permit it to change the level at which the plant capacity is utilized; a period of time not long enough to enable Firms to enter or to leave an Industry (*see*).

Short-run aggregate supply curve — The aggregate supply curve relevant to a time period in which input prices (particularly nominal wages) remain constant when the price level changes.

Short-run competitive equilibrium — The price at which the total quantity of a product supplied in the Short run (*see*) by a purely competitive industry and the total quantity of the product demanded are equal and which is equal to or greater than the Average variable cost (*see*) of producing the product; and the quantity of the product demanded and supplied at this price.

Short-run farm problem — The sharp year-to-year changes in the prices of agricultural products and in the incomes of farmers.

Simple multiplier — The Multiplier (*see*) in an economy in which government collects no Net taxes (*see*), there are no Imports (*see*), and Investment (*see*) is independent of the level of income (Gross domestic product); equal to one divided by the Marginal propensity to save (*see*).

Single-tax movement — The attempt of a group that followed the teachings of Henry George to eliminate all taxes except one that would tax all Rental income (*see*) at a rate of 100%.

Slope of a line — The ratio of the vertical change (the rise or fall) to the horizontal change (the run) in moving between two points on a line. The slope of an upward sloping line is positive, reflecting a direct relationship between two variables; the slope of a downward sloping line is negative, reflecting an inverse relationship between two variables.

Smoot-Hawley Tariff Act — Passed in 1930, this legislation established some of the highest tariffs in United States history. Its objective was to reduce imports and stimulate the American economy.

Social accounting — (*See* National income accounting.)

Social good — (*See* Public good.)

Social insurance programs — The programs that replace the earnings lost when people retire or are temporarily unemployed, that are financed by pay deductions, and that are viewed as earned rights (rather than charity).

Social regulation — The newer and different type of regulation in which government is concerned with the conditions under which goods and services are produced, their physical characteristics, and the impact of their production upon society; in contrast to Industrial regulation (*see*).

Sole proprietorship — An unincorporated business firm owned and operated by a single person.

Special Drawing Rights — Credit created by the International Monetary Fund (*see*), which a member of the IMF may borrow to finance a Payments deficit (*see*) or to increase its Official international reserves (*see*); "paper gold."

Special-interest effect — Effect on public decision-making and the allocation of resources in the economy when government promotes the interests (goals) of small groups to the detriment of society as a whole.

Specialization — The use of the resources of an individual, a Firm, a region, or a nation to produce one or a few goods and services.

Speculative motive — Keynes' term for the Asset demand for money (*see*).

Spillover — A benefit or cost associated with the consumption or production of a good or service that is obtained by or inflicted without compensation upon a party other than the buyer or seller of the good or service; (*see* Spillover benefit and Spillover cost).

Spillover benefit — The benefit obtained neither by producers nor by consumers of a product but without compensation by a third party (society as a whole).

Spillover cost — The cost of producing a product borne neither by producers not by consumers of the product but without compensation by a third party (society as a whole).

Stabilization funds — International monetary reserves (*see*) and domestic monies used to augment the supply of, or demand for, any currency required to avoid or restrict fluctuations in the rate of exchange; in Canada held in the Exchange Fund Account by the Bank of Canada on behalf of the government.

Stabilization policy dilemma — The use of monetary and fiscal policy to decrease the Unemployment rate increases the rate of inflation, and the use of monetary and fiscal policy to decrease the rate of inflation increases the Unemployment rate; *see* the Phillips curve.

Stagflation — Inflation accompanied by stagnation in the rate of growth of output and a high unemployment rate in the economy; simultaneous increases in both the price level and the Unemployment rate (*see*).

Standardized product — A product such that buyers are indifferent to the seller from whom they purchase it so long as the price charged by all sellers is the same; a product such that all units of the product are perfect substitutes for each other (are identical).

Staple — An exported raw material.

State ownership — The ownership of property (Land and Capital) by government (the state).

Static economy — (1) An economy in which Net investment (*see*) is equal to zero — Gross investment (*see*) is equal to the Capital consumption allowances (*see*); (2) an economy in which the supplies of resources, technology, and the tastes of consumers do not change and in which, therefore, the economic future is perfectly predictable and there is no uncertainty.

Store of value — Any Asset (*see*) or wealth set aside for future use.

Strategic trade policy — The use of trade barriers to reduce the risk of product development by domestic firms, particularly products involving advanced technology.

Strike — The withholding of their labour services by an organized group of workers (a Labour union).

Strikebreaker — A person employed by a Firm when its employees are engaged in a strike against the firm.

Structural unemployment — Unemployment caused by changes in the structure of demand for Consumer goods and in technology; workers who are unemployed either because their skills are not demanded by employers or because they lack sufficient skills to obtain employment.

Subsidy — A payment of funds (or goods and services) by a government, business firm, or household for which it receives no good or service in return. When made by a government, it is a Government transfer payment (*see*) or the reverse of a tax.

Substitutability — The ability of consumers to use one good or service instead of another to satisfy their wants and of Firms to use one resource instead of another to produce products.

Substitute goods — Goods or services such that there is a direct relationship between the price of one and the Demand for the other; when the price of one falls (rises) the Demand for the other decreases (increases).

Substitution effect — (1) The effect a change in the price of a Consumer good would have upon the relative expensiveness of that good and the resulting effect upon the quantity of the good a consumer would purchase if the consumer's Real income (*see*) remained constant; (2) the effect a change in the price of a resource would have upon the quantity of the resource employed by a firm if the firm did not change its output.

Superior good — (*See* Normal good.)

Supplementary labour income — The payments by employers into unemployment insurance, worker's compensation, and a variety of private and public pension and welfare funds for workers: "fringe benefits."

Supply — A Supply schedule or a Supply curve (*see both*).

Supply curve — A curve that shows the amounts of a good or service sellers (a seller) will offer to sell at various prices during some period of time.

Supply factor — An increase in the available quantity of a resource, an improvement in its quality, or an expansion of technological knowledge, which makes it possible for an economy to produce a greater output of goods and services.

Supply schedule — A schedule that shows the amounts of a good or service sellers (a seller) will offer to sell at various prices during some period of time.

Supply shock — One of several events of the 1970s and early 1980s that increased production costs, decreased Aggregate supply, and helped generate Stagflation in Canada.

Supply-side economics — The part of modern Macroeconomics that emphasizes the role of costs and aggregate supply in its explanation of Inflation and unemployed labour.

Supply-side view — The view of fiscal policy held by the advocates of Supply-side economics that emphasizes increasing Aggregate supply (*see*) as a means of reducing the Unemployment rate and Inflation and encouraging Economic Growth.

Support price — (*See* Price support.)

Surplus — The result of a price floor or price support: a minimum price set by government above the Equilibrium price (*see*).

Switching Government of Canada deposits — Action of Bank of Canada to increase (decrease) backing for Money supply (*see*) by switching government deposits from (to) itself to (from) the Chartered banks (*see*).

Tacit collusion — Any method utilized in a Collusive oligopoly (*see*) to set prices and outputs or the market area of each firm that does not involve outright (or overt) collusion (formal agreements or secret meetings); and of which Price leadership (*see*) is a frequent example.

Tangent — The point at which a line touches, but does not intersect, a curve.

Target dilemma — A problem that arises because the central bank cannot simultaneously stabilize both the money supply and the level of interest rates.

Tariff — A tax imposed (only by the federal government in Canada) on an imported good.

Tax — A nonvoluntary payment of money (or goods and services) to a government by a Household or Firm for which the Household or Firm receives no good or service directly in return and which is not a fine imposed by a court for an illegal act.

Tax-based incomes policies (TIP) — An Incomes policy (*see*) that would include special tax penalties for those who do not comply and tax rebates for those who do comply with the Wage-price guideposts (*see*).

Tax incidence — The income or purchasing power that different persons and groups lose as a result of the imposition of a tax after Tax shifting (*see*) has occurred.

Tax shifting — The transfer to others of all or part of a tax by charging them a higher price or by paying them a lower price for a good or service.

Tax-transfer disincentives — Decreases in the incentives to work, save, invest, innovate, and take risks that allegedly result from high Marginal tax rates and Transfer payment programs.

Tax "wedge" — Such taxes as Indirect taxes (*see*) and pay deductions for Social insurance programs (*see*), which are treated as a cost by business firms and reflected in the prices of the products produced by them; equal to the price of the product less the cost of the resources required to produce it.

Technology — The body of knowledge that can be used to produce goods and services from Economic resources.

Term deposit — A deposit in a Chartered bank or other Financial intermediary against which cheques may not be written; a form of savings account; part of M2, M3, and M2+ (*see all*).

Terms of trade — The rate at which units of one product can be exchanged for units of another product; the Price (*see*) of a good or service; the amount of one good or service that must be given up to obtain one unit of another good or service.

Theory of human capital — Generalization that Wage differentials (*see*) are the result of differences in the amount of Human capital investment (*see*); and that the incomes of lower-paid workers are increased by increasing the amount of such investment.

Theory of public choice — Generalizations that describe how government (the Public sector) makes decisions for the use of economic resources.

***The* rate of interest** — The Rate of Interest (*see*) that is paid solely for the use of Money over an extended period of time and that excludes the charges made for the riskiness of the loan and its administrative costs; and that is approximately equal to the rate of interest paid on the long-term and virtually riskless bonds of the Government of Canada.

Third World — The semideveloped and less-developed nations; nations other than the industrially advanced market economies and the centrally planned economies.

Tied selling — (*See* Exclusive dealing.)

Tight money policy — Increasing the Rate of interest (*see*) by contracting the nation's Money supply (*see*). See also Contractionary monetary policy.

Till money — (*See* Vault cash.)

TIP — (*See* Tax-based incomes policies.)

Token money — Coins that have a Face value (*see*) greater than their Intrinsic value (*see*).

Total cost — The sum of Fixed cost (*see*) and Variable cost (*see*).

Total demand — The Demand schedule (*see*) or the Demand curve (*see*) of all buyers of a good or service.

Total demand for money — The sum of the Transactions demand for money (*see*) and Asset demand for money (*see*); the relationship between the total amount of money demanded and nominal GDP and the Rate of Interest.

Total product — The total output of a particular good or service produced by a firm, a group of firms or the entire economy.

Total revenue — The total number of dollars received by a Firm (or Firms) from the sale of a product; equal to the total expenditures for the product produced by the Firm (or Firms); equal to the quantity sold (demanded) multiplied by the price at which it is sold — by the Average revenue (*see*) from its sale.

Total-revenue test — A test to determine whether Demand is Elastic (*see*), Inelastic (*see*), or of Unitary elasticity (*see*) between any two prices: demand is elastic (inelastic, unit elastic) if the Total revenue (*see*) of sellers of the commodity increases (decreases, remains constant) when the price of the commodity falls; or Total revenue decreases (increases, remains constant) when its price rises.

Total-revenue–total-cost approach — The method that finds the output at which Economic profit (*see*) is a maximum or losses a minimum by comparing the total receipts (revenue) and the total costs of a Firm at different outputs.

Total spending — The total amount buyers of goods and services spend or plan to spend.

Total supply — The Supply schedule (*see*) or the Supply curve (*see*) of all sellers of a good or service.

Trade balance — Balance of trade (*see*).

Trade controls — Tariffs (*see*), export subsidies, Import quotas (*see*), and other means a nation may employ to reduce Imports (*see*) and expand Exports (*see*) in order to eliminate a Balance of payments deficit (*see*).

Trade deficit — The amount by which a nation's imports of merchandise (goods) and services exceed its exports of merchandise (goods) and services.

Trade surplus — The amount by which a nation's exports of merchandise (goods) and services exceed its imports of merchandise (goods) and services.

Trades and Labour Congress of Canada (TLC) — The federation of Craft unions (*see*) formed in 1886 and affiliated with the American Federation of Labour (*see*); amalgamated into the Canadian Labour Congress (*see*) in 1956.

Trading possibilities line — A line that shows the different combinations of two products an economy is able to obtain (consume) when it specializes in the production of one product and trades (exports) this product to obtain the other product.

Traditional economy — An economic system (method of organization) in which traditions and customs determine how the economy will use its scarce resources.

Traditional view of advertising — The position that advertising is persuasive rather than informative; promotes industrial concentration; and is essentially inefficient and wasteful.

Transactions demand for money — The amount of money people want to hold to use as a Medium of exchange (to make payments); and which varies directly with the nominal GDP.

Transfer burden (effect) — The outflow of interest and dividends abroad resulting from foreign investment.

Transfer payment — A payment of money (or goods and services) by a government or a Firm to a Household or Firm for which the payer receives no good or service directly in return.

Tying agreement — A promise made by a buyer when allowed to purchase a patented product from a seller that it will make all of its purchases of certain other (unpatented) products from the same seller.

Unanticipated inflation — Inflation (*see*) at a rate greater than the rate expected in that period of time.

Unconditional grant — A transfer to a province by the federal government that goes into the general revenues of the province to be used as it sees fit; such grants are made for two reasons: (1) as an Equalization payment (*see*) and (2) to make up for the general inadequacy of provincial revenues in relation to provincial responsibilities.

Underemployment — Failure to produce the maximum amount of goods and services that can be produced from the resources employed; failure to achieve Full production (*see*).

Undistributed corporation profits — The after-tax profits of corporations not distributed as dividends to stockholders; corporate or business saving.

Unemployment — Failure to use all available Economic resources to produce goods and services; failure of the economy to employ fully its Civilian labour force (*see*).

Unemployment insurance — The insurance program that in Canada is financed by compulsory contributions from employers and employees and from the general tax revenues of the federal government with benefits (income) made available to insured workers who are unable to find jobs.

Unemployment rate — The percentage of the Civilian labour force (*see*) unemployed at any time.

Unfair competition — Any practice that is employed by a Firm either to eliminate a rival or to block the entry of a new Firm into an Industry and that society (or a rival) believes to be an unacceptable method of achieving these ends.

Uninsurable risk — An event, the occurrence of which is uncontrollable and unpredictable, that would result in a loss that cannot be avoided by purchasing insurance and must be assumed by an entrepreneur (*see* Entrepreneurial ability); sometimes called "uncertainty."

Union shop — A place of employment at which the employer may hire either Labour union members or workers who are not members of the union but who must become members within a specified period of time or lose their jobs.

Unitary elasticity — The Elasticity coefficient (*see*) is equal to one; the percentage change in the quantity (demanded or supplied) is equal to the percentage change in price.

Unit labour cost — Labour costs per unit of output; equal to the Money wage rate (*see*) divided by the Average product (*see*) of labour.

Unlimited liability — Absence of any limit on the maximum amount that may be lost by an individual and that the individual may become legally required to pay; the maximum amount that may be lost and that a sole proprietor or partner may be required to pay.

Unlimited wants — The insatiable desire of consumers (people) for goods and services that will give them pleasure or satisfaction.

Unplanned investment — Actual investment less Planned investment; increases or decreases in the inventories of business firms that result from production greater than or less than sales.

Unprosperous industry — (*See* Declining industry.)

User charge — A price paid by those who use a facility that covers the full cost of using the facility.

Utility — The want-satisfying power of a good or service; the satisfaction or pleasure a consumer obtains from the consumption of a good or service (or from the consumption of a collection of goods and services).

Utility-maximizing rule — To obtain the greatest Utility (*see*) the consumer should allocate Money income so that the last dollar spent on each good or service yields the same Marginal utility (*see*); so that the Marginal utility of each good or service divided by its price is the same for all goods and services.

Value added — The value of the product sold by a Firm less the value of the goods (materials) purchased and used by the Firm to produce the product; and equal to the revenue that can be used for Wages, rent, interest, and profits.

Value-added tax — A tax imposed upon the difference between the value of the goods sold by a firm and the value of the goods purchased by the firm from other firms.

Value judgment — Opinion of what is desirable or undesirable; belief regarding what ought or ought not to be (regarding what is right or just and wrong or unjust).

Value of money — The quantity of goods and services for which a unit of money (a dollar) can be exchanged; the purchasing power of a unit of money; the reciprocal of the Price level.

Variable cost — A cost that, in total, increases (decreases) when the firm increases (decreases) its output; the cost of Variable resources (*see*).

Variable resource — Any resource employed by a firm the quantity of which can be increased or decreased (varied).

VAT — Value-added tax (*see*).

Vault cash — The Currency (*see*) a bank has in its safe (vault) and cash drawers; till money.

Velocity of money — The number of times per year the average dollar in the Money supply (*see*) is spent for Final goods and services (*see*).

VERs — (*See* Voluntary export restrictions.)

Vertical axis — The "up-down" or "north-south" axis on a graph or grid.

Vertical combination — A group of Plants (*see*) engaged in different stages of the production of a final product and owned by a single Firm (*see*).

Vertical intercept — The point at which a line meets the vertical axis of a graph.

Vertical merger — The merger of one or more Firms engaged in different stages of the production of a final product into a single Firm (*see*).

Voluntary export restrictions — The limitation by firms of their exports to particular foreign nations in order to avoid the erection of other trade barriers by the foreign nations.

Wage — The price paid for Labour [for the use or services of Labour (*see*)] per unit of time (per hour, per day, and so on).

Wage differential — The difference between the Wage (*see*) received by one worker or group of workers and that received by another worker or group of workers.

Wage discrimination — The payment to women (or minority groups) of a wage lower than that paid to men (or established groups) for doing the same work.

Wage guidepost — Wages (*see*) in all industries in the economy should increase at an annual rate equal to the rate of increase in the Average product (*see*) of Labour in the economy.

Wage-price controls — A Wage-price policy (*see*) that legally fixes the maximum amounts by which Wages (*see*) and prices may be increased in any period of time.

Wage-price guideposts — A Wage-price policy (*see*) that depends upon the voluntary cooperation of Labour unions and business firms.

Wage-price inflationary spiral — Increases in wage rates that bring about increases in prices, which in turn result in further increases in wage rates and in prices.

Wage-price policy — Government policy that attempts to alter the behaviour of Labour unions and business firms in order to make their Wage and price decisions more nearly compatible with the goals of Full employment and stable prices.

Wage rate — (*See* Wages.)

Wages — The income of those who supply the economy with Labour (*see*).

Wastes of monopolistic competition — The waste of economic resources that is the result of producing an output at which price is greater than marginal cost and average cost is greater than the minimum average cost.

Wealth effect — The tendency for increases (decreases) in the price level to lower (raise) the real value (or purchasing power) of financial assets with fixed money values; and, as a result, to reduce (expand) total spending in the economy.

Welfare programs — (*See* Public assistance programs.)

(The) "will to develop" — Wanting economic growth strongly enough to change from old to new ways of doing things.

World Bank — A bank supported by 151 nations, which lends (and guarantees loans) to less-developed nations to assist them to grow; formally, the International Bank for Reconstruction and Development.

X-inefficiency — Failure to produce any given output at the lowest average (and total) cost possible.